Freedom

From Fear to There

By

Eno Mondésir

ISBN: 1-4033-4827-8 (e-book)
ISBN: 1-4033-4828-6 (Paperback)

This book is printed on acid free paper.

Editors: Paula J. Waters and Zaundria M. May
Cover and book illustrations: Charlot Lucien
Printed by Advanced Print Management, Inc., Wilmington, MA

Mondésir, Eno
Freedom: From Fear to There/by Eno Mondésir

1stBooks — rev. 10/29/02

SPECIAL NOTE FROM THE AUTHOR

Using a psycho-social approach, as well as some concepts borrowed from natural sciences, this book is framed within a context that deals with almost every aspect of **Personal Growth, Empowerment, Wellness, and Achievement**. It is intended to give to the reader some new perspectives about his or her attitude and belief toward himself/herself and life in general. For the most part, it aims at helping the individual focus on the obstacles from a new dimension. Moreover, from the point of view of concept and language (vocabulary), the material is presented in a way that will stimulate a broad range of audiences, going from people in academia to all those who are at the point of becoming self-conscious. The last chapter reflects mainly on the previous chapters; however, by no means does it cover the discussion of any part in its entirety. Therefore, it is NOT a shortcut through the work.

A challenge to you!

So far, have you identified your mission and goals: short, medium and long range? Are you pursuing them? Do you care to have one, or have you ever started a project but got cold feet or became so discouraged and threw everything out of the window? Perhaps, so many odds seem to go against any plan that you ever conceived: age, socio-economic circumstances, illnesses, politics of destabilization, a pregnancy, somebody else's ignorance, race factors, gender differences, family background, family breakdown, migration, not enough support/money to get the education that you want for you and/or your children. Maybe somewhere along the line, you have lost confidence in your own ability to carry on your vision, or no one believes in you! Unfortunately, all these things can happen even to the best of us; and I agree, they seem to outnumber all the reasons why you should go forward with your plan (s). However, very often our battle is already won and our success confirmed, and it is a matter of standing fast and walking the extra mile or just flipping the coin over to unveil the prize. Also, it would be a failure on my part not to mention that life

in general is made of trial and error. We may succeed if and only if we dare take the risk and try!

Lastly, even though the material in this manual focuses on the individual, if you work in the field of education and would like to find innovative ways to encourage and stimulate your student body, you ought to try this book. Maybe, you are doing community intervention and want to help the people empower themselves, or you are a minister/priest and you envision growth in your local congregation, I recommend that you read this book!

It is said that "success is failure in reverse". So, don't be stuck in a gear; this book will challenge and assist you in making the move forward.

Dedicated to
all those who
believe and engage
in the
pursuit of growth
as a lifetime process
and are
interested in maintaining
a healthy lifestyle

CONTENTS

❖PART SIX❖
The Magic Triangle: You, Your Culture & Beliefs

❖PART SEVEN❖
The Bottom Line

ACKNOWLEDGMENT

In recognition of their contributions to this work, I would like to extend a special thanks to:

Reverend Paula J. Waters, Twelfth Baptist Church, Roxbury, Massachusetts

Honorable Carl McCall, New York State Comptroller

Attorney Anthony Mondésir, private Law Firm in Chicago, Illinois

Mr. & Mrs. Andre Mondésir, Haiti

Miss. Eunice Mondésir

Miss. Vallerie E. Mondésir

Mr. Jason Mondésir

Mr. Jamal Mondésir

Dr. Loretta J. Williams, Assistant Professor at Boston University

Dr. Charles Austin, News Reporter, WBZ-TV, Boston, Massachusetts

Mrs. Avis Turner-Ricketts, BU School of Social Work and Bethel AME Church, Jamaica Plain, Massachusetts

Ms. Nerlande Sanon Germain, Department of Social Services, Massachusetts

Dr. George Thyvelikakat, Chairman of Chemistry Department, Oral Roberts University, Tulsa, Oklahoma

Ms. Rhoda Johnson-Lyn, Boston Public Health Commission, Boston, Massachusetts

Dr. Abede Alexandre, Psychologist and Theologian, currently practicing in Massachusetts

Ms. Virginia Pratt, Boston Public Health Commission, Boston, Massachusetts

Dr. Renald Raphael, Haitian-American Public Health Initiative, Mattapan Massachusetts

Ms. Lynn Diniz, Boston Public Health Commission, Boston, Massachusetts

Dr. Eustache Jean Louis, Dir., Center for Community Health Education & Research, Boston, Massachusetts

Ms. Winnie May, Lemuel Shattuck Hospital, Jamaica Plain, Massachusetts

Mr. Charlot Lucien, Massachusetts Department of Public Health
Reverend Doucet Deronvil, Port-au-Prince, Haiti
Reverend Felicien Felix, Miami, Florida
Professor Jean Claude Saint Louis, Roxbury Community College, Boston, Massachusetts
Mr. Riche Zamor, The Medical Foundation, Boston, Massachusetts
Reverend Gaspard Matheus, Lehigh Acres, Florida
Mrs. Nirva Mondésir, B.S.N., R.N., Massachusetts
Ms. Cathy Wattley, Boston Public School, Boston, Massachusetts
Mr. Robert Edwards, Boston City Hall, Boston, Massachusetts
Reverend Jean Wilner Guerrier, Jeremie, Haiti
Dr. Thierry M. Muanza, Internist at Jewish General Hosp., Montreal, Canada
Mr. Carl Dreyfus, Ercolini Insurance Firm, Boston, Massachusetts
Ms. Denise C. Dabney, ABD, Heller School, Brandeis University, Waltham, Massachusetts
Reverend Othon O. Noel, Haitian Coordinator for Southern N. E Church of God, USA
Mrs. Nicole Muller-Cesar, Psycho-social Counselor, CCHER, Boston, Massachusetts
Dr. Nanette Graham, Assistant Professor of Criminal Justice and Criminology, Northeastern University, Roxbury, Massachusetts
Janine Walker
Reverend Dr. Michael E. Haynes, Boston, Massachusetts
Reverend Soliny Vedrine, Eglise Baptiste Missionnaire de Boston, Roxbury, Massachusetts

Thanks to the following for their special support and encourage-ment:

Dr. T.L. Nicks, Ph.D., U.S. Public Service (Retired)
Professor Jean Claude St. Louis, Roxbury Community College
Mrs. Lucia Jean Charles, Bacteriologist
Reverend Nicolas Homicil, United Methodist Church of Waltham
Mr. & Mrs. Joseph Bernard, Massachusetts
Mr. & Mrs. Edzer Derilus, New Jersey

PREFACE

Sometimes in the summer when I am driving on country roads, I find myself settled into ruts created by the snows, rains and thaws of winter and spring. I am reminded of these deep ruts where it is sometimes easy to drive when I catch myself in settled patterns in my life and in my very thinking. Sometimes we humans settle too long in predictable ruts in the way we approach life and living. Yes, it is understandable—a coping device, perhaps, given that the world is complex. The familiar seems easier than negotiating an alternative way. Yet, the ruts in our thinking and action may be to our detriment.

Freedom: From Fear to There offers possibilities for getting out of those ruts. It is about the possibilities of and for personal transformation. Eno Mondésir, an astute and whimsical public health professional, maintains that we humans continuously place locks upon our very own potential. By stepping back from some of our taken-for-granted assumptions about ourselves, our present plight, and our future possibilities, we can remove those locks, he says.

I approached this text with some trepidation. Why another treatise on freedom??? Probably another person worshipping unduly at the altar of individualism, I thought. The language of "freedom" can sometime conceal the violence of the ways things are, and the legitimating myths undergirding them. I found to my delight a multifaceted discussion of ways to move from insularity to self-understanding, and then on to self-transformation.

This book will "jog" your thinking. We all are familiar with jogging as a way of moving towards physical fitness and wellness. In that same vein, we human beings can do with some mental jogging—ways that take us away from our familiar habits of thought. New vista open up.

A vista point provides a place from which one can survey the view all around, and sees that patterns that can only be guessed from down on the ground. That's what this book does—it creates a place to see the larger whole of ourselves, our way of life and living.

Mondésir has a poet's imagination as he offers readers a variety of **scientific facts, then feisty parables, then metaphors, then pithy**

quotes and true stories. Along the way, he illumines some of the murkiness in our thought patterns and in our actions by provoking us with challenging questions and examples.

Mondésir holds that ambiguity is the stuff of life. We lack ease in situations that are unfamiliar, or where difference is a factor. We tend not to think about the standard we are using from which "difference" is measured. We are often ill-prepared to negotiate conflict. Our habits of thinking, says Mondésir, may block our shedding the protective armors that are strangling us. **Demonstrating a gifted familiarity with the world of social psychology and hard science, with faith, perspectives and folklore, the author takes us through reflective planning for alternative growth in our lives.**

He's opinionated, yet he does not rail at his readers. Instead he offers fresh ways of looking at the ways we may be holding ourselves back. **You have options, he argues. Yes, there is hard work ahead, but the reward for the journey is an audacious hope.** We stretch our views of ourselves, and of possibility, as we read through the various chapters.

You, the reader, will benefit from this discussion. Much change occurs under the surface of visible things—as when an underground irrigation system transforms a desert into arable land. So, too, can we be nourished and transformed.

Mondésir urges us to work to change our perceptions, so that we can move into a larger world. We would be free, yet often we fear our own intent in our living. We would be free, but familiar habits are so routine that their oppression blurs from our thinking. We would be free, but we have enslaved ourselves.

I recall Gwendolyn Brooks, poet laureate, offering a reading. One of the first poems she read caught my attention: "I was thinking that we are so used to dealing with shadow that, even if a sun would manifest itself to us, we wouldn't recognize it." Much is packed into that brief sentence. Fragility and resiliency both are part of human composition. In the face of the complexities of life and the universe, new connections can be attempted. New pathways can be forged.

Self-help books can sometimes deplete energy. Not here. This book made me reflect back on the wisdom expressed in an African American hymn that I learned in Sunday school: "Clim'in' Up The

Rough Side of the Mountain." The only place to get a toe-hold as one attempts to climb a mountain is where the side is ragged and craggy.

Some will call Mondésir's approach thinking outside the box. He makes us more deeply aware of how much we are influenced by the dominant culture and its cynicisms. Freedom is a constant struggle; yet it can and must be striven for from all sides. We can handle the paradoxes and contradictions.

Indeed we can. As the Hebrew text says: "Faith is the assurance of things hoped for, the conviction of things not seen." *Freedom: From Fear to There* is written with faith and a generosity of spirit. We are people on a journey—people-in-progress.

Thank you, Eno Mondésir, for reminding us so clearly of the many ways we can shape our future.

Loretta J. Williams, Ph. D.
Sociologist, Boston University
Boston, Massachusetts

PART ONE

Fear is to Ignorance
as Knowledge is to Freedom

Eno Mondesir

❖ CHAPTER I ❖

Fear: Its Roots and Consequences

Taken to its extreme, fear is usually expressed with some form of tension and it often accompanies a feeling of apprehension and anxiety. It conveys a sense of unpreparedness and inadequacy or inability to fulfill the task at hand efficiently or to face life's challenges. It also portrays uncertainty and insecurity and may lead to a state of emotional paralysis where the subject of that fear becomes temporarily dysfunctional or is unable to function properly: emotionally, mentally, psychologically or even physically.

Generally, certain types of fear are often described depending on the object (s) of fear. Among such categorizations, we find:

Agora-phobia: fear of being in open or public places
Andro-phobia: fear of men
Claustro-phobia: fear of closed space
Hydro-phobia: fear of water
Acro-phobia: fear of heights (high elevations)
Algo-phobia: fear of pain
Astro-phobia: fear of storms, thunder, lightning
Arachno-phobia: fear of spider
Hemato-phobia: fear of blood
Mono-phobia: fear of being alone
"Decido-phobia": fear of making decisions
Myso-phobia: fear of contamination, germs
Nycto-phobia: fear of darkness
Ocholo-phobia: fear of crowds
Patho-phobia: fear of disease
Pyro-phobia: fear of fire
Xeno-phobia: extreme fear of strangers, foreigners
Homo-phobia: fear of humans
Cyno-phobia: fear of dogs
Ophio or Ophicio-phonia: fear of snakes

"Crescento- phobia": fear of growth
"Fortuno-phobia": fear of success

In fact, you can create your own list of phobias, since there is an infinite number of objects, animals, and things that one may choose to interact with. Fear in its strict meaning is defined as an unpleasant, often strong anticipation or awareness of danger; that is to be afraid or apprehensive of, to have anxious concerns. Anxiety, on the other hand, constitutes a generalized feeling of fear and apprehension. Sigmund Freud has described three (3) types, namely:

1. **real anxiety,** which is the arousal from danger or threat in the external world
2. **neurotic anxiety,** one that is caused by the Id's impulses, threatening to break through the ego controls into behavior that will be punished in some way
3. **moral anxiety,** according to Freud, arises from a real or contemplated action that is in conflict with the individual's superego, thereby arousing feelings of guilt. And it is both, a signal provided by the ego that a dangerous impulse has been activated and the motivated force behind the deployment of defense (Coleman, J.C., 1988).

Later in this work, we will address the following terms more thoroughly, but for now we wish to throw at you their definitions. Id represents the instinctive drive in an individual. Ego is a mediator between the id and reality of the external world (Coleman, pp.60-65). The superego stands as the conscious component of the psyche that is developed from learning the myths and the moral norms or values of society. It thus helps us determine right from wrong.

As one's fear is internalized, it can take on several aspects which may even be classified as personality disorders, depending on its severity. It may affect the mood of a person, causing him/her to not only be alarmed (looking around himself/herself for an object of fear) all the time, but it could also help create the right kind of environment that houses such characteristics as being insecure, deprived, lonely, pessimistic, defensive, provocative, hopeless, helpless, upset, discouraged, or depressed, to name these few. As fear persists, a person may experience tension in his/her muscles, fatigue, restlessness, difficulty sleeping, irritability, dry mouth, inability to make visual contact when talking to someone else, or inappropriate body posture. Physiologically, there may be internal changes that set the tone for the individual to observe the following signs and symptoms: rapid heart rate or pulsation, high blood pressure, frequent urination and/or bowel movement, shortness of breath, headache, dizziness, angina or stomach/back pains (Calron, N. R., 1988; Coleman,1988). Let me just mention that shyness, a mild and more specific type of fear, can make a person uncomfortable especially in social settings, thereby generating many of the conditions listed above. As we just described for you, fear may be as real as our shadow!

gure 1.1 A fearful shadow

Depending on whether or not we are in real danger, or there be some frightening object to really be afraid of, otherwise, we might be simply trying to run away from our own shadow, which is to me an irrational endeavor. Now, as far as I know, there is no threat coming from that other than what you and I wish to create. Our shadow is the friendliest, non offensive representation of ourselves; we need to get in touch with ourselves and our emotions more often!

Fear in any form or shape will definitely put a certain amount of stress on the individual, and failure to successfully develop effective defense mechanisms or coping techniques will leave a person highly vulnerable. We reserve a special chapter in this book to talk about stress in general, considering that it may also be a direct result of what we try to describe here. However, before going much further, we would like to provide you with some suggestions in dealing with fear, per se.

Generally, there exist several ways to effectively handle fear or the stress resulting from it. First and foremost, you must identify the source of your fear, what causes you to be afraid! If you can recognize or acknowledge it, there is hope if you will take appropriate steps to correct it, or else you may deny that it ever exists. Denying that we have a problem does not make it go away, and neither does that help us look for possible cures or treatments. For one thing, we are rational beings, but we often fool ourselves and end up on the wrong side of the fence, messing up our lives. While some people may view denial as a coping mechanism, the other side to it is that they just set themselves up for failure and mock themselves with a **"K.I.S.S."** or Keep It Simple Stupid. Denial is not a solution; it simply provides a basis for the problem to exacerbate or become worse. Secondly, let me say that if your fear is strong enough to cause disturbance in your mood and affect your performance vis-à-vis the task at hand, you definitely need to assess every situation where you are most likely to experience fear. Thirdly, every time a fear arousal is generated in you, it will probably increase your stress level, at least temporarily. To help you deal with your fear more effectively, we are proposing the following:

1. If your fear revolves around failing a test or under-performing a particular task, make sure that you prepare yourself by receiving adequate training. Also, building self- confidence is a great tool in helping you overcome most kinds of fear, either rational (a well founded feeling) or irrational (unfounded or imaginary, no good reason). Otherwise, you can nurture your fear by doubting your own capabilities. If you internalize your fear, and don't do something about it, other than sitting on it, believe me it WILL NOT GO AWAY. Instead, it will be a constant source of trouble to your mood and your health in general. That is why we are urging you to identify your source of fear right now; then use appropriate techniques to help you overcome such a feeling. Develop and practice healthy habits which will assure you greater control of your person.

2. If your fear has to do with entertaining a large audience or crowd of people, you want to prepare yourself adequately before performing. Some people seem to almost always experience anxiety when they become exposed socially, especially in dealing with an unfamiliar crowd and in areas where they seem to lack expertise, and self assertiveness. Many times people experience this kind of fear, because they do not relate that well to their audience, or to the message that they are about to deliver. Instead, they focus on themselves, how they will be judged by their peers. That creates panic attacks in them and eventually shatters their ability to contain themselves (exert a certain amount of control over their own emotions) and perform. You need to capture the attention of your audience (listeners) by treating them as friends rather than judges. You also need to master the situation by demonstrating that you are in control. <u>Continued and uncontrolled fear can be a great source of disturbance.</u> You may want to find a way to make your audience laugh at the beginning of your performance, as well as during your presentation in order to create a friendly atmosphere and break the anxiety cycle.

You also want to feel relaxed and show them that you are. You can even make joke about being shy or anxious in delivering your message. If you experience fear before you talk in front of a group of people, try your best to organize your thought processes beforehand; and on the stage, take a few deep breaths.

3. Some people are afraid of objects, SITUATIONS, or animals, including other human beings (better known as homophobic). One way to desensitize yourself is by frequent exposure to what causes you to fear in the first place. You are afraid of dogs, then play with them more often. You are afraid of flying, fly more often. In both cases, take your best friend with you, or someone that you are comfortable with, especially somebody who is not in the same predicament as you. You can teach yourself out of fear by constantly visualizing yourself in the environment with the object of fear. You can also rationalize by doing mental exercises like playing down your feeling and by telling yourself that you are not afraid, which is different from denial.

The other kind of fear and the most important one that we wish to help you come out of has to do with self-expansion, self-imposed limitations, which is generally grounded in our perception (how you see, understand and interpret different things or situations). This often goes against any fresh idea, any new belief system that encourages personal growth! Another aspect of it is that sometimes some of us may feel as though we have too much to lose to allow any kind of changes to take place in the system or the environment (conflict of interest). Therefore, we choose to maintain the status quo by going through everyday motions, practicing the same old routine when we could be on our way to the greatest discovery ever. Whatever comfort we now feel, we are resigned to it. Other people are simply too ignorant or too narrow-minded to even conceive changes. Still others just don't care about improving their lives. Therefore, they opt for no kind of behavior modification. In other words, they do not look to make any significant investment in life. For them, life takes no further course. They either inherit a situation, or they confine themselves to a menial task in life. Then, they fall in love with it. As a result, they cut short or waive the probation process by becoming intimate and make the position permanent and rule out any other possibilities or opportunities that might arise. All is finite or final, no renovation or innovation, no incentive to reach any higher than to stay where they are at, which may be just steps from the umbilical cord. So far, two distinct patterns have been suggested in dealing with people as they go through life.

One pattern focuses on one group of people that is task-oriented, up-beat and receptive to new opportunities. These individuals are able to face day-to-day challenges objectively, whether it be real obstacles, their object of fear, or the stressor. In the end, they take appropriate steps to resolve the issue (s) at hand.

The other pattern looks at those individuals who always come forth with a defense-oriented mechanism or strategy. In which case, they simply react to different situations by developing all sorts of unrealistic approaches such as: denial, repression, emotional insula-tion, overcompensation (spending so much energy in the wrong way), regression (going back to stages that they have already outgrown), acting out, etc. (Coleman 1988; Myers, D.G., 1987; Mondésir, E. 1993.)

What is the big deal about fear? We wished that we had all the nice things to say about it. Unfortunately, if we don't address it properly, we will do a disservice to humanity itself and we could not live in peace with our conscience. Constant fear can destroy one's emotional well-being, and if it is allowed to become internalized, it may progress to more advanced stages thereby throwing out of balance many of an individual's bodily functions. Suppose that you affront a fearful object or obstacle, your neurological system will be activated, causing many glands to release different hormones into the blood stream, especially adrenalin (epinephrine) and noradrenalin (norepinephrine) from the Adrenal medulla and the cortex, respec-tively. As the channels transporting these hormonal secretions remain open for an extended period of time, the person's heart rate will go up, blood pressure will increase and perhaps will stay up until it is treated, the situation reverses itself, or until the point of exhaustion is reached and the entire system shuts off.

Furthermore, while a person experiences fear and or stress, one of the many outcomes could be that an increase in systemic imbalance becomes noticeable. For example, the sweat glands may secrete unnecessary amounts of sweat. At times, the person may feel uncomfortable, hot, cold, restless, and might even develop migraine headache. In some instances, when people are in fear, they lose control of their bowels (Hole, John W. Human Anat. & Phys. 1987. PP. 465-478) Sometimes, their body becomes shaky (just as a friend of mine whose legs shake like someone who has a seizure or Parkinson's disease). Occasionally, there are few people whose mouths might produce additional amounts of saliva, otherwise, the opposite is more likely to happen. Their mouths become dry.

I like to feel that I am in control at least of my own body. So, if you are like me, you may struggle to regain control. Thank God, there are not that many objects or obstacles that generate fear arousal in me.

People who are very shy or who feel quite insecure watch their surroundings, and try as hard as they can to prevent being exposed. This could be a learned behavior, especially for those individuals who grow in cultures where there is strong indoctrination about power figures and paternalism, and very domineering social classes (Fairholm, GB. 1994; Miller, J.B. 1972). In the case of children who have been trained not to look older folks in the eyes or ask questions (complete subordination, total submission), these individuals grow up having difficulty to really stand up and defend their position until they become liberated, until they liberate themselves. That is why we say that such is one's frame of mind, such is one's thinking; because the whole idea of paralyzing fear or enslavement has to do with your mind and your perception of things, how your thought process operates.

In academic settings, fear may keep students from asking questions which are relevant to understanding their teachers, their professors, or their course materials, thereby preventing them from achieving higher marks. In front of a judge, or anyone who happens to be in authority over them, they are quiet or withdrawn. It can be quite a weary situation to find oneself in. Asking questions and coming across firm or assertive is the key. There are many settings in this world where you may be perceived as guilty every time you fail to take a stand for your rights or articulate your positions. Some people will always be there looking to profit from your position of weakness. From that perspective, we say that "one man's failure is another man's success". If you refuse to or cannot do it for yourself, someone will take advantage of that. The kind of fear that we are talking about here may last for a life time, if you allow it to happen. Consequently, you may not come to full personal growth or maturity, and your accomplishments will be scarce.

The sooner, the better. If you would like to expand in any area in your life, you've got to overcome your own fear by taking the lead. Yes, but how does one do that? Well, you just do it. Remember the response of former US First Lady Nancy Reagan to kids using drugs? That was quite a test in itself. However, certain things are easier said than done. And getting rid of our irrational, unfounded fear is achievable if we mean to and learn how.

During my childhood, there was a boy who used to physically attack me. As a result, I used to feel very stressed out every time I would meet him on the street. Then, I viewed him as my giant, my Goliath. However, one day I finally decided that my relationship to him would be different once and for all. As usual, he attacked but this time I convinced myself that I would no longer resign myself to the situation, and I did not feel powerless any more. I fought back and beat him up. That put an end to his harassing me. His aggression stopped, and never has he bothered me again. I had to take control and teach him a lesson. Every time you see yourself as powerless, as hopeless, and as helpless, you are most likely to be defeated or destroyed by the circumstances.

I was told the story of a particular woman who despised her husband. Every time the wife was not pleased with something that he did, did not do, or said, she would grab her stick and beat him up. You are talking about real physical abuse. This was a woman who knew how to take care of her man. However, one day the husband decided that he would change the situation. He anticipated a scenario where he is being the victim but with one thing different. He visualized his dearly beloved wife coming at him with the whip as usual; then, he prepared himself. Now the usual situation lent itself once again. And as the wife got closer to lynching him, he jumped out of his customary suit, pulled from the closet a piece of pine wood specifically designed for the incident. He lit it up, pulled up his own hidden whip. He used the fire to create an optimal space between himself and his wife so she would not easily get through to him. With one hand, he held the lit torch and with the other, he spanked her to his liking. As his fear ended, so did his misery. Now, I am not in any way suggesting that this is what you should do if you are having problems with your wife or husband. You might want to disarm him by lovingly taking the belt away from him, or you, husband, might want to gently remove that venom from her tongue and prevent further gossiping or verbal harassment. I hope that you will be able to accomplish all of that in love and gentleness. Before going any further, I would like to address a positive aspect of fear.

A. Healthy or Positive Fear

Thus far, you probably have been told that all fear is bad and irrational. On the contrary, scientifically it has been shown that we need a little bit of fear to operate. It is almost exactly what some men say about their spouse that they can't live with them and they can't live without them. If you notice, that is not my saying, otherwise, I would have stated it the other way to sympathize with the women.

Too much of anything hurts, so they say, and dealing with fear is not an exception to that golden rule. By raising our anxiety level and the pumping of a little bit of adrenaline in our blood stream, fear in a minute quantity can help us carry an assignment to term. It may as well redeem us from a potential source of danger.

Consider for instance that your house caught fire and you seem to not be able to locate the door to escape. You and your family are inside, the flames and the smoke make it very difficult for you to look for and rescue family members. Suddenly, a bright idea comes to you to not only escape from the fire but also to contain it or make that 911 call (wherever and whenever applicable) and get help. To flee from the fire, you either jump through the window or locate the fire escape (stairways) just in time, which is quite adventurous. Well, without that amount of fear being generated, you probably would not have the strength to do anything that could save your life and that of your family. Whether to risk your life by staying in the house or to jump out of the window and break your leg, you choose the least of the two evils. There is a Haitian proverb that says "Tout bet jennen mode." What that means is if you push even a docile animal to a corner leaving it no way to escape, it might create its own line of defense, including jumping on you! This may sound a bit sensational or perhaps, scary to some of you. However, that's not out of place.

In the so-called science of life, biology, we learn about a concept termed "Fight or Flight". That means that for any animal, including humans, whenever confronted by an obstacle or potential danger the tendency is to react either by displaying some type of aggressive behavior like attacking (fighting) the obstacle or by running away from it, which is synonymous to flight (fleeing). I will provide another example about containing your fear or using it constructively and after that I'll move on to something else.

Remember when you were in school, if you ever developed a phobia with respect to taking an exam, you turned that obnoxious feeling into a healthy one. You applied yourself and used the same energy in a positive way. You spent time studying the material, and on the day of the test, you just walked in and passed your exam. You probably told yourself beforehand that you would pass, which is recognized as the power of positive thinking. Have you ever surprised yourself that way? I am sure that's an affirmative (a yes answer). That fear of failing, which could be very demoralizing, was turned into a productive force, just like a catalyst. My goal in writing this book is not necessarily to convert you to Christianity; nevertheless, it should come as no surprise to us that the Bible admonishes the adept to the Christian faith against disbelief; and Peter (St. Peter), one of the disciples, made history as the first and only human who literally walked on water. He believed. However, the instant he doubted, he could no longer remain afloat but started sinking (Saint Matthew 14: 25-31.). Along with doubt that was mounting up inside Peter, he developed what we call healthy fear. Whichever way you might look at it, you will find a way to deal with the emotion constructively.

14

After all, too much of anything tends to leave a negative taste in our mouths. Having said that, let us continue with the other aspects of fear.

B. Unhealthy or Negative Fear

There is a saying which goes as follows, "Once you lose control of your temper, you diminish yourself in front of your peers". Well, that is true probably not because anyone expects you to be perfect or emotionally guarded at all times nor that you are necessarily antisocial. It means that the way you react in front of other people makes them think twice about you. On occasions such as that, they may feel that you do meet their expectations. Whenever you allow that to happen, fear can make you act very strangely. Unless you become desensitized by keeping your fear in check, you tend to turn into a volcano, reacting to everything, including people that you come in contact with. The truth of the matter is that you engage in the wrong kind of reaction. With time, you find yourself acting in a pattern that is totally unhealthy. The obstacles, as you perceive and translate them into your own belief system, take control over you, instead of you dominating them.

While fear can well be no more than a mindset, freedom is the way. Fear can paralyze and keep you hostage in your own home. You will not believe how much damage fear can do to you! It can be very draining and counterproductive. It may even be a source of depression in your life. Open that compartment over there and feel the pain. That is definitely not a way that anyone should live. May I ask what your source of fear is? Are you comfortable with that? Perhaps you don't know any better. Maybe you have lived in constant fear all your life and have identified with it to such an extent that it almost becomes normal for you. Just like people who always take abuse mercifully, there comes a time when they no longer consider that an issue; they condition or resign themselves to it until one day, they just explode. How many times have people been ridiculed or discriminated against for whatever reasons, but choose not to do anything about it! Sometimes, we see it and know what to do but feel too powerless, too helpless to say or do something. Other times, we are too preoccupied, feeling self-pity, or too busy contemplating the obstacles.

If not all, most of our fear is unfounded, irrational, and self defeating. Our perception is often a distorted but powerful indicator to see things differently from the way they really are. In a way it feeds our ignorance and helps shape our beliefs and attitudes about ourselves and life in general. You are talking about a very inaccurate measurement. Fear at its extreme can resemble paranoia, a form of personality disorder where subjects experience delusions and they hallucinate about the world coming after them, looking to harm them.

When we allow fear to penetrate our world, it does not take long to manifest itself to other people around us who in turn may use it against us and to their advantage. So, we often set ourselves up by not realizing the impact of our actions/reactions. Note that the greater your phobia or your fear, the greater is your vulnerability. As someone said, "Better fear a danger once than be always in fear". In his writing on the anatomy of melancholy, Robert Burton (1577-1640) indicated, "The fear of death is worse than death".

C. Overcoming Your Fear

1- The Agony of Fear

People who study war and those who are infatuated with securing peace, argue that the best way to maintain peace is to prepare for war. I am not so sure that this always works to one's best interest. For one thing, we can never have full control over what happens in the environment. Secondly, peace is not always secure by having weapons in our home, for oftentimes they are used against us or members of our own family. Thirdly, unless we wish to become a society of savages, there are better ways of maintaining peace in our home, our neighborhood, and around the world other than piling up destructive weapons which once they are made we have so little control over. However, desperation is often a child of fear. You cannot be wrong in being assertive, which is what most people lack. Also, you <u>do not want to trouble trouble until trouble troubles you</u>. Nonetheless, to secure your freedom, sometimes you may need to put a question mark over certain traditions in the ways that they harbor the status quo. Do you ever wonder what it is like to have opportunities taken away from you simply because you did not prepare for it or due to your lack of assertiveness?

If fear is characterized by a real or an imaginary feeling of being threatened, or being intimidated by someone, some object, some situation, you must look for its opposite, which is the assurance of being in control, of being self-assertive. Then, freedom can be thought of as an imposing statue standing on a dominant tower, or as a compass or a lighthouse which provides guidance along the sailor's path. In other words, even though freedom is not a license to do as one pleases, it gives you the pleasure of acting on your own account and on your own terms.

Many of us have allowed fear to control every aspect of our lives, thereby reducing ourselves to subservants, living in abject poverty. Consequently, we never amount to what we ought to be. Once we are subdued by our fear, we become resigned to whatever socio-economic and/or spiritual conditions in which we find ourselves, thinking that the Good Lord thus created them that way and that such boundaries ought to be revered and kept in place. We deny ourselves the right to exist and live in dignity: our personal growth becomes stagnant. Our psycho-social well-being as well as our economic growth remain feeble and shallow. A lot of us are afraid or feel incapacitated to follow our destiny by taking the lead or moving to the highest possible stage of our development. And we make sure that we find every reason not to do so. As time goes on, every single opportunity passes us by. We become sessile and we just sit there watching our whole existence being wasted.

2- Shaking it Off

I just want to tell you that you must first cast out any fear or doubt which has crippled you, and establish your own identity before anybody else can acknowledge your existence. When fear knocks on your door, as if it is about to impeach you, you need to curse it, give it the death wish, and take control immediately or forever live in your misery and tragedy.

People may want to or at least try to deny you access to a lot of opportunities, but you are the only person who can give the okay or the permission that such things be done to you. God really did create us equal; however, in our own fearful way and through ignorance we have too often substituted (replaced) humility by humiliation. Then, we subject ourselves to lead a life that is far less fulfilling than our maker ever intended it to be. Many of us love to say that we are surviving! Surviving what? I haven't the faintest idea! If you surrender the key of your existence or well-being to your fellow human beings and allow them to exercise the power of attorney over your own assets, I guarantee that they will gladly assume charges. They will even tell you when you may eat, what to eat, when to sleep, where to live, what kind of education you and your children are entitled to, or how far below or above the minimum wage you can earn.

I know that it is easier said than done. However, some of the most remarkable achievements that any of us can make in our lives include being assertive and eager to learn new skills that will make us remain necessary, and having the willingness, as well as the motivation to develop and implement a system that provides room for our own personal growth and maturity. Which in turn will lead us towards interdependency and autonomy instead of total dependability on an ineffective and yet an inefficient system!

I do not know what constitutes a phobia in your life and hinders your self-promoting ambitions. Nonetheless, whatever it may be, real or imaginary, we urge that you find the positive component of that force to overcome your fear or it will negate your personality, and distort your vision and your image. Consequently, it will deprive you of all the opportunities by taking them away from you and replacing them with obstacles. Fear is a feeling which we must bring under control or it will subdue us and cause our downfall.

Only as we apply ourselves in this life will we be able to experience the fullness of joy, personal growth, self-satisfaction, new spiritual dimensions, wellness, and success, whatever our definition may be. That is also the way we will find freedom that will make us whole.

❖ CHAPTER II ❖

Are Bondage and Freedom
Two Sides of the Same Coin?

Sometime prior to his ascent (rising) to the presidency, Mr. Nelson Mandela of South Africa said, "I will not leave South Africa, nor will I surrender. I will continue fighting for freedom until the end of my days."

Mr. Mandela went from living as a civilian with some freedom to an inmate (with almost no freedom) where he spent twenty-seven years and ultimately to occupying the highest office in the land. This is not magic or luck. We are talking about someone who not only believes in positive thinking but who also acts on it while keeping his motivation high until the goal is reached and the prize is won. He is a living symbol of pride and excellence. Though destiny might have abandoned him in the jail cells of South Africa's old apartheid regime, by his determination, his persistence to pursue standards of equality for himself, his people, and humankind, and his courage to rise beyond the obstacles, Mr. Mandela lives a life that has some powerful lessons for those of us who often think that we are powerless in life's situations and therefore have to resign to whatever complexities may come our way.

Before the proclamation of the great American emancipation proclaimed by President Abraham Lincoln on September 22, 1862, black people were not allowed in many public places and facilities such as: schools for higher education (colleges and universities), restaurants, amusement parks, and rest rooms. They even had to have their own church to worship a God who condemned bigotry, hatred, segregation, racial inequalities or what have you. And until Ms. Rosa L. Parks decided that it was too much and openly resented the idea, black people could only sit in the back of the bus on public transportation. They lived, worked the land, and contributed to the wealth of the country; however, they barely had anything to do or say about the

19

assets that they helped produce. They were part of the system in terms of production but when it came to the distribution of the wealth, their rights stopped short. They were prohibited from exercising their rights such as independent living and voting which is a fundamental necessity due to the fact that all people are created equal and should be able to freely pursue their destiny. I should mention that while voting may not mean much to all of us in the U.S. and other parts of the world where elections are relatively free, it is a right that some people too often take for granted. Unfortunately, freedom of self-determination (that is the responsibility of each one of us to pursue and achieve socio-economic independence) depends on our individual choice and we must labor tirelessly to engage in the fight all the way, which also includes voting. If and when we choose not to exercise these rights, I guarantee you someone else will be more than happy to do it for us. Talking about voting, how many of us realize that every time we have the opportunity to participate in the affairs of our country and don't take it that somebody worse than we ever imagine will get elected and mess up everything? Am I being prophetic? Sometimes, all that a particular candidate needs to win an election is that one additional ballot vote over the opponent. Therefore, those who decide not to vote indirectly but automatically support a candidate.

Realistically, it is somewhat inconceivable for us to want what we do not know or what no other human ever dreamed of. That is to say that our individual pursuits reflect what men and women collectively aim at. Hence, once we become exposed to something that we appreciate or develop a taste for, we might very well want it for ourselves. Also, imagination gets its price; oftentimes, we need to start from scratch and build on. For lack of creativity, we spend a lot of time going backward and lusting after what others have worked very hard for!

As much as Karl Marx with his communist might has made many of us Westerners uncomfortable, we can grow up a little bit to appreciate a statement that he made, and which we might even agree with, being true to ourselves. Marx said, "A house may be large or small; as long as the surrounding houses are equally small, it satisfies all social demands for a dwelling. But let a palace arise beside the little house, and it shrinks from a little house to a hut."

If none of us were free or concerned about freedom, or perhaps if everyone had the same amount of resources, then at least for a while things would be fine since people could afford food to feed their families and supply many of their basic necessities. Now, the notion that "all men are created equal" makes us long for things that other human beings possess. On the contrary, bondage tends to suppress in some ethnic groups these basic human aspirations and if it were possible it would even eliminate their humanity. Slavery can be either self-imposed or somebody may force us into it. Many of us have the idea that enslavement can only be physical, not realizing that whoever and whatever controls our mind also regulates our whole person. We better believe this and incorporate it into our knowledge bank or we will just be everyone else's fool and attempt to walk in everyone else's shadow.

Both slavery as well as freedom have their demands. Whereas a slave is deprived of his or her free will and the serf's basic needs are often supplied by a master, a free person, on the other hand, assumes responsibilities and decides on his/her own. In domineering relation-ships where one person literally dictates what everyone else in the family/society ought to do, a role that is most often attributed to men (in a male dominated world) or occasionally to whomever the bread winner happens to be. When a person is deprived of his or her freedom or his or her rights and privileges as a result of another human being's infringement, we cannot talk about mutual relation-ships or partnerships because only one individual or group of individuals make all the decisions for the rest of the people. This kind of uneven relationship also resembles what goes on between employ-ers and employees or between nations where one nation, usually the smaller and the weaker, does not enter the round table negotiations as an equal partner but is pressured to accept the conclusions drawn by the stronger partner (s) or to go along with whatever decisions have been made on its behalf. Now the question is should freedom always be desired or preferred over slavery? As you answer this question, please make sure that you keep it within its proper context, or you might create a situation where you choose slavery over freedom. I will agree with you, though, if you said that you like to do the right thing at the right time and in the right place. However, slavery has no other name, it is denigrating and diminishing. Most of all, you decide how much abuse or harassment that you are willing to take from anyone. Also, I would warn you not to run from crisis to crisis or from slavery to slavery. Sometimes, we run from a bad situation to only fall into the worst one.

According to biblical history, the Israelites were granted freedom from the Egyptians in the 13th century B. C. (Before Christ) after serving them some 400 years. After the nation of Israel's exodus from the land of servitude (slavery), it headed toward Canaan, the "Promised land" via different deserts, including Mount Sinai, according to the biblical scholar, Reverend Paula J. Waters. It occurred that while they were in route that they experienced food and water shortages. Then, they cried out saying, "Why did not we stay in Egypt, serving the Egyptians? At least, we would have food to eat" (Exodus 16: 1-4). The complaint of the Jews about possible starvation in the desert, and their idea of taking the yoke of slavery upon themselves once more seems to come as a desperate cry, lacking some logic and justifying bondage over freedom! Obviously, the thought of going back and being fed by their former Egyptian masters versus sitting in the desert is a two-edged sword or it looks like choosing between two evils. What do I mean by that? In either decision, death seems to be eminent. In other words, they can either choose to die of starvation with dignity, or go back, be fed, and die under the gun and in humiliation.

Based on our discussion here, it would seem illogical and irrelevant for anyone to want bondage over freedom.

In the United States of America, the Constitution guarantees the rights of all citizens to proper physical care and medical treatment while they are incarcerated or during involuntary confinement. Ironically, it seems that in recent times, few hopeless individuals would rather give up their freedom and go to jail so they could be cared for! Maybe that is not a bad idea, after all; free meals, a free room, free medical care, free everything, even free handcuffs, free chains. For anyone who feels desperate, that may seem the only way to go and acquire what he or she needs.

By definition, bondage (slavery) means: the quality of being bound, a restraint of personal liberty by compulsion (force), voluntary subjugation (willfully); the tenure or the service of a villain, serf, or a slave. On the contrary, freedom is defined as the quality or the state of being free, and not being constrained by fate, necessity, or by circumstances in one's choices or actions. In other words, a free human being decides for self, thinks for self as well as acts in one's best interest, whereas the slave is to be told what to think and told when to or not to move. Someone has taken control over someone else's life and therefore makes all major decisions for that person. In one of his assertive speeches, Dr. Martin Luther King, Jr. cried, "Free, free at last..." Many other great leaders and advocates of the emancipation believed that freedom was the only way out, the only choice. Now, even if Webster and other authoritative figures in the area of linguistics were to misguide us, we would still have to decide whether we want to be the estate or the possession of someone else.

Thus far, I probably have led many of you to believe that slavery deals only with the physical or that one could only be subdued by other people. Bondage affects our mind as well and in many occasions, we become a slave of our own beliefs and ignorance.

A- Freedom From the Umbilical Cord (the Navel String)

With the privilege of being born also comes the need to grow, mature, produce, and even become detached or independent. I am not all so concerned with the physical aspect of this, because given the proper nurturing and time, physical growth will happen. Moreover, by the time we are prepared to move on and be on our own, our parents usually provide for our needs. Thank God for the umbilical cord. It was an excellent apparatus for the time being. It has served its purpose well, but after all we reach the age where each of us must come to the realization that we can no longer rely on Mom or Dad or any surrogate parent (s) to care for and provide for us. One question we might ask ourselves is the following: should we fault our parents for not handing everything to us so we could live without having to take on so many responsibilities on our own? And if they did, could we ever mature and become responsible adults? Absolutely not. Our obligations towards ourselves and our fellow human beings demand that we fulfill our individual tasks, or life is meaningless: no challenges, no aspirations, and no progress beyond what our parents have made.

Fig. 2.1 Gratitude/Dependency linked to servitude

Freedom is not hereditary or something that a government or a country necessarily and equally gives to all its citizens. To obtain their freedom, some people fight to death, and sometimes not even their offspring live to tell the story. If anybody owes something to us adults, then it must be our name. Anything else is on us. We have no excuse for not doing something to help ourselves. As Sidney Smith said, "It is the greatest mistake to do nothing because you can only do a little. Do what you can."

For everything under the sun, there is a time. Our time to be born was yesterday; today is our time to grow and mature emotionally, psychologically and spiritually. Today is the time to break away from the umbilical chord and look to become self-sustained socioeconomically.

A chicken egg that goes on for months without hatching is certainly defective. Contrary to scientifically-based knowledge, the Haitian popular wisdom and mysticism tend to believe that a woman can carry a baby in her womb for more than a year. Nonetheless, a human embryo can develop in the placenta for only nine months plus or minus two (2) weeks. Once the baby is born, it must automatically assume certain responsibilities on its own like breathing and having a pulse and a heart rate. Also, that baby must be able to get rid of the debris of food metabolism through urination, perspiration, and defecation. Past several months postpartum (after birth) infants are expected to show some sign of mobility like trying to crawl or even standing up by holding on to some device. These little ones must be encouraged so that different aspects of their development can take place. They will require some adult supervision and nurturing until they become fully developed. However, one thing is not possible. Contrary to what some unrealistic parents and a few interest groups would want, once the fetus comes out it cannot reenter its mother's womb or be reattached to the cord anymore. Life must go on.

Different ethnic groups tend to vary in their approach to socialization. Some cultures advocate greater dependency than others as the way to life. The higher the level of dependency, less of a desire will a person have to grow and obtain freedom. In addition, with a teaching that emphasizes the wrong concept or idea, a person may early on develop low self-esteem and an inferiority complex. That is one of the reasons why psychology warns us about what we feed to our kids. If they grow up in an environment where they are constantly being put down especially by adults whom they perceive as their role models, and if they have been ridiculed or looked at as inadequate, then they grow up believing that. It takes strong-willed individuals to teach themselves out of that culture and achieve any significant accomplishment in their lives. The status quo and traditions that many rich and poor people cherish represent a sign that they belong to a system. The rich often think that the only way to maintain their wealth is by getting more and more, regardless. The poor, on the other hand, who are already at a disadvantage sometimes do nothing other than sit and complain about everything and everybody else. If there is no one or nothing to blame they soon invent one.

25

The socio-political, cultural, and economic constraints which are designed within existing establishments oftentimes represent contributing factors that prevent underserved, underrepresented groups from reaching their goals. Once these factors are in place they usually become barriers that cannot be lifted easily by outsiders or those at a disadvantage. Other times, nature itself may set the tone, thereby putting some people in very awkward situations. However, for the most part the foremost handicap and obstacle which can prevent us from growing and succeeding in life is our own self, our own perceived limitations, our own beliefs. In all three instances, we need to make an assessment of our situation, and if need be try to do the necessary damage control, all for the purpose of putting our life on the right track and moving ahead. To every problem there is a solution.

Just like a race that is undertaken by a great many athletes at the beginning but to be disqualified later, during our life's journey, most of us start at the same point and with the same opportunities, but get bogged down, sidetracked, or lose our motivation. Which leads us to believe that to a large extent, the focus must be on us instead of on the others, what they did or did not do for us. Other factors that restrain an individual from ever reaching his or her goals are his or her own inabilities to dissociate from the womb (the womb or the umbilical cord being anybody, anything or any ideology used as crutches) and view life in a brand new dimension.

Other than Adam and Eve, we all can relate very well to the analogy of cord, placenta or womb, because we carry the scar. During pregnancy, the human fetal tissue remains attached to the woman's womb via the umbilical cord, which is intended to be but a temporary support system. For that matter, the relationship is not a perfect one and can neither be permanent. A fairly identical analogy that resembles the relationship just described above has to do with those welfare recipients who rely permanently on government or on somebody to care for them. Therefore, they selectively create a deceptive, faulty comfort zone or a cage that houses their entire imagination. Consequently, they do not allow themselves to look beyond that habitat or pursue any other avenue that would help them break the yoke of dependency. It is as though they force themselves into a real jail cell that has no way out. Stated otherwise, we might say that they try to confine themselves within the walls of the uterus with no intentions of ever growing beyond that, which not only violates a natural law (that limits the length of stay for any individual human being regardless of race, gender, sexual preference, national origin, religious creed, or marital status to a maximum of nine months, plus or minus two weeks grace period), but it also jeopardizes the very existence of the dependent person and further threatens the welfare of his or her neighbor.

Now, no matter how unethical or arrogant that might sound, the unborn or the dependent species is at the mercies of the caregiver. Case in point, many argue that a fetus cannot be viewed as a person because of the absence of the individual will. Taken a step further, there is a high risk that whoever relies on such people's mercy might be flushed out of their system without prior notice.

The relationship between the mother and the fetus is not so important for us here. We continue to use it, however, as a way to draw your attention on the issues of: freedom versus bondage, personal growth versus dwarfism (socially speaking), socio-economic and spiritual uplifting versus stagnation, or interdependence versus a state of total dependence (leading towards abject poverty).

We know that from a physiological (the way in which the body functions) standpoint, the umbilical cord via the placenta allows the two individuals to develop a unique relationship. Actually, whatever substance enters the mother's body reaches the baby that she carries, which is another reason why pregnant women are discouraged from using illegal drugs (substances) and alcohol, for fear that they might cause damage to their unborn baby. However, we wish not to expound on this issue at this point. Given the intimate relationship that these two human beings share, it creates an environment for the fetus, the unabled, the unspoken, to be one hundred per cent (100%) dependent on another person, in this case the mother. That unique way of survival necessarily ends at approximately 266 to 280 days following the last menstrual cycle of the woman, and then the two, mother and fetus, can no longer hold on to each other.

May I say that we enjoy being part of a secure environment, away from all sources of danger and disturbances. We must know by now

27

there isn't any perfect system that exists in our world which can provide complete, lasting satisfaction; not even the one we just described above. Certainly, it is the safest, the most reliable for that particular period of time and given the existing conditions. Ultimately, the separation between the two individuals becomes inevitable, whereby this newly fashioned creature departs from its temporary haven or shelter. The intimate bond which once existed is somehow severed, thereby reducing the level of dependency. To reiterate, such a breakaway occurs automatically. It was made that way and will remain as such; when we try to keep it going longer than it ought to, we just mess ourselves up.

King Solomon said it and our own experience proves it. Paradoxically and ironically, "To everything under the sun, there is a season…" A time to be born, and a time to die; a time to build, and a time to tear down; a time to hate, and a time to love; a time to make friends, and a time to depart from friends; and even a time to grow and mature.

Many experts recognize growth as a process that can be painful at times. However, by not allowing ourselves to undergo the normal process, we cause much more harm to ourselves first, then to our loved ones, then to humanity as a whole. We disrupt our own personal growth by relying on the environment or more specifically somebody to come along and do for us what we alone are responsible to do for ourselves. When a person suffers from malnutrition, we refer to the condition as "kwashiorkor." In other words, that severe form of nutrient deficiency prevents usually a relatively young person from reaching his or her full body size.

Sometimes, this aspect in the development of a person takes place, but does not accompany any other kind of growth. For example, a great number of people limit their mind as to what they can think of, accomplish, or achieve. They take their minds and sequester them in miniature boxes. What good is it to reach a full body size and have a mind in captivity. Many people wait around to see if somebody would come by and tell them that it is okay for them to think in a certain way, to dream of or to pursue certain goals. Others realize what they must do to enhance their growth, but get scared or distracted and ignore the fact that practice makes perfect; still others convince themselves that some people are exceptionally and naturally gifted, and that is the only determining factor in their high achievement in life. While there may be some truth to this, no one is as gifted as the person that persistently follows through on his or her dreams. In general, either individually or collectively (usually as a group), people base their existence on a concept called "self-fulfilling prophecy" in that they develop and nurture a belief system that matches whatever expectations they have of themselves: high, low, or none. They advocate for bondage instead of freedom; then, they live accordingly. They reduce their entire existence to a shell-like life and walk in someone else's shadow. I cannot think of a better illustration than the following one. There would never be butterflies in nature had the larvae not hatched from their cocoon, a kind of growth that is often referred to as metamorphosis! An individual species uses all the resources that it can allocate in order to ensure it does NOT live a stagnant life but remains in constant evolution, reaching out for excellence and/or perfection, if such a thing as perfection exists on earth. Then again, I am referring to a broader meaning of the word. By that I mean to say that one is constantly working towards living a fuller and a more complete life. It does not matter that a person may be born in a ghetto, but may apply himself or herself so he or she does not remain there vitam eternam (Latin), meaning indefinitely. I am sorry to say that to a great extent this is an individual choice, a willingness to jump higher and take on new vitality by tearing down obstacles, as in the case of the movie called "Forrest Gump" portrayed by Tom Hanks. This character, the main actor, was being chased by a bunch of naughty boys, school mates. Handicapped by a cast on one leg, the actor almost fell in the hands of his assailants. However, he used the power that was at his disposal to break that thing open and rise beyond the obstacles. The transformation of our lives clearly resembles that of a caterpillar.

I view the process rather fascinating, and almost the same phenomenon applies to other egg-laying animals. Without the hatching of the eggs, no new individuals can develop. Consequently, the entire species would head towards extinction. Even we humans cannot escape such reality, when we really think of it. The whole human race probably will not disappear as a result of this particular behavior

29

alone; however, before you and I may be able to experience growth in the full sense of the word, we must hatch or let go of our bondage which is our fear and our self-defeating beliefs.

Another intriguing fact is that no transition can be made without some sort of nuisance or some degree of disruption in the system. To put it mildly, there are risks involved when we engage in any kind of growth process, be it physical, mental, psychological, emotional, spiritual, social, political, economic, etc. Besides a few obstacles in the physical environment (such as diseases or being detained in jail indefinitely, in which we may not always have control over what happens to us and risk-taking fear) lack of motivation seems to be one of the main reasons why people are afraid to look for freedom. They are scared of growth or any kind of change. As I indicated earlier, some people in the United States admit that they would rather lose their freedom by breaking the law so they could be arrested, put to jail, and become dependent upon or be taken care of by the government instead of choosing to undergo changes that would eventually lead them into the path of independence. Like many others, those individuals refuse to liberate their minds. Contrary to creating opportunities for themselves, they decide to just retain the status quo by resigning to a life of stagnation or one that has no purpose or meaning and which leads nowhere. They're born and live and die in the ghetto; or they're born poor, live and act poor, enjoy being poor, and ultimately die poor. And since they continue to live and consume resources that someone else sweats for, not only do they become part of the problem but also, they automatically place themselves in the category of people who are "socially handicapped" or "socially disabled", *dependent state or a public nuisance and expect to be provided for.* With no offense to low achievers and those who perceive themselves as poor, it is somewhat unlikely for someone to always behave contrary to his or her belief. Who would like to match the two at a cost?

There is a price for freedom. Everyone has to sweat in the pursuit of his or her own freedom. "Nobody wants you to walk in their shoes", does this sound familiar? No one will voluntarily hand freedom to you. You have to want it and be willing to fight for it. And to know what you want, as well as how you will obtain it, helps you focus on a whole new dimension. That is why some conservative folks prefer to control what you and I are being taught. For the instant you acquire knowledge, it's like a "mind opener" which will guide you toward freedom. They have a real problem accepting another person stepping into that free world. It should be theirs and theirs only. However, if you really care about your personal growth and well-being, you need to do what you have to.

B- Enslaved to a World of Apathy and Greed!

While we are talking about people who freely accept to become or remain part of a welfare state, we cannot and will not ignore that greedy world out there. Anyone who has lived in it for a few decades and who is true to himself or herself can appreciate such a statement. Personally, I have seen quite a bit and experienced first hand a lot of bias, injustice, and social inequality. Of course, every culture, every society, every nation, and for that matter, every government that ever existed has embraced certain values aimed at promoting some kind of internal growth within that group, and eventually removing barriers that prevent growth at least for a collective minority, with respect to the rest of the world. In many instances, anyone who is not considered part of the group may not be granted free access to the readily available resources. However, whoever possesses a kindred mind can develop his or her own resources. It may require a lot of time to observe any significant result, but eventually, it shall come to pass where your creativity and persistency will pay off. The trend is not to be overly distracted, as you often will. Otherwise, whatever you conceive in your mind you can make it happen. For example, if you feel too restrained, maybe you are in some form of bondage. And if you recognize it as such, it might be detrimental to your personal growth and well-being. Then, you may want to identify whom or what you are enslaved to; and afterwards, try unceasingly to secure your release. Again, most kinds of servitude are self imposed. If you do not like a situation, try to create alternatives for yourselves. Don't be cornered in a box, as we often are. To every problem, there is at least a set of solutions. Let us consider for instance the following problem:

31

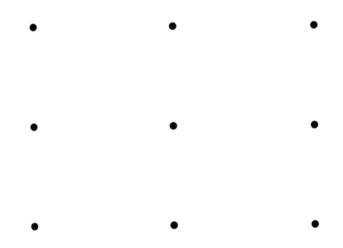

Fig. 2.2 A limited box for the unlimited imagination

If you count them, you will notice that there are nine dots set in a cubical form (a cubical, as you remember your geometry, is an object with six sides of equal dimensions in every direction: height, width, and length). Now, you are asked to draw four straight lines that will unite all (9) points without ever lifting your pen from the drawing. Do you think that you can find the solution? Hint: don't cage yourself in a box. Be willing to look beyond the boundaries. I will patiently wait for your answer at the end of the book. Thank you for your cooperation! May we go back to serious business?

It is first of all a disservice to each of us and then to society as a whole, when we choose to forfeit our rights to freedom, whether it be individual or collective. Sometimes, we have to work together to not just achieve but to maintain it too, since one influences the other. Not to forget that even freedom has boundaries, which may lead to its misuse or abuse, as well as the loss of the privileges that come with it.

By setting your spirit free, and by using it to your benefit and that of humankind, you will never stop growing, for as long as you live. Bondage is a form of physical, mental, psychological, spiritual, as well as emotional limitation, and it can be self-imposed, or it could be directed towards you. Self-imposed limitations may exercise a far greater influence on us if it is a state of mind, because in the course of human history, many people have been subject to extraneous physical servitude or enslavement but survive. Before anything or anyone can destroy you, they have to first disrupt your mind. Resigning to poverty or any kind of social deprivation, for instance, and not doing anything to either change or improve the conditions will eventually lead to physical, mental, psychological, emotional and spiritual debilitation. Obviously, we cannot win every single battle in this life, but at the same time, it does not mean that we have to give into every one of them. Choose them conspicuously or intelligently, and you will probably win more than you ever imagined.

You may recall earlier in this chapter we referred to the liberation of the Jews from the Babylonian rulers. Prior to that, they were told by the mighty king Pharaoh not to seek their freedom or he would see to it that their labor automatically increase. Later, while Egypt was being plagued by various disasters and the Israelites kept pushing for their emancipation, the king returned to his decisions so many times. At one point he told them that they had the choice of leaving his country, but empty-handed. Now, the Jews lived under slavery in Egypt for over 400 years, and at some point they helped the country prosper a great deal. Also, they did share some of that wealth. However, upon the king's order, leaving Egypt meant that all the assets that belonged to Jews would be confiscated, which by the way the slaves did not buy. They were persistent in their demands, and as the story went, Moses, the Jewish commissioner, presented their plea as was commanded by their God. After severe casualties were impounded all over Egypt in terms of human lives and livestock, the Babylonian monarch finally allowed all Jewish subjects to vacate the land with all that belonged to them (Exodus Chs. 7-11.) A slave has no real say over his/her person nor his/her estate, but the master does reserve all the rights. The servant does the dirty work, while the master reaps the benefits. We can even relate to that here in America, if our memory does not fail us. Those of us who did not live the era at least read about it. And the Reverend Dr. Martin Luther King, Jr. looking at the social justice in this country said and I quote:

"There is nothing more dangerous than to build a society with a large segment of people in that society who feel that they have no stake in it; who feel that they have nothing to lose. People who have stake in their society, protect that society, but when they don't have it, they unconsciously want to destroy it..."

Now strangely enough, many times the master is not a distinct person from us, but a mindset which we ourselves develop and which in turn prevents us from freely engaging in the road to personal freedom. A mindset shapes our belief system and affects how we perceive ourselves in the realm of things, whether or not we can get ourselves out of the present situations, or look hopeless and give up. Our captor may even be inanimate objects in the environment that we have allowed to take control over our lives. Some people have a lot of money; however, they are the servants and the money is their master. Bondage may be very subtle and it can cause great damage to our development.

After a careful personal inventory, we should be able to discover ourselves. As we get to know ourselves, then we may begin to undertake steps to liberate self and work toward self-determination, that is to develop our resources, educate ourselves to become better able and equipped, capable of caring for ourselves and our loved ones. Freedom from whatever and whomever is a process. President Alberto Fujimori of Peru used the best tool which he thought was at his disposal to free hostages from the Japanese Embassy (April 22, 1997.) Sometimes, our eagerness to win freedom may suggest difficult twists. It is often best that you work stepwise toward removing all real and perceived obstacles that may have held you hostage, by **1)** starting to identify the captor or captors, which may include your own emotion, your own beliefs, your own state of mind. **2)** evaluate the strength to be dealt with. **3)** develop specific strategies to deal with issues. **4)** reconcile, and negotiate first with yourself and/or anyone else that is involved as an important aspect of the process. **5)** find different alternatives to arriving at your ultimate goal, which is securing your freedom. We will devote some more time later to address the issue of negotiation, and conflict resolution;

but for now, a piece of advice to you: don't go half way and quit, thinking that you have initiated the process and the rest will take care of itself, you have just defeated the purpose right there. What you start, you must also complete. Don't be another quitter, unless it is a vice or a bad habit that you try to get rid of.

Beside your creator, you are the architect of your destiny. An athlete that is lazy, unfit, and does not apply himself or herself in such a way as to rise above all obstacles won't receive a prize.

May I say that a great many people don't know what they want in life. In other words, they set no goals for themselves, or have no specific reason for being alive. To reiterate, too many of us never really tried hard enough to grow beyond the cubicles or develop to full maturity, which also means growing way beyond the placental cavity. Among those who have attempted that great walk to freedom, so few have been willing or barely have much incentive to pursue with enough momentum. The majority concedes loss when they get so close to see the shining light at the end of the tunnel, they turn the opposite way and back to square one where they started. Let us be real and not kid ourselves. As Jean Jacques Rousseau stated: "...lacking all sense of right and wrong, a child can do nothing which is morally evil, or which merits either punishment or reproof." We must grow, mature and make sound decisions for ourselves. Our involvement in securing our own freedom is sine qua non. By that, I mean there is no other way. Each of us has the primary responsibility to sustain our own level of motivation, even if an external source does exist. You can never be too sure that you will always access that support whenever you need it. And not to be cynical, you don't always know the motive of those who claim to be sympathetic to your cause, especially when they might be competing with you for the same resources! You need not be greatly alarmed, but beware that for some people, their success means your failure. Some of us do like to maximize their result but at the same time would rather see others move at a much lower pace. The former US Supreme Court Justice, Thurgood Marshall, looking at the progress being made in the American social justice system said:

> "...I believe in gradualism, but ninety (90) odd years is gradual enough..."

To every rule there is an exception; however, the road to our own socio-economic progress will not be paved by the "Good Samaritan". Everything has a price and that rule has almost no exception. If you need something and need it bad enough, you may not be able to afford it immediately, but that is okay. Just don't get discouraged should you fail at first. Practice makes perfect. Keep on trying, and build on your strength but not on your weakness, lest you fall miserably. Even if it means taking one step at a time; babies do crawl before they develop muscle fitness and articulation to walk properly. It takes a great deal of trial and error for a human baby to learn how to walk. A baby that never falls may never walk either. Yet for many of them who do not succeed, they often attribute their downfall to some strange cause or to an external source.

C. Yeah, Blame it on Them, the Scapegoats

An encounter with the writing of someone by the name of Toni Morrison provides us with the following quotation, "If you can't count, they can cheat you. If you can't read, they can beat you."

I am sure that you may be able to come up with all the good reasons why you failed to make headway. When it is somebody other than us who fails, we attribute the cause to something inside the person (we might say that he or she was lazy, incompetent, or he/she did not try hard enough), however when it comes to describing our own misfortune, we point to an external source. Sometimes we go as far as saying that someone out there must have meant evil against us. Nevertheless, when our neighbor is faced with the same hardship or obstacles that we ourselves confront, we attribute his/her mishap to internal factors or agents. We see him/her as being either lazy, careless, unintelligent (not so smart) or whatever imperfection we can dig out of him/her. We often see what is wrong with people around us, and usually we can pinpoint what they did wrong.

By the same token, it's certainly true in this society that we do not always give credit to whom credit is due, or people do not always appreciate us for what we really are but instead for what we have accomplished or what we can offer them. It seems as though we are looked upon as machines of production, and the instant we can no longer produce we are discarded as obsolete or useless merchandise. There is a materialistic giant in most of us. Consequently, we tend to love things and use people. Moreover, we often and deliberately look for scapegoats and make them responsible for whatever happened or did not happen to us, good or bad.

At this very moment, I invite you to search your personal baggage and try to identify your own belongings. And when you have completed your search, I suggest that you take credit for the entire package. Do not displace your discontentment toward somebody else.

For instance, without picking on any one person, a particular ethnic or a specific nation, I know that my fellow Haitians contribute many good things to society. They are bright and represent the first group of blacks to earn their independence in the world. In fact, following their emancipation (freedom), their technicians: educators, engineers, physicians, agronomists were on demand in many parts of the world to help provide services for, train, and educate other citizens of society, which by the way they hardly ever get credit for. They work hard for the most part. They often settle for what will make them feel proud of themselves. However, in their socio-cultural perception and their political wisdom, their ideals seem to be distorted oftentimes, in that they always blame their misfortune on somebody other than themselves. So and so is the cause of their problems; not realizing that only one finger points away, the other four turn towards themselves! That smells so much like the recipe that Adam and Eve cooked in the garden of Eden after God confronted them, asking why did they disobey (Genesis Ch.3: v9-13).

Frankly, I firmly believe this kind of bondage, a mentality, stands in our way causing us to become blind or limited in our vision. Thus, it prevents many of us from looking at our own life's situation objectively and come up with the right reasons why such obstacles stand in our way! That is sad, very sad indeed; because this form of denial causes much damage. For one thing it prevents us from dealing with the real issues; other times it appears as though we never had a problem in the first place. Moreover, many times when we blame the wrong person for what he or she did do, he/she often laughs in our face and accepts the credit as if he/she really exercised control over our life. Just recently, I had a conversation with a minister, a friend of mine and who told me a story about the devil. On a bright Sunday morning, a group of Christian believers were on their way to church. Suddenly they saw the devil sitting by the road weeping; a sister in the group opened her mouth and asked, "What is the matter with you?" The devil answered, "They have accused me for things that I have not had a chance to do."

Freedom is mainly a mindset. In order for you to obtain it, you must have an open mind and a kindred spirit. Right now, it is 12:30 AM, Tuesday, December 23, 1996, just hours away from Christmas, a date that Christians adopt to celebrate the birth of Jesus. Then many people will be exchanging and opening presents. I must say to you, do not be a fool and think that freedom is a gift, that someone would want to give you! To obtain and maintain it requires a lot of personal effort. As your own person, only as you realize the role that you have to play in your destiny, and only as you try to identify and rid yourself of your phobias will you be able to dismiss misconceptions from your mind. Only as you arm yourself and fight the odds will you come to the realization of securing your freedom. That is not a given.

More importantly, you are as free as you believe that you are. Let's not resemble flies that after numerous attempts to escape from the sealed jar resign themselves to sit at the bottom of it even though the cap has been removed providing a way to escape.

If you must live a free man or a free woman, then you ought to identify your real adversaries and at the same time decide what kind of message you will allow your ears to listen to: negative or positive; I can or I can't. As Lord Chesterfield of England, in a letter to his son, stated, "…Let dull critics feed upon the carcasses of plays; give me the taste and the dressing" (1696-1773).

In conclusion, "Blame where you must, be candid where you can, and be each critic the good-natured man" (Oliver Goldsmith, 1728-1774). I say all this to say that if you ever attempted an adventure and quit after the very first time you failed, then you really have no one else to blame but yourself.

❖ CHAPTER III ❖

Freedom: An Expression of Independence and Maturity

"Necessity is the mother of taking risks," said Mark Twain. In fact, the whole idea of us searching for freedom (working toward our personal growth and creating socio-economic opportunities for ourselves and our community), starts with our determination to set sail and discover freedom, not knowing exactly what lies ahead. However, we must not forget that wherever we may be, certain rules apply so much so that we cannot consider freedom as a license to do as we please. It is just like driving our own motor vehicle on public property, we need to know the traffic regulations and try to abide by them

As a robot, a car has no will to undertake any action. It remains grounded in one place and is not liable for itself. Someone who takes possession of that vehicle first needs to learn how to operate one. Then, after completing a driving test, he/she may have the privilege of moving around in that car but in no way does that permit void the road signs or any traffic regulations that might relate to operating this vehicle.

We advocate for freedom, because without it no one would be able to achieve any kind of social progress or growth. However, everyone must keep his/her own liberty in check so as to avoid the abuse or the misuse thereof.

Once, I was told the story of a boy who owned a toy boat. Somehow, the boat was stolen from him. However, one day as he was shopping at a market place he spotted and recognized his little boat in a store. And since he loved his toy so much, he redeemed or purchased it back from the seller and called it his twice. In this life, certain things are worth fighting for, including our freedom.

In America, the culture seemingly provides a certain "class of freedom" to distinct groups of its citizens, namely the teenagers.

39

Many from this population cannot wait to turn 18 or 21 years of age (depending on the state) to legally gain access to a bar or a liquor store to purchase alcoholic beverages. Moreover, they should not consume any such product either. Also, as an adolescent who lives on the United States soil approaches his/her 18th birthday, this young adult soon becomes legally free to decide where he/she wants to live, whether he/she wants to continue to stay under the same roof as his/her parents. Upon their 18th birthday, American youths are no longer considered minors, and they automatically can be prosecuted as adults for any wrongdoing, although the law in some States makes special provisions prior to an offender's 18th birthday, depending on the nature of the offenses.

I am sure that many parents would not put their kids out of their home, but obviously, many others long for that date to arrive and many teenagers wait with great anticipation to see it come where they may free themselves from those <u>domineering</u>, <u>stupid</u> and sometimes abusive parents whom they sometimes feel lack sense. At that time, the young adults assume their own set of responsibilities as granted by the Constitution of the United States of America. This is not the best example of freedom. It looks more like running from one situation to another, and the process can be just as painful for the young freedom seekers as for the "freedom holders" (parents). While it is encouraging to teach young people civic responsibilities and duties, as well as how to become independent, it works best when we have a supportive environment in place and a thorough plan of action. It also helps to know what we are running from and to. Running from a home just for the sake of it may not be the smartest idea. So, yes, some parents need that freedom, that peace of mind from their teenagers who think that they have already conquered the world, and perhaps some teens do need that freedom to avoid constant conflict or misunderstanding between their parents and themselves. However, freedom cannot always be fought and won in isolation. Some of us learn that lesson the hard way. We depend on each other for moral support and other things. Unfortunately, even when that is lacking, if need be, we must do without.

You will probably agree with me that every country and every culture in the world sets different guidelines for or have varied expectations of their citizens. Thus, in relation to time, we all need to reach that point where we're no longer breast-fed or rely solely on someone to give us fish. To everything under heaven, there is a time: a time to be bound and a time to be set free. Time and circumstances influence us and each other, but what is tied today must be turned loose tomorrow.

Freedom is not one hundred percent guaranteed. In other words, just because you won it once does not mean you will always have it. You must work unceasingly to retain it. Secondly, just as much as different areas in our life relate to one another, freedom from lack of self-esteem relates to but is different from that of being discriminated against. It is like saying that we can prevent birds from making their nest on our head but we cannot stop them from flying over. When we talk about freedom, we need a context. Just as I explained above, I may need to fight low self esteem, which differs from fighting racism. Though they may show similarities, these represent a different set of animals or battles and therefore must be fought either separately (on a different battle ground, with different strategies) or simultaneously but independently. Can you think of them being draining? You bet.

Those individuals who have experienced freedom of speech, freedom of mobility (not being incarcerated) or even of ideology but lost it afterwards might even feel compelled to let go of or forfeit some of their material possessions in order to recover such liberty once more, just as the story of the little boy and the boat at the beginning of the chapter. There is something about freedom which makes most of us cherish it, and we do not want to let go of it easily. Even though such decisions might bring severe consequences later, the joy of being among those who live free outweighs them. After all, the price that one pays to secure one's freedom can never match the amount paid for being enslaved.

Freedom is everything. It means power, independence, authority, individual growth, be it physical, mental, psychological, or emotional. It also includes spiritual as well as socio-economic well-being, which we cannot emphasize enough in this book. Some cultures are more conservative than others, but each one addresses the issues of freedom in their own way and within their own frame of reference. As individuals or communities, we often express it through distinct choices that we make for ourselves. Be it the choice to select our own place of dwelling, place of employment, type of profession, or the person we want to be our mate versus someone else making that choice on our behalf. Unfortunately, some people make the worst kind of choices, especially the one of depending on the welfare roll for a life time. We have an undeniable responsibility to educate ourselves as well as our children in order to become productive members of society. However, we also have the choice to: K.I.S.S.= Keep It Simple Stupid or more directly to keep ourselves in the abyss (the pit)! Education does not include just traditional schooling with a degree at the end. As you can see nowadays, many people may be walking with degrees in their hands and not be able to secure jobs. So, any technical or trade school that gives solid job skills plays a pivotal role in the lives of men and women in society. One sad thing about freedom sometimes is when people make totally deliberate or blind choices. For instance as they look to be accepted or acknowl-edged by a particular culture or clan, they may compromise all previous values that they have cherished.

To me, being able to determine one's destiny or promote self-determination represents an inherent, God-given right that each of us should strive to die with and not be deprived of unless it be removed from us on the grounds of gross misconduct or by reason of insanity, which makes us not just a threat to ourselves but to society as well. We might argue that individual freedom can be described through three distinct but inclusive components. They are:

1-freedom of self determination, self actualization; freedom to think with an open mind, and with objectivity, hoping that as you reach this level of growth and maturity you will take the liberty to develop and exercise that right.

2-freedom to not just react on a rational level to situations in your surroundings, but to also act responsibly and pursue your own destiny; for we are all created with endless potentials.

3-freedom to express or voice your opinion not arrogantly, not destructively or violently but in a constructive manner, what some folks would call "freedom of speech".

As you define yourself or your ideals before society and strive to preserve them so shall you fulfill these three aspects involving individual (personal) freedom. Nonetheless, to coordinate the three types of freedom simultaneously requires a great deal of self-control and discipline, as well as an enormous amount of external stimuli or encouragement, especially early on in life's developmental stages when the support of parents and loved ones is most critical. Hopefully, the level of care that they are able to give may help shape our young people's attitudes, behaviors, and values, which will then influence their belief system. After that, it becomes the burden of each of you as individual citizens to define what your freedom will look like: great, small; self-imposing freedom or one which tends to make us imitators of someone else. If you do not know yourself (which is not so easy either) and set your own goals as the great Master would want you to, you will just be a passive follower, leaning in whichever direction the wind blows. You need that personal drive, a sense of commitment, perseverance and patience. More importantly, we would like to emphasize that all three aspects of freedom may be achieved through biological, psychological, emotional, and sociological development with respect to time. Some of us may reach a certain level of freedom faster than others, but the point of the matter is not to allow ourselves to wander around and become desperate and destitute. Many experts on the topics of personal growth, psycho-social and economic development or freedom would probably agree with me that the capacity of an individual to live a life of co-dependency (versus absolute dependence) has to do with how a person formulates his/her logic and perceives his/her role in the environment.

As we all know, for human subjects especially, physical growth is largely affected by genetics (heredity) and external or environmental factors such as food, nurturing, caring, and encouragement from other people. By the same token, intelligible sounds or speech that we humans develop usually starts within the first year of life. Then, our vocabulary keeps expanding with time. For example, an infant (0-12 months) often starts saying "Daddy". Between 9 and 12 months old, he/she usually vocalizes two more words in addition to "Mama" and "Baba". A child of about 18 months, is often capable of maintaining a conversation and constructing 8-10 word sentences at a time. At about 24 months, a child may have an expanded vocabulary as vast as 300 words. By the time the child reaches 6 to 12 years of age, the individual develops complex sentences and mastery of language. (Jackson, D. B. and R. B. Saunders. Child Health Nursing. J.B. Lippincott Co. Philadelphia, 1993.) Also, it should be specifically stated that by 36 months (3 years), the average child acquires 80% of intelligible speech and some thousand (1,000) word vocabulary. At 48 months (four years), language is well established (Vander Zanden, J. W. Human Development. 5th Ed. McGraw-Hill, Inc. New York, 1993.)

Free speech is one way that we demonstrate our freedom, and the first amendment to the United States Constitution says that: "…Congress shall make no law…abridging the freedom of speech, or the press". Therefore, even with the extensive and sometimes stringent power-sharing between the two houses: the US Congress and the executive branch (also known as The House of Representatives and The White House, respectively), freedom of speech is protected. However, what does that really mean to the average citizen? Does it allow him or her to say anything, to anyone, anytime, anywhere? Are there boundaries that one must not cross? Or if there exists such a thing as an absolute free press, in how many places around the globe do we find it?

A- Where Does our Individual Freedom Begin and End?

To the people living under dictatorship/authoritarian type of government where few enjoy the values of an intrusive cultural setting, freedom may be perceived much more as an illusion. In other words, in those states individual freedom of the average person tends to be greatly compromised, and few members of the community have absolute power in their hands to dispose of other people's lives as though they are properties that can be owned. On the contrary, those who live in a "democratically oriented society", such as the US, often put more emphasis on freedom and think of it as an inherent part of their birthright. They also believe that boundaries can be expanded.

And sometimes, some people do challenge the rules governing individual freedom and see no boundaries whatsoever.

As we enter the 21st century, more than ever before, modern technology allows us to deal with many issues on a much larger scale. Thus, it facilitates the displacement of many values and presents a challenge to all such limitations and the source of authority itself. Nothing personal, I just want to make a point. Cellular phones are becoming more and more popular and perhaps those individuals who can afford carrying one on their person feel more in control and have a false sense of security. Moreover, with extremely powerful satellites in place, people throughout the entire planet have the potential to watch instantly or simultaneously an event taking place in a remote location of the world. Computer technology, specifically the superhighway provides even more freedom, and a world of information seems to be at our fingertips at any time we might want it. However, some individuals lacking the resources would not be able to utilize such technology to their own advantage and may even see it as a threat. For example, how many people in the work force whose training has increasingly become obsolete are being disposed of and being replaced by robots? The merging and trimming down of companies, thereby shrinks their manpower and forces many of their senior staff into involuntary retirement, which may translate into loss of earnings and/or less buying power. How can these individuals regain the freedom once they are deposed from their previous employer? Can they or are they willing to start life anew? How likely will they secure another job which offers decent benefits and the flexibility that they might need to pursue other interests and lead a balanced life?

Moreover, we have seen the Soviet block power crumble and the new world order is gaining momentum. Many so-called dictators have failed; and the seven most industrialized nations, better known as the G-7 (which of course includes: the United States, Canada, France, Great Britain, Germany, Russia, and China), exercise greater power and freedom by taking the lead over the world market economy. On another foot, we have much to expect from the emerging (rising) of a united Europe; meanwhile, most of the developing countries are experiencing a dragging, staggering and even a suffocating economy, facing more and more hardship in their ability to provide for the basic needs of their citizens.

More money = more power = more freedom, at least that's what it boils down to in a world which elevates or values things more than they value people! Evidently, while some people gain freedom, others lose theirs. And at times, it makes you wander whether or not those operating under the banner of this elusive freedom, or who have greater buying power recognize any limitations at all, as their approach to consolidate their power and extend their empire often suggests a lack of or any concern for those people who are constantly being compressed or pushed towards the lower end of the socio-economic spectrum!

Another unusual aspect of the erosion of freedom is seen in the area of derogatory speech and disrespect for human lives (organized crime against and continued massacre of innocent citizens). In some political settings, some people are obliged to stick their feet in their mouths in other to avoid being smashed by their foes. Culturally speaking, however, with moral decay and the many people who are experiencing freedom of expression for the first time in their lives, profanity in their every day conversation, hateful wishes against other members of society and disrespect for life, as well as for those in authority, keep rising. The decline in moral decency is more than ever taking its toll. Many young people and even some adults don't know how to tame their anger, let alone their tongues.

Recently, I stood by and listened to a conversation between a friend of mine and someone else. In the course of their discussion, my dear friend said to the other person, "I own my mouth". I took her to task or I kind of teased her, and she backed down. Another way that we often hear people say that is, "I speak my mind".

By all means, if you feel that's the way you may restore your individual freedom, go right ahead, and speak. There is nothing wrong per se to actually own your mouth or speak your mind especially if your rights are being compromised or violated. In fact, even though I have been around now for few decades, I am still trying to own my mind!

Language is a powerful tool that we have at our disposal, if only we could coordinate our thought processes and our emotions to deliver our message eloquently, respectfully, yet decisively and with tact (if you want to call it diplomatic language, I have no problem with that whatsoever), we might make our voices heard in the depths of rocks and in the skies above and win the sympathy of many hearts! By acting, reacting, or responding too quickly, we might do more harm than good to ourselves and that can happen to the best of us! Many times in my own life, when I am faced with unpleasant situations and confronted by people with inappropriate behavior toward me as a person or toward my ethnic minority, my heart would speed up causing adrenalin to be released thereby changing the tone within me and giving utterance to my mouth. I may feel like giving them a piece of my mind or taking matters into my own hands. However, my brain would automatically take over, guide my intellect, and help organize my thought and speech patterns, preparing me for the right thing to say. It is clear that I do not want to be aggressive or abusive. Whereas some of my close allies consider that a distinct mark of wisdom, those who have limited encounters with me fathom with the notion that I am SHY!

Perhaps that's true, even though I strongly disagree, and I believe that it all depends! It has to do with time, circumstances, places, the audience, and the subject matter being discussed, as well as a quick assessment on my part on the potential damage which could result from my hasty response. These are some of the important elements that one has to pay attention to before verbalizing one's thoughts. Even when you have the right language, you need to watch for the appropriate time and the right environment. You have to focus on ways you wish to deliver your message as well. Back to me being perceived as "shy", has to do with perception of the person doing my evaluation; however, I can assure you that my temperament, personality, and approach do keep me out of trouble and help me entertain as well as maintain different crowds for great lengths of time without having to apologize every so often.

In this day and age, too many of our young folks feed their minds on trash. Therefore, they ruminate on that and bring forth assaults as they open their mouths. They just talk trash, no matter when, where, and who is around! Having said this, we should ask a very important question. Does freedom of expression operate under any kind of rules, and is there such a thing as self-respect involved in the kind of language that we use as we express ourselves?

In a free society, self-control and mutual respect do apply, even when we talk. I think that it is a terrible mistake when we are exercising our freedom and are not being mindful of our actions and speech. Many people either lose their tempers along the way, or they have not been properly trained to tame their emotions and carefully choose their words. Thus, they move solely under the impulse of the moment. By comparison, they share some of the basic characteristics of fluorine, one of the most reactive chemicals in nature. They look for the least amount of excitement to explode. And if none were to come their way, they would serve their own bias and create a situation to get themselves excited and display their poor mannerisms.

They gossip, curse and take no heed as to the environment that they are in. Oftentimes they represent the most talkative, loudest orators (speakers) in the entire neighborhood. They may even blast their radios and disturb the whole block! You can have all the freedom in the world; however, it makes no sense whatsoever if you try to convey any message without bringing into the picture the 5 W's and the How!

Just like nature has its own set of rules that we ought not violate if we are not prepared to deal with the consequences. By the same token, being free means a new set of conduct; new set of rules to live by. Freedom obeys certain principles, and without their implementation the world will never be suitable for living. No matter who we are, where we come from or what we may look like, if we apply those rules, even though people may wish to resent us at first, in the end we will necessarily command or capture their attention.

Of course, there are exceptions to any rule, even to the application of freedom as it relates to who, when, what, where, why (the best one, according to my Reverend friend, PJW), and last but not least, how. By the end of this work, you may feel like calling these "The Mondésir's Principles to successful communication and freedom", and you don't even have to pay me to use them. No plagiarism, no copyright violations (as to the use of the 5 W's and How, everything else, yes). A message with appropriate content (What), to be most effective must be carried out in a certain way (How), to its target audience (Who), within a certain time (When), in a distinct environment (Where), and with a particular purpose (Why). It is very funny to see what ticks some people off. The tone (How) in which you deliver your message is just as important as the vocabulary that you use, if the former is not even more important.

Among the human attributes or values, freedom of expression has its own merit, and it ought not be taken for granted. It has real boundaries; and therefore, recognizing and acknowledging them is often the best way to play it safe with our equals. I would allow no one to shut me off when the time comes for me to express myself and defend my rights. However, I do know that one cannot consider oneself free without one's ability to use discretion. Good manners and self respect, as well as being considerate of others go hand-in-hand with personal freedom. Many people who get themselves into some form of trouble do so not because of their action, but rather by what they say with their mouth.

In his wisdom, King Solomon said: there is a proper time and procedure for every matter under the sun (Eccl. 8 v. 6), which mature individuals and clever politicians know full well. A way that the latter group deals with it is by adopting a non-committal language, so no one would make them accountable for what they do not want to. Because by using the wrong word or language, they know that it can backfire on them, creating chaos that can be politically suicidal for them. If you did not, now you do know why politicians, especially, are usually emotionally guarded. After they search their environment, they wait for the right moment to deliver the right kind of speech. When you think of it, deliberate use of words is not a trademark of moderate or skillful politicians.

In effective communication skills (Communications 101), we learn just that. Unfortunately, people who are underrepresented in mainstream society, and or who have been discriminated against do not always possess the best tools to effective communications. Hence, many times they give more reasons to their opponents to discredit them and keep them disenfranchised. The ability to effectively (with calm, firmness, and in due respect) say what you have to and exactly when you need to, carries a lot of weight to good communication and interpersonal relationships. It also helps create an environment conducive to individual freedom, whether it be socio-economically, spiritually, politically, or otherwise. Language represents a powerful means of communication and freedom, if only one knows how or cares to use it adequately and effectively. It opens doors that one could only dream of and it can help build bridges where no possibility seemed to have existed prior. At the same time, it is given great admonition to people who cannot tame their tongue (James Chapter 3: v.1-6)

In the Haitian creole language we find a proverb that says: "Bouch manje tout manje, men li pa pale tout pawol." I almost got carried away into the spirit; I better stop and translate what is being said. Literally, the phrase means that one's mouth may eat anything, but ought not say anything. In other words, we need to weigh our thoughts before our mouths speak out words. Sometimes, you may feel that you have a case to make when in fact you have not, or perhaps you do but ignore the rules, let alone the slurs and the filthiness that often serves as seasoning or spice flavoring the speech that is even aired on some of the talk shows.

Given all that we know about language and of course free speech, we humans have the capacity to make such an impression through verbal communications. Then, again like any airline ticket, certain restrictions do apply as you talk. Watch it! There may be dead weight or personal baggage that your carrier will not accept from your mouth. Check with your agent for further details. You may even need a course to help you enhance your verbal communication skills. Freedom of expression does not ensure a license to say as we please at any time and place. Even in America where the constitution guarantees free speech, you may not become legally liable simply on the content of your language, however you may be caught using indecent language, profanity or defamation. Case in point, just last night (Friday, December 27, 1996), I was riding on a public bus on Blue Hill Avenue (Boston). At one of the stops, a group of teenagers got on the bus and started cursing loudly and using inappropriate language at the bus driver. She would not move the vehicle until after the police came and had those young passengers vacate the bus. We need to watch our language or someone else will do it for us.

B- Democracy and Freedom

It may sound cynical or even ironic to many people reading this work, but that is a fact. Some of the individuals who become rich instantly do not always know how to behave. You may have the wealth but lack manners, and therefore are subject to being ridiculed by your peers. What happens if someone who grew up in poverty and never received an appropriate education suddenly becomes rich? Since in many ways money is power, the newly wealthy person has yet to learn how to conduct himself or herself with that kind of asset.

Democracy and freedom are mutually inclusive. In other words, one does not do well without the other. With the former being a process, it takes time and education to teach the governing rules to the newly exposed individuals. We may try to help people adapt to an ideal model of democracy; however, we cannot just transport it from one ethnic group or from one group of people to another. It must burgeon among the people and follow the transitional phase or phases. Without education and that transition, people might just think of democracy as synonymous to anarchy where the absence of all authority reigns.

When the rules are properly laid out for the people for whom democracy is being advocated, hoping that they follow such rules, then they will discover true freedom, and that will redefine people's new territory or their sphere of influence. In layman's terms, as individuals or a nation walks towards freedom, both will keep discovering new boundaries, which will dictate the size of their space: individual or national. Even though we are for individual, community, and even national freedom (power) in this book, it is false for anyone to think of that as having no limit at all.

For argument's sake, let us consider the Crusaders. They went from place to place conquering other people and brutally colonizing them. Once they did that, they set new boundaries for themselves and laid out guidelines that their subjects were to follow. And the conquered always adapt to the culture and always have to learn the language of the conqueror. That is mainly how many languages became widespread. If the French colonized another country, that country ended up speaking French. If it were the Spaniards or the

51

British that conquered, their subjects ended up speaking Spanish and English respectively. We say all this to say that power is often an outcome of freedom. You cannot have freedom and not exercise your influence, which is one of the reasons why some people do not like for others to have any kind of power, and sometimes they will try to prevent or limit the freedom of other people. National freedom is not too far different from the individual's, except that one is sought collectively, while the other is individually focused. On the national level, one of the main goals may be to try to expand geographically, while the individual may put emphasis on improving his/ her skills, learning new techniques or a new profession, which is our main goal in this book.

In our search for freedom, we all would like to exert a little more power and have more space at our disposal, whether we really need it or not. Some people call it portable space, others call it personal space. But the truth of the matter is that it's a sign that we are somewhat free agents with inherent rights to do or act at will. All of us are entitled to such a claim under God and the Universal Human Rights Declaration in the United Nations Charter.

Freedom is ours and by not claiming it, someone else who needs it most may take it away from us. One of my former professors, and in fact, Chairman of Chemistry Dept. at Oral Roberts University (when I was attending school there) who is originally from India told me that if you want to find how much power people have in their homeland, just look to see how many keys they carry on their key ring. Usually, more keys equal more power. In the Roman Catholicism, Saint Peter represents the one to whom God gave the power key to open the gate of heaven and allow fervent Christians to enter.

In our discussion, may I say that freedom is a key in itself. When properly used, it may open any door before us. The problem with us sometimes is that we are not sure that we have it. Also, at times, we either abuse, misuse or simply do not know how to use it to our own advantage. Moreover, freedom is not a one way street, in that it imparts privileges and responsibilities as well. I do not know how you get your news; however, I usually access mine through reading the newspaper and by listening to the radio. Now as it relates to the written media, the pages are often bombarded with promotional ads offering you free this, free that. Then, if you take the time to look far enough, you will discover the very fine print telling you that you are not really getting the item (s) absolutely free. Many restrictions apply, and you'd better familiarize yourself with these ads or you may be in for a big surprise when you receive your "free gift". Similarly, freedom is not an absolute commodity that we earn for life. We have to work hard to preserve it. Secondly, it is neither a license, nor does it issue any licensure to any one person or nation to do as it pleases. It has finite boundaries. That is where the idea of freedom seems to be an disillusion, especially for those with the wrong concept of what it means or stands for.

Without really misleading anyone, I would like to tell you that you are as free as you think you are though you may be limited in some of the things that you would like to do, or in what you would want to say. Secondly, contrary to what some people might have been told or believed, freedom may appear to be one of the birthrights which is passed on to the heirs of a monarchy. Unfortunately, just a few kingdoms exist in the world today. To reiterate, freedom is something that we have to work hard for in order to achieve and preserve. Due to its significance it won't be handed to us by anybody.

Some of our life's pathways would have been a whole lot easier had we believed in or applied some of the concepts in psychology as it relates to freedom. It is quite fascinating to understand why we behave the way we do. Some of the concepts in psychology may be inaccurate and even erroneous just like any other field or discipline, but you cannot experience freedom apart from the applications of some basic and practical psychological means or model. Plain and simple!

Some people cannot appreciate any of the works by Sigmund Freud, the father of psychoanalysis, a branch of psychology that deals with mental processes, dream interpretation and free association. In part of his theories, Freud has attempted to describe the power and the dynamic (psyche) of the human mind. He thus described three separate aspects of the human psyche and they are:

1- the ego, which represents self; example, self-esteem, who we are and how we feel about ourselves

2- the id, the instinctual aspect of human character, the basis of unconscious power drives and needs

3- the superego, the house of internalization of conscience and rules of society which also functions to reward individuals for their actions that bring a sense of guilt.

Within this context, I would like to remind the readers of this great work to search for their freedom and to grab it once it is found. In contrast, I want to caution them as to the use thereof.

Freedom is not an unlimited or an extensive attribute of human possession. It brings rights as well as responsibilities. Moreover, real boundaries do exist; and whenever you do not see any of them, you may want to build a few layers of insulation around you for your own good, lest you deliberately want to be run over by the person next to you. You cohabit or share this planet with approximately five billion (5.0×10^9) people who also exercise their own rights to freedom. That is why we need some boundaries. If we disregard it and allow our next door neighbors to draw it for us, they will definitely raise their fence over our own territory. And if we try to operate without boundaries, sooner or later, we will find ourselves in a terrible posture with authority and other fellow human beings. Then we may be forced to give up all that freedom that we worked so hard for. In the pursuit of your destiny or the realization of your dreams, you must see freedom as your right and a just cause. In your mind, you may conceive great dreams, and you may even see them materialize as long as you believe that you can. Bear in mind that physically, your freedom ends where somebody else's begins. Use your language, choose your words discretely and appropriately. Exercise your freedom to the extent that it does not demolish or undermine some-body else's. Respect begets respect. There is nothing wrong with peacefully pursuing our goals in life, and only we can limit ourselves as to how high we can fly or how far we can reach. Just like driving a vehicle, you can drive it whenever and as far as traffic regulations allow, granted that you violate none of those rules, or else your driving privileges will be removed from you.

Words and actions are very compelling; and you have the freedom of speech and you also have the freedom to act as an independent individual, but responsibly or with respect for other people. Your selfish and careless actions may cause harm to your fellow human beings. Therefore, do not act as though you are the only person that exists in the whole world. Kindly, live and let live.

C- The Human Rights Declaration

This section deals strictly with the Universal Human Rights Declaration, as stipulated in the United Nations Charter, dated December 10, 1948. It applies to both individuals and groups (nations). The following is the complete text as it is found in the charter:

"WHEREAS recognition of the inherent dignity and of the equal and inalienable rights of all members of the human family is the foundation of freedom, justice and peace in the world,

WHEREAS disregard and contempt for human rights have resulted in barbarous acts which have outraged the conscience of mankind, and the advent of a world in which human beings shall enjoy freedom of speech and belief and freedom from fear and want has been proclaimed as the highest aspiration of the common people,

WHEREAS it is essential, if man is not to be compelled to have recourse, as a last resort, to rebellion against tyranny and oppression, that human rights should be protected by the rule of law,

WHEREAS it is essential to promote the development of friendly relations between nations,

WHEREAS the people of the United Nations have in the Charter reaffirmed their faith in fundamental human rights, in the dignity and worth of the human person and in the equal rights of men and women and have determined to promote social progress and better standards of life in larger freedom,

WHEREAS Members States have pledged themselves to achieve, in co-operation with the United Nations, the promotion of universal respect for and observance of human rights and fundamental freedoms,

WHEREAS a common understanding of these rights and freedoms is of the greatest importance for the full realization of this pledge,

Now, Therefore, THE GENERAL ASSEMBLY **PROCLAIMS**

THIS UNIVERSAL DECLARATION OF HUMAN RIGHTS as a common standard of achievement for all peoples and all nations, to the that every individual and every organ of society, keeping this Declaration constantly in mind, shall strive by teaching and education to promote respect for these rights and freedoms and by progressive measures, national and international, to secure their universal and effective recognition and observance, both among the peoples of Member States themselves and among the peoples of territories under their jurisdiction. "

Half a century after this statement was made, and three years before the new millennium, men and women everywhere are still working hard to make sure that Human Rights Declaration becomes a reality to all mankind!

D- A TRIBUTE to Rev. Dr. Martin Luther King Jr. by H. Carl McCall

"...Dr. King was our teacher. He taught us about human freedom, dignity, and justice. He inspired us to dream of a world without prejudice or oppression, and he demonstrated how one life dedicated to the non-violent pursuit of righteousness can change an entire society...How we can work together to make his dream a reality...to build a better, more peaceful world, where all people can be free...prosperous, and productive...

Today, in these very troubled times, we can pay tribute to Dr. King by following his example...Each one of us can be witness to the transforming power of the Lord...We can teach the world the language of love and the power of peace...There is no question that Dr. King would be greatly cheered...but also saddened...by what he would see here today.

In many ways, this is the best time ever for African Americans. Some 60 percent of African-Americans now earn middle-class incomes. Before World War II, just five percent did...Let's look at a few more numbers:

— In 1995, 13 percent of Black adults held bachelor's degrees, up from 8 percent in 1980.
— Today, there are seven times as many Black college students, nearly 1.5 million, as there were in 1960.
— And, among college-educated full-time workers, 28 percent of Blacks have executive, administrative or managerial jobs.
— Meanwhile, as hope among the Black middle class blooms, so does despair among poor Blacks and other minorities.

And there are other disturbing numbers:

— In 1996, 33.3 percent of Blacks and 29.3 percent of Hispanics lived in poverty...compared to 11.6 percent of Whites.
— 21 percent of Blacks have no health insurance...among Hispanics that number was 33.3 percent.
— 50 percent of the prison population is Black, while Blacks constituted just 12 percent of the general population. 30 percent of Black males are in the Criminal Justice System...more than are in college.
— In recent years, the AIDS case rate among Blacks has been almost three times higher than among the general U. S. population.
— Drug and alcohol abuse are too common...Dropout rates are 53 percent higher than the rate for Whites...HIV infections are three times that of Whites and growing...and African-American teenage girls are four times more likely to have children, babies having babies, than Whites girls.

Aside from these on-going troubles, we are facing fresh troubles of anti-attitudes. From Africa, Asia, Latin America...Black, Brown, Yellow...attitudes have changed. Systematically excluded...systematic inclusion. People on welfare are being punished...What is needed is training, child care, and jobs.

A study by the Glass Ceiling Commission, which was set up by George Bush, and sponsored by Bob Dole, recently reported that:

— White males continue to hold 97 percent of senior management positions in major corporations.
— African Americans hold only 2.5 percent of top jobs in the private sector and Black men with professional degrees earn only 79 percent of the amount earned by their White counterparts. Comparably situated African American women earn only 60 percent of the amount earned by White males...

And, we can't forget the lessons of Dr. King...the spiritual nature of our strength...He said in 1960...
'Quite often we say the church has no place in politics, forgetting the words of the Lord, The spirit of the Lord is upon me, because he has [anointed] me to preach the gospel to the poor; he has sent me to heal the broken hearted, to preach deliverance to the captives, and the recovering of sight to the blind, to set at liberty those who are oppressed.'
As Christians we need a mandate. We must be political. Register to vote. Recognize the importance of political action. Save our children. Let them know they are special. Invest in them now. Education not incarceration.
We must be involved in politics, in the struggle for social justice and equality, Black people and White people, Christians and Jews, men and women.
All people of good will made sacrifices and played a part in tearing down the vestiges of segregation. For the Martin Luther King holiday, we must come together, not to celebrate the triumphs and struggles of the past, but to make it possible to build a future of hope and opportunity.
We shall overcome. Dr. King has taught us to have hope with the Lord's help, to believe in ourselves, to help others." (*Remarks prepared and delivered by **The Honorable H. Carl McCall, New York State Comptroller**, during King's Day Celebration, January 20, 1997.*)

Conclusion

Freedom does not mean the absence of law and order. In fact, when people who search for or believe in democracy try to live in the absence of or abuse the law and completely disregard other human lives, they abruptly reach the point of social disintegration and anarchy. True, democracy advocates for and supposedly guarantees the freedom of all human beings. It does not however eliminate all the law and order, and the principles that govern society. As someone said, "There is no liberty but liberty under law. Law does not restrict liberty, it creates the only real liberty there is..." (William Sumner, in his piece entitled <u>The Forgotten Man</u>). As individual human beings, we are free to seek and follow the orientations that promote personal growth, give us a sense of well-being, and which guarantee our welfare. Nonetheless, there is a proper place and order for everything. In order to fully enjoy our liberty, we need to also think of other people around us who share the same rights as we. Consequently, we can be free, live freely, and act freely. However, the minute we start abusing our freedom, we tend to create disturbances and disrupt peace and order which once existed. So, feel free, think freely, and act freely without interfering with or destroying the governing principles. Note that your freedom stops where someone else's starts. As stated by that famous philosopher, "If ye would go up high, then use your own legs! Do not yourselves carried aloft; do not sit yourselves on other's backs and heads!" (Fredrick Nietzsche, 1844-1900; in <u>Thus Spake Zarathustra</u>).

❖ CHAPTER IV ❖

Freedom of Self-determination, Self-actualization

Figure 4.1 Our Influence over the Environment and vice versa
(One bird descending its nest, the other entering a no fly zone)

In life, we have to set goals and even standards for ourselves. If we do not stand for ourselves, no one else will and there is a lot of truth in this saying, "He who stands for nothing falls for anything". I would like for you to compare the two pictures displayed above and see if you can explain the difference! It is very important that you look at the details. I will come back to assist you in case you run into difficulty interpreting the scenario. In the meantime, I'd like to give you an overview of my personal story which may in part explain why I make it my obligation to write and dedicate this work to you, knowing that my efforts and your fight won't be in vain.

An excerpt of my personal background (an autobiography)

I do not want to sound arrogant, but I simply would like to share with you some of my personal experience with the intention that it might help you through, at the very least.

I am the first born of the two children of a humble family in rural Haiti, and for a good part of my life I have conditioned myself to look in the forward and upward directions. And at this particular juncture in my life, I cannot say that I have accomplished all that I had hoped to. If God grants me longevity, I still have a long way to go. However, if I may say that I have traveled a great distance. I have a past history of "Boat People" (I am sure you know what that is) where I ended up in the Bahamas at the age of sixteen. Needless to say that I could not finish my high school education at the traditional (standard) age because of economic hardship within my family. My persistence toward reaching a higher realm has helped me get this far.

I remained in the Bahamas for about one year and a half and managed to sporadically secure a few days of work here and there. I do not regret ever going in the Bahamas; but if history were to repeat itself, I certainly would NOT like to find myself once again stranded under the exact same conditions. At such a young age, and for the very first time I found myself dissociated from my relatives, my homeland, and my loved ones. Confined alone in a one room habitat, I learned to make friends, meet my needs and do all that I was able to on my own in order to survive. I became very involved in church activities, which generated a new family for me. I met some very important people there: Haitians and Bahamians, especially some ministers whom I would love to pay tribute to in this book. However, I did not seek their permission to mention their names here. And shortly following the Bahamian independence from England in 1973,

I decided to go back to Haiti. Still frustrated by the same conditions that prompted my traveling in the first place, I just learned to hang on. Upon my return, I found the socio-economic conditions of my parents unchanged, and all that I brought back to Haiti with me was less than two (200) hundred U. S. dollars.

It did not take me long to spend that. Then, I began to travel regularly between the Island of La Gonave, my hometown and Port-au-Prince, the Haitian Capital in search of a new outlook and new dimensions for my life. For a moment, I thought about resuming my high school studies, but there I was facing the everyday reality of not having enough of anything to help meet my basic living expenses! With some English that I was able to learn in the Bahamas, I started looking for work especially in a place where I could use this little knowledge. For a while, I tried to be a Tourist Guide but that too did not work well. By 1976, after completing the prerequisites, I was hired at Grace Children's Hospital in Port-au-Prince (the town of Delmas, to be exact). I started my first paying job back at home as a Medical Lab Technician, then after a year or so later, I resumed the process of my formal schooling. For the most part of my high school, I was also working. At one time, while I was still at the hospital, I also worked as a part-time translator/interpreter in the English language for a religious organization in Haiti. A couple of years later, I worked as a supervisor at an artificial flower plant where I oversaw some sixty or so employees. I did not stay there very long; I moved into education where I taught a couple of subjects to high school students while serving as assistant principal at the same facility. After I migrated to the US, in many ways it was like starting over.

I remember working by myself in a gas station as an attendant one winter. There was snow on the ground and it got so busy at some point that I could not even take a break. By the time my shift was over, I had frostbite in my feet. History is quite long, when I do my autobiography, I will be able to give you a more detailed version. Having confronted almost insurmountable obstacles, I transferred from Rutgers University in New Jersey to Oral Roberts University in Tulsa, Oklahoma where I completed my bachelor's in natural science. After that, I attended Boston University where I earned my master's in public health. At the present time, I still harbor other ambitions and am currently pursuing a graduate degree in clinical psychology.

Neither age, nor the color of my skin, or my nationality, my family roots, my religious conviction, or anything else can prevent me from reaching my dreams, unless the good Lord allows it. Factors such as socio-economic and other external constraints may arise against my plans as they have in the past. However, I must keep my visions alive and pursue them. Also, I must make choices and take calculated risks. As I do that, I need to keep assessing my life, and wherever necessary postpone some of the immediate or "shallow gratification" so that I do not get overwhelmed by obstacles and lose motivations and sight. Slowing down to reenergize, and reevaluate your plan and strategy is perfectly all right and very different from quitting.

Very briefly, I would like to share with you one additional piece on the personal side. There is a place where I used to work at a job entry level, or as a case manager while I was in grad school. Upon graduation, I left to conduct a still pending AIDS research project. But two years later, I returned to that same place and assumed directorship of an entire department. Now, This may not mean much to many people, but I consider all that a move in the right direction. And in a way, I call it self-determination, being able to overcome some of the barriers and make myself a bit more productive to better serve my community, my fellow human beings. Why do I say all this, aside from being encouraged by Charles Austin, a friend and TV News Reporter from WBZ in Boston? In order that you might better relate to this work, I feel that nothing could so succinctly or precisely help me do it other than my personal history. Having said that, I will continue with this present chapter by asking you some questions: That way, you can air part of your opinions. By the way, you are safe with me, I promise not to chase you around. Despite our diversity of opinions, we can still respect one another and work together, too.

Where are we in terms of our individual rights? Is freedom an illusion, or are some people freer than others? Who or what determines that someone is free to pursue one's destiny and act in one's best interest while others can't?

One author made the following statement: "There were some who said that a man at the point of death is more free than all others, because death breaks every bond, and over the dead the united world has no power." (Fenelon, 1651-1715, in the piece called <u>Telemachus</u>).

My argument is not that we cannot experience freedom in this life. In fact, if freedom ever exists it must be here and now; for we know not what tomorrow may bring and we have no idea what will happen after death. It is true; death represents the most impartial judge that treats everyone alike, regardless of race, social status, religious conviction, cultural background, and gender type. It does not even discriminate against nationality. It intervenes when it wants and wherever it feels like it, and it carries away whomever it chooses. People may attempt to and perhaps succeed in shutting doors on our face, blocking our way. However, the ultimate responsibility remains with each of us to enhance and improve our human conditions through constant efforts and better planning.

As I typed the above paragraphs, I turned around and asked the Reverend and theologian friend of mine, P. J. Waters whether we could talk about some people being freer than others. In principle we disagree, but technically there seems to be a philosophical difference in the degree of freedom that we all have or believe that we have. Taken a step further, the attempt here, at least for many people, would be to say that not only is freedom transferable or transmissible (meaning that it is passed to a future generation from a previous one or from one individual to another) but also it is finite or fixed and is a given. Therefore, the determinants (factors) leading to freedom are all external or environmental. Though many times it feels like those individuals who for one reason or another have the upper hand socio-economically (money, social status, fame, political power, national origin) are the ones to decide for the rest of the world. While that may be true to some extent, if you believe that this is the case and that there is nothing you can do as a person or as a nation to improve your living conditions, you are doomed to failure. Socio-economic, cultural, and spiritual changes happen mostly because people believe that they can make a difference, therefore they decide to take some risks and engage in activities which would bring about improvement in their lives.

If we decide to simply sit around and wait, hoping that something will happen, of course some naturally occurring changes will definitely take place, but probably not all that we would hope for! Let's consider, for instance, the formation of rainfall in the atmosphere (which is also a recycling event), a natural process that brings hydrogen and oxygen atoms together to give us the most precious, most consumed beverage:

$$H_2 : _2O_{1/2} \qquad\qquad H_2O$$

*Figure 4.2 Hydrogen and Oxygen reaching
out to each other's heart*

Naturally speaking, changes occur when hydrogen atoms get close to oxygen atoms. The two elements (agents) interact and finally, after reaching a mutual agreement, get married and form the union that gives us one of the most important substances in nature which we call water. One other chain of events that continue to happen in our lives involves our heart. Physiologically, this organ has been set to keep blood circulating throughout our body; and unless we interfere with the process or some adverse conditions disrupt it, the cycle goes on even though we may not pay attention or be fully conscious of all that is happening. However, on a conscious level, we can actually monitor our heart rate and cause it to work at a slower pace and more efficiently through different activities and exercises, thereby reducing some potential risks of high blood pressure and heart disease. So even though this particular process seems to occur automatically, we can influence it, thereby messing it up or monitoring it and cause our cardiovascular system (heart and blood vessels) to be more effective and to work more efficiently.

Almost every kind of activity that we engage in is somewhat behavior-related. We decide to work, sleep at a certain time for some length, eat certain amounts of produce at a given time, may even choose to have a spouse and children, and we bathe (which is quite helpful for at least some of us). We decide whether to learn how to operate a motor vehicle; we even accept role playing, hoping that something good will come from it and benefit us. It all relates to a belief system that we either create for ourselves or adapt to as we interact with the world around us.

As you grow and mature, you may have your own rationale or your own ways of interpreting what is happening in and around you. As we all do, based on our own personal tastes and values, we may wish to be associated with certain people and places, or we want to reflect on certain changes or events, good or bad, which happened to us in the past or are now taking place in our lives. However, after all, we don't like to be held accountable for our actions, especially when that involves error, mistakes, or failure. It suits us to look for someone else to blame for what happened or did not happen and excuse ourselves. Also, I must admit that what we do either individually or collectively (as a group) often has an impact on other people's lives. However, while we may find a basis or reason (s) for us to make certain associations which may be relevant, to a great extent we are individually responsible for our own actions and behaviors as well as for not reaching our potential or getting our work done.

As part of our developmental process, we will formulate attitudes of our own, just like we shape our personalities. Attitude becomes part of self, and it generally precedes or dictates our behavior to such an extent that we may try to justify whatever we do in order to fit our own beliefs. There is something called self-serving bias; that we believe and do certain things in a certain way regardless of their irrelevance to the facts, but when we are confronted to give an explanation, we simply try to justify everything based upon our own beliefs, just like the way that certain traditions are passed from one generation to the next. In addition, we also encounter another expression called Self-Fulfilling-Prophecy, a tendency for our expectations to occur as we predicted, usually on the negative side. An example of this might be telling someone how inadequate he or she is, and as the person listens to the repetitious note and believes in what is being said, he or she will eventually act it out. True but sad isn't it?

Along the way, the environment through the process of socialization will influence and help shape our beliefs and attitudes. It may even attempt to mess with us by playing with our minds, and by trying to slow down or delay our progress as individuals or as a distinct group of people. However, for a few moments I would like to focus your attention on the pictures displayed at the beginning of this chapter.

You will notice one human and two birds. In the picture, one bird literally tries to nest on the person's head. The other bird is flying over the person's head without being able to lay its nest. As you can tell, by the picture, one bird seems to just want to fly over the person's air space. The other bird, more distracting by being more intrusive, looking to lay its next trash over somebody's head. In either case, that can certainly distract someone and cause him or her to expend energy in an unproductive way. But that individual should never ever allow himself or herself to forget what his or her original goals were at the beginning to the point of making that bird his or her object of preoccupation. Certain things we cannot prevent or control, like a bird flying over our air space; but we certainly can prevent it from building its nest on our heads, from messing up our hair, our minds and everything else. Let's take this a step further and move even deeper into the idea of self-determination.

You must be familiar with the expression that "someone is chasing the wrong rabbit." Many of us seem to specialize in chasing rabbits, and we do it so well that the main reason we do not possess our own zoo farm filled with this animal is because we never stop and think about which one to chase and therefore they all evade us until it is time for them to once again interfere with our well-being. Please, a word of admonition: don't go crazy about looking to see how many of those rabbits you can actually catch, all right! Let me pause here and say that my intention for writing this book is NOT to encourage people to continue to spend their energy in futile or trivial pursuits, and for that matter I intentionally leave out or briefly mention some of the causes to a particular problem. Now, back to the rabbit business. We CANNOT afford to chase every rabbit because we would not have enough time and energy. We NEED to learn how to coexist and operate alongside some of the so-called rabbits without being intimidated, constrained, inhibited, or consumed by their presence. Obviously, it demands great strategies to build a safe zone where we may continue our work and not have to constantly worry about being disrupted by them. (Rabbits = Interferences/Obstacles)

We all need to constantly remind ourselves that it is pointless to try to undermine every cause to our problem (s). I would not say never, but I promise that beyond this I will not mention the word rabbit again in this book, unless you did not get the idea the first time around. While you cannot run in every direction, sometimes chasing a particular rabbit with some specific purpose in mind may lead you to where you need to be. In other words, it is determination at work. There are problems that we just have to learn how to live (coexist) with. For others, we have to have a cohort of friends and an entourage to help us solve them. Still for others, we need to deliberately take time to set boundaries and keep them away for good and be done with them.

Your ability to succeed in the pursuit of your dreams greatly depends on how well you are able to utilize the talents which your creator has entrusted you with. I know that I am not dealing with paranoid people here but I'll say this, not all birds flying over your heads represent obstacles or carry the sword of Damocles. You have heard that "the failure of one man is another one's success." And you have also heard that two bodies cannot occupy one space at the same time. That is true to some extent; for instance, there is but one seat at the White House for a president. So it's either Bob Dole or Bill Clinton but not both of them at once. So, in that sense, one man grabs the seat and the other one fails to secure it and has to look elsewhere until the next time around (make sure to vote for the right guy, then). Bill grabbed it over Dole. As for you, don't be overly concerned by fear to think that every time you face a particular challenge or did not get through with your goal somebody out there other than yourself should be held accountable. Otherwise, you may suffer from a psychological condition called paranoia or bipolar disorder; that is when someone does not have it all together, at least temporarily.

Mr. Dole had in mind to really win the election. As far as determination goes, you can tell by his relentless efforts to make the chase until the election date, except that for whatever reason (s) he stopped short in his list from catching all the significant rabbits or the right kind, but I am sure that he can see where he has gone wrong. Next time, he may come out the victor. Some opportunities come by more than once, and perhaps greater success lies ahead not just for Mr. Dole but for all of us who are willing to follow our dreams through.

Again, not all obstacles that we encounter are necessarily designed by some expert witness in a lab or made by a fashion designer. That may have everything to do with our perception, as we often create our own case scenario, set our own stage, and become entrapped in our own ignorance and misdeeds. The other thing is that if we do not have real vision, and if we do not set goals for ourselves, how can we expect to get anywhere in life? If we do not feel that we are hungry and look for food, how would anyone know that we are in need? I am sure that God never told Adam and Eve, "Oh, you are hungry, therefore come let me feed you". The food was already being provided, but instead of resigning themselves or living in denial, it was their responsibility to eat and look for food or ask their provider. Religiously and spiritually committed or not, I don't believe that it is the responsibility of anybody else (deity or human) to actually think for us or to constantly program our database (in this case, our mind). That's the whole reason behind us having a brain so as citizens we may have an active role in the administration of our country as well as in our own personal growth and well-being. And how can we expect to live responsibly and successfully if we won't even stand on our own feet and try to take steps forward? In the development of any human being, the ability to walk independently has always been considered a natural process and the expectation is that all human babies will, after a certain time postpartum, develop articulation, crawl, and then start walking, a process which may take up to 14 months of age to complete (Villee et al. Biology. Saunders, 1989.) At that point, the cycle stops, and there is very little need for the individual to go back into crawling or learning how to walk. However, as far as I know there is no age limit into thinking and using one's brain. Unless a person is brain dead, he or she is expected to do that on his or her own throughout life expectancy or until some circumstances arise beyond the person's ability to continue to function properly. So where do some of us get the idea that they ought not think, dream and carry out visions throughout their existence? I would like to know if that is a new age revelation!

Along our lifelong journey, we are supposed to develop and maintain the ability to adapt. However, once we try and fail, we lose motivation and we have no determination to grow and reach higher goals. We simply resign ourselves to the "Survival Mentality", which in turn harbors the Culture of Poverty. Then, we keep wondering why things are so difficult. Of course, they will and perhaps they'll never change until we see ourselves as agents of change, and not just passive, irresponsible, and hopeless beings. That's what we mean by freedom of self-determination. We may be conditioned to view our inner strength and ingenuity as miniature and sizable objects; however, our ability as individuals to excel in life is dimensionless (bottomless, topless, and sideless). We just cannot put a price on it. No matter how constrained and competitive life may get, as it often will (to the point of discouraging anyone), we only run out of options and ways of being creative when we stop thinking or do not take those decisive steps leading to the next level.

I find it hard and inconceivable at the same time for so many of us to live from one day to the next without setting goals or with no purpose or dream. I agree that not everyone who shoots for the stars actually reaches, for many times we encounter difficulties beyond our control, but much could be expected from someone who is willing to take some risks than from somebody who gets cool feet or procrastinates all the time when it comes to initiating a new move which would eventually engage him or her in some new steps towards achieving a career path, or becoming a better and more productive individual. I don't care who you are, self-determinism will work for you as long as you want it to. If you believe in the providence of God and have a problem with the idea of self-determinism, let me say that it does not matter who you believe in, if you do not have an active (working) faith, you are living in a delusion and are contradicting your own belief. To take this a step further, have you ever heard of the expression, "the way that you make up your bed is how you lie in it"? If you fixed it crooked, your body posture will most likely take the same shape. Contrary to belief, faith seems to be a word that many people have a problem with, probably because of its religious connotation or root; however, it goes hand in hand with self-determination. In his book entitled <u>Keeping Faith</u>, which focuses on the Memoirs of A President, ex-President James Earl Carter, Jr. (better known as Jimmy Carter, born October 1, 1924 in Plains, Georgia) talks about some of his successes and disappointments as Head of State, and more so his aborted efforts to secure the release of 50 or so American hostages from Iran, and his loss for a second term in office. However, a lot can be said about his faith and determination. In summary, Mr. Carter who was well acquainted with a life on the farm climbed from there to the US Naval Academy to the Georgia Senate in 1962. From there, he made a leap to the Office of Governor of this State (1970) and all the way to becoming the 39th President of the United States of America in the November 1976 Election, unseating the incumbent President Gerald Ford, a victory that has been termed "Sheer tenacity" (The Democratic Presidential Legacy, January 20, 1993). Disappointments with life's situations have the potential to bring your spirit down and keep it there, but self-motivation always picks you up and drops you a few steps closer to your destination, that is if you had one to start with. Having talked to so many people along my path, I quickly discovered that some of them vaguely remember where they are from and hardly know where they are going, which explains at least in part why you see many folks sitting in the same position year after year; and all burdened.

Very briefly, let us go back and take a look at the picture ahead of the chapter. You may not be able to prevent the birds from flying over your head, but you can stop them from making their nest over your head. Secondly, the idea of the bed which we spoke about earlier could be further elaborated upon in order to emphasize a critical concept. For example, where you live and work, the kind of friends that you have, and the organizations which you are affiliated with have a great deal to do with your personal choices. Remember, we make choices and live with the consequences.

I realize that oftentimes, you and I may be forced to lie in a bed which we did not make and which does not meet our ideals. If push comes to shove, so be it. Do what you have to do. I am definitely too conscious of these situations involving making decisions against

71

one's own will. As they say, between the two evils, you choose the lesser one.

In the scheme of things, certain events occur in our life as a consequence of somebody else's action or behavior. We end up paying someone else's tab. That is not unusual; however, no matter what the circumstances may be, you do not have to remain in the same predicament for the rest of your life, and do not be trapped in your own shortsightedness (what some would call tunnel vision). Know your needs and create new ways to deal more effectively with your our limitations. Try to have an understanding of the world around you, how it functions, how you relate to each other. It may be hard for many of us to rationalize, but basically what I am asking you is to break your present situation (s) into pieces and analyze each part individually and then try to come up with some solution.

The answer to the problem which you are confronted with may sit near you or it could be found at a distance. Somehow, most of the problems that you face are not restricted to you alone; someone before you had already gone through them perhaps in a slightly different setting, but they found a way out. There is nothing wrong with you thinking globally, but you need to start somewhere. It helps you focus on yourself and your immediate surrounding; that way you have an opportunity to address your basic needs, evaluate your talents, strength, and inadequacies, and find out where you should make changes or adjustments. To succeed in life, you need not be super human like Mr. Somebody; but most importantly, you have to have a vision and the determination to pursue it.

Arthur Godfrey once said, "Even if you are on the right track, you'll get run over if you just sit there." At times we all need a lesson on humility, including myself; however, we must be mindful not to confuse that with humiliation, which often denigrates our humanity. Learning how to have your needs met is what self-determination is all about. And you do not have to forget your past when looking forward; in fact, if you did, you might not have a future to build into. What I mean to say is that you may have come from the ghetto or you might be part of a subculture or a subgroup and you are in search of self-identity, which is fine; however, I resent the idea of looking down on ourselves or following the wrong crowd, one that lives in despair, with vision deficiency, vices, and which takes us further and further into self-destruction. At times, we might even feel that we were born of a family whose nickname was similar to poverty, germ carrier, the cursed, or the serfdom and that we cannot contemplate any great idea or invention. First of all, that's humiliating to label anyone that way because that's discriminatory in nature. Second of all, such association and epithets matter only to the extent that you respond to them and make no effort to reverse that.

Earlier in this chapter, we used a figure of speech and referred to someone sleeping in a bed that was improperly made or poorly designed. Every time you try to sleep in that bed, it causes your body to ache, and it creates nightmares for you. You might have inherited that stupid bed or someone gave it to you as a charitable gift. However, while you can still be grateful that someone wanted to be helpful it may work to your best advantage to just use a mat and sleep on the floor, or simply stand on your feet until you find or make yourself another more suitable bed. Using this defective piece of furniture may take away all your incentive to look for something better. When you settle for less, you run the risk of not meeting your quota or falling below the mark.

The whole idea that we are addressing here has to do with a poor belief system, low self- esteem, lack of self-assertiveness, and negative self-image. All are associated with low achievements, lack of enthusiasm and commitment to higher education, and lack of basic skills to confront life's challenges. We have come to tell you that life may not have been fair to you, but you don't have to be or feel destitute and helpless. You can try to change whatever conditions that you find yourself in, when you start building self-confidence and develop habits and a positive attitude which in turn will promote a greater sense of self-worth and inner strength. Any human being who can be held liable on the grounds of moral accountability for his or her own action has the obligation to make his/her life a bit shinier.

Freedom of self-determination is a term that developed around the 18th century by philosophers and social scientists and is widely used to make people more aware and more responsible for themselves. Now whether or not these people in question saw themselves as having all the necessary means to do so is totally a different ball

73

game.   Under self-determination, the burden is placed on each individual human being to pursue and advance his/her own destiny. Determinism, Will-Power, Freedom and Responsibility are not terms that can be altogether dissociated (they're not mutually exclusive.) In other words, one influences the other and helps us assume certain roles. On this ground, a slave can determine whether to use his or her Will-Power to fight for freedom (Live Free or Die), in which case he or she becomes responsible for the actions taken. On the contrary, if one sees himself or herself as irresponsible for his or her actions, that person will most probably make somebody or something other than self responsible for his or her own behavior. Therefore, there is no moral obligation which will influence the individual to commit or not to commit a violent act.

From that perspective, we would hope that every human being is capable of assuming responsibility for his or her own actions, as well as adapting to a lifestyle that envisions personal growth, a constant task and an individual endeavor. According to this school of thought, all of us may choose to develop ways that would open doors before us and enhance our likelihood of succeeding in life which will eventually further the cause of the human race. Even a religious person who believes in Divine providence is given a set of responsibilities which will help the individual improve his/her quality of life here on earth. Unfortunately, every time we fail to find our purpose in life and pursue it, there is the risk of us digressing towards becoming a dependent state or an indigent society.

So often we come up with these rhetorical or the wrong kind of questions: Why is life so hard? Why didn't so and so do this or that for me? What can I get from the system? In other words, who is doing what for me? But we hardly ever ask ourselves the question: What are we doing to change things for the better! How can we as individuals improve our living conditions? This is a legitimate or the right kind of question we should raise.

There is a famous saying that chance made our parents, but we choose our friends. Put otherwise, we are stuck with our parents; however, we have the option of choosing who we want for our friends. Greed and lack of creativity on our part, as well as our own ignorance, often portray us as a community made of predators and preys where the former try to live on the latter, thereby creating disturbances and causing an extra amount stress in the system. Moreover, despite the complex nature of and the dynamics that govern the needs of human society, too many of us are self-defeating in life. Even when we raise the right kind of questions around the issues dealing with our lives, we place such limitations on ourselves. We do not approach matters with such an open mind and motivation; instead we foster our own personal biases, look for the easiest way out, and settle for less. In the end, we oftentimes cast the blame of our shortcomings to external sources. It is nobody else's fault if you went for the cheap shots. Someone said, "Only as high as I reach can I grow. Only as far as I seek can I go. Only as deep as I look can I see. Only as much as I dream can I be..." The Reverend Jesse Jackson once stated, "If my heart can conceive it, I know that I can achieve it."

For those of you who ever got around the kitchen and cooked something, you know how you accomplished all the necessary steps leading to the preparation of that dish. A significant phenomenon in the whole process of cooking is the fact that once the intermediate steps are completed, you turn on the stove and place the pot on it (I guess you can put on the pot, then turn on the stove. I do not know, ask the chef). Anyway, given the appropriate time, the surrounding temperature will rise causing the temperature of the pot and its contents to go up. And neither the pot nor its contents has any control over their own fate.

This example would be an extremely poor representation of our human attributes because it displays two different objects being acted on. On the contrary, God has given us the power and the will to make our existence here on earth worthwhile. Even though it is not absolute, we have some control over ourselves, our body and mind. We dictate the behaviors and actions that we would have them engage in, and that is true in many respects. For instance, we probably cannot do a great deal in our power to influence our physical growth (especially our height). Most of it is pre-determined by the genetic make-up of our parents and what their ancestors passed onto them. However, when it comes to our socio-economic conditions and our spiritual, personal, and emotional growth, we possess most of the power necessary to be where we should. We have the capacity to decide what we want to be, and individually, we have the ability to make choices which can promote and protect our well-being and welfare.

In fact, to a large extent, not only that you and I have the capability but also we are given the responsibility to determine our course of actions and the positions or roles that we play in society. We can just sit there doing absolutely nothing to make our life worth living, or we may choose to follow someone else's dreams. Intimidation from those around us may take over and make hostage of a great many of us. However, as we continue to live and strive for a better quality of and fruitful life, opportunities will multiply and become endless. Nonetheless, we must start with a mission or a purpose. We have to take time to define ourselves and develop an identity of our own. We also need to stick to the goals that we set for ourselves and pursue them. Too many people are so comfortable with the level of growth that they have achieved so far and have no intentions to grow beyond mere survivorship. They are stuck in a gear or unable to reach a plateau, and it is as though they stop living. They make no more effort to attain any higher in life. These people tend to become very difficult mates unless they find partners of their caliber with no further aspirations. As for me, don't tell me to stop breathing before I stop living, but let me live and fight till my last breath.

"Life is a journey and not a destination." Therefore, we must continuously set goals and search to fulfill our visions. Note that whether we choose to grow or not to, there are consequences associated with such decisions. Pursuing one's goals and dreams is an ongoing process. To live and enjoy life fully requires a conscious effort on the part of the individual to remain focused and keep his/her dream peg in check until death comes.

Taken a step further, to follow one's dreams is like climbing a ladder. Getting to the top of the ladder requires some strategic planning. You don't jump from ground zero or from the first echelon to the top. There is nothing wrong with taking one step or one echelon at a time. As a matter of fact, that is a very smart way different people have successfully completed it. The most harm that anyone can do to him/her is not necessarily climbing in a stepwise manner but rather the unwillingness to ever taking the steps.

We wish to acknowledge however, that the very first step usually represents the most difficult one. Once you complete that initial move, chances are that you can continue to build strength and keep on going. There is a concept called "The Foot-in-The Door Technique". It emphasizes the idea and the importance of that first step. You may perceive great difficulties at the start and even encounter many challenges along the way, but chances are that once you have made your way past the first move you will be able to keep going in the direction that will carry you to the end of the tunnel. Don't be a procrastinator and don't be stuck in the rut of indecisiveness. That is a malignant tumor which will viciously and dramatically invade your existence and expediently carry you to the grave head down.

Hint: self-determination means that you know what you want and where you aim to arrive at in life. You may not have all the clues on how to get there (and I encourage you not to tarry or wander around until you see a vivid picture of the beginning and the end). Each route that you travel and every decision that you make may not be the right one, but you are willing to take some risks, and that in itself is a giant step in the positive direction. Similarly, the fact of not choosing is already a choice in itself, and claiming the status quo can be riskier and more damaging to your individual development and health than taking some steps forward and making few mistakes.

Do you ever wonder what it would feel like for you to have a child that never develops. Ten, twenty, thirty, or forty-eight months after birth, that child never walks, never grows teeth? Or better yet, can you imagine a woman becoming pregnant and the fetus never develops to term? I never got pregnant before, and I am not looking forward to, at least not in this life, but *as a human*, I can sense the agony of someone going on and on with a pregnancy and can never give birth! All I want to say is this: we walk through this life only once, we ought to decide how we may best use our talents and resources. We must find what our mission is supposed to be; and we must lay out goals and visions and bring them all to term. There are but a few insurmountable obstacles in life. All the rest is a matter of perception, making choices, and taking a certain amount of risks.

It is as tragic as any tragedy can be that we remain passive and let all the decisions concerning us and our future be made on our behalf by somebody else. Once in a while, it does not hurt to be part of somebody else's agenda or to have a joint goal that we are pursuing collectively with another person or a group. As you will find, in many cases, collective efforts often bring better dividends or greater profit; the ants are great examples of that. However, to their own embarrassment and misfortune some people go around and never ever give themselves the chance of carrying out a clear vision. Unfortunately, I gladly declare this is **not** an element or a part of self-determination, which we already defined as people pursuing, taking control of their destiny; people playing an active role in their own development and their community. We are referring to those individuals who choose to become part of their own socio-economic and political developmental process and who engage themselves in being part of the solution instead of the problem. Please, don't be fooled by the idea of waiting or looking for the time when all obstacles are removed. Some of which will be there. They may be imaginary (created by your own perceptions of life) or they may be real (thrown along the way to distract you and divert your attention so you do not keep your mind on the prize).

In social (global) politics, self-determination doctrine precludes the rights of a people, a nation, or every individual human being to seek their own identity and pursue their own future. Now, given that my target audience, for whom I am writing this manual, is not religiously based, I do not expect every reader to adamantly acknowledge God's omnipotence, omnipresence, and providence in their lives, even though the idea can be a rewarding experience. Therefore, I will attempt to present this work in a way that is more catholic or universal in nature.

Having said that, let us move forward. Suppose your parents died and left you and your siblings an enormous amount of wealth. Furthermore, imagine that you are living in a country where the law of the land recognizes the full rights of children to possess the estate of their deceased parents. Unless otherwise stated in a will signed by those parents, then their offspring duly become the legal beneficiaries of whatever heritage they left behind. However, a right is as valid as the person who has it believes in its validity. Should the children never exercise such rights or undertake any action whatsoever to claim that wealth, they may never, ever have access to it. In other words, if they forfeit their rights, they lose it.

You may argue with me on this, but I must say it. You are imparted an enormous amount of autonomy, which is self-directing. Once you know your rights and pursue or claim them, you are well on your way toward self-determination. Such freedom will lead you in the directions that will help make you divorce being part of a welfare state, a dependent society to an independent community, a free nation.

All human beings are predestined to live, work, and eat of the fruit of their labor, and seek their level of comfort. Whatever your goals and priorities may be, as time goes on, if you do not discipline yourself, set boundaries for yourself and pursue your destiny, but instead you choose to perform at a low level, that may be dangerous to your health.

As human beings, we have the freedom to move around at will, live where we choose to (hopefully), seek and practice the profession that we deem suitable for us. Remember, we are focusing on each of you individual citizens (regardless of what country you were born in), what you can accomplish for yourself instead of encouraging you to keep your eyes on the obstacles that have for so long surrounded your life. It is so sad to see how many people spend their lifetime pitying themselves, putting themselves down, walking with their heads down all the time, and who never consider the unprecedented accomplishments they could have made!

That is a fact of life, if you spend all your time fooling around, or sleeping, then sooner or later, you may die of starvation. Equally, if you feel that you must live to eat instead of eat to live, you may turn into an elephant, or you may end up dying of all kinds of diseases including: cardiovascular, atherosclerosis, high blood pressure, and all kinds of other complications which are preventable. Similarly, if you never engage in ventures that promote self, but instead you remain focused on the obstacles, you are guaranteed to miss all the opportunities. Consequently, you do not experience any substantial personal growth; instead you condition yourself to a life of resignation, vision deficiency, "a Survival Mentality", deceit, and silence.

There will always be obstacles around us to slow or to tie us down while life goes on. Therefore, it is pointless for us to try to eliminate them. We need to learn how to live with them and function more effectively. Many of us miss the train, others miss the boat, but it all boils down to us missing the opportunities. There are times where we can no longer rely on our loving and caring mom to spoon-feed us. Much less, can she really fulfill our needs and wants? Physically, psychologically, and emotionally, all babies must grow up and mature past the stage of being fed and cared for by an adult. Please do not go any further. Stop right here!

Have you set any goals for yourself? What are they? How far are you from reaching them? Hopefully, no one, absolutely no body actually takes up the following as their sole goals in life: eat, rest, marry, have babies. These are fun when other necessary means are available, otherwise, they can be like self-fulfilling prophecy, self-deceit. And you know what? Nobody will promote you until you actually learn to do it yourself. It's your choice.

A- The Freedom to Choose

We live and make choices. No one can say that he or she never takes a side of an issue. Some of the decisions that we make at times are critical and bear severe consequences. Unfortunately, no one may claim expertise in every field. Obviously, this leads to taking the wrong turn at times, and burning the very bridge which we should cross. In spite of it all, we continue to take risks.

Have mercy on yourself if you feel that some of the choices which you made are not on the merit. That means you are human. One other thing that you are to remember however, is that some of the choices that you have made may be reassessed so you can make adjustments wherever necessary. You should give yourself that window of flexibility; as they say: **success is never final and life is a journey but not a destination.**

I don't know if you ever purchased airlines tickets, they can be very expensive; yet they may carry just enough restrictions to cause you to mystify the airlines industry. One of these restrictions may be a partial loss of the money you have spent to buy the ticket, if for whatever reason, you decide to cancel your trip! Isn't that painful? Sometimes, it seems as though you just cannot win. The same thing holds true when making decisions. The fact of not choosing is already a choice in itself. The more demanding the choice, the more costly it might be, which leads us to ask the following question: Which choice (s) do you want to make, and how much information do you have about the subject matter prior to you making the decision? If you are a cautious person, you may weigh the pros and cons so you can make informed decisions or take calculated risks. For example, I know of many young women who make decisions early on to choose a career path and become excellent in their respective fields. Unfortunately, for some of them that may come with a high price. They either choose not to have an intimate relationship at all or postpone being committed to someone until they have reached the end of their career training.

Based on their socio-cultural background, these women may have to go outside their immediate ethnic circle to find a bachelor, a man. The same thing might be applicable for men too, however, educated single women who are older do not have an equal chance as their male counterpart to develop a committed relationship. It is proven that females who go for higher education and who delay creating a family until they reach their thirties have difficulty finding ideal or qualified men. That is a disadvantage in a male domineering world, because not having an education or a profession can also prevent a woman from finding a man. Nonetheless, for the women who seek a career first, I believe that is the right choice. There may be pressure or time constraints coming from society and which may interfere with a woman's dreams or priorities. However, I have news for you, if you find yourself in that predicament. If you end up with a career and not a man to share it with, you may feel sad or unhappy, but you could also have the man and be unhappy without a career. I personally prefer having a woman with great visions or who has her head on her shoulders, a woman who can be involved in making rational decisions with her mate for the betterment of their family. Where does that leave men?

You might make the wrong choice at the wrong time in your life. Perhaps the choice might be right but timing is off. It is becoming more and more difficult to make a living and provide for a family. That seems to be a major problem in the family setting when men engage themselves too early in life where they either lack basic skills, a profession, or an appropriate education. Note that there is no such thing as a stupid profession; if you master the techniques, perform well, and remain on top of things you will have a job sooner or later.

I love freedom because it gives me latitude to make certain decisions on my own, to be creative, and exert a certain amount of control over my life and my destiny, and I am sure that you do too. It can prevent us from experiencing some of the humiliation that we might otherwise encounter in life. On the other hand, freedom brings responsibilities with it. That is just the way life is. You either transfer your rights to somebody else and let him or her decide for you, or you make the decisions and enjoy the privileges and assume responsibilities for your actions. Whenever you do not take charge or make significant or smart choices for yourselves, guess what? You end up at the bottom of the pit with everybody else's dead weight and baggage all over your face! That is one of the reasons why physical freedom alone, without the necessary means to live an independent life has no merit. Of course, the slave can enjoy a moment without having to think of the whip on his/her back, but freedom goes far beyond the physical realm. Someone who has a kindred mind, though that person may have physical infirmities (impairment or limitations of some sort) is far better than someone who seems to have control over his/her body but no place to go and no power to act in his or her best interest. Because as far as I am concerned, this person remains the estate of somebody else, and never amounts to anything. After all, life is what we make it, and time well spent is a treasure to one's soul.

B- Jubilee: Free Yourself

For the purpose of our discussion, we might think of Jubilee in reference to a slave or to an inmate. In fact, that is exactly what we are going to do. Some jails operate under maximum security, so that prisoners who are perceived as dangerous do not escape too easily. In a "democratic" society where the rule of law prevails, jail term may be strictly enforced according to the violation or as determined by the presiding judge. Once the jail term is served, the said offender regains his/her freedom. By now, you understand the ecstasy that O.J.

Simpson experienced after he heard the not guilty verdict from his criminal trial. For those of you who had access to a TV monitor at the time that the sentence was read, you could observe the jump in the air that Simpson made.

On the contrary, in a culture where the rule of man prevails over the rule of law, justice and freedom are dependent upon the discretion of the master's gracious gesture, the prisoners are not freed until such mercy is shown. They are deprived of all rights, and they may not even be treated as humans. Now, here are some million dollar questions for you. How could anyone in his/ her right mind forfeit his or her own rights and become an outcast? Number two, how can a human being hold another captive? And third, a question that is almost similar to the first; what about keeping oneself captive?

As we search for the answers to some of these questions, we might say that we tend to become the slave to whom we obey. Conversely, as we assume roles and responsibilities upon ourselves, we benefit from the entitlement that pertains to them. Secondly, human nature is such that it elevates us over everything else in the universe; thereby it allows us to acquire a taste for power, on the one hand, and enjoy the assimilation of a certain amount of wealth for ourselves. Undoubtedly, you must be familiar with the expression "power coerces". In other words, power can influence our ability to make decisions and cause us to act very strange sometimes. As a result, we not only use power, but abuse and misuse it very often. Having developed a taste for such power, some of us will go out of our way to find means to exert our dominion. Please note that I did not say to exert authority, for the latter is a title which may be conferred upon someone with specific terms and conditions. Then the power elevates such persons to a higher sphere of influence. Being in authority is not bad; it depends on how one uses the power which one has. Consequently, one may be demoted from one's function or become a slave of one's own bias.

Freedom entitles us to a certain amount of power over our own lives and destiny just as it confers responsibility. Those of us who want freedom of self-determination and who are willing to pay the price can get it. There lies the risks of losing it all or setting ourselves free once and for all. Just as the expression says, "Live Free or Die".

Since it does not always work in the slaveowners' best interest to voluntarily free their captives, more often than not, struggle between the two parties prevails, wherefore mediation through peaceful resolution is not an option sought. Therefore, heavy casualties usually result when the two must sever the existing linkage. Remember, until we acquire the freedom of the mind, we are not free. In some situations, those with whom we have to negotiate our freedom impose on us such heavy penalties that we may be tempted to forfeit our rights and remain bound. Though we may not always have the monetary means to pay our way and avoid going to jail, there exists other aspects to freedom that are just as important, if not even more important. And let me tell you, money does not procure this kind of freedom. You acquire it through your sweat. If you want it, you work and fight for it. Many nations and a great number of individuals such as Toussaint L'ouverture and Jean Jacques Dessalines from Haiti, General George Washington from what we now know as the United States of America, Mahatma Gandhi from India, the Reverend Dr. Martin Luther King, Jr., the slain civil rights leader, Nelson Mandela from South Africa, and many more have fought and obtained partial freedom for themselves and their fellow citizens. Now, they have long gone and in order to pursue and maintain freedom in the full sense of the word, it is up to the present and subsequent generations to expose their lives.

In the Judeo-Christian tradition, land and slave owners were required by law to either set their subjects free or let the land rest after so many years of service (Leviticus 25; Psalms 96). Jubilee then became such a significant word in the vocabulary of nations. The term literally means, to set free. Nowadays, almost no country that we know of openly practices the kind of slave trade which was once a lucrative business. What we continue to have through the 21st century is a renewed attempt on the part of those who control the wealth of the world to secure more assets for themselves, leaving less and less for the rest of the people. In so doing, they may be able to control your pocket for a while, and perhaps for a very long while. With the emergence of the neo-liberal movement over the world, I think that we are observing another form of slavery, small businesses are being forced out by the giant industries and corporations. Secondly, the way that new technology is being used does not necessary serve the workers with the least skills. Consequently, the "little men and women" experience such a hardship providing for their family.

While this picture looks gloomy on a global scale, people all over the world can still obtain their freedom. It keeps on crying in the streets, upon the hills, in every corner. If only the captives are willing to work at it and be set free, they can achieve it. There is an issue of choice involved in the whole gimmick. Too often, we cut ourselves short of change. We must let go of our old, unproductive mind set, which is filled with impossibilities and self imposed limitations. No one can indefinitely keep you hostage against your own free will. Your consent, your acceptance of, or your resigning to the existing conditions is what keeps the circle going. By not acting now, you tend to remain captive as long as you sit there in your misery, expressing your hopelessness, feeling sorry for yourself and thinking that nothing on your part will help bring changes or remedy the situations. We can understand why many of us are socially: unproductive or underproductive, economically deprived, illiterate, and lack the most basic skills to live a life that is more independent. Therefore, we are doomed to remain captive permanently, until we decide to set ourselves free.

That also implies freedom from our own ignorance for it represents one of the most fearful and fiercest of all masters which we could have. We need not always take no for an answer, and we may not have to corner ourselves in a box, thinking it through is the only way to find the solution to most of our problems. Each set of problems has its own set of solutions. It is almost similar to saying that there are many ways to skin a cat (by the way, you own that cat, therefore you skin it the way it pleases you, and don't let anyone tell you that you are a criminal or commit "Catocide" vs. genocide. Too often we are caught in our own fear of failure or being criticized by others or crippled by our lack of vision. When it comes to physical growth, either our parents or we will strive to ensure that we don't go one day without eating something, hopefully some nutritious meals. However, socio-economically, politically, and spiritually, we usually don't engage ourselves with the same degree of enthusiasm and determination. We have been **conditioned** to think that way, which is the essence of our underproductivity and our lack of resources to live on. That is partly true for those living under the "culture of poverty". Against such malady, we are mainly our own physician. Once we free ourselves, we will be able to experience personal growth. Then, we may be able to exercise the full power of our mind, which will then boost our (intellect) thinking process and spirit so we can create a vital environment that is conducive to personal growth and a higher level of productivity. As you get to make choices, and personal decisions, hopefully you will make some of the right ones and as a result, you will increase your life skills and competence level. Hence, you may be able to make greater contributions to humanity.

The Reverend Jesse L. Jackson said, "The only way to avoid genocide is to remain necessary". Try harder and make something better of your life, and you will enjoy it. Whatever you can learn, apply yourself and be good at it, and other people might need your service some day.

Besides everything else, you need to create a positive belief system for yourself, without which you cannot hold for long. Once you create it, you must take appropriate actions toward preserving it. John C. Carlhoun stated, "It is harder to preserve than to obtain liberty". I find it equally stimulating to bring you another quotation. Harriet Tubman said, "I would fight for my liberty so long as my strength lasted, and if the time came for me to go, the Lord would let them take me". There is an old saying which concludes that life is not fair, but God is good.

Sometimes, as much as things change the more they seem to remain the same. Who gets what in this system of things? Terence (Publius Terentius) eloquently stated, "How unjust it is, that they who have but little should be adding to the wealth of the rich!"

There may never be a system of fairness that will grant socio-economic immunity to the disenfranchised and the underserved factions of society. However, we ought to believe that our own effort can and will help make a difference.

Freedom, Freedom, Freedom!!! Freedom for all! But it won't come to us; we must pursue it. US Supreme Court Justice Thurgood Marshall could not be any clearer in his statement. He said, "I do not believe that the meaning of the Constitution was forever 'fixed' at the

Philadelphia convention…To the contrary, the government they devised was defective from the start, requiring several amendments, a civil war, and a momentous social transformation to attain the system of constitutional government, and the respect for individual freedom and human rights we hold as fundamental today." I think that this clause can be summarized to say that we cannot believe in everything that we hear or in everybody who says that they will help us. We all need to start by examining ourselves and where we are in life and come up with our own strategies on how to promote ourselves. Hopefully, we will be cautious not to design a repressive model but one that makes the world a safer and better place to live.

"Knowledge is indeed that which, next to virtue, truly and essentially raises one man above another." (Joseph Addison, 1672-1719.) Stated otherwise, knowledge is power, and that is why Alexander the Great (356-323 B. C.) said, "I assure you I had rather excelled others in the knowledge of what is excellent, than in the extent of my power and dominion." My interpretation of this particular statement is that true power resides in knowledge.

There are those individuals who advocate that what they ought to become has already been cut out for them. This school of thought leads to what is better known yet as "predestination", and people don't really have to work hard. If they were meant to be, they eventually will be. Unfortunately, if that were to be accurate, then everyone who is born and raised in the most socio-economic hardship is doomed to remain in that state, and there is nothing he or she could do to improve his/her life. Therefore, humanity itself would be left to despair. Furthermore, if that were to be the case, then what would those people answer to Shakespeare's saying, "I am a true laborer: I earn that I eat, get that I wear, owe no man hate, envy no man happiness, glad of other man's good." (1564-1616, in <u>As You Like It</u>, III ii, 78.) Moreover, how would we argue over the following?

"There is no real wealth but the labor of man. Were the mountains of gold and the valleys of silver, the world would not be one grain of corn richer, no one comfort would be added to the human race." (Percy B. Shelley, 1792-1822, in Queen Mab notes.)

In an article reported on Thursday, January 9, 1997 by "The Bay State Banner" on the celebration of Haiti's 193rd anniversary of independence, Lynn Granger, the Banner's reporter quoted an artist as saying, "Our minds are still enslaved even though we are free..."

In this business of self-determination, freedom of the mind is the focal point of an evolutionary process. Each individual has the distinct responsibility to pursue or create his/her own destiny as far as life on this earth goes. There is no way that we can just sit there and expect a good fortune to fall over. You may well believe in winning the lottery before you die, but remember, you may reap that prize only in your other life. By then you won't even know what to do with that money.

It is through our hard work and continued effort that we may be able to bring about positive changes. Every day is important in our lives, and no matter what our inner feeling may bring into our mood, besides God, we remain the sole architect of our destiny. As said Cicero, "One day well spent is to be preferred to an eternity of error." (106-43 B. C.), in Tusculararum Disputanionum.)

Predestination, if it exists, is how far you want to travel or how high you wish to reach. And then, self-determination emphasizes when and how you choose to get there. We will have to deal with whatever reality that may exist; however, much of our success depends on our perception and state of mind. For some of us, motivation is what stands in our way; we do carry a vision. Some other people have none, and still others procrastinate and allow themselves to be distracted so much that they never get to start a project or bring it to term. These factors are not only carcinogenic (cancer causing) but extremely lethal to our very soul and existence. I could not agree more with William James who said, "There is no more miserable human being than one in whom nothing is habitual but indecision." (1842-1910, Psychology.) I believe that I have discussed self-determination at great length and I will continue to do so throughout this book; however, as I bring this chapter to a close, I would like to reiterate the quote from James De Lille, "Chance makes our parents, but choice makes our friends" (1738-1813, Piety). Lastly, if you really want to develop your wings and fly, just like the butterfly, you must come out of the cocoon!

PART TWO

The Reverend Jesse L. Jackson Recipe: "We Must Turn to Each Other and NOT on Each Other."

Freedom
From Fear to There

❖ CHAPTER V ❖

Freedom from Self-incriminating and Dangerous Behaviors

At one time or another, we all interchangeably appear in different scenes where we get to perform our role in the great theatre of life; moving from being actors to spectators or vice versa. And as we try to fit into our parts, our individual role-playing then takes a major toll on our lives, which then shapes our personalities and leaves its footprint on us.

From these perspectives, if we try to underline the interactions between different players, we will notice the remarkable influence that every actor exerts on the rest of the world around him/her. Such influence provides the basis upon which we build, live our lives, and attempt to formulate our belief system. In other words, the way in which we behave, do things, or relate to the environment is not mere accident, but it derives from the personality that we have developed over the years. And that personality results partly from our genetic make-up and partly from what we feed on in the environment. As we grow, mature, and search to develop our own identity, we watch other actors perform, and we interact with them. Hence, based on how we intercept and absorb the information that we receive, we may develop a vivid picture in our mind. We then process and incorporate it in our own personality.

Though personality may remain fairly constant once we develop the belief system which suits our individual needs for self-identity and our desire to belong to or feel accepted by other human beings, as we continue to live, and interact with the environment, our knowledge bank tends to modify with new information that will shape our belief system. As a result, our behavior will be impacted and undergo changes, hopefully for the better. This is an evolutionary process that goes on for as long as we live. As time goes on, we tend to adapt by finding the most acceptable, most comfortable pattern of behavior that suits us or that responds to the norms of a distinct group which we identify with (the later adjustment is called conformity) and that is why peer pressure becomes so critical for adolescents because they live in the most transient world and the need to belong to and please others is urgent.

One important observation that can't easily be dismissed is that people with strong personalities tend to change less, but overall, we look to create a habitat (portable space, personal space, or sphere of influence, as different scientists call it) that provides us and our loved ones with a safe haven. Sometimes, we also refer to this safe zone as territory, which may be expanded to include other people with similar belief systems (as you have heard, "birds of a feather flock together"). First of all, we often carry on our person a **social face** (the one we usually display in public or among unfamiliar crowd), a **personal face** (what we would like to be or how we perceive ourselves), and the **real face** (the true self, as stated in the work of psychoanalyst Sigmund Freud). Second of all, there are not two individuals with the same personality. Consequently, we all tend to act differently at times, and react to situations based on our own perception or personal experience, and we also respond to the despair of the moment. By that, I mean to say that our emotions (part of our animal instinct) can also take over and dictate our course of action. Therefore, individually or together, these factors may constitute a base from which undesirable behaviors may evolve. That is an important point to understand in trying to match different personalities with distinct behavior patterns. Lastly, people who might have been raised in authoritarian homes and who go on developing domineering personalities themselves may resent authority and display uncontrolled behavior. In addition, those who have been brought up with little or no parental guidance may experience difficulty later in life to abide by the rules set by society which expect us to have such orderly conduct. Other ways that beliefs influence behaviors have to do with how people go about satisfying their own selfish motives such as getting even and unwillingness to assume responsibilities for their own actions. Sometimes, peer pressure can be of great significance in assessing dangerous or risky behavior particularly among individuals with very high needs to socialize and who want to feel accepted in a group or in a clan. They will do almost anything that they are asked to so they may show their zeal in becoming and staying members of a group/organization. By the same token, individuals who grow up feeling that they have been deprived of their rights or alienated may at some point start acting in ways that are offensive not just to others but to themselves as well. Because aggressive, repressive, or undesirable behaviors do not simply cause problems to other people but also to us. Equally important, perceived hostility coming from the surrounding, unforgiving spirit in dealing with self and others may feed our moods and the way we choose to interact (act and react) with the rest of the world. Sometimes to support our own unfounded hostile conduct, we first create the portrait of a hostile environment so that we may justify our flaws in a face-saving mechanism.

The belief system really plays a pivotal role in shaping a person's life. Certainly, we've already indicated that any belief is subject to change. New information, new ideas and the perceived needs of an individual to comply or change may influence the ways existing beliefs are being deleted, depleted, and replaced. Hence, once the new concept is (internalized) put in place, the individual will develop a different attitude toward self, others, and perhaps toward life in general. First of all, I must say however, as it relates to moral issues, many times people will experience conflict both internally and externally and rage war at themselves until they are able to reconcile the whole self together: intellect (area of logic and reasoning), spirit, and emotion. Secondly, the same statement can be made for those who are struggling with low self esteem and who feel insecure anytime they face new challenges, especially if they cannot predict the overall benefits they will gain if they have to make changes. Along with other issues that we have already mentioned here and what other researches have found out, these two factors can turn a person's temper into a boiling pot or a smoking gun. Otherwise, some people simply develop a mischievous spirit or become resentful of the environment. Consequently, they have tension that builds up which, when it is not ventilated or properly dealt with, may produce frustration. And someone who experiences frustration may occasionally feel outraged with society. Finally, he or she may burst out in anger and demonstrate an unfit personality. The associated behavior is said to be improper and it negates a person's image, making it hard for him/her to be sociable or to be dealt with outside his/her own clan. We are focusing just on some specific causes of violence here.

Self-abasement, aggression, harassment, and violent temper are issues that we humans often have to deal with almost on a daily basis. As you probably notice, rarely ever are we attacked by extra-celestial hosts or by wild animals and other creatures that we share this planet with. It is often other human beings, our very own species, that prey on us. Not only do we attack our own kind, but also we destroy ourselves in many ways.

A- Self-abating, Self-destructive

Under this heading, we may well start with young children, an innocent and yet a vulnerable group of individuals. Although these young lives evolve in their own little world, too often they are disrupted by the adult or the grown-up world. Put otherwise, these youngsters do not grow in isolation. They share, observe, and model themselves after the adult world. As a result, they grow up living what they see and later become what they practice. They tend to demonstrate or display whatever behavior they pick out there. Moreover, many studies show that children who have been put down constantly, especially by adults, end up having low expectations of themselves. The message that they hear most is usually the one that they seek to identify with and eventually register in their mind. Therefore, if they have been fed on negativism, low self-worth, feelings of inefficiency, powerlessness, vindictiveness, aggressiveness, and violence, they tend to reproduce that and perfect themselves in it as they practice. Just as we cannot expect to reap apples on a mango tree or oranges on a fig tree, it is inconceivable to expect from our kids the opposite of what we teach them or what they observe. In psychology, there is a theory called self-fulfilling prophecy. It implies here that children who have been told that they're no good or that they're stupid end up believing it and acting in ways that will confirm it. The Bible says that you cannot get fresh water and salt water from the same source (James 3:12).

95

Adults can also become that way later in life after they have gone through different obstacles and many defeats. By then, they've learned all about cynicism, for they have tried to turn things around but failed. As a result, they may be driven by their emotions and interact in a certain way that makes them fall short from showing the standard behaviors or as that might be expected by society at large. Instead, they dissociate themselves from people who would help them develop a positive self-image, self-worth, and identify with those who may reflect any subgroup characteristics: shy, impulsive or aggressive, pessimistic, self-incriminating, self-destructive (perhaps violent-tempered) or they represent values that are not widely accepted by society. They become part of a stagnant world; they live and function in an environment but contribute nothing that we could call growth and advancement. They clash with authority as they perceive the latter to be a hindrance to their future. What a way to live!

These individuals present characteristics which may be looked at either as symptoms or root causes of what is wrong with our society, **(hopelessness, learned helplessness, poverty on the one hand, and greed, pride, hatred, and violence on the other hand)**. A vast majority of people fall into these categories. At one point, we hope that some of these folks will see the need to change their attitudes about themselves and life in general. Unfortunately, a large segment of them will require continued leadership, education, skills-building (rather than jail cells), and guidance in order to initiate any move in the positive direction. It so happens that many nations and governments around the world waste a lot of money and other resources dealing with symptoms that manifest themselves in our midst rather than providing education and self-help programs to citizens. Nonetheless, we must assume responsibility for ourselves individually; because should help never come from somebody else, life will go forward, regardless.

Therefore, we owe to ourselves the benefit of rising beyond the challenges and obstacles in order that we may pursue the best yet in life. Let us not settle for second best or anything less because we might as well wind up with the mediocre if that is what we aim for. And we also owe to our fellow human beings any kind gesture, comfort, and encouragement which might make their journey more bearable, more enjoyable. It is also very detrimental for us to write-off other people, especially those who are very negative and nonchalant about life, or to marginalize those who look differently from us, talk different from us, and who very often may seem responsible for all the misery that is our lot. Fortunately, none of us reading this book are like that.

Now, going back to what we may call a "culture of violence", the perpetrators and repeated offenders resemble people who are addicted to some sort of drugs or chemicals and who lack the power to free themselves. Their imagination seems to lead in the downward direction. Something always goes wrong in their world, and they hardly ever view life optimistically. Without any intention to blame those who might be victims themselves, I feel that each and every one of us needs to take a personal inventory to see where we have faulted and to try to make reparation. Who forms the C.O.V. (The Culture of Violence)? Who are those villains? Are they isolated individuals, extra-celestial bodies who descend and invade our planet every now and then? Are they ordinary citizens that society has failed, or do they just choose to commit random acts of violence on somebody that happens to be in the wrong place at the wrong time?

I would buy into any of these arguments; however, the closest ones to my heart would be those which convey a society in default. We do not have to travel to the end of the world to take notice of crime going on. Violence erupts in our community and our neighborhood almost intermittently or around the clock, and many such acts are premeditated! As civilized people, where is our sense of decency? Why can't we strive to handle our frustrations and our discontentment in different ways other than through violence? It is quite unhealthy and costly at the same time to commit crime. And just like a society of addicts, each of us has the responsibility to learn how to tame our senses and rid ourselves of or better ventilate our anger.

B- Freedom From Abusive (violent) Behaviors, Turning the Dead Heat Around!

If only we were able to develop an accurate tool which would enable us to identify what motivates people to either display or engage in abusive behaviors and make them turn on each other, and if we were able to install a spy satellite or a radar system having the capability to detect all serious and potential offenders beforehand, then we would probably set the limit at two attempts (strikes) and they would be out. That would also cause each of us to be more in touch with our own emotions and feelings. However, human behavior is so uncertain and so unpredictable that we can barely tell in which direction it might blow at any given time, or in any given moment.

Imagine for a while, if you will, a sailboat being driven by opposing currents and winds. That leaves you with no indication as to where and how far this vessel might travel before being stormed by the driven forces. This analogy may help you grasp in a deeper sense the human behavior, the way that we choose to act or react at times. It does not mean, however, that we are passive animals and that we are driven by our emotions or whatever other forces that are acting on us! Though it may look that way sometimes, nonetheless, we set ourselves above all the other species. We take credit as to the fact that we are more intelligent than the rest of them; we even call ourselves rational animals. I wonder whether evolution was kind enough to the degree that it specifically chose us to exemplify a hierarchy or a higher order over everything that exists, which to me would be mere chance. Or could it be that we are in fact created in the image of an absolute God who surpasses us in intelligence, power, might and wisdom! Anyway, that is food for thought.

We are addressing certain human behaviors being a major contributing factor to many of the problems affecting the environment. And when we fail to apply the rule of self control and allow our instinct to take over, it causes a lot more pain, a lot more suffering and agony, and it incurs (creates) much more disruption in the social order, more than anything else has ever done and ever will. If only the world's great leading bodies and institutions would want to invent the miracle drug that could cure and eradicate in us the predisposing factors associated with problem behavior, that would definitely resolve almost all the issues that you and I have. However, until then each of us has the responsibility to assess his/her behavior and make corrections as well as concessions wherever and whenever necessary.

While some people instinctively act and react based simply on their feelings, others may do so as a habit in that it becomes automatic (like a computer, they're programmed) for them to respond the way they do. Still others just do not know how to reconcile with themselves and keep their compulsion or their emotion in check. However, in either way the results are the same. In every aspect and every sense of the word, negative or destructive behaviors are a major setback to human safety, peace, and happiness; therefore, we must appropriately and efficiently deal with it. Whatever and whoever our source of frustration **may seem to be,** we should avoid taking it out on somebody or on ourselves through suicides.

By the end of the chapter or at the end of this book I hope to be able to help those individuals with such behavior find ways to channel the dead heat being generated in them, thereby converting it into some productive force and energy. In the meantime, I shall proceed with the issues being addressed: abuse, aggression, and violence.

We hold very dearly to the notion that human life is sacred, yet we turn around and behave quite differently; we kill, we destroy our neighbors, and then come up with a thousand and one reasons as compelling evidence to justify our actions! Given the chance, I believe that even the gun, which was used to assassinate president John Fitzgerald Kennedy in 1963, would tell its side of the story and try to find all the justifiable means to kill another human being! What causes our priorities to shift? Instead of loving people and using things, we reverse the process; we dearly love things and we disgustedly take our wrath upon our fellow human beings. It does not take anything to use them or hate them! To our own shame, we are often involved in role displacement in that we don't intelligently and creatively use our brains (as well as our senses) to focus on new ways that could help us match the right kind of thinking with the right kind of behavior, which in turn would result in us making the move that would further the cause of the human race. On the contrary, we devour our own kind whenever we feel like making them the cause of our unhappiness or whenever they happen to be at the wrong place at the wrong time. I am not even referring to cannibalism for that is too strong a word; but we literally aggress, oppress, attack, impeach, and oftentimes kill each other for our own selfish gains!

While some people have the vague idea that crime of violence is very remote and does not affect their own community, more and more we are seeing the evidence that no one is safe, no matter who they are, where they live, and what their level of education and social status may be. My heart goes out to the Cosby family in the recent loss of their only son Ennis, the victim of a violent crime occurring in a rich and affluent neighborhood in California.

If we think that crime and violence are the other community's affairs and we don't do anything to try to bring global solutions to a global problem, we are deadly wrong. We might indeed become the next victims! Building more jails, is that the solution? I doubt it very much! Investing more to provide better education for people and create greater opportunities for them, will offer a better chance to help fight violence.

Shear aggression and madness should always be condemned and not be tolerated. Individuals should be held accountable for their actions if society as a whole has any responsibility toward maintaining whatever kind of social order by building more prisons to punish crime perpetrators. For every jail being built there should be an education facility or a learning center annexed to it where defenders could receive appropriate training and learn how to handle different crises and deal with their emotions. However, because many of the social problems that society is confronted with are not properly addressed and resolved, we attempt to deal with the symptoms and put bandages and masks over the underlining causes. Therefore, we stand ineffective in fighting violence, and it becomes more and more prevalent every day. The widow of Malcolm X, Betty Shabazz, 63, suffered third degree burns over 80% of her body due to a blaze that is believed to have been set by her 12 year-old grandson (*The Boston Globe*, June 2, 1997. pp. A1 & 4). Timothy J. McVeigh remains the prime figure in the Oklahoma bombing of the Federal Building on April 19, 1995, causing the death of more than 163 lives. If in fact he acted solo to carry out the bombing, or if there were other assailants plotting the coup with him, it is so unfortunate and my heart goes out to each and everyone who survived the attack, as well as to the relatives of the victims. This proves that no place is too big or too small, too affluent or too poor, too white or too black to escape the scene of a crime. Let's reflect on Boston for a minute.

City of Boston - Part I and Part II Crime - 1992 through 1996

Crime Category	1992	1993	1994	1995	1996	Yearly Average
Violent Crime	**11,675**	**10,843**	**10,664**	**9,568**	**9,154**	**10,381**
Property Crime	**44,728**	**44,712**	**42,414**	**42,709**	**35,557**	**42,024**
Homicide	76	98	85	96	59	83
Rape	537	480	453	379	414	453
Robbery	4,765	4,081	4,245	3,597	3,470	4,032
Aggravated Assault	6,297	6,184	5,881	5,496	5,211	5,814
Burglary	8,718	7,982	6,799	6,671	5,052	7,044
Larceny	24,599	24,798	24,375	26,002	21,234	24,202
Vehicle Theft	11,411	11,932	11,240`	10,036	9,271	10,778
Total Part I	**56,403**	**55,555**	**53,078**	**52,277**	**44,711**	**52,405**
Other Assaults	9,719	9,730	9,696	9,687	9,411	9,649
Vandalism	10,010	9,478	9,520	8,984	9,199	9,438
Weapons Violation	629	477	469	389	386	470
Prostitution	1,901	1,073	970	866	803	1,123
Drugs	4,468	4,504	4,786	4,725	4,714	4,639
DWI	781	675	589	527	565	627
Disorderly Conduct	2,221	2,221	1,740	1,387	1,320	1,778
Other Part II	26,380	25,869	25,615	26,017	27,768	26,330
Total Part II	**56,109**	**54,027**	**53,385**	**52,582**	**54,166**	**54,054**
Grand Total	**112,512**	**109,582**	**106,463**	**104,859**	**98,877**	**106,459**

Note: Part I crime date are based on the criterion established by the F.B.I.'s Uniform Crime Reporting (U.C.R.) Program and may not reflect the complete incident workload of police personnel (e.g. excludes rapes against males). Other Part II Crimes (s): Forgery and Counterfeiting, Frauds, Embezzlement, Stolen Property, Sex Offenses, Gambling, Offenses Against Family and Children, Violation of Liquor Laws, Vagrancy, All Other Offenses, Parking Violations, Violation of Traffic Motor Vehicle Laws.

Source: Boston Police Department, Boston, MA

Reported Personal Crime in the City of Boston, 1974-1993

Year	HOMICIDE	RAPE & ATTEMPTED	ROBBERY	AGGRAVATED ASSAULT	TOTAL PERSONAL CRIME
1974	134	351	7,195	2,582	10,262
1975	119	453	7,778	3,036	11,386
1976	81	392	6,125	3,290	9,888
1977	75	408	5,655	3,284	9,422
1978	71	475	5,635	3,854	10,035
1979	92	464	6,600	4,236	11,392
1980	91	484	7,526	4,376	12,477
1981	100	531	9,248	4,192	14,071
1982	93	366	7,217	3,980	11,656
1983	90	367	6,713	4,195	11,365
1984	82	460	5,539	4,476	10,557
1985	88	532	6,232	5,036	11,888
1986	106	516	6,225	5,549	12,396
1987	75	550	5,408	5,920	11,953

1988	95	558	5,233	6,291	12,177
1989	100	483	5,866	6,471	12,920
1990	152	539	6,022	6,960	13,673
1991	113	486	4,784	6,446	11,829
1992	76	537	4,765	6,297	11,675
1993	98	480	4,081	6,184	10,843
Yearly Avg.	97	472	6,192	4,833	11,593
*	28,9%	-10.6%	-14.4%	-1.8%	-7.1%

*indicates the percentage change in 1993 over the 1992 calendar year
Source: Boston Police Department, Boston, MA

In recent times, Gary, a relatively small city in the state of Indiana, has attracted national attention as the "murder capital of the United States." That prompted immediate action from Governor Evan Bayh to order the dispatch of state troopers equipped with helicopters and a blue-and-white mobile command center to "patrol violence-racked Gary", where the homicide record has reached a total of 96 cases as of the end of September, 1995 (*The Virginia Pilot*, Tuesday, October 3, 1995. pp. A4.)

What are the causes of these problems? Has the heart of humankind become necessarily and increasingly evil? Why is violence becoming more and more prevalent in our society? What explanations do we have for the increase in intolerance due to diversity, and why does society become so lenient in its dealing with mores and values? We find that people turn on each other more frequently nowadays than they ever had before! Are we more frustrated with life, less resourceful and less willing to invest in building stronger communities?

None of these questions has easy answers. The defense attorney, in his/her passion to exonerate or prove the innocence of his/her client thereby files insanity pleas unless he/she possesses the comparable intellectual and the legal stoutness/savoir of a Johnny Cochran; then, he/she might say not enough evidence found. Or the prosecution team, in its effort to punish for a crime being perpetrated, may be too busy to reach the guilty verdict and therefore files all the reasons he/she could think of except the real one. The law enforcement officers may just want to vilify the suspect and conclude that the latter did not cooperate or that he/she misbehaved, therefore he/she must be the perpetrator. The professional politicians who find it too costly to focus on the real issues, may see aggression or violence as a sign of corrupted and unproductive people; therefore decide to order more cops on the streets or inject additional tax dollars into building more prisons to keep offenders locked up. From behind the pulpit, the charismatic preacher may have a simple explanation which might coincide with the scriptural passage that says, "All (humans) have SINNED and come short of the glory of God" (Romans 3: 23), or he/she might otherwise state that "the heart of men [Humans] is necessarily evil..." (Eccl. 8: 11), which Aleksandr Solzhenitsyn seems to have experienced personally, for he said, "If only there were evil people out there, committing evil deeds, and if it were necessary only to separate them from the rest of us and destroy them. But the line dividing the good from evil cuts through the heart of every human being."

Other people who feel that it matters to know some of the root causes of crime and violence might suggest different hypotheses or possibilities. Hence, some suggest overcrowding as a potential source for the aggressive behavior that is often observed in some people. Experiments conducted using rats and other animals suggest that, when a geographical area becomes overpopulated, individuals constrained to that space display a marked increase of aggressiveness. Now, considering those findings with respect to human subjects, are we dealing with direct causes or effects of other underlining problems?

Population explosion which results in decreasing the amount of square meter (m^2) in personal space per inhabitant confirms a theory of English economist, Thomas Malthus. He basically said that while population grows geometrically, resource availability increases only arithmetically. In order words, growth in population size tends to exceed the amount of goods that are readily available for consumption. Taken a step further, this explanation kind of coincides with Charles Darwin's theory of "survival of the fittest", where people compete among themselves in an attempt to secure as much material wealth as possible for their individual uses. That raises the question of human nature as being selfish, ignorant, and lacking creativity.

Some other researchers have come up with the notion that a gene must be responsible for the aggressive, violent behavior that we observe in people. Especially male aggressiveness has been linked to the Y-chromosome; however, that neither accounts for female aggression in particular, nor does it address the fact that we all have a bit of evil in us which can affect our character and behavior as individuals. Still other studies point out peer pressure as an enabling factor leading to certain crimes. We have a great deal of information on the pressure felt by people who want to fit in or be accepted in a group; and therefore, they will do whatever they are asked to. Also, increased madness and insanity pleas seem to be making their way to many court rooms, with emphasis on the American judicial system and a lot of offenders wish that they could present such claims and be acquitted on charges brought against them! Another contributing factor to crime and violence that does not seem to make too much headway for itself is frustration. Perhaps it is because everyone gets to that point at times. However, people can become frustrated after they have failed so many times to find plausible answer to their problems. I would say that most domestic abuses and offenses are probably committed in conjunction with frustration over some matters. Consequently, after they tried different things, including drugs and found no consolation, they either commit suicide, turn on each other, or engage in crime against other people. Self-defense then becomes a paradigm that we often hear after a crime is perpetrated. A great number of individual offenders including attorneys representing them make this claim. Several years ago, Bernard Goetz while traveling the subway system in New York unloaded his pistol on a group of teenagers, killing at least one and injuring several others. Even though the presiding judge upheld his decision in this particular proceeding, the assailant claimed self-defense for the shooting. While violence undoubtedly begets more violence, we too often neglect to put emphasis on these principles that bring peace among us and to unconditionally and positively reinforce or praise all the peace-seekers/peace-makers. At times, we even create a tense atmosphere between brothers and sisters or neighbors causing them to become divided and so while they are busy fighting among themselves we may advance our agenda and satisfy our own ego. Unfortunately, sometimes these fellows are too docile to even realize what is happening to them!

I hope that history is on my side here. Throughout human civilization, it seems that the first homicide to have been recorded is the one where Cain, filled with jealousy and anger, killed his own brother Abel (Genesis Ch. 4.) From that point on, violence has escalated to a proportion far beyond imagination. The precedent has set the tone for the never ending vicious cycle! And while we may not be able to disregard any of these potential causes as it relates to a particular crime or violence in our society, certain conclusions are just too simplistic, thoughtless, or unfounded for the intelligent mind and those who love justice. On a similar vein, it is obvious that while many of the causes attributable to crime might be warranted, I believe that a lot of time the real causes to violence are overlooked or not thoroughly addressed.

While ignorance and individual greed might be the two most common causes of crime that we often commit, it seems as though that under the best human scrutiny some offenses will never be associated with one specific factor. Moreover, other major causes of violence in our society have to do with existing institutionalized discrimination, the lack of knowledge of many people to be able to establish cause and effect, and unresolved socio-economic problems, as well as geo-political differences among various groups of people. It seems that sometimes we deliberately choose to ignore the existence of such issues. Last but not least, racial tensions account for quite a bit of crime and violence all over; yet people in authority who should be sensitive toward dismantling these evils often have their ears clogged up, and they pay lip service to the cry of the oppressed and potential victims. Sometimes it makes you wonder whether they are part of the problem rather than part of the solution. A concerted effort on the part of all these individuals who occupy positions of power in society would have made our world a much safer place to live. Unfortunately besides pursuing their our own personal agendas, they often have their priorities mixed up. More and more money is being spent for building arms arsenals, and so many resources are being allocated for space missions when so many people starve for food on a daily basis, and they cannot afford a better education which would improve their socio-economic conditions so much! However, regardless of these pitfalls violence just does not pay. It may look like it in a short run, as in the case of someone who seems to have been ignored and who decides to seek revenge by taking matters into his/her own hands. Two wrongs do not make a right! You must know of this famous case scenario. For whatever reason, the employer was unhappy that day and decided to fire employee D. Employee D becomes irate with the boss and could not retaliate, but instead went home and took it on Mr./Mrs. D, who felt safer at the time to take on the children. Since the children could not avenge themselves by hitting the parent back, they passed their anger on to the dog who took it on the cat, which then passed it on to the mouse.

A deliberate attack on any human being is indeed destructive behavior. It is unethical (amoral) and therefore should not be tolerated in any human society. Most countries have common laws that punish the perpetrator of any repressive acts against other members of society. While punishment may sometimes serve as a deterrent mechanism to prevent further violation of the law and other people's rights, it is not the most effective tool in reducing crime and violence. Now, whether or not this conventional wisdom fails us, we cannot afford to lower our standards and become our own destroying force.

No matter where you live: in inner American cities, in some of the slums in Haiti, in France, in Bosnia-Herzegovenia, Africa or else-where, you can observe and hear the depressive news. Every day, the news media from around the world is filled with cases of physical abuse, rape, violence, homicide, suicide, etc. The world cannot continue like this, or we will all likewise go down. Something must change in our character. For more statistics, please refer to the appendix section.

C- The Self-centered World of "ME" and "MINE"

In the early 90's, a judge in the New England judicial system after weeks of deliberation concluded that Pamela Smart premeditated to kill her husband and succeeded in hiring an ex-high school sweetheart to carry out the murder act. Having been found guilty, Pamela was then sentenced to a number of years in jail.

Likewise, when we go back and review the trial of Cain mentioned earlier in this chapter, we discover that this cold-blooded relative of Abel was charged with manslaughter with intent to kill. There is no question that the offender was a self-centered, sociopath who thought of himself to such an extent that he had to take away the life of his very own brother. He exploded in anger simply because he was not chosen as the prize-winning recipient. He could not live with the fact that his brother was such a recipient either. He pretty much wanted to be the Honored persona at that particular occasion.

Sometimes, some of us wear over and over that same suit of pride and self-centeredness. As a result, if it is not "US" or "ME", the chosen one, then it must not be anybody else, as if we are the most important person on the face of the earth. Almost too much of anything can be a nuisance.

There is nothing wrong with the desire to succeed or having the determination to improve our living conditions. In fact, that is what life is all about, a time for everything under heaven; a time to be born. Then comes the time to grow and mature. No one was born to remain stagnant or to be filled with despair. We are co-architects of our destiny. I am not aware of any law which bluntly states that some human beings must refrain from pursuing their own happiness and fulfillment. However, if we become envious or jealous of others' achievements and we have difficulty accepting the success of our fellow human beings, that is very dangerous and it poses major problems. When people start attacking and even shooting down their own kind for their selfish gain, it really makes you wonder about the future of any such generation. Many of us, instead of being the possessor of material things become possessed by them, and as a result, we lose control over our own minds. Many young people today become involved in gangs while others chase their prey for reasons that most of us would consider futile. Many of our young people today take very little pride in who they are. Instead of delaying some of their wants or working a bit harder to provide for their needs, they fight over anything that their eyes can see or whatever their minds can perceive in the possession of someone else. Moreover, Whites cannot live with Blacks or vice versa; Catholics cannot get along with Protestants or vice versa; the Christians have little tolerance for their Muslim brothers or vice versa; those who possess the wealth of this world continue to exert stronger control and neglect the poor who sometimes feel that the only way to secure something for themselves is by engaging in violent, reprisal acts. Politically, it suits a great many people's ego and ignorance to create rivalry and sabotage the would-be opponents and destabilize the very system they claim to protect. Leaders must strive to be good examples to the people whom they represent, and they also have the responsibility to educate themselves and their constituents.

Long live President Nelson Mandela of South Africa who, despite 27 years of incarceration and torture, does not seek revenge against his foes but instead rises up above them and makes it a priority of his to help bring peace to his nation, his compatriots, and neighbors. I am convinced that he could find more reasons than any of us that would make him angry and bitter and which he could legitimately use to either get even with those who hurt him or to undermine their success. Many countries across the globe remain very volatile politically and move from crisis to crisis because their would-be leaders have no idea why they are there. They have zero tolerance for anyone with a different view or opinion. They lack all leadership qualities and oftentimes their own selfish agendas take precedence over the people's whom they claim to love dearly. A very brief note on my observation as it relates to the so-called dictators and some authoritarian heads of states: they tend to be blind and deaf at the same time. They almost always make the same mistakes as their predecessors or their colleagues.

A political leader or any leader, for that matter, cannot only have good intentions all the time; he or she must also empower himself/herself and rise beyond the entanglement and obstacles so as to deliver what he or she has promised. As they say, "Even the gate of hell is paved with good intentions."

Sometimes, the motive behind human actions and behaviors does not lend itself to simple explanations. Just as the human mind, our personality and our behavior are quite complex. Our mental capability as well as our psychological fitness play a major role in the way that we conduct ourselves. However, too often these days do we find people who commit violent crimes and afterwards try to be exoner-ated (acquitted) under insanity pleas.

A violent act opens the door for more violence to happen, and before we know it, that permeates the entire neighborhood, the entire community, and a whole nation. Then, we turn around and start asking why there is so much violence going on! Out of every situation, a few people will always gain something; however, what good is it if they cannot find any peaceful environment to live with their assets? What goes around comes around. And if we can smell what is cooking over there in that neighborhood, it may be just a matter of time before it reaches our court. Consequently, if we can, we better do something to prevent it from ever getting started. And if it has started, we should look for corrective measures or else it will get out of hand and we will all be paying a price.

Violence in any form or shape should not be tolerated, especially from those who initiate it. I understand that self-defense is a legiti-mate course of action against someone who seeks to harm us. Perhaps, if somebody walks up to us and deliberately insults and harasses us, we might not have or think of any further options at the moment than to fight back. However, if we feel threatened or sense any immediate danger as a result of somebody's violent behavior, we can try to avoid direct confrontations with the person by walking away or by taking legal actions. Whereas retaliation might be a last resort or tactic which may well save some lives under certain circumstances, oftentimes, it is simply a face-saving mechanism. Especially, when dealing with individuals, we should never neglect to call on the law enforcement officials for assistance, instead of just taking matters into our own hands.

May I say this to those who experience emotional stress quite often and who have difficulty calming themselves down or ventilating the heat or the anger. Do something about whatever problem you might have before it gets out of hand and becomes nasty. Let's imagine the worse case scenario. Now you sit in a restaurant, at your house or you find yourself in a place, and then someone walks by and starts shooting or seeks to subdue you against your own personal will. If you can help it try to defend yourself as you call for assistance (and 911, wherever applicable). This is an example where somebody other than you has a behavior problem. That person may be too incoherent or too emotionally distraught (agitated) to respond to logic; therefore, it might prove pointless to try to reason with him/her.

When someone else does not or chooses not to behave properly or he/she acts in ways that cause disruption in others' lives, most likely you have limited control over what the person does. As for you, there is a lot you can do to correct undesired behavior; violence does not have to be communicable like TB, HIV, STD's or even like in the example starting with the employer firing Mr./Ms. D. Self-discipline or self-control will greatly influence your emotions and keep you out of trouble.

The following are some suggestions that you may want to practice for future use. Some of us grew up in the wrong environment and have learned the wrong chapter and experimented with the wrong methods. However, if your behavior causes you embarrassment, it may be time for a personal inventory to liquidate the excess baggage and reconcile with yourself in the first place.

Secondly, the environment may be unhealthy and cause you to be immature in ways that you handle different matters. Perhaps, you tend to make premature decisions without thinking about consequences. It could mean that you are not comfortable in certain areas or around certain people and you become too sensitive as you are exposed to them; therefore you develop some level of susceptibility which expresses itself in outbursts of anger and discontentment. Somewhere along the line a change of environment might not be a bad idea. And at whatever cost, avoid being in the company of those who breathe violence.

Thirdly, if you usually feel unhappy with life in general and if you are very pessimistic, you may become frustrated easily, which can make it difficult for you to experience joy in life. You may need some professional help to assist you in developing a more optimistic view about yourself and life's situations.

Fourth, your work, your daily occupations and the family setting create additional stress in your life, making it hard for you to effectively cope. Should this be the case, then you need to evaluate your situation very closely and find ways to solve problems; you may need professional help in doing that. If it involves other people, do not assume anything about them, and don't start by making threats and don't become hostile; you may have to approach them by pointing to what you believe to be wrong.

Fifth, one of the greatest tools in mediation and conflict resolution is communication. We all need to communicate clearly and vividly with those that we relate to in any significant way. You may spend a lot of time talking but you just beat around the bush. Communication means the ability to listen to the other party's concern. It also means making your points respectfully without being so offensive, so defensive, or with irony and sarcasm as these may simply complicate matters and make your opponent resentful of you.

Sixth, trust is another important element in negotiating; you will gain your opponent's trust in ways that you respond in your choice of words but more-so in gestures and body language. At some point in our mental and intellectual development, almost all of us become equipped with a device that I am comfortable calling "a lie detector sensor". I believe that it is more than just intuition, which some of you might call it; but anyhow, it helps us detect when someone might be playing with our intelligence.

Seventh, then find out what ticks you off more often, and see if you can change or modify your lifestyle or become a little bit less susceptible. Chances are that you can do something about it. Talk to someone whom you can trust. Seek professional advice if you are unable to resolve issues on your own.

Eighth, find some low risk exercise/activity that you can do to help alleviate or channel tension in your muscles. Walking is the safest of all; ten to fifteen minutes, three to four times a week may be quite helpful. Swimming or jogging may be agreed upon with your doctor.

Ninth, instead of punching somebody, kick a ball, enter into the bathroom, and scream.

Tenth, if you can stand it, taking a lukewarm/cool bath or shower may be very therapeutic against tension that is being built up inside of you.

Eleventh, any music that is not prompting you to violence can be an effective tool towards reducing your stress.

Twelfth, for young and relatively young people, learning to perform martial arts can be an enhancing experience in mastering self-control.

Thirteenth, do not suppress or internalize your feeling of anger. Acknowledge it in you but, if something bothers you, whatever it may be try to ventilate by talking to somebody who is mature and confidential enough.

Fourteenth, practice some relaxation technique such as rhythmic breathing. Find a comfortable position. Then, try to breathe in forcefully through your nostrils versus through your mouth. Breathe in and hold your breath for about five (5) seconds, then, exhale (release the air) slowly. Repeat the cycle for about five (5) times and throughout the day or as needed.

Fifteenth, when you are too tired or stressed out, you tend to be short tempered; do not engage in conversation which may be confrontational in nature. Avoid any argument that has no basis and that does not lead to constructive, productive outcomes.

Sixteenth, this may be a hard one; reflect on your attitude to see if you are not the problem. If you are honest with yourself, you should be able to figure that out. Then, reconcile with yourself. It feels much better when you can tame yourself or contain your anger and not explode on other people.

Last but not least, if you have to defend yourself, try to avoid violent action, whenever necessary. Never seek to be the aggressor, leave it to somebody else. We could add more to the list, but we feel that we have offered you adequate choices.

All of us may lose our temper sometimes because we are human. Nonetheless, before engaging in any repressive act, we usually catch ourselves, which I hope we can all practice someday. Now, what about these individuals who carry out violent acts while under the influence of illegal drugs and alcohol? It is up to them if they choose to put themselves so low, but our foremost duty as responsible citizens is to maintain our own sanity by not giving in to toxic substances that can destroy our lives, our reputations, or make fools out of ourselves. (*Hint:* if you are what some people refer to as social drinker, know your limit as to how much you can handle). In general alcohol is no good for your body anyway but each person's level of tolerance depends on: 1) body mass 2) drinking history, how much you have had in the past 3) the alcohol content of previous consumption 4) the altitude (environment) where you're drinking; in the air or at high altitude, you weigh less, therefore the more vulnerable you become.

It seems as though we (human beings) are evolving towards a more dangerous, more violent species. Our society has never known so much crime and violence. It is faced with a real dilemma of power control. There seems to be a lack or an absence of strong authority figures. We even experience the abuse of power by many of those who are supposed to be examples. We really need to do a better job reeducating and recivilizing ourselves, as well as providing more positive role models to our kids and young people so we may help build a more humane world and enjoy a safer environment. We also need to do a better job in dealing with our differences. Otherwise, we shall sooner or later turn this place into a real jungle where all of us become hostages of our own undertaking. When we are unhappy with ourselves or with our fellow human beings, and when things go wrong as they often will, before we jump the gun let us reason and come to our senses, lest we forget that we call ourselves the most intelligent, most civilized, and most advanced of all the animals. Let us leave violence in the hands of the barbarians, and may we act as people with character, self-esteem, self-control, pride and decency!

A case scenario: if you happen to catch your spouse in the act (in your bed or in some bed) with your neighbor, before you are overcome by your emotions and kill both of them, pause. Then, ask them if they would rather be each other's mate, that will determine whether or not you have something to live up to or that is worth fighting for. Should your boss fire you from your job, don't take it out on your poor spouse or your kids. Make an effort not to react at the spur of the moment. Besides other advice which I have given you earlier, sing all you can. Take a long shower, if that's not against your religion or problematic to your health. Go hunting, or watch a good comedy show. You, fellow, your wife stays home all day and does not cook, or you wife, your husband decides to end the relationship. Before you start knocking each other's heads against the walls, take a walk or do whatever else you can to help release the tension. Then, come back. At that point you should have ventilated that dead heat. Remember, you never have to take it out on each other; there's always a door next to you. If you have to, exit but do not punch, which is the worse human response. You may be disagreeable on matters but agree on some civil ways to solve all your differences. If anyone wants to call you a coward, while you may feel offended, show him or her that YOU have self-control.

❖ CHAPTER VI ❖

Socio-cultural Intolerance/Hostility

"**W**e must be constantly vigilant against the attitudes of intolerance and injustice. We must scrupulously guard the civil rights and civil liberties of all citizens, whatever their background."

Each idea that ever comes into being almost always starts in a single mind and remains at the level of thinking until it is put into action. Occasionally, a conspiracy plan may spring almost simultaneously in the head of several people. The Bosnian-Serb ethnic cleansing which broke into wars in this last decade of the 20th century provoked the indignation of many world leaders. Hence by the end of 1995, the United States, under President Clinton's administration and the European community through NATO (North Atlantic Treaty Organization) have taken significant steps into bringing the fight and the killing to a halt. During Adolph Hitler's reign in Germany, the world witnessed a similar trend except that the target of hatred in the above two countries differ markedly. In Germany, it was more like a war to cleanse the country of a particular undesired and perceived as unwanted nationality, namely the Jews. In Bosnia, the war reflects more on national ideology which creates social divides among a population. Right there, we might as well mention the old South African regime of the apartheid and the wars in Ireland between Roman Catholics and Protestants. Lastly, during the slavery days, black people were reduced to absolute objects. They were forced to work and build a system that even alienated them more from civilization.

In every race, every culture, and almost in every ethnic group or clan, we find distinct elements of ideology that people use sometimes to define themselves, and secondly to identify, categorize, isolate and/or minimize other groups that are different from them. The irony is that the same factors and values that unite society and different groups of people together are the exact same ones which constitute forces to create social disparity, divisions, chaos, dissension (quarrels) and segregation, whichever one might choose to call it. For that matter, our society could be viewed at times as an aggregate mine-field, against which each individual human being, each nuclear family, and each country needs to use caution during interaction because of the possibility that someone or a group may be designing some divisive machine to try to disqualify and uproot a neighbor. Sometimes you even wonder if it would not make sense that we all wear a warning label admonishing our neighbors not to get too close to us or to approach at their own risk!

We might argue that the relationships between relatives (nuclear and extended family members) represent the polar bond which necessarily designs the back-cloth of the social order. From this interaction, people come together and build communities which can expand to include different cultural elements, different ethnicities. Furthermore, the whole concept of nation focuses around a group of individuals who perhaps live in the same geopolitical stratum and who share similar goals and aspirations. Last but not least, we encounter conglomerates of people who form a race and as a result, you and I talk about white, black, yellow, and red people. Such a description is used oftentimes to socially elevate one group of people over another, to promote the interest of one group over another and if possible to isolate, devalue, or denigrate/dehumanize a group.

In the makeup of that intra and inter lateral (with self and others) unity, the magic word which makes such binding possible in the first place is called socialization. Without this notion, no human being could ever relate intimately to one another. Other relationships would still be possible, however. For example, the wolves in a jungle do relate to other species, or other animals in the environment but on a parasitic level; they live at the expense of the latter group (s), which they will sooner or later drive to extinction. There is another type of relationship which can be developed among species that is called commensalism, whereby one group lives on the account of another without necessarily destroying it or causing great harm to it. For example, the bacteria that live in our intestinal tract. More accurately it means that only they benefit in the relationship. It is not a recipro-cal or mutual relationship where both parties involved draw equal benefits, as in the case of family settings where relatives live together, care for each other, and share resources.

Aristotle made the statement that we (human beings) are political animals. At the dawn of human civilization, another yet powerful statement was made and that states, "Man is not made to be alone..." (Genesis, Chapter 2: Verse 18). The need and the ability of each individual (man or woman) to interact with his or her peers in the first place will then create the kind of environment conducive to social bonding. As a process, socialization comprises several elements or steps. These are 1) Attraction vs. Repulsion (withdrawing), 2) Tolerance vs. Prejudgement (Prejudice), 3) Means of communication (verbal, non-verbal), 4) Self-evaluation vs. Cross-examination, 5) Compatibility vs. Incompatibility, 6) Mutual understanding vs. Self-centeredness, 7) De-individuation vs. Collectivism (togetherness), 8) Perception of needs: new values vs. the old ones, 9) Conformity (adaptation) vs. Non-compliance, 10) Acceptance vs. Avoidance, 11) Interdependency vs. Individuation, 12) Conflict (friction) resolution vs. Marked resistance (diverging forces), 13) Adherence vs. Break-age, 14) Personal growth vs. Social Stagnation (mal-adaptive), and 15) Activism vs. Hostility. (This hostility is usually directed against non-partisans or members of different groups.)

Socialization represents the backbone of our social make-up and it provides us with the support that we need to continue to live. It gives us a sense of belonging. That also helps us enjoy humanity or life, if you will. Had it not been for social gratification, very few of us could survive for any length of time. Remember the story of Adam being alone in the Garden of Eden (Genesis, Chapter 2: Verses 18-20). It is further stated that, "No man is an island". In Aristotle's term we read the following: "Man is a political animal". Political here implies being sociable. And thanks to God that not only men but women are also political in nature. I should warn you, however, that socialization has other downfalls besides those mentioned in the chart above.

A- "Can We Talk?" A Rodney King Version

Earlier in this chapter, I brought to your attention that every idea starts in the mind of one single individual. Once the person generates the idea, he or she will probably struggle with it through a process of acceptance vs. avoidance not only in an attempt to make sense of it but also to try to establish a moral basis for it. Having passed this stage, either out of mere curiosity or boldness, the person will seek to confirm the birth of this fresh thought by communicating it with other members of his or her own social milieu. Then, that idea may well be on its way to becoming a milestone of that group, and perhaps making it one of its new endeavors. It does not have to be like that however, it may give way to some resentment and cause a split between the proponents and the opponents of this undertaking; and the stronger the disagreement here the more defined the separation within the group. However, as we pick our battles, our allies will eventually join in helping us carry the load. Then, who or what are we up against: the old culture, the implementation of the new one, the people who see and think differently from us?

Intolerance of or hostility against members outside one's own clan is hardly ever an isolated incident. It often requires more than one person to build an arsenal, to validate and execute a plan of action aimed at reaching a certain target. For example, there is no way that Hitler could have carried his extermination plan against the Jews or no one person alone could promote and perpetuate the slave trade. There must be allies who support those ideas and who are willing to advocate for and carry them to term.

May we use an analogy here. Just like pregnancy (wanted or unwanted) and/or STD's (sexually transmitted diseases/infections) are the product of sexual intercourse, so too, hostility precedes aggression and violence. It gives birth to discriminatory behaviors which is an end product of our thoughts and the environment in which we evolve. Hostility also represents the offices which lodge our aggression against those individuals who look different from us. Oftentimes, the hostile individual engages in a mission of self-fulfilling prophecy, in that he or she may justify his or her own hostility by acting it out. In other words, to sustain his or her bias, he/she must portray the other person as the hostile one in the first place and then make allegations against him or her. Perhaps I can use this French maxim as a metaphor or an analogy to further explain how hostility works. The French say, "Quand on veut noyer son chien on dit qu'il a la rage".

Translated literally, it means, "If one wants to drown one's dog, one will find any just cause to carry such action".

In this analogy, the dog represents a figure of speech. Sometimes, we complain about the other people not because they have done anything to us or that they have anything against us, but just so that we may be able to justify our own prejudice and carry hostile plots against them.

Violence penetrates every segment of our society and becomes almost a normal course of our daily life. Regardless of who you are and where you live, no one is exempt. We may be identified either as assailants or victims. As civilized people, how can we allow ourselves to become so low, or is it part of our contemporary culture and civilization?

On a daily basis, violent acts claim some life either in our family or in our neighborhood or our community. One never knows from one day to the next who the next victim (s) will be! For any silly idea, we turn on each other. Where is our pride as people, and where is the respect that we once held for our fellow human beings? Despite the fact that it may sound like a million-dollar word, most people nowadays might not have even heard of the **sanctity of human life**, never mind asking them to explain what it means! What is our hope for tomorrow? Everyday, we witness more and more violence! And, as a society, where do we stand in terms of homicide, euthanasia (mercy or assisted killing), suicide? Are we leaning towards becoming part of a *culture of assassins?* What kind of values are we teaching our children and what legacy do we intend to pass onto the future generation?

B- A Human Repellant

Crime and violence have long reached epidemic proportion in our society and have become pandemic. No one is safe. It is a scary scene for public officials and a major public health concern, as well as for clergy! Habit, said Horace Mann (an American educator, 1796-1859), is a cable; we weave a thread of it every day and alas we cannot break it.

Time magazine, on the cover of its February 14, 1994 issue portrayed the head of a pig with a human trunk in a suit and tie and entitled it "Are Men Really That Bad?" In the actual article, it is mentioned that <u>World War I wiped out some 8.5 million men in Europe (pp. 56-57).</u> <u>The Nazi movement in Germany exterminated about 6 million Jews; and the count for blacks who, in the name of civilization, were murdered either on the African soil, in ships during transport to the plantations or within their respective colonies, will never be known.</u> The question that one might ask is not so much about 'Thou shall or Thou shall not kill', but seemingly 'When is it okay to kill?' The second most important one becomes 'Who shall kill whom?' Obviously, who shall live is implicitly understood, as we may deduce from the questions asked.

The other day, as I was driving on Blue Hill Avenue in Boston, Massachusetts, I spotted a bumper sticker on a car which read as follows, "Hell was full so I came back". It would seem somewhat logical to think that there exists different levels of hell, considering the place where that person went and got the chance to come back, and also in an attempt to portray the one in which many of us may be living in here and now! I am not trying to be funny! I guarantee you that, for the problem is too overwhelming to make fun of it!

Based on another article published on July 14, 1996 in *The Boston Globe*, not counting any other form of violence, firearms alone are responsible for some 40,000 homicides and suicides among teenagers each year across America. That accounts for more deaths per year than what is recorded for all the diseases combined for this particular age group. The article went on to say, "Gun-related homicides rose 18 percent in the past decade and by 30% among people ages 15 to 24" (p.19). Meanwhile, German authorities are trying to curb Neo-Nazi propaganda that is rampant in the nation (*The Boston Globe*, Feb.7, 1996, p.4.)

Law student Yigal Amir confessed to killing Israeli Prime Minister Yitzhak Rabin. When asked about his motive for the murder, he indicated that was his obligation, his religious obligation. (*The Boston Globe*, November 7, 1995, p.3.) That is a great tragedy of all time, people killing people in the name of religion.

Bronson Alcott (1799-1888) in 'Table Talk' said, "Civilization degrades the many to exalt the few." Judith Martin, a newspaper columnist, recently said, "People are fed up with the tone of society now, so much so that, finally, they are calling for civility." She went further to talk about rescuing civilization and the need to liberate society from instability, anger and violence (*The Boston Globe*, June 26, 1996, pp.41,44).

To prevent ourselves from being eaten alive by insects, we have developed what is commonly called insect repellent. By spraying such a chemical over a surface area of our body, we keep those insects from attacking us; thank God, at least we have one problem partially solved but we are still flanked by other ones. At times, human behavior, for instance, constitutes a major barrier against social progress. When a particular behavior is associated with the person's belief system, it thus becomes part of self and is reflected in the individual's everyday attitude. It is no question that our behaviors and attitudes affect how we relate to people. They even stand in the way preventing us from trusting and getting along with each other. Common sense tells us to keep a certain distance from these individuals who show great potential to carry assaults against us. Then, their behavior becomes like a repellent; it keeps people away. Thus far we find at least three reasons why we are uncomfortable with other human beings. The first is behavior that is considered problematic, which a person previously displayed and has caused some harm to us. A second reason is our own personal bias toward that person or an entire ethnic group. Third, our own limitations and ignorance get in the way sometimes, thereby decreasing our consideration of other people. Hence, at times our level of tolerance toward each other is almost zero; we have no patience to sit down next to someone who looks different from us, talks different, and who has different opinions from ours. In other words, the person looks foreign to us and we are ready to cut him or her out of our lives. As a result, we often do not take time to properly address issues on which we disagree. We throw constructive dialogue out of our vocabulary and we embrace the cheapest possible road to solve our differences or get rid of our frustrations. Most violent crimes feed on emotion which often builds up and transforms itself into anger and ultimately bursts into violence.

It is all right to disagree and, in fact, hardly ever do two human beings agree one hundred percent on any issue. However, there is a way to handle things, which will create a safer, more productive and a healthier environment for us all. Dr. Martin Luther King, Jr. said, and I quote, "We must learn to live together as brothers or perish together as fools". No matter how rough life gets, violence does not have to be our way of living. There are just a few reasons for that. One reason is that violence is definitely not healthy for us or the environment. There is no net gain in violence; plus it incurs a lot of pain. After all, what goes around comes around. Please, do not turn on each other. Violent behaviors can be viewed as human repellant except to the person who displays it, and I know that no one likes to be labeled as having a quick temper or be called violent.

C- Socio-cultural Intolerance and Insensitivity

Many violent actions in this place can be traced through socio-cultural intolerance, frustration, and insensitivity. These factors constitute the basis for the kind of apathy, hatred, and disguise that you and I often experience out there and they probably account for most crimes being perpetrated. Sometimes, just because you walked in a hostile territory where people express very little sympathy for your being different, or you step in a wrong place at a wrong time or perhaps you step on someone's toe by mistake, then you get harassed.

It should be no surprise at least to us who have grown up a bit to notice these things. People call you names, try to stereotype you, or they treat you like the scapegoat or even like a third class citizen. I think that we have no other choice but to call it by its full name: bigotry/hatred, discrimination; whether it be racial, gender, national-ity, or discrimination based on one's religious beliefs, political conviction, or low achievement in life. In that case, you feel as if you are a victim of circumstances. Many times people will belittle you or shut doors in your face based on the reasons mentioned above. What do you do then? What is your right course of action? Do you give them a piece of your mind, grab them by the neck and choke them, punch them in the face, or pull them by the hair? Or do you spray them with bullets or exterminate them by whatever means available to you? Let us think for a moment. What will that accomplish and what kind of message will it convey to our children? Could it be that we're telling them that it's okay to hate?

I agree with you that there is much pain and suffering in society today, and sometimes you try to endure some of it. However, even that can't go on for ever; then you feel like retaliating, which seems to be a legitimate course of action. Moreover, a lot of the suffering comes about as a result of oppression whereby some people feel that they own the world and the best way to ascertain that it remains their possession is to dictate and control the lives of or destroy everyone else! No sense of respect for human lives and definitely no room for cohabitation. Sometimes, those same individuals turn around and ask why other people are so hostile toward them, when in fact it is their own hostility to which they are reacting. You just cannot win, sometimes!

So many people are unhappy and feel powerless in front of the situation that they oftentimes face. More importantly, even though they live in a world filled with people, they can experience just as much loneliness as if no one else ever lives around them. They may use that as an indicator to draw the conclusion that nobody cares about their problem, no one listens to them, and there's no one to confide in. This is a time where many may contemplate suicide. That is a pretty sad situation and extremely painful. There has to be better ways of handling those hypercritical moments. That is enough to engage our attention on and around the obstacles and nothing else. Some of these obstacles are mere perception but great many of them can be substantiated eloquently; and believe me, there are enough out in the world to make any one person feel powerless, dispossessed, offensive, and defensive.

Now, may I say this. While you may not have much or any control over someone else's behavior, there are steps which you can take to ensure that your own behavior does not create unprecedented, embarrassing situations that lead you to trouble.

Obviously, in a confrontation, at least two parties may be identified:

1) The aggressor or the assailant
2) The one being assaulted, aggressed or oppressed.

Occasionally, you may get a slap from someone, perhaps from someone that you least expected. It could also come about at a time and place where you least anticipated it to happen. You were already upset that you or someone in your family has just been diagnosed with a terminal disease. Maybe you just got fired from your job and your boyfriend, girlfriend or mate has just turned his or her back on you. The only thought you have been able to entertain is **revenge**. Thus, the above assault comes like a stimulus and ignites your anger, you have just about had it. You may say to yourself at that time that your best bet is to retaliate by slapping the person (s) back. Since you were not the attacker, it would be your right to take revenge; however, this is not the ideal choice. In fact, it may be the worst reaction on your part, and we are not even thinking about anarchy yet.

Remember that people are also ignorant and therefore they just act stupid, not even knowing the reason why they acted the way they did a minute ago. Other times you and I need to watch ourselves so we do not become hypersensitive and respond to any petty things and let them disrupt our peace. It may be easier said than done, but it is a cause worth pursuing, especially when we know that things will go wrong at times.

D- On to Developing Healthy Ways to Channel Our Anger and Frustration

Just exactly how we will behave or react in every situation we face in life is unpredictable. However, as we grow and become more mature, hopefully we will know ourselves a little better to understand what triggers our anger and what does not, what we can or cannot live with. At the same time, it would be a great idea to work on our emotions so we do not lose our temper too quickly and go out of control. That way, we may be able to retain our lucidity and a certain clarity over our thought processes. Hence, we can reflect on and rationalize what had happened and choose the proper course of action, which will help us deal with the issues at hand somewhat more effectively.

Although I am not about to prescribe a "sine qua non" medicine that will prevent or immunize everyone from ever getting into trouble, some hard to deal with behaviors may be kept in check even in most troublesome circumstances. The way to accomplish that may vary (differ) from people to people, but there exists a general formula or a partial but yet effective vaccine against violence. But first, allow me to arrange it into a fat equation and then turn it to a tiny pill or syrup suitable to go down any throat.

Step #1: Allow yourself to know who you truly are, not the way the society sees you (your social component) or your ideal self (what you would like to be) but who you really are. It may be hard for you to accept but that's the first step into shaping your self-identity and building a positive self image.

Step #2: Learn about your emotions, how well you are able to interact with people and things around you. Some of us just do not know how to calm ourselves down. In chemical terms, such a characteristic could be viewed as explosive. In a psychological setting one might use the word compulsive. Socially speaking, such words as antisocial, sociopath, or unstable personality may be used. (*Note*: the worst way you could choose to make your point is by either blowing your top or by hitting someone. That really negates your image. And please, no "four letter words".)

Step #3: Some of you may have to do it more often than others, but all of us need to monitor our emotions. It is like our blood pressure; as long as we live, we will have a blood pressure level. However, when it gets too high, it may become lethal or suicidal. So monitor your emotions by trying to keep it under control so you're not too quick in your reaction. If you feel too angry to talk, then it may not be the proper time to take actions or make decisions.

Step #4: Ventilate some heat if need be, which will help! Exercise, listen to some form of soothing music; sing along. If it is something that bothers you or makes you unhappy, discuss it with someone or the person causing it.

Step #5: Having accomplished step three, you may not have all the tools in place to rationalize what has happened because you need to reason before taking action. For this, whenever possible, try to remove yourself from the situation so you may be able to look at it with greater clarity. That will also help you practice self-control.

Step #6: The reaction stage. This is a critical point because you may blow it, solve the problem, or leave it as is for now or for a later date. Let us take a concrete example. a) Your friend may call you a jerk. An instinctive reaction might be to jump on him or her, in which case, the situation degenerates into a fight, and if a weapon is involved the incident may turn out to be fatal; bad business. b) You work the first five steps and at step #6, you figure that you need to sit down and talk with the person who called you a jerk. It is better to be called coward than to burst into flames. Most of the time we could solve our differences amicably by keeping the line of dialogue open. c) Lastly, you could ignore that the person ever called you a name. What we respond to matters more than what people call us. However, if that bothered you and you never received an apology, there may be repetition of that later on. So if you wish to maintain the friendship without hypocrisy, I suggest that you choose point b.

Step #7: Some of us are hypersensitive to criticism. We do not tolerate too well people talking about our downfall; we tend to handle praise a lot easier. But our ability to deal with criticism effectively is a sign of maturity. Also, what you need to realize is that there are constructive and destructive criticisms, and you always get one or the other. So, learn to deal with both in a constructive way.

Step #8: Be considerate and tolerant of others' points of view; we are all entitled to have our own opinion.

Step #9: Be objective. Do not draw your conclusion until you have all the relevant facts, and remember that there may be many and better ways to solve a particular problem. It is better to be slow in your reaction than to cause more harm by acting too quickly, which I've seen too many times. Now the whole equation into a pill or syrup:

Know Yourself
(Be in touch
with yourself)

The reaction
stages

**Learn About
Your Emotions**
(How reactive
you are)

Try to rationalize
or reason about
what happened.

Make it your
priority not to
base your
decisions on
hearsay

**Monitor or Keep
Your Emotions
Under Control**

Ventilate some of
the heat, if need
be.

Be slow to anger.
Stop, think, and
listen. There may
be more sides to
this one issue.

You cannot change anybody else, but you can change yourself. Ventilation. Release some of the tension or the heat that has accumulated. There are an array of activities that can help you do that, some of which may sound too simple to be true. What works for one may not work for another; however, out of them all, you will find the one (s) that do apply to you.

Before an act of violence is carried out, unless it be voluntary or premeditated by perhaps a cold-blooded individual, there is tension being built up within the person. If that feeling lasts long enough and if it is transformed into anger, it carries within it the potential of causing internal (within you) damage or external outburst. In summary, here are some of the activities that you can do:

— Do not internalize everything. Share what happened with someone you trust or someone whose judgment you value.
— Take a walk or do some kind of physical exercise if that is suitable for your body.
— Listen to music, sing, laugh, or watch a comic movie.
— Do some rhythmic breathing. Take some deep breaths; hold and release slowly. Repeat the cycle about five times.
— Read a book or newspaper.
— Forgive yourself, forgive others, and let go.

You can also think of other things that you enjoy most and do them during those circumstances. Basically, you entertain your mind by keeping it preoccupied with other things while diffusing the anger, or tension. The main focus is to do something relaxing.

Trying to give others a taste of their own medicine usually sets the tone for a vicious cycle. Hostility begets hostility, and people who have been mistreated have a tendency to mistreat others, or the oppressed of today tend to be the oppressors of tomorrow. Let us learn how to make the world safer, less violent, and more loving and caring. Please note that today's enemies may be tomorrow's friends. That is another reason to rid violence.

Also, only a percent of all violent actions being committed deal with specific types of discrimination. That is the reason I attempt to address the issue from a broader angle. Marcus Garvey said, "Hungry men have no respect for law, authority, or human life." With respect to violence in domestic settings: "If you are wise and seek to make your house stable, love your wife fully and righteously…kindness and consideration will influence her better than force" (The Husia). I believe that this applies to both men and women, because both genders carry the potential for being abusive.

In conclusion, let us all strive to make the world a safer place to live in. As said by James Baldwin, "Remember, to hate, to be violent, is demeaning". It could mean that you're afraid of the other side of the coin, to love and be loved. Socialization is a process which can lead to growth. It revolves around several steps:

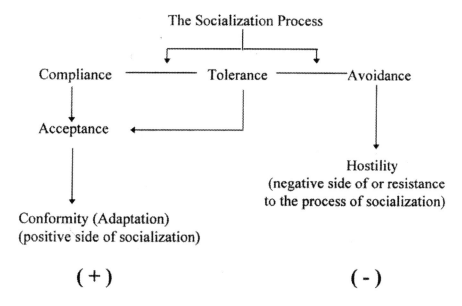

It was Horace (65-68 BC) who said in the Epistles, "No one is so savage that he cannot become civilized, if he will lend a patient ear to culture". Except that culture is made of people who are biased. Culture tends to undergo certain changes over time and it is as good as the people who make it. However, the central message is to live and let live. "Be civil to all, social to many, familiar to few." (Benjamin Franklin (1706-1790) in <u>Poor Richard's Almanac</u>.)

❖ CHAPTER VII ❖

Conflict Resolution: Improve Your Negotiating Skills

Before going any further, I would like to lay out to our prospective readers some of the important terminology that will be used in this chapter:

A	B	C	D
Interaction	**Perception**	**Self-centered**	**Collaboration**
Communication +	Conflict +	Hostility +	Conflict resolution +
Dialogue +	Attitude +/-	Finger pointing -	Negotiation +
Cohabitation +	Perception +/-	Sarcasm -	Mediation +
Building bridges +	Expectations +	Mind set -	Amicable climate +
Tearing walls +	Run away from -/+	Scapegoat -	Agreement/Contract +/-
Attentive listener +	Power struggle -	Face saving tactic -	Goal setting +
Apologetic +/-	Giving in +/-	Personal baggage -/+	Overcoming barriers +
Diplomacy /	Competing -/+	Offensiveness -	Reconciliation +
Courtesy +	Decision making +	Defensiveness +/-	Mutual ground +
Open-minded +	Obstacles +/-	Individual interest -/+	Common interest +
Focused discussion +	Disagreement +/-	Name calling -	Promotion +
Mutual respect +	Facts vs. Opinion +	Susceptibility -	Concession +/-
Interaction +	Passive Listener -	Individual pride +/-	Cooperation +
Flexibility/Change +/-	Acting +/-	Reacting -/+	Compromising +/-

Fig. 7.1. Words to think about when facing conflict. Within specific context, + means positive outlook; - means negative outlook. So, +/- means either.

Conflict is such a common phenomenon in our daily lives that we cannot just disregard it and not talk about, as if it does not take place or doesn't exist. Most of the stress that you and I experience comes as a result of that. We may be in conflict with ourselves; for example, part of us wants to have an extra piece of cake, while another part keeps flashing the word <u>overeating</u>. We may have conflict over relocating, or moving on to another job. We may feel pressured to sever an abusive/stressful relationship. Your spouse puts you out or threatens to leave you. Perhaps you signed a contract with someone who does not show any cooperation in keeping it and you are not getting your share from the deal, or your country's rights have just been violated by another. All these can be looked at as conflicts which require some immediate and serious attention.

The most difficult type to acknowledge is when we are in conflict with ourselves. It is more soothing that we remove or dissociate ourselves from anything which can make us look bad or ridiculous, and put somebody else (a scapegoat) in there. It takes a lot of courage to address the fact that something is wrong with us, and that no one else is to blame for it but our own self. To resolve this kind of conflict, we must be in touch with our own feelings and emotions and be willing to deal with the real issues more rationally. Otherwise, the more that we try to run away, the more frustrated we become; it's like trying to run away from our shadow, it does not work! Then, the next thing, we start having an attitude towards other people, and before long we raise those walls of indifference around us, isolating ourselves from the world and causing our stress level to go up. Because, **number one**, we have not been honest with ourselves; we internalize whatever issue is bothering us. **Number two**, by not being truthful to ourselves, we tend to develop a hostile view against those that we make accountable for our problems and then we turn around and portray them as hostile. I hope that you don't get upset with me, for I am simply saying it as it is. This particular kind of conflict which I have just described is easier dealt with; it may take you a while but since you are the problem, you are at least part of the solution also. Perhaps, the condition may require you to see a counselor, psychologist, pastor, priest, minister or whatever your religious convictions embrace.

On the contrary, many times we face conflicts which result from the process of social interactions. And even though our perception may still play a great role here, our individual and sometimes our collective (as in the case of one ethnic or one nation against another)

131

interests may be in jeopardy. As we pursue our own goals and aspirations in life, often we are reminded not to lay a personal claim over the world or its resources but instead, to live collaboratively regardless of where we happen to be in the universe. That's a hard reality to deal with, and every day I make it a rule to remind myself that I am not alone in this place and whatever I do impacts other people; therefore, I try to live in a way that reflects such a philosophy. However, even that has the potential to generate conflict between other people and me as our philosophies may often clash.

Our lack of understanding of each other's positions and our own ignorance and inability to effectively communicate to each other too often pose serious problems by blocking the line to constructive dialogue and collaboration. And despite our civilization and our claim of superiority over the rest of the animals, we do not always seem to convey such clear differences in ways that we often respond to each other.

A- How Do We Respond When Things Do Not Go Our Way?

On Saturday, June 28, 1997, in a boxing rematch between former heavyweight Mike Tyson and the actual champion, Evander Holyfield, the world once again witnessed a rather peculiar behavior. Whatever our source of information: primary (television), secondary (radio, newspaper) or tertiary (third person), the fact remains that those of us who lived the event know the outcome. I will not elaborate too much on that; I'll simply take a few quotes from the media to make a point. We get our first citation from **Mike Tyson**: "He kept butting me. **Holyfield** is not the warrior he claims he is..." The second citation, from Holyfield as he refers to Tyson: "He spit out his mouth-piece and bit me in the ear. I think he was afraid and this is what fear can do, make you do things like that. Fear causes people to do the easy thing, the quickest thing." And the final quote in this series is from **Ron Borges**, a newscaster: "Tyson disqualified for taking a piece out of Holyfield's ear..." (*The Boston Sunday Globe*, "It's a bite to the finish", June 29,1997, pp. C1 & 3). Instinctively, even though Holyfield's statement about Tyson may be substantiated, there exists another underlining issue such as uncontrollable anger which might help explain the above behavior. I don't think that fear alone can be attributed to or explain the whole incidence of eating off or chewing on another human being's ear two consecutive times.

In biology, there is a theory or a principle called "The fight-or-flight response." What does that mean? When animals are challenged or feel threatened by obstacles (be it the same or different species of animals), they tend to respond either by fighting back or by running (flying) away. We humans do not always behave too differently from the rest of the animals. In fact, many times the way that we interact (act and react) with each other seems to suggest only these two options! By saying this I am not denying or suggesting that we are limited to just these two choices; I don't believe that anyone would make such a claim; nonetheless history speaks very loudly. Not one day has gone by without a violent episode being reported among us: domestic violence, rape, gang and or street violence, organized and or institutionalized crime, suicide, homicide, you name it! One remarkable observation is that most of the time the lower (other, a better word) animals chase or attack a different species; but we have the most difficulty getting along with our own kind. And from the beginning of civilization to date, God alone knows how much resources we have wasted to wage war against each other or to try to build a defense that would deter potential assailants thereby providing us with a sense of security until they in turn invent a stronger and more potent system. Then, it becomes a vicious cycle where every nation either keeps building a weapons arsenal or is constantly sucking up resources to innovate its military might. And so far, almost every country that, for whatever reason (s), as a deterrent measure or in the name of self-defense, ever engaged in building up/stockpiling weapons has subsequently used them at one time or another against its own citizens or its neighbors.

Thus, from nations to ethnic groups to individuals, we always come up with presumably irreconcilable differences which we virtually base our decisions on and take arms against each other. Even though we have problems domineering our own senses and inadequacies, <u>we love to dominate over everyone and everything else</u>. And since we all possess the same inherent rights to live and pursue our own interests and happiness, we have not fully learned how to coexist in a symbiotic relationship with mutual respect and an open-mind, flexible to changes. We specialize in disagreeing or competing with each other. The kind of power struggle that goes on in between oftentimes prevents us from building bridges, tearing down walls, and seeking common interests. Despite all the sophisticated machinery and technological advances that we have been able to make, we still face tremendous difficulties promoting better communication skills and greater dialogue.

We do need money and other material things to live on or make ends meet, and I do encourage anybody and everybody to try to secure a certain amount of wealth for himself or herself. However, money alone does not provide the kind of self-worth and it certainly does not have the necessary values that we need to help us set standards for ourselves. And contrary to the kind of indoctrination that many of my Christian brethren have received, after all, the Bible does place certain responsibilities on each and everyone of us, in that it says: "…In the sweat of your face you shall eat bread till you return to the ground…" (Genesis 3, vs. 19. RSV) It further indicates that: "…If anyone will not work, let him (her) not eat." (II Thes. 3, vs. 10. RSV) does that preclude fist competition? In other words, as we look to develop our self-identity and individual pride, what kind of legacy do we wish to build for ourselves and leave for our children? How can we establish a world where violence does not become the norm or the weapon of the strong or the weak (depending on whose judgment call we uphold)? In other words, what are the alternatives to violence?

B- Conflict Resolution: The Real Superiority Class of Humans

In the opening statement of this chapter, we talked about two different responses or reactions being accounted for under biological sciences, namely: "The fight-or-flight response". These represent two generalized responses, but of course there exist more than just these two. Certain ways that you respond to a perceived or real threat may be more effective than others, and your ability to peacefully dissolve or reduce such a menace can greatly increase your credibility and prominence among your peers. May I side with the male chauvinist for just a fraction of a second? When it comes to choosing a woman, men used to say, "You cannot live with her, and you cannot live without her." Okay, what is the point? I do not know whether that is true or not; perhaps you women say the same thing about men. I wish to exercise my constitutional rights by abstaining from taking sides. However, I am a firm believer that if we cannot live with or without each other, then the next best thing to do is to learn how to coexist because after all we do need each other. If any one person could destroy everybody else and claim ownership of everything, he or she would soon be bored and powerless without any one to dominate and would equally face isolation.

Now, before looking into the other alternatives to violence, let's consider for a moment the two options supported in biology. In the real world in which we live, we cannot function without ever facing some form of conflict. Secondly, no matter how powerful our arms get or how agile our legs become, we can neither be fighting nor running away constantly. We have to negotiate with whomever is involved and reach some form of agreement or compromise. By the way, some people always see the latter word through a negative eye. When you work out a compromising plan, it does not mean that you are weak or that you necessarily have to throw your values out of the window. We do it every day and at different levels, and almost no one gives without any expectation of reciprocity. The expectations may not be a kiss for a kiss, or a dollar for a dollar. It could be for something totally different. However, there are so few instances where anybody keeps giving unconditionally; that's human nature. We do want to preserve our individual pride, we want credit, which may be legitimate.

Moreover, we need to be able to live decently, having access to resources and making decisions leading to self-determination, and not feel that we are at the mercies of someone else or being taken advantage of. Undoubtedly, we can come up with an infinite number of reasons to disagree with the world, for that matter! Nonetheless, we can resolve almost any existing conflict among us without ever taking arms, but some ground rules must be laid down and all the parties involved need to agree to and abide by them in order for the

135

plan to work. In my opinion, fighting represents the most barbaric way to try to overcome our differences and disagreements!

We do dispose of other means to meet such challenges, but there has to be some willingness and some initiatives to pursue these ends. *First*, the conflict must be clearly identified by all sides. What is the nature of that conflict, or why does that conflict exist? Who is involved, and how did it get started in the first place? *Secondly*, how do the parties relate to each other in the midst of it all? One may not be up to the level to develop the kind of dialogue needed to resolve the conflict; however, no one can downplay the importance of non-biased communication for effective exchanges.

Good communication skills require good and attentive listeners, and not someone who selectively chooses what he or she wants to hear. If this is the attitude, you are not quite ready as yet to resolve the conflict. You may need to take an inventory of your personal baggage, which may be a hindrance to the very plans that are being developed. *Third*, there has to be mutual respect and consideration from all sides. Avoid derogatory language and offensive or defensive tactics for they will only make it difficult for your opponent to negotiate with you. *Fourth*, in some instances, this may not be necessary, but based on the complex nature of the conflict and the degree of comfort that you experience, a neutral ground with a third party mediator (with direct interest in the deal) may be necessary. Some conflicts involving spouses, for example, may be resolved without line item # 4; but the problem may have deteriorated too far for just the two of you to work out a peaceful settlement. *Fifth*, avoid putting your opponent in corners where he or she has no options or feels humiliated; he/she may build resistance towards any further proposition which you might have. Dr. William Ury, author of many books and professor at Harvard Law School says, "You want to bring the other side to their senses, not to their knees" (William, Ury, Getting Past No: Negotiating with Difficult People, p.111, 1991). *Sixth*, show the other party that you try to understand where he/she is coming from. It may not be the easiest thing to do; however it may probably create a far better climate, free from hostile tendencies, and one that increases receptivity on both sides. Acknowledge your opponent's feelings. *Seventh*, try to differentiate opinion from fact.

You need the latter for a breakthrough. It is a lot easier dealing with factual information than personal opinion. _Eighth_, the other party may be trying to get you upset by making ridiculous personal remarks about you. You have to let him/her know that you understand what he or she is doing and that your goal is to resolve this conflict, but his or her attitude makes it difficult for the negotiation to continue successfully.

Dr. Ury talks about going to the Balcony. Sometimes in between talks, you may need to change the pace by taking a short break, and then come back to the table afresh. _Ninth_, if at the end nothing works, still acknowledge the presence and participation of the opponent, letting him/her know that you would make another attempt to resolve the issue. Ask him/her for his or her opinion as to what might work. Also ask him or her why he/she thinks that the negotiations failed. You do not want to be apologetic, but it does not hurt to accept your own shortcomings. Lastly, if you succeed in negotiating a plan, you need to nurture it and make sure that all sides agree to the terms. Any plan is as good as those who design it. Do not feel embarrassed to point out to your opponent any doubt that you might have over the agreement. Don't be too hasty in reaching conclusions that may fall through later. Give yourself time to think it over, and if need be, call another session to clarify the part that may not be clear to you. Hopefully, having gone through this process, you may be able now to live together or at least coexist. If all attempts to solve your differences fail, as much as it depends on you, make it your responsibility that life continues beyond the irreconcilable point. Remember, you will not be able to please everybody. As much as you can, always try to play your part in good faith without any attempts to "bring your opponent to his/her knees." Otherwise, you might be up to a tougher battle, and with many more oppositions, including walls of resentment, frustrations, personal ego/pride, face-saving tactics, etc.! To pursue, restore, or establish harmony within ourselves and with others does require work, mutual understanding, and dialogue, as well as commitment from the parties involved. These are key elements in reducing tensions, maintaining good rapport with our neighbors, and avoiding barbarism.

Maslow's Hierarchy of Needs

Self-actualization
Aesthetic appreciation; order, structure, beauty
Intellectual achievement: understanding and exploring
Self-esteem: approval and recognition
Belonging: love and acceptance
Safety: physical and psychological security
Survival: food, water, shelter

In no way are we advocating that people live to eat but the other way around. When human beings try to make it through days or weeks without eating/drinking, they end up as dead bodies. Therefore, it is important to eat and drink constantly in order to sustain life. The million dollar question comes up then, how do we go about having that need met on a regular basis? We might as well raise the questions relating to the 5 W's: Why, Where, What, When, and Who.

In the present chapter, we wish to help our readers arrive at how to get their needs met on a consistent basis, including the ways that their food supplies are provided for. You can be your own provider or you may depend on someone else to provide your food. You can get trained to catch your own fish or you may pass the responsibility on to someone else to learn how to fish and feed you from what he/she catches whenever the person wants or if he/she ever feels that there is enough for himself/herself and for you. Now <u>Who</u> would be interested in giving us fish indefinitely and unconditionally? If we are not so concerned about catching our own fish, <u>Why</u> would anyone else go catch it and bring it to us? Why would we indefinitely depend on someone? <u>Where</u> is our pride and dignity? <u>What</u> kind of fish are we being fed and what will happen to us when that provider decides to no longer feed us or what if he/she dies or simply decides to no longer be the god of our lives? It is one thing for us to determine that we wish to be off the providers' black list but to be told that we will no longer be provided for, perhaps at a time when we least expect, can be fatal. If we depend on others to feed us, <u>When</u> can we eat, on our time or on their own agenda?

A- Who Cares to Feed Whom?

To some degree, it is no doubt that we have all adopted and developed our coping mechanisms and survival skills, otherwise we would no longer be alive. And when we consider the environment (the ecosystem), the kind of interaction among all living things and animals, we discover a sophisticated pattern of relationship that allows resources to be made available. We can talk about the food chain, a theory which attempts to explain how food is provided for all species that are represented in the chain. We find: producers, then primary, secondary, and tertiary consumers (we are part of the latest category). Should we consider the theory of natural selection which supports the idea of the survival of the fittest, or "only the strong survive"? In which case, we may be bound to describe the environment in a dichotomy or in a dual facet where we have predators and preys.

Generally, several kinds of relationships have been recognized. 1) Commensalism. A commensal relationship involves two or more individuals or two or more species co-existing in one place where one feeds on or lives at the expense of the other, with no apparent harm to the host or to the individuals being lived on. 2) Parasitism. A parasitic relationship is one where one party draws all its living expenses from another while causing the later to suffocate and die. 3)We also discover mutualism which represents a form of relationship where all parties involved equally or satisfactorily benefit in the deal.

They co-exist and develop in the same environment; one does not inhibit or impair the growth of the other (s).

When it comes to us human beings feeding ourselves or having our needs met, we often take it upon ourselves to provide for our own: our family, relatives, and loved ones. That is a responsibility that most of us have. Now whether we live up to that task or whether we have the means to do so represents a totally different ball game. Some of us labor and gain our existence in a legitimate, responsible way. Others find every kind of crooked way that they can think of to ensure their survival. In most instances, competition is the name of the play. People compete among themselves for readily available resources, especially when they lack the creativity to generate new ideas which will help meet their aspirations.

To some people, it becomes customary that they dominate others and try to monopolize everything for themselves. Others have, over time, developed a mentality that makes it extremely difficult or almost impossible for them to grow and become independent and self-sufficient. They believe that God assigned them the present position that they find themselves in and that they cannot change things. Of course, there are needs for humanitarian organizations and philan-thropic groups to exist because some people need their help to make the transition from where they are to where they ought to be. However, it defeats the purpose when agencies function within the frame of mind to keep people on a continual state of dependence. That is not a service to neither the organization that provides the assistance nor the person receiving it. Maybe another way to look at it is that if there were no needy people, there would be no need for such organizations to continue to exist! While there may be some truth to that, I think that is short-sightedness, and I personally would never want to live my life as though I lost my faculty to breathe on my own and I have to be put on a respirator or any other similar device when I know for a fact that I have all my senses, all my faculties, and I am healthy.

When you care to feed yourself and know what you want to eat, you may look for it. Perhaps someone along the way will help you find it, but if you do not know what you want and perhaps don't care, it is a very sad situation, trusting your belly or your whole person to someone to supply your basic physical needs, someone who might even need the space where you now stand. They'll buy you out, granted that you allow them.

B- Why Rely on Potentially Contaminated Food?

I am pretty sure that there exists more reasons than we can possibly describe in this one volume. One answer to the question is that between two evils, one must choose the lesser one. I understand that if someone may be starving and is offered a stew made of rats, that person finds himself/herself flanked by two devilish ideas, the one of dying of starvation and the other of feasting on something that may be contaminated. Then, if the decision is to eat the rat stew, the person may virtually do so, maybe not, but at least he/she put some food in his/her stomach and can now go to try to find a job. Then, he/she may no longer need to eat that stuff again.

Sometimes, we make bad choices in life and we have to live with the consequences. That, too, I understand, and if that is the case I think that people have a legitimate cause to bend over backward and swallow something that they normally wouldn't. For instance, your marriage did not work out the way you would expect and you've tried everything to try to save it but nothing seems to work; or you invested all your assets in the stock market or a venture and you lost everything. You may have to start all over again; if that is what you have to do, so be it. Jesus had to die to save us sinners. So, be practical and not dogmatic or stagnant.

Some people are legally and scientifically diagnosed with a disability or deficit (physical or mental). Then they may have to be provided for, that is fine and we hope that the provider (s) can still offer humane treatment, a treatment with dignity.

On the contrary, take for instance these individuals who for one reason or another have received welfare assistance. While some welfare recipients seem to live well, most fall under the poverty line, as defined by the United States National Center for Health and Statistics. (*AJPH*, Oct. 1996, vol.86. pp.1401-1405). What often happens is that these people who get some kind of state benefits are considered too poor to survive on such income but too rich to receive other assistance. What a paradox!

Anyway, the point that I really want to drive at is this. Some welfare recipients are <u>physically able bodies with no history of mental impairment,</u> which means that they could live on top of the world if only they were willing to learn some job skills and find work. Again, I am pro welfare benefits to those who for one reason or another have to receive them as a means to an end. However, I consider it a waste of human resources when young, energetic, and able people enjoy the free meal, not realizing how much harm they are causing to themselves. For truly, anyone living on welfare checks most likely has a limited budget that he or she must carefully watch. Whereas, if they were to join the workforce there would be no real limit imposed on their earnings and on how they choose to spend.

C- What Kind of Fish is in Your Plate?

Figure 21.1 *Catch Your Own Fish*

Despite our arrogance, when we allow ourselves to be fed by other people, it becomes a favor that they do for us. We cannot force them to give us what we feel like having. It is basically up to them to decide what they want to give us. It could be a small portion, due to the fact they are sharing what they have with us. It could also mean that's what we seem to deserve. In addition, what they are really giving us raises very significant concerns. Many times when people give you things, they tend to view it as charity. Some people will respectfully choose the kind of product that they offer to you, others would just give what they do not need; that's the difference between humility and humiliation. If that is no good for them, maybe it is no good for you either. And you have the option of accepting or refusing the offer. Nonetheless, can you really afford rejecting it, given your present state? Also, there is another damaging side to getting help all the time; it can be addictive. Once it becomes a habit to live and act in a certain way, a cycle leading towards dependency is created. Then, the recipients or the persons receiving the service become paralyzed in their ways of thinking, which makes it very hard for them to consider alternate choices.

Do you want to make sure that you will eat the right kind of fish? You also want to assure yourself that you will have enough to meet your actual needs; that may not satisfy your wants. However, the choices remain yours. If you want to go to the moon or you wish to succeed in a career, just find out what it takes to get there and be willing to make some sacrifice. The road may be long, but make this the least of your worries; just keep on doing what you have to. Other than the choice to become a fool, an idiot, or incapacitated, nothing good or excellent comes easy! Everything makes you sweat; even if you were born a hero, life would soon disqualify you if you failed to maintain your proper pace and place. Have you watched any champion being thrown off track? Therefore, keep on, keeping on! The fight is not over until **you** say so. Now, let's move on.

D- When Can You Eat?

Who calls the shots sets the clock as to when such events must occur, when you and I may eat, rest, etc. That can be anybody willing to assume responsibility for self and others. Some people are simply limited in the amount of care that they can give you. Others have their own agenda that they must comply with, then everything else and anyone who is not a part of the agenda becomes secondary, which we often call prioritizing, and that is not exceptionally wrong. It simply means that certain things or certain people occupy a certain place in these people's lives or on their priority list, and don't let anyone fool you about that.

When you can eat becomes a more important question at this stage of the game. For a human fetus or an infant that is automatically decided by the pregnant woman or the care giver as the case may be. In some instances, a baby will cry to express its needs for food or other things.

As adults, **supposedly** we are on our own, and we assume complete responsibility for ourselves and for our actions. However, there are some exceptions to the rule. Adult life is certainly associated with the idea of being independent and having the ability to make sound judgments, as well as maintaining the freedom to move around as we feel like it. The question is can we lose that privilege? Absolutely, voluntarily or involuntarily! It may be taken away from us by someone who wants to exercise control over us, and we are forced to relinquish our individual rights (that's involuntary, of which slavery is one expression). The other way we can be decompensated or disenfranchised of freedom is when we decide not to live up to our responsibilities. And occasionally some of us need to make special arrangements to transfer our authority to some specific people for specific reasons, as in the case of a terminal illness, for instance. Then, we delegate the power of attorney to somebody hoping that he or she will take up the responsibility which we have entrusted him or her. The funny thing about responsibility is that some people back off; others love to assume it and then take total control of the situation. One vivid example is when people or citizens of a country do not take charge of the environment, and if the government or some interested party sees the opportunity for potential gain, they step in. While they take control, most likely they are there to stay and dictate when and how things are to be done.

When someone else provides your fish, they are the ones to know the time the product ought to reach you. If they decide that your share should go to some other persons out there, you have no say in the matter. When you learn how to fish, you know when you are hungry. Then you can decide what kind of fish you want to eat, when, and you have a legitimate reason why. But none of this matters if you do not know how to fish and do not bother to learn. Perhaps somebody out there needs to hear this!

E- Where Do You Fish?

When you go to visit other peoples' homes, you are not at your house, no matter how comfortable they make you feel. Obviously, there are restrictions and boundaries that you shall not cross. Where you sit may even be determined by the owner of the house. In addition, as you know, when food is served outside your own home, usually the owner of the house sits at the head of the table. This is not a rule that I am imposing but proper etiquette teaches it; so it is often best to leave the seating arrangements in the hands of the host, or the person or the family giving the dinner. However, things are different in your own home. Where you choose to sit reflects how you decide on your territory or how you exercise your sphere of influence. Some people claim not to have any power at all. They simply don't see or don't get it. They are willing to delegate whatever is theirs to someone else, and some people love to feel and exert their power.

I must say that this is a matter of perception and whether we accept it or not. We do carry a certain amount of personal space around us. When we are with friends, it is reduced but tends to increase when we interact with strangers. The same principle applies when we stand on our feet whether to use our freedom to defend our rights or to create opportunities for ourselves. And someone certainly did not do any special favor for any of us by bringing us into this world. Therefore, white or black, Greek or Roman, more educated or less educated, physically attractive as well as physically unattractive, we all share equal rights and belong to where we are. However, we have to claim it so that no one else pushes us or bounces us around. The only thing is that if you don't have any skills, no education, no willingness or motivation to improve your own living conditions, it may seem as if you belong nowhere. As a result, you seem to have no rights and nothing to live for.

If you are here, it is not by accident. Fight for what you duly believe in, most importantly for equal rights and opportunities for yourself, and the others. Your fish is right next to you. You just need to convince yourself that fishing for your fish is not inconceivable or inconsistent with our human values and aspirations. Ask to be taught or learn on your own how to catch your own fish, and don't be too hasty accepting a fish from someone. It takes less resources to teach someone or to learn how to fish than it requires to keep feeding that same person. After all, it destroys someone's self image when he/she is constantly being provided for!

❖ CHAPTER VIII ❖

Fear of Rejection

People who have strong fear of rejection usually feed themselves on the notions or the feeling that:

1. They are not as good as someone else and they do not have much to offer
2. They are not sure about themselves; they doubt their own ability and feel insecure
3. From their own perspectives, other people seem to be more proficient than they
4. They cannot match others' expectations
5. They cannot match up with others. They belittle themselves and play back negative messages to themselves, such as "If only I were as good as other people."
6. They must impress and capture everyone else's attention. They have a hunger for other's approval and end up focusing too much on themselves
7. They will lose their chance to fit in, if they make mistakes. These individuals can be so preoccupied with perfectionism that they live with that fear of messing up and not matching other people's expectations of themselves

<u>Self-assertiveness</u> is definitely not part of their characters. By their own standards, they cultivate a sense of personal dissatisfaction or a lack of self-worth, possibly due to psycho-social traumas that they have experienced in their early childhood. It could also be a failure to develop their self-identity and carry on a successful and healthy transition from adolescence to a more mature adult life, as it may relate to Piaget's Stages of Cognitive Development (A. E. Woolfolk, '1990', 4th Ed. pp. 38-75). Therefore, they are constantly comparing themselves and their performances with others. When they fail to notice such pairing up, they tear themselves down and re-enter their niche to come out later. This is not the book in which we want to address personality disorders, and we do not wish to claim expertise in the field, but it is important to briefly mention a particular trait vis-à-vis self-identity, personal growth, and the fear of rejection as they move towards building interpersonal relationships. We are referring to what is called in psycho-social research a "<u>Histrionic Personality Disorder</u>." People with this particular diagnosis may have the following behavior patterns: signs of immaturity, emotional instability, craving for excitement, self-dramatization, and/or excitability. Such a personality may also be characterized by dependency, helplessness, and self-centeredness (possessiveness). A person may also be overly reactive, vain, insecure, and extremely concerned about other people's approval of them (R.C. Carson et al. 8th Ed. pp. 222-237.)

Overall, people who experience fear of rejection move in a cycle that keeps repeating itself until they realize what they are doing to themselves and perhaps seek help. These individuals can nurture constant craving for others' approval, and consequently, they always want the reassurance that they are doing well. As we said, they do not take much pride in themselves and their achievements. You will probably detect them in a room all by themselves even with other people in their surroundings. They are most likely to be loners or to feel lonely. Such folks tend to be shy, very reserved, introverted or withdrawn, and afraid of taking many risks that would reveal themselves. For that matter, they are very self-protective, making it hard to know whether they are sick, uncomfortable in the environment that they are in, or whether they simply have a personality problem. They may appear to be task-oriented, but mainly they want to gain attention and please other people in order to feel accepted.

They hardly reach out to make new friends because of fear of being turned down. At times when they step out of their shell to start a relationship, they will probably be overly cautious and may even leave it up to the other party to first extend an invitation. They scrutinize people to find these few who might like them. Though they may want to be included in social events, when asked to do something or participate in a function, they may decline on the grounds that their presence could not make much of a difference.

They are super-sensitive to criticism. Their susceptibility level can be exceedingly high. Such a characteristic does not make it any better for them. In fact, since they tend to feel lonely and need approval of others, it makes them very vulnerable. The reason being that once they perceive someone who shows signs of a friendly attitude towards them, they may jump too quickly on board their ship and do not take time to cultivate the relationship and watch in which direction it is going. They just give into it. In the interim, if they get hurt, they become hypersensitive or very tense and are ready to blow their tops on anyone or hibernate or disappear for a while. You are talking about people who are afraid of growth!!

They experience difficulty expanding their horizons, and by secluding themselves in their own little habitat, they do not allow themselves to discover the wider world out there. They take a very small number of risks to go out and meet people and are emotionally guarded.

When they start a project their primary aim might be to get attention. Once that attention is being given, they will most likely quit the task or drag it along while they pursue the relationship. If they perceive completing the task at hand as the only means to getting the relationship going, they may finish it a lot faster. This type of behavior which they displayed by bringing their goal to the end is one that we call operant conditioning. It simply means that an individual expects a pleasant reward once he or she completes the task at hand. The reward presets the tone or becomes the stimulus behind the driving force.

These individuals could be fun to get along with. They can show very truthful and sincere friendship and may respond well to social activities that do not expose them too much. In addition, they may cooperate well with those who are in leadership positions since they tend to look for people they can follow, granted that they do not feel too threatened by them. However, as you may already imagine, those are people who show substantial evidence of emotional instability. They have great difficulty accepting changes within their environment and will probably do all they possibly can to hold to the other person just for the sake of the relationships. Besides being emotionally unstable, there is that inferiority complex which keeps the person in a cage-like environment. Although the person has a drive for social acceptance, fear of rejection prevents him/her from making the proper move to go out and meet new people.

The usual and often unconscious way that people get de-sensitized over this kind of fear is by:

1) Experiences that bring pleasant and unpleasant memories, but the ones that brought the greatest satisfaction to the person are mostly remembered and tend to reproduce themselves over time. In other words, if the experience was perceived as good, the person will tend to have it again. During that time some personal maturity is gained.

2) Age. As people grow older, certain fears tend to disappear automatically, including fear of rejection.

3) Gender. This too tends to make some difference. As males and females feel the needs for companionship, and courtship, they will mostly look to the opposite sex to fill the void or the emptiness being felt.

A- Building Up Fear of Rejection

Fear of rejection and the drive for social acceptance grow beyond the boundaries of individual perception. However, before we get ourselves into laying out some of the causes, we would like to start with a diagram that shows the cycle. Deep fear of rejection does not just come and go away.

People who display fear of rejection may attempt to internalize it, and at times, they might feel the pressure coming from within. However, that is simply a response to the object of fear based on previous experiences. There is a direct relationship between a person's psychological state and his or her physiological functioning. As you remember, the neurological pathways include a sympathetic and a parasympathetic system (if you can't remember which is which, just know that one gets you high and the other gets you down). They work in opposite ways. One increases your heart rate and the other decreases it or brings it down. When you get ready to fight or fly again, your sympathetic system is stimulated through a very complex mechanism in your brain. The response is the release of adrenaline in your bloodstream to help do the job and make it complete. You send messages to your brain that things are okay and you want to cool off. Then, the parasympathetic counteracts and brings you to land safely. All that is tied to psychology and neuropsychology, two parallel fields that tend to explain personalities and nerve functions.

Your actual role as an individual is to ensure that your systems are running as smoothly as they should. And fear of rejection just helps you do the opposite of that. You would like to loosen up but are emotionally guarded. Nonetheless, no matter how your fear originated, it is a feeling that you must overcome. Let me bring you back to the diagram you saw a while ago in Chapter 7. First, fear starts on the outside of a person (see letter A) and drives the person inside out. Fear of rejection is a personality problem and it can come about when children are raised in authoritarian homes and where they are usually not allowed to take a stand or express themselves openly. Secondly, those who have had traumatic experiences in their childhood may grow up with a feeling of inadequacy in public speaking. Thirdly, young adolescents who have been molested by adults may also act that way. Fourthly, people can simply develop that fear if they come out of low social status families and try to step in a world of uncertainty and hostility. All these possible causes leading to fear of rejection are identified under the letter B on the diagram. For the letter C, we can attribute fear of rejection to parents or guardians who themselves show very poor self-esteem to their kids and who also put them down as they (kids) grow up. There are other factors such as failure early on to satisfy or meet the expectations of others and perhaps they are being ridiculed or made fun of. However, we simply select these few. In addition, in Chapter 6, we attempt to show how fear overtakes its subjects, and once it is internalized how it progresses in a cycle. As pointed out, there are 10 steps in the cycle which show what happens when the subject tries to rationalize his or her fear. Briefly, let me add that the diagram portrays mainly the unpleasant aspects in the behavior of a person trying to go through her sensations.

B- Tearing Down Fear of Rejection

Fear of rejection is one of the greatest enemies of individual growth, for it limits the person's exposure to the outside world. It prevents one from taking risks of opening oneself up. It causes a young man to date just a particular girl because of the fear of being turned down by others. Along with socio-cultural values, fear can prevent a young woman not to be the first to reach out to a young man that she would like to have in her life. It keeps many other doors closed. Usually, we create opportunities, they are not freely handed out or just come down to us by the generosity of other people. We often make them through human interactions.

No man is an island and as Aristotle put it, "We are political animals". In other words, we depend on society to develop, grow and survive (the word interdependent is very significant here.) It is a disservice to you first, and then to society when you, for one reason or another, cannot develop interpersonal relations. And when you cannot stand up to defend your own rights, or speak for yourself, you are likely to pick up the left-over pieces from the mouth of society if you are even permitted around the table. Many people just survive because they give up too easily and are set up for anything in life. There is a saying that goes right along with it, "He who stands for nothing falls for anything". This is not the sole setting where that can happen to you but you must recognize certain things about human interactions. When you cannot look people in their eyes and tell them what you need to, not only will you fail to convey a convincing message, but also you will have problems putting your thoughts together. In which case, you receive much less attention and you are likely to be served after everybody else has presented their case. First things first. Everyone needs to overcome his or her fear of rejection. During your lifetime, you may never be able to gain the sympathy, respect, or the approval of everybody, and I hope that this is not one of your goals. However, you may learn how to live up to face anybody and present/defend your case whenever need be without having to think of how people will consider you, whether they will accept you or reject you. Here is one way to accomplish this:

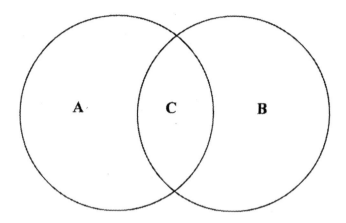

A= Your uncompromising self   **B**= The world in itself, without you
C= You and the World interacting

Figure 8.1 Bifocal Diagram of Interpersonal Relationships

This diagram is made up of two circles but depicts three distinct areas. As you meet people and interact, one part of your life will become exposed and open up to criticism. The other portion remains your private property. You alone will know or need to learn how much of yourself to expose and how fast. You've got to prevent yourself from being invaded. Another thing, your role as an individual is not to force people to accept you or enter a relationship with you. If you see yourself doing that, virtually you will end up with your character being assassinated. Plus, you will not be able to keep such a friendship going for long. Remember, a relationship is a two-way street. All parties involved must work at it. On the contrary, I realize that this discussion goes beyond just opening up, but that is the way it ought to. There is no question that we are all indebted to the world around us since none of us can survive in isolation. We voluntarily commit ourselves or are forced to interact with our environment and influence each other. As a result, we lose part of our self-identity as in area C where we share some common elements and carry a certain resemblance of each other with respect to personality and conduct. Unfortunately, not everybody will be attracted to you just as you won't be attracted to everybody else. You will get along with some people better than others. If you are shy and lack self-confidence, if you are withdrawn/introverted, non-conforming, rigid in your manners, immature, and homophobic, then you will probably walk a lonely road most of the time.

As you learn how to get rid of your fear of rejection, you may be able to accomplish more than just building relationships. You will find yourself in the workplace, in school, in other human activities, and it works to your advantage to develop the ability which will allow you to mingle with different kinds of personalities and handle various levels of interpersonal relations. Let us see if we can help you develop a menu, starting from where you are.

Individuals who receive positive feedback from family and peers early on are most likely to have a sense of self-concept and who they are. If they choose to, they have the ability to develop very good positive attitudes and they are able to get rid of their unhealthy fear or any feeling of inferiority. They feel good about themselves and have high self-esteem. Having reached that sphere, they will show signs of maturity and personal growth. These are critical in forming ideals or goals in life. These individuals who reach that stage will display their own value system and monitor their progress while they establish themselves emotionally. Once they release themselves, they have no difficulty relating to other people, meeting other people, and developing new relationships.

Although territory comes with political, economic, and intellectual influence and power, we all need to reach the point where we create a comfortable space around ourselves. We may choose to call it our territory, portable or personal space. It does not really matter, as long as it is there and is not being violated. Then, we can be ourselves there and form our own opinion and won't have to just follow other people along. We will have dreams of our own. With that in mind, do not let anyone tell you or make you feel as if you do not belong there. All men (humans) are created equal and you cannot but claim that right. Also, you do not need to wait until you get to heaven or purgatory to do so. Do it right here on planet Earth. Good, responsible, and productive citizens down here will make good citizens for the heavens. Do not be fooled by the rhetoric that the Good Lord made you to be the slave of another man or that you are poor because He created you to be that way. You need to know who you are and what to believe in, which is the whole reason why you ought to walk out of your fear, fight humiliation, and raise your head high toward heaven, not in arrogance but with a bit of pride, dignity and self-worth. That's nobody else's responsibility but your own.

In conclusion, let me say this to you. You will never succeed trying to make everybody love you. No matter how nice you can be or how candid you present yourself, some people will always give you a cool response. And sometimes, it may not be anything personal. So you should not take offense every time you do not get a warm reception. Remember, fear of rejection has everything to do with how you feel about yourself. Stop focusing on what you cannot do, bear in mind that you must first accept and appreciate yourself the way you are before others can accept and acknowledge you. Do not carry on your shoulder the burden of not being liked or appreciated. That's what keeps you down, the craving for approval of others which may not come. Some of us may look undone or a little devilish on our outer appearance, as that may also be deceiving at times. However, as we look for ways to bring forth our intrinsic values, improve our standards of living, and care for this body of ours, anybody would want to be in our company.

Your role is to make sure that you feel good about yourself. You can try to be articulate and be a bit concerned about dress code too, especially on your first meetings with people. Work on your attire. All that cannot hurt you but instead it will help you focus more on your self-image. When you have high self-esteem it is unlikely to have fear of rejection at the same time for they are indirectly/inversely related. How you feel about yourself is how you present yourself. Get out of that mode of fear by showing that beautiful and healthy side of you. There is an approach called the foot-in-the-door technique. It focuses on the notion that the first step is the most difficult. Therefore, maybe the first time you meet somebody, you may not try to say too much, maybe you can just say hello and how are you to the person. That will usually get you through the door and lead the way to deeper conversation. When you feel shy or intimi-dated by others, just greet them or say to them something like, "I have a lot of respect for you". Do not always be so concerned with impressing other people. In fact, it's better if you do not think about it for a moment, and people will start accepting you naturally. Note that you are not particularly looking for people to like you, if they do, be grateful to God; however, it is also their right if they choose not to as long as they do not interfere with your individual rights to exist and pursue your happiness! You cannot prevent birds from flying over your head. What you can do though, is stop them from taking residency over your head. Nobody has to like you, but we all share a common space. You might just try to relate to the other individuals and not look to be liked, and who knows, it might end up being just that. Your skin color or the color of success may raise concerns in your mind at times. However, first things first; let's get down to business. Then, further on we will address the issue of color (green pigment, brown pigment, white pigment, red pigment, yellow pigment, whatever pigment) and success. In the meantime, I invite you to focus on an extraordinary task, one that will change the outlook of your world.

❖ CHAPTER IX ❖

Fear of Shedding One's Shell

Oftentimes in this life, people are faced with difficult issues which relate to cause and effect; then they pause and ask, "Which comes first, the chicken or the egg?" The argument could lead in either direction. It all depends at what point in time those individuals presenting and defending the idea decide to jump (come) in. Perhaps, while some may argue that the egg comes first, others may present convincing arguments that without the chicken there is no egg. Therefore, the chicken must come first! The importance of the chicken over the egg does not matter for the simple fact that if one needs to make an omelette, one would have to use eggs, and by the same token if one is interested in eating poultry, then chicken is what one would need. Therefore, let us not look to make a case relating to mere analysis of difference in the state of matter, at least not now. We all know that H_2O (water) exists in three states (solid, liquid, and gas) and depending on what we want to accomplish, a specific state might be needed over another.

Suppose the egg comes first. A fair argument here is to ask oneself how many chickens producing eggs can one have to provide even more eggs just by having the first ones hatch. Then, that raises another issue of great significance for us; how does one maximize one's assets or resources while looking at cost effectiveness and time involved to raise a chicken farm. Obviously, you earn more by selling a dozen of the animal than you would by selling a dozen eggs. Now, if you were asked based on the amount of money which you wish to make which might be more efficient to sell, I sense that you know it is the chicken. The more chickens you sell, the more money you make. Hence, it becomes imperative to have as many eggs hatch as possible.

Here, we are not literally concerned with the issue at hand, but instead, we wish to use it per analogy or as a comparison to raise a more significant point.

A- Failure to Grow Up, a Dis-ease

Psychologically, when someone is diagnosed with a certain deficiency, including mental, we often refer to that state as a form of mental retardation. Physically, if someone is underdeveloped for his/her age, as a result of being malnourished, then, we say that the person suffers from kwashiorkor (usually in relation to children). Socially, we have several names when referring to someone who has not matched certain norms and standards. One of which name is immature; another one is unsociable. Other times, based on the circumstances and the person passing the judgment, one may be labeled a social outcast. From a religious vein, the unbeliever may be classified as atheist, pagan, impure, or simply a heathen, especially with respect to the Christian faith. Intellectually, we call those who cannot comprehend or reason appropriately idiot or imbecile, and we relate to those who are too proud or ride on their high horse as arrogant. The politically incorrect or undiscerning individual may be seen as undiplomatic, or ignorant, or corrupt, for the politician who violates the trust placed in him/her by the constituents. All these terms have one thing in common: their negativity. People with the above characteristics are perceived as sickening or abnormal, ambiguous and loose terms often used synonymously to the word disease by some medical personnel. Therefore, explicitly or implicitly, directly or indirectly, the idea of malady is being communicated.

Fear of growth contributes to so many of us not reaching our potentials to such an extent that more specific courses around this topic should be developed and taught at every level in our educational system. In the community agencies and every organization which claims to work around the issues of self-worth and empowerment (whether the focus is the individual or the community at large), this kind of nurturing should be fostered. There is no good reason why our colleges and universities could not help every freshman in his/her focus on becoming mature, competent, and somewhat independent human beings. Unfortunately, we live in a system whereby a great many people would rather give a fish to someone instead of teaching that person how to catch his/her own fish. Let us take this a step further.

Once this individual becomes dependent, then he or she is conditioned and has no incentive to try to grow. I am pro welfare in that I believe that if for any reason, citizens are debilitated, physically and or mentally disabled and not able to provide for themselves for any length of time, then it becomes a public domain (government) to care for them. However, those people with no known abnormalities should be taught and encouraged to develop their skills so they may become self-sufficient, which I consider part of the role of the educator.

On the other hand, there are those who would like to take up the challenge and grow, but are given neither the opportunity nor the encouragement. Also there exist a few folks who cannot stand growth. While we cannot force the latter group towards taking initiative on their own, we are responsible for picking up their expensive tabs. They have no medical diagnosis of physical or mental deficiencies. They rather fall in a category of people that we might call socially and psychologically dysfunctional, which at a later date may lead to economic hardship and medical complications. I am in no position to say that individuals who find themselves in these predicaments are necessarily hopeless cases, because as long as one lives, there is hope (Eccl. 9:4); but the longer they remain sessile or hooked on a support system, the less likely they will be able to function independently. They will go as far as becoming a welfare state, holding on to the **survival mentality**. And generation after generation they will learn the self-fulfilling prophecy, meaning that <u>this is what we will ever know all our lives</u>. Our relatives depended on the system and so do we, as long as we tell ourselves that there is no other way for us to make it. In other words, that is called learned helplessness.

Many great minds have wasted away in this process. That gives rise to a sizable world population being born below the poverty line, causing medical problems and mental retardation in some, impaired physical growth in others, or both. For many of these individuals, especially children born in this environment, their suffering starts very early in life, many of whom survive to only take up delinquent behaviors, causing more trouble for themselves and for authorities. They have neither been told nor realized on their own that they can grow and that it is okay to do so. Research proves that when the muscles in our body are not active or do not exercise they atrophy; in other words they waste away. That's a price we pay when we neglect ourselves in every way that we can think of. For a moment it might seem that the caterpillar is better off staying in the cocoon. I know that some people will attempt to argue that it looks peaceful in its environment compared to a very mobile and even a turbulent life of a butterfly, when in fact the sessile stage of the species is so much more vulnerable. I understand how the road of uncertainty may influence our decisions to the extent of jeopardizing everything for which we have lived; however…

B- Everything Is A Risk, Why Not Hatching?

What does it really mean to hatch one's shell and how is that accomplished? Let us begin by saying that before a baby can actually walk, it first crawls (at least most of them do). Moreover, it must be nurtured and cared for. To the babies, growth is a process that they experience with time. They need the proper environment, the ideal stimulant (nurturing) or encouragement. They need to acquire articulation or muscle fitness. One of the reasons we call them babies is that they depend on older folk to help provide for their needs.

For a human adult, any kind of personal growth requires several factors:

1. A person must recognize the need to grow.
2. He or she must be willing to accept challenges and criticism.
3. He or she must focus on the positive side of growth.
4. Each of us must strive to create an environment conducive to growth. Portable or personal space is very important; and over-protection (being overprotected) inhibits personal growth. An environment suitable for growth is important.
5. Growth is a process and not only does it require time but also, it may involve different phases. Short cuts and a search for immediate gratification usually do not get us there. Therefore, such transformation or transition could be painful for the individual at times, but life itself is that way.

6. Also, for anyone to grow, it requires support of some kind and understanding from loved ones. They are not to be judgmental, overprotective, or cynical.

7. Mistakes will be made. That's part of the process itself and cannot be at all costs avoided. Just be willing to learn from the mistakes and move on.

8. Personal growth should occur in the upward direction or toward maturation, focusing on the ability of a person to accept responsibility, to live and share the environment with other people without lashing out at them all the time. Being able to give and receive affection, becoming more patient, tolerant, and accepting.

9. It is ideal for the individual to know that certain things in life cannot change and will remain as is. However, he or she can entertain the thought that many things can in fact change by one's initiatives, motivation, determination, and persistency (by being persistent). Put otherwise, "When life gives you a lemon, you make lemonade with it."

10. Personal growth also calls for accountability. Inability to acquire such growth or maturation suggests some underlying problems which may be traced back to childhood. They may have to do with traumatic experiences during adolescence or early adulthood where certain stages have not been reached. Also, people who have never been allowed to make decisions on their own may resent taking such challenges in life.

This represents a very interesting point in our discussion, because it opens the door for another solid argument. Let's face it, one of the definitions (or the classification) of being a bird is the ability to fly with one's own wings. Birds are made to fly and if a bird does not fly then the definition does not hold. And I indicated earlier, as one tries to fly or to grow, one may encounter great danger. However, the danger may be even greater by not being able to fly (to grow). At the beginning, the mother bird may be able to provide and the male species may take it upon himself to care for the mother and the young bird (s) by bringing food supply and by giving affection. Nonetheless, as time goes by, there may be catastrophes which may call for their sudden departure from their parents and/or providers. Perhaps, the adult birds may want to go on procreating and caring for their much younger babies. In which case, those young ones that never applied themselves to flying will not survive. Many grown up among us humans fall into this category of young birds.

If you ask me, I will tell you point blank that many times in life I wished that I had not grown. However, coming to my senses, I realize that I had no choice in the matter and I still don't. Growth is not an option for me and therefore, I must grow at some (all) costs. If I don't, then I might as well return to my mom's womb, as said Nicodemus and which is absolutely ludicrous and even insane! Would you like to go back there again? I do not believe that someone at the corner over there says yes! You wished that you could, too bad! Mom won't let you. God forbid you could go, what would your father think of your mother when he gets back home? You probably run a much better chance trying to enter your dad's womb, should he have one. Once you come out of the womb, you are on your own.

Let's get serious for a moment, shall we? In our activities, we become self-defeating, lethal to other human beings, and dangerous to the environment. Ecologically, there is no question. It seems that we are quite capable of destroying anyone or anything which tends to represent a potential obstacle in our way. And believe me, I am not prejudiced, that is not in my system and I am not a real hot fan of Mike Tyson. Nonetheless, if he did not get that $25 million in 89 seconds, he would eventually get it the next second over. So, to him it was a matter of taking control over a situation. There is an African proverb which says, "When the elephants have their fights, its the grass that pays the consequences". Do you know why? The elephants are quite strong animals, pitiless, and the grass has always laid down or it is always at the bottom. How would you like to be the grass, always being walked over?

Let us consider another example. It has been a fascinating experience for me to watch butterflies move through the air. I think that they look so pretty. Oh, they make me want to fly but I have not acquired such ability or this is not one of the human characteristics. If you have never watched these insects fly, I urge you to do that when next summer comes or if ever you have the chance to travel to a tropical country where you can actually observe them all year round. The funny thing though about butterflies is that they represent a more mature and advanced stage of caterpillars. That is to say that caterpillars and butterflies are not two distinct species or two different insects. The former is the larval stage and the latter represents the adult species (individuals). In an environment where there is so much human activity going on, butterflies have a greater chance of survival compared to caterpillars which are at a high risk of being stepped on and destroyed by all kinds of animal activities. At this stage, the species is quite defenseless, and therefore reaching the developmental stage into adulthood becomes a necessity if the insect wants to perpetuate or prolong its life span.

Just for the science majors, this insect belongs to the order of lepidoptera, a specific taxonomy or classification when naming biological species. Now passing the preceding stages, the insect reaches the larval phase, which is also called the nymphal stage. During that period, the animal is kept and protected by a silk-like envelope that we commonly designate as the cocoon. This is a sessile or stationary phase where many of the organs undergo severe modifications. At the end of the stage, the envelope or the cocoon breaks open, transforming the caterpillar to its evolutionary phase of adulthood, the butterfly. As you can see, we leave the heavy science portion out. We are interested in giving the necessary information that is conducive to your individual growth. Hence, we do not want to overwhelm you with other things. We make it our foremost responsibility here to fully engage your mind in the developmental process and see you through the initial steps. The very first obstacle to overcome in preparation of getting there is your own fear, and there isn't one more minute for any of you to keep living in denial. The more you tarry in taking actions toward building your future, the longer will it require of you to reach there. Each moment, each day that passes by is an opportunity for you.

C- From Fear to There

As the caterpillar undergoes the transformation that allows it to come out as a very beautiful animal flying in the air, needless to say, it attracts more attention at this point because its visibility increases by more than 100%. Who would go in the bushes looking for a darn cocoon unless he or she carries some ulterior motives? Secondly, butterflies are more useful to the environment. They help farmers get rid of some other insects that cause a nuisance to gardens. It is your right not to believe that an ugly caterpillar gives rise to such a beautiful, agile, elegant, and useful butterfly. However, we have given you the truth, all truth and nothing else but the truth. Take a step at once. Break your cocoon open and don't let anyone tell you that you can't evolve or grow!

Life, being a process, requires that every human being (for our discussion here, but all other species do, too) evolves, becomes transformed, adapts, or makes adjustments in order to reach the stage of adulthood, that mature height which leaves the individual susceptible to growth and this process ends after one dies. I should point out that certain deaths come prematurely, because of carelessness, stupidity, resentment to growth, and silly mistakes.

One can easily step on a caterpillar; however, one might be lucky to catch a live butterfly. Even though the environment may not always provide all the necessary elements for growth, the caterpillar must try to come out of the cocoon before it can claim independence. A larva is conditioned to live on the object where it is attached. Having not attended its maturity, the animal would literally spend its entire existence at the larval (or nymphal) stage, and never be able to know such joy to explore nature, lay on beautiful flowers, and all the other advantages and disadvantages that come with it.

Let me ask you a question. Ignoring the impact or the influence, do all caterpillars have the potential to transform their world? Are they all created with the capability to grow? I do not know about you, but I would say yes. However, do they all develop into butterflies, having wings to freely move?

See, freedom is there, you just need to know and believe that's what you want, and that you can achieve it. No one on earth will decide that for you. From our perspective, every child is born with the ability to become somebody. All of us are imparted with special potential to be born, grow, and be productive. I recognize that conditions may sometimes exist beyond our human capability, thereby preventing us from reaching higher. And many of us may really believe in shooting for the stars but do not reach altogether. Nonetheless, we will either aim at getting somewhere, or choose to remain stationary, sessile, and dependent. Without motivation and individual determination, we will always remain in the cocoon which cannot move on its own. Break the shell open at once. For that is our only chance to go forward, in every way you look at it.

In conclusion, you must be ready to be ridiculed by some and confronted by others. Some of us just cannot stand other people growing around us. As someone said, "There would be no great ones if there were no little ones" (George Herbert, 1593-1633). That is an irony of real life despite the fact that we hold to the idea that all humans are created equal. If you know what you want in life, people may attempt to oppose you, or they may help you get there. However, they certainly will not create for you the kind that you would really go for. Furthermore, people may choose to call us whatever they feel like; however, "It's not what they call us, but what we answer to that matters" (D. Juka). Lastly, we were created with enough talents to invent a world after its own kind. It does not matter which category you fall under, just choose one; and as said Shakespeare, "Be not afraid of greatness, some are born great, some achieve greatness, and some have greatness thrust upon them" (Shakespeare, 1564-1616, in *Twelfth Night*, II: V.56). Let Freedom, Peace and Justice be our greatest endeavor for such is our only hope.

PART THREE

Freedom from the Bondage
of One's Own Mind

❖ CHAPTER X ❖

Nelson Mandela's Recipe

"**I** have cherished the ideal of a democratic and free society in which all persons can live together in harmony with equal opportunities. It is an ideal which I hope to live for to see realized. But, if need be, it is an ideal for which I am prepared to die" (Nelson Mandela).

Be all you want to be, for there is nothing, absolutely nothing under heaven that you cannot accomplish, given that you set your mind to it. The obstacles have been and are here to stay. In fact, they represent your test, and you just have to be persistent in the pursuit of you goals. Now what supermarket or court of law does one go to in order to acquire the freedom of mind?

In a chronology of events, The Danville Register and Bee, a daily newspaper in the State of Virginia (USA) opens with the following statement on its front page: "O.J. Officially a Free Man Again" and went on to say that as of Monday, October 21, 1995 the estimated cost of O. J's trial is about $8.5 million, the number of days Simpson spent in jail is 473, the number of attorneys involved in the case is 11 on the defense side, and 9 on the plaintiff's (Wednesday, October 4, 1995, pp. 1, 10-11A.) The Globe Magazine made the remarkable heading: "I Can't Believe They Let Me Walk" (Globe, October 17, 1995).

The verdict has been reached. Whether or not O.J. Simpson was wrongfully acquitted, that is not our task to decide. We simply want to mention that this was probably the longest and most intensively watched trial of the century and perhaps the most expensive one ever. For others involved in the case, they may be of a different opinion. However, for O.J., it had everything to do with his freedom and only. Briefly, what is freedom and can one achieve it?

Freedom is the liberty to self-determination that an individual or a community has. Freedom to choose, freedom to speak, freedom to live apart from others' infringement is a fundamental right of every human being. However, there are socio-political constraints being placed on people's lives that annihilate this right, thereby forcing such individuals to inhumane conditions. The opposite of freedom is enslavement which can be physical, mental, psychological, emotional, spiritual, etc.

A- Physical Enslavement

A particular country may be invaded by another and its people taken as slaves. That is one form of physical enslavement. In another form, people can be locked up in a jail cell under strict supervision where no relatives are allowed for visitation. Physical enslavement can lead to some of the other forms just mentioned above and vice versa; and any of them can be just as suppressive. But for now, our focus is on the physical.

From 1964 to 1990, ANC (African National Congress) leader Nelson Mandela was thrown in jail in South Africa under the apartheid regime. Like other prisoners, he was forced into slave labor and lost his total physical liberty. Another outcome of his incarceration relates to his poor vision due to working in the minefield. There is no question that 27 years in jail will have a lifetime impact on any human being. Some of us would not endure that long. Once we are physically confined, our mind would disintegrate, plunging us into absolute despair. Then our physical and mental health might take a toll on us leading to our grave fast. Partial or total loss of one's freedom can greatly impair one's health or well-being, to be more inclusive, and I hope that everyone reading this book comes to the realization of the severity of the mind being incarcerated for that stands as the very root of almost all the evil involving human kind. The imprisonment of one's mind may even explain the many forms of violence that permeate our society. Some people become restless after they experience the pain that punctuated their lives by being deprived of their spiritual freedom (freedom of the mind) and then try to run away from it simply to fall into further disaster. Others, in the attempt of seeking attention, end up perpetrating violence, which is of course detrimental and self-defeating. Instead, they need to find ways to make a positive impact on society, which in turn will be far more rewarding. Still others are either fed up with everything, have not learned how to deal with their anger, or they have been abused or simply don't know any better way of securing their freedom. As a result, they choose to express themselves through violence. One of the laws of physics says that for every action there is an equal and opposite reaction. For every form of behavior, there exist consequences whether or not we are conscious of them. Therefore, we may escape but for a moment. Let's set our minds straight about taking control of every situation which we may be driven into. This book is filled with examples of how one can go about achieving these endeavors. Violence may be a symptom or a mere reflection of other underlining factors resulting from spiritual bondage (again the mind.) Many people literally fill their minds with trash. They do it either by medicating themselves on too many tranquilizing agents based upon their inability to deal with the real issues or by allowing the environment (society) or culture to feed them with erroneous messages, thereby reducing their lives to a sea of limitations, a valley of impossibilities, and mountains of obstacles. There isn't any accurate instrument by which we can measure quantitatively and qualitatively the degree of success achieved by men and women when they use their minds constructively and productively. However, we encounter on a daily basis numerous lives that are adversely affected when people fail to efficiently use that mind or the brain which God gave them. In fact, some of us see very little use for it, as others try to destroy it by various chemical substances such as crack, cocaine, marijuana, excessive consumption of alcohol, etc.

The United Negro College Fund has emphasized that "The Mind is a Terrible Thing to Waste." Between your mind and your body, which would you rather lose first?

Obviously there is not one without the other, but your mind has the superiority over your physical body in that it gives you the ability to rise beyond the obstacles and bring you to a place where you may be able to at least create a buffer zone or a safe haven, a place where you can find temporary relief. Had it not been for the gift and the proper use of our minds, our world would not look too different from that of the other animals. Evolution may have something quite the opposite for us or at least for those believers of macro-evolution. If other forces combine together to make bondage inevitable for a time, perhaps the best we can do is to prevent bad things from happening to us in the first place. However, there are instances where we cannot escape. If we could, we might even attempt to eliminate the source of bondage altogether or move away from it. As these two options become unfit, we may analyze the situation and try to find a way out or we may attempt to adjust. If we fail in all that and the condition persists over time, it might escalate, bringing us toward exhaustion, the end stage.

B- Freedom is Yours to Achieve

Now how is President Mandela different from the rest of us, or is he different? Where was his mind while his body was being held captive?

I firmly believe that there exists but one Nelson Mandela. There cannot be another one or the exact same personality twice. Put differently, no one will be able to fit in his very shoes. Perhaps the subject matter discussed in this book will point you in one direction while trying to compare your life experiences with that of Mr. Mandela leads you to another path. As long as you are not confused, that is fine, because one thing which we should be comfortable doing is to take different situations, analyze them, and try to find in what ways they resemble our own situation and use them to shape our lives. Nothing could be farther from the truth by asking you to walk in Mr. Mandela's shoes or someone else's. However, we may both agree on this. If you can picture his experience as vivid in your daily fight, then you may be able to relate to the obstacles that he went through. And as a result, you may become stronger in building more internal resistance and remain focused on the success to come. As some say, "Success is failure in reverse". Someone else said, "A man can succeed at almost anything for which he has unlimited enthusiasm" (Charles M. Schwab). "If you become a legend, so did John F. Kennedy" (Mrs. Jacqueline Kennedy, in a tribute to her husband, Nov. 1964).

Mr. Mandela is no ordinary man. However, the strength which he had to endure sufferings while in his jail cell comes from his mind. Just like many of us, while he was in there he could have said, "The fight is over for me," in which case he would have given up and dug his own grave. Instead, he conditioned himself to see beyond those walls and grills. In John C. Calhoun's words, we read the following, "It is harder to preserve than to obtain liberty." We can, in fact, overcome psychological, emotional, physical, political, cultural, and social barriers that prevent us from reaching our freedom.

As far as my memory serves me, I do not know too many people in human history who have walked out of prison after 27 years of incarceration and lead a combatant fight to occupy the highest office in government. That is quite remarkable that newspapers around the world portrayed Mr. Mandela standing next to Queen Elizabeth of England.

Figure 10.1 President Mandela and the Queen of England

We all have the responsibility to contribute to our freedom. As US military General Douglas MacArthur put it, "The inescapable price of liberty is an ability to preserve it from destruction." On that same line, we must add that, "He that would make his own liberty secure must guard even his enemy from oppression" (Thomas Paine, 1737-1809). If at one time, the current South African President was forced to live among the criminals and all kinds of villains, he made his prerogative not to live a life of desperation and resignation. Instead not only has he entertained his mind with various exercises but also he avoided being fed on discouragement hoping that as time goes on, he would rise beyond the walls of the jail into freedom. What about you? What is your formula to secure your freedom?

Many times, I would want to believe that I cannot do anything to change my conditions, but I know that is a big lie being sung in and around me. Therefore, I do not feed myself on that notion. Just as there are too many slaves of greed and materialism in the world, there exist far too many prisoners of learned helplessness in our society. In addition, too many people out there keep playing the wrong tape in their minds, telling themselves that they can't! It is time that you stop sending the wrong message to your mind. You have listened to that tape for too long. Freedom can only be yours if you believe that you can achieve it. If you don't believe that you can succeed, then you accomplish what you believe in. You fail. The redemptive plan of Jesus Christ for His disciples, according to the Bible, was the sacrifice of His own life, which further indicates that there is a price to be paid and a vision to attain. Freedom, whether it be social, economic, spiritual, intellectual, psychological, physical, or else, has its own merits and requirements. It could prove to be costly, but if you want it you can get it. Moreover, freedom is not a license to do as one pleases. Much less, it is not taking vengeance against your foe. As it is said, "We wish to plead our own cause. Too long have others spoken for us...Our vices and degradation are ever arrayed against us, but our virtues are passed by unnoticed" (John Russwurn Samuel Cornish, 1827).

No human being can ever claim to have all the answers, it's only through an act of faith that we may set sail through life's journeys hoping to discover the road that no other men/women have set their feet on and conquer the unimaginable. The road to freedom may be long and solitary, which may often lead to discouragement and sometimes to disappointment. However, what is a better cause to die for than what one believes in? If you should not die for freedom, you are appointed to die anyway; would you rather carry the yoke of enslavement indefinitely and succumb to it? Life can be much more beautiful and gratifying if we dare think the unthinkable, touch the untouchable, search for the unreachable, and see the invisible! If I may, what is the best way to learn to walk other than trying to walk? Your own childhood experience with walking might not have left you with observable scars; however, such exercise is often associated with falling and injuries. If you recall the nine (9) dots which were presented to you in a previous chapter in a box form, and which you were asked to join by drawing four (4) lines through without lifting the pen off the paper. The answer was not possible if you simply looked to draw the lines over the dots by picturing a box in your mind.

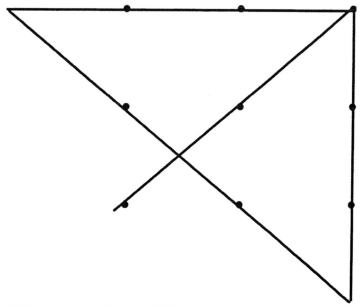

Figure 10.2 Answer made possible by attacking the problem in a diagonal

Solution to the problem given in Chapter II. As you can see, if you remain confined within the walls, or if your imagination can focus only within the confines of this hypothetical box, then the probability of you finding the answer to the question as worded is none. Hence, my advice to each and every one of you out there is the following: allow your mind to take you beyond this box!

❖ CHAPTER XI ❖

A Mind Held Captive

When people think about slavery, they often conceptualize the physical realm. That is the most known and acceptable form of servitude that society at large acknowledges. It was also common practice every time a nation led a successful conquest against another that the citizens of the latter would be colonized and serve the former. That was started very early in human civilization. Some of the oldest civilizations include the Mesopotamian, the Egyptian (African), Palestinian, Greek, the Oriental, and the Roman, from Republic to Empire. Some of the latest ones started with the building of Europe in the early Middle Ages (476-1000) and we found the Frankish (or French, later on), the Germanic, the English, and so on and so forth.

Civilizations may have taken many forms or shapes over the course of human history; however, they have shared one thing in common. They have all used slavery to advance their cause so much so that citizens of the besieged nation would be reduced to mere subjects of the conquering nation and automatically accept their new servitude role and language of their master. We are all familiar with this kind of insane practice, for we cannot rewrite the pages of history.

The notion of captivity and hostage taking are highly condemned in the charter of individual nations and the United Nations Organization which started around the World War II era (1948) with less than sixteen member nations. The evil then seemed to be over, but unfortunately, that is not the case.

A- The Captivity of the Mind, Another Disease

Within the realm of the enslavement of the mind, there is a range. And it is rather difficult to talk about or vie the enslavement of a human mind without any comparison to other humans. The possibility of doing that, however, resides in the fact that every human being presents a certain uniqueness; therefore we can see each person with his or her own merit. How this person develops and functions within that culture and his or her relationship with other elements within that particular culture often dictate the way that individual is very important, since we operate so much based in relationship to and rely so much on social constructs (approval of others) to survive.

Sometimes our uniqueness goes unnoticed and often it is over-shadowed by the performance of other individuals. So, it is within this framework that we sometimes talk about the captivity of the mind. Unfortunately so, but before we were born, certain boundaries have been set for us on how to behave, what we may or may not do. During our developmental stages in life, we try to form our own identity, and make sense of the environment. Consequently, all of us at one time or another struggle with the issues of self versus society, what we want and what society expects of us. The way we understand, process and interpret the information that is being displayed on our screen (meaning our intellect) makes us better orators and finally our audience has a chance to make an opinion. It tells us how our program was intercepted, its quality and its particular impact and we become very conscious of all that. So we end up carrying our own baggage and whatever we decide to pack along the way. In addition, can it happen that we carry only other people's stuff? The more of this personal baggage that we have in our possession, the harder it will be for us to grow and breathe freely. Furthermore, even though we may carry empty baggage which can be counterproductive for us, the contents of the bags that are filled also have great significance. That can help determine how well we are doing in terms of personal growth and how free we are. And of course, all this has to do with how we live and function in society.

Besides being conquered by or subdued by another person, another nation or power, physical and mental infirmities represent a second force which can reduce our ability as people to operate freely, thereby putting us in a position of weakness or enslavement. Thirdly, slavery can be self imposed. That may be accomplished based upon our state or frame of mind and our level of perception, a work that can be done on us by the baggage which we referred to earlier. If we were to translate the contents of the bags into messages being relayed to our radar system (meaning our anatomical brain) and on our screen (meaning our mind), most definitely we would find that not only do we function on exclusivity and selectivity but also we allow ourselves to live and operate on many false premises. We do certain things certain ways as if that is the only way to do them and there are many things which we should be doing that we are not. We become conditioned or locked in gears like machines and get to the point where we willfully and voluntarily commit to conditions that may be inhumane, self-defeating and detrimental. Thus, we assume new roles and resign ourselves to them. When we resign ourselves to a particular condition or a cause, not only do we train our body to fit in but also we adjust our mind so we may be able to respond accordingly.

Due to the fact that slavery (physical) was perceived as wrong, the subjects complained and few rebelled against it, forcing their owners to modify the rules of the game. I say modify because rendering just physical emancipation or liberty to people does not take them too far. It is a good gesture, a noble one, but it falls short on some aspect of rehabilitation which should be more or less a holistic model comprising body, mind, and spirit, as we identify with these. You are no longer a slave but a free person, physically! This dealing usually overlooks many fundamental issues of slavery, the psycho-social ramifications (consequences), and therefore often takes a simplistic route to try to address a very complex problem.

When people live in a system and identify with it, as a function of time they develop a certain degree of dependency. For that matter, whenever you decide to bring new ideals into the picture, you need to know how they will fit with or into the elements of the old system. One of the evils of slavery is found in this simple expression, **K.I.S.S.**, an acronym which stands for **K**eep **I**t **S**imple **S**tupid. We may as well accept "It" to represent the slave, since the relationship there is unequal and somebody is being treated or looked at as less than a human being. Education therefore was never a part of slavery for the simple fact that the subjects were necessarily inferior to their masters. That system degraded the serf and encased the person's faculty or capacity, which he or she would need to live and function independently. If people are to be free and live on their own (and not

179

on welfare), they ought to have the proper ammunition, some of which has to come from them but the rest has to be provided to them, and they ought to be viewed as people instead of a bunch of numbers (black numbers, white numbers, red numbers, yellow numbers, male versus female numbers).

Let us consider the portion to be provided to these people. I have never been on welfare and I am not saying that I am better off than those on welfare; however, the current changes in the system make me quite nervous. In all due respect to President Clinton, whom I support, and to those who work quite hard to prepare a new version of the American welfare system, but I believe that some important aspects in the package have been left out thus far. Many of these people need some form of assistance until they can be trained to catch their own fish, if that is a priority or if it has any significance at all! See, it is sickening for someone to remain attached to the umbilical chord indefinitely and never acquire maturity to live an independent life. However, it is even more sickening to just cut off the chord and separate the person from the system without providing him/her with adequate education, technical assistance and skills as well as psychological training. Just job training won't do it; an integrative model is what we need to create. Left the way it is, the new proposed welfare model will just represent another, and it will split the recipient population at least into three subsets or categories:

1. A marginal number that will be better off due to greater survival skills.
2. A larger number that will remain the same. This group will make some arrangements and adapt to the new model.
3. An even larger category that will become poorer due to lack of preparation and motivation to face new challenges.

Honestly, this kind of dependency should never have been allowed to go on in the first place, but the system created it. Responsively, many recipients have used and abused it, thereby causing them to become handicapped, socially and psychologically. Of course, some people have convinced themselves that they are truly handicapped and that they need crutches to lean on and to help them move around for as long as they live. That idea corresponds to the principle called self-fulfilling prophecy, meaning one behaves as one believes.

This is not at all blaming the victim. We are familiar with the idea that such is one's frame of mind, such is one's thought. Ambition may well be a vice; however, it could just be the father of virtue, as the Roman philosopher, Quintilian (40 B.C.-100) believed.

The individual responsibility component. As it stands, life is a constant struggle. We cannot just sit there and expect things to happen. Yes, something will definitely occur, but not what we would hope for. Our mind is the lighthouse or the guide of our intellectual ability and motivation, hence thinking, reasoning, decision-making. We cannot do any of these life transforming, life renewal activities if the light switch is either off or is not functioning properly. That is a major reason why so many people have problems looking and going forward in life. Once in a while, or occasionally they will use their mind. Research shows that most people on average only use 10% of their brain capacity. The remaining 90% simply vegetates or goes down the drain.

Be as it may, we cannot afford an ill mind, at least not for an independent living. It reveals much too costly to us and to society. So, we just can't do that, even though we may be convalescent in our body.

I realize that sometimes, due to accidents, diseases, and naturally occurring phenomena, we will get sick in our body and require help to move around. Physiologically, our mood may be affected by internal factors (including hormonal), and changes in the external environment may combine at times to reflect on our state of mind, which ultimately may impact our reasoning and perception or our mental and psychological health. Moreover, psychologically and sociologically, we interact with the environment and as a result, we may engage in certain changes conducive to our own personal growth, or we may remain passive with very little acknowledgment of our being present. In contrast we can strive to make our presence felt by getting involved and keeping our mind engaged. Otherwise, external forces, toxic and pathogenic ideology can invade and contaminate our mind, messing it up, thereby keeping us hostage indefinitely until we do something about it. In comparison, in the same way that one may lose his or her sobriety due to alcohol and other drugs, causing one's vision and thought process to become impaired, once we feed our mind the wrong idea or concept, we tend to lose our autonomy and enslave ourselves. Alice Walker said, "Never offer your heart to someone who eats hearts." Many of us are careless with our heart sometimes entrusting it to the wrong person, at the wrong time, in the wrong place, and under the wrong circumstances.

I would make the same inference with regard to your mind. Many times we let in the wrong messages by not being careful or not knowing how to sort them out. A lot of signals and radio waves are constantly airing different messages around us, which can really be deceiving by twisting our mind. Don't let anything mess you up, and don't let obstacles run you down. All the faculties that you have to make decisions or accomplish tasks, small or great, are affected by the state of your mind. It is not without reason that the United Negro College Fund creed says that <u>a mind is a terrible thing to waste</u>, which is what many of us allow drugs and circumstances to do to us. Just like diseases can ravage our own bodies, if a mind that is not properly entertained but instead is allowed to go to waste, either by improper utilization or under utilization, that can be very detrimental to our growth and welfare.

B- The Consequences of an Enslaved Mind

When we examine the crime scenes in the world, we tend to dis-cover a pattern. Most of the perpetrators that commit crime seem to act under the influence of some sort: be it greed to conquer and dominate, the use of drugs, self-centeredness, temporary madness (insanity plea), mental disturbances (illness), ignorance, vengeful attitude, pressure to identify with and conform to the ideals of a distinct fraternity or sorority, intolerance toward other individuals or groups, or simply to attract attention. Once the mind concedes (or gives in), or acknowledges such force (s) and favorably responds to it, it becomes conditioned and loses the power and its objectivity to reason in a non biased manner or act logically or rationally. That leaves room for gross human errors and misconduct which in turn may reduce safety as a whole and increase the vulnerability of self or the environment. We cannot deny the relationship that exists between the psycho-social instability and the prevalence of violent crime in our society today. If we do not engage our mind into doing positive or constructive work, we then tend to allow it to be used as a weapon of destruction.

Put mildly, people who have allowed their mind to be influenced and/or controlled by the environment have a tendency to become dependent on the object of influence. Once such dependency is developed, it carries the potential to create a vicious cycle that resembles a reactive gas or agent being compressed in a semi-permeable container awaiting the right conditions and time to explode. The dependent subject (s) internalize (s) the concept at hand and incorporates it into their belief system. An array of topics can derive from that, for instance we have previously talked about self-fulfilling prophecy, learned helplessness, culture of poverty (the C.O.P.), depression, potential hazards to cite a few.

The whole ordeal looks like real disability except that it relies on the individual's perceptions or views and how he or she understands and interprets them. All of our actions have underlying causes whether we look for them or not and whether or not we are capable of making relevant diagnoses and accepting them as such. Taken in its deepest sense, a mindset can lead to paralysis, thereby disabling the individual to grow or move up the socio-economic ladder, to reach higher spiritual or intellectual dimension of his or her life. We human beings can grow in three different ways: deep and wide (vertically and horizontally), which apply to body size, how tall we get and how big our waist expands. The third way a person grows is in his or her mind or intellect. While the physical components of growth may take a definite shape, direction and size, mentally or spiritually, psychologically, growth has neither direction nor dimension. In that sense, only one can prevent oneself from growing.

Oftentimes, even in the absence of any medical diagnosis, people can be pronounced disabled either by self-imposition or by societal constraints. Let us consider for a moment that teenage boy who, in the movie entitled "Forrest Gump" wore a cast on one of his legs. As his mind was set on the perceived disability, he could not really take control of the situation and break away from the gang members who were literally chasing him. In contrast, the minute after he was able to convince himself that for no reason would he let those gangsters catch up with him and possibly break up every one of his bones, he regained consciousness; he became aware of himself, and his ability to remove himself from the mess was obvious.

Now, what he once perceived as a disability became a strength. Immediately he jumped, shook that cast off, and ran even faster than a "Greyhound" (whichever one you wish to compare the new boy with, the bus or the real animal). Around the world, in every culture, in every race, every community, people accept role playing either consciously or unconsciously. From that perspective, many of them give up not only their individualism but they also forfeit their imagination or creativity. Consequently, they write and practice their concession speech which they ultimately deliver to Mr. or Ms. Genus. They go as far as endorsing his or her ticket with full rights or privileges, to take possession of the moon and the stars which they could ascribe to themselves. And the best they do is resign themselves to whatever chance or good luck may bring or whenever the good Lord feels like dropping some manna for them from heaven.

Even if I decided to deny my past and say that there are no real obstacles, my very present state would categorically betray me. Therefore, I know what it is to face true obstacles and for doors to be slammed in my face. But I have learned that as long as I do not stand for my rights, it will be taken away from me and whatever people are dropping on my lap they will keep doing it until I am buried under their load of trash. I also learned that a door closing down is another opportunity opening up. As one said, "Success is failure in reverse."

Unfortunately, too many of us are prevented from seeing it that way. We either give up the first time we try it and fail, or we insulate ourselves, our thoughts and imagination into our own little niche with no opening into the larger universe. Then, we really would be talking about personal needs, problems, different levels of distress and depression, poverty, illness, etc. It is a shame, the amount of human resources going around under-utilized, which ultimately wastes away.

A mind held captive is worse than a body being thrown in a jail cell under heavy chains and maximum security; for if the mind is free, it will work to secure the freedom of the whole person. On the contrary, a mind that has not been emancipated can cause the destruction of the whole individual. And that emancipation comes from within. It is God-given and dimensionless. No one can take it away from us unless we voluntary allow them to control it.

I cannot fathom any benefit that a person may gain by letting his/her mind become captive to his/her surroundings, other folks' ideas or myths, one's own feelings, one's own emotions, much less circumstances. I cannot overemphasize the notion of perception and its impact on our overall development. And very seldom has any human being been prohibited by another from using his or her mind. Sometimes that occurs in classroom settings where traditional instructors do not welcome creativity from their "pupils". Also, the socio-cultural and political system in which we live and operate can be framed in such a way as to try to exclude or shut some people off. That can constitute a real burden when you are trying to establish yourself and do what you believe to be the right thing. My suggestion is that you do not quit just because things are hard to achieve. Believe what you believe and fight for it until you obtain it. Besides these few boundaries mentioned above, it is our own infirmity, our ignorance, self-inflicted limitations that prevent us from developing our potentials and excelling in life. And that obviously has a price on it, which is the very freedom that we are defending. Mr. Mandela resisted being mentally and spiritually incarcerated. I am sure that it was not an easy thing for him to do, to be locked up in a prison cell with no assurance when if ever he will be set free! However, aside from his kindred spirit, which kept him going in his isolated cell, he also left behind a network of believers, people who had a relationship with and who were sympathetic to the same cause as he. Whenever we resign ourselves to whatever life may bring, we mean that we have conferred our freedom to someone or something else and taken up despair, hopelessness and suffering. Somewhere in this book I have already mentioned the idea that "who stands for nothing falls for anything." What kind of obstacles have held you captive this far? Where would you now be had you moved them out of your way?

PART FOUR

Opportunities Come After Struggles

❖ Chapter XII ❖

What Do You Perceive Your Goliath to Be, Defiant?

Special note: Those limitations (boundaries) which we have allowed ourselves to be entrapped by due to our own inadequacies and/or our ignorance represent the very weapons that cripple and render us ineffective in our day-to-day fight!

In the preceding chapter, we have talked about a mind held captive. In this current section, we would like to draw an analogy between real life's challenges and your perception of them and perhaps help you reach the stage where you won't faint at Goliath's feet or at the foot of the mountain. Instead, you must realize that no victory is finite and no enemy is invincible. You may lack resources and ammunition at this particular point in time to face the challenges, nonetheless that's no reason for you to give up hope. You may be just steps away from winning this present battle. **Effective strategies, determination, and patience** represent three great elements that we need to combine in order to win any number of battles in a given war, be it psychological, emotional, physical, mental, or socio-economic. Equally important, you want to be in a **state of war** until you know that it is finally over and that you have not only disarmed the enemy but you have also positioned yourself on a much firmer ground than you were initially. Now, how do you do all that? May we guide you through the remaining steps?

All along we have held you, the individuals, accountable for your own destiny, at least we have attempted to do just that. We do not want to sound as though we are minimizing the potency of the adversaries. However, we know that perception has everything to do with how you approach life's situations and carry yourself through. For example, everyone around me may conclude that I hold a pencil in my hand when I stand alone, trying to convince them that I have a real sword in my hand. They may not necessarily change their position from the notion that I hold a pencil to accepting my idea of a sword, but the fact that I hold dear to that belief reflects on my perception and it conveys a particular message at least to me. Please note that I am not talking about me being in denial, which could very well be the case in other instances. This particular belief of mine will affect my attitude to the point of creating a behavior modification in me. And as long as I do not yield to anyone else's idea, I may do well defending myself with my pencil against any potential foe. What I am trying to do here is to help you focus deeper into your environment so you may see what lies across your path, how your perception can shape your belief and attitude.

If you have a distorted view of a situation, and if you happen not to recognize it but instead draw your final and conclusive decision based on the limited amount of light shed on the matter at that time alone, you probably set yourself up for disappointment. Please allow me to give a working definition to the following words, since they constitute the central elements in this book:

Disability: real or imaginary impairment that causes a person to see or convey himself/herself as incapable of accomplishing a particular duty or task.

Perception: (according to *Webster's*) a mental image, a physical sensation interpreted in the light of experience. For our purpose of discussion, I will define it as a descriptive representation of an object or idea based on reality or fictitious beliefs and limited knowledge at the time.

Growth: (unless otherwise stated within a specific section of this book) it means the expansion of one's mind and intellect, one's ability to approach a situation in a broader scope, beyond a narrow vision. The capacity to acknowledge one's limitations and a willingness to take risks and accept failure as a step toward finding the real solution to a specific problem.

Belief System: belief itself is defined by *Webster's* as a state or habit of mind in which trust or confidence is placed in some person, object, or thing. A belief system comprises the socio-cultural values and moral characteristics by which a person may choose to live, interact with the environment, and have his or her needs met. A person holding a particular belief may not even know the why and how that came about, but that belief satisfies his or her desire to belong to and identify with other members of similar faith.

Freedom: the liberty to think openly, act in one's self-interest and exercise control over one's own actions. Self conceptualization, self actualizing.

These five words summarize almost the entire concept that we try to convey in this manual. People who suffer from real disabilities have to be accommodated by relatives or their government. However, for those with imaginary dysfunctions or disabilities, they alone can cure themselves. They may receive a prescription such as this book but they alone have the power to change things affecting their lives. Growth opens our horizons, allowing us to look for more pertinent and possible answers. Freedom itself represents the medium that facilitates growth and that helps one to distinguish between the two kinds of disability. That is why freedom is so important in life. It will take a person from his/her state of hopelessness to one of self-assertiveness, from a state of fear to self actualization, thereby turning things around, from the position of ambivalence to the level of decisiveness, from weakness to strength, from skepticism to optimism, from retrogression to progress, from stagnation to growth, from object poverty to selective living. As Robert Browning stated, "As is your sort of mind, so is your sort of search. You will find what you desire." (*Social Psych*. D. Myers. p.177).

Perhaps you have been hearing negative clichés and epithets all your life, and you may have unconsciously made them a part of your belief system which then works against you. However, I am telling you this now. It is the right time to examine yourself and your life and decide whether you want to be free and grow or remain stagnant. It is up to you to either live and reach your potential or simply survive and suppress your ambitions, talents, and your imagination (creativity) by focusing too much on the obstacles while denying yourself all the opportunities that open up to you.

It is very unfortunate that most people do not realize the power behind positive thinking (thinking positively). Throughout its entire existence, Israel as a nation always had enemies, some very powerful and some not too powerful, but they could all cause damage to the stability of the Israelites. Obviously, one day they had a very fearful warrior that no one dared attack. In almost everyone's mind, this man named Goliath who led the Philistine army, a neighboring country of Israel and located on the southwest of Palestine, was invincible. No one among the Israelis seemed to want to affront him. Out of them all, one "insignificant person" then had a different perception of the giant warrior. Just because someone has never done it before does not mean that you cannot succeed in doing it, and just because other people have underestimated your strength does not mean that you are incapable or incompetent! Whatever the dream may be, if you can believe it, you can realize it. David, the King to be, had that confidence.

Now the argument could go both ways. Some might say that David, the only person on the Israeli side who felt that he could do something about that Philistine Army Commander, was positive and self-assured. Or the opposite thinking may conclude that the whole scheme was orchestrated by the supreme power or force acting in David and that he was just a passive instrument which happened to be in the right place at the right time, being used to defend that cause or any others. I disagree with the second argument. First, we must understand that David was focused. Secondly, due to the simple fact that everyone else who was in the Israeli camp had their eyes on Goliath, the obstacle, David had very little support either from his immediate family or from his fellow countrymen. As he saw things differently, he decided to act solo. Sometimes, the very people that you love so dearly and whom you are willing to make all the sacrifice for may be the ones that resist your every move. This was not better for Moses who put his life on the line to defend his fellow brethren and it was not different for David whose entire family turned up against him. The same situation applied for Toussaint L'Ouverture (also known as Pierre Dominique), a former slave and Haitian emancipationist who fought for the freedom of his other enslaved brothers who later betrayed him and caused his capture by troops loyal to the feudal system and the status quo, and to this very day the self-defeating mentality prevails among the people, no trust, no spirit of collaboration! And the tolerance for diversity of opinions is non-

191

existent. What a defeat for freedom and the freedom fighters! All that is a great lesson for you and me or anyone, especially for people in leadership positions. David then went alone beyond and in front of the Israeli army, by the restricted zone. He developed a belief system which allowed him to look for solutions when there was not one readily made up. How many times in your life have you come up with new ideas and instead of trying them, you simply strangle and abort them?

When faced with whatever obstacles in life, our first question should never be "can we really come out," but instead "how will we come out or succeed?" Too often we look around for ready-to-go answers but are too eager to find a quick fix (instantaneous or immediate gratification) and not enough patience and the willingness to work the problems out ourselves and arrive at the best possible conclusions. As you can see, the first question not only puts to test our strength to stand the difficulties, but it also casts doubt on our ability and competence level to affront the challenges and come out as victor.

During our lifetime, we will have many battles to fight, even to just remain alive. Evidently, we will not win every battle; however, you and I have to decide as to which battles we are willing to fight. If we are smart enough, we will negotiate around those which we believe have the potential of laying extreme casualties on our sides. There exists a great difference between giving up a fight and a negotiated settlement; and usually one man's failure is another man's success.

What would be the casualties laid on Israel by the Philistine had David, like everyone else, focused on the magnitude of the problem? Goliath was a true, skillful warrior who acquired his experience in the battlefield; he was no neophyte in the matters of war. Physically, he had a profile somewhat similar to a football or basketball player like Michael Jordan. All that put together, he could scare anyone who could not see beyond the physical realm. Goliath enjoyed scaring people, and to make matters worse, when no one in Israel would defy him, he mocked, insulted, and ridiculed them all (I Samuel 17). And because everyone was too threatened by Goliath's size and his defiant personality, they allowed him to take control of a situation and he kept the entire nation of Israel under siege for quite some time.

Most of us live under siege and persistent fear of circumstances. We allow them to take control over our lives. Too often we feel defeated before we even try. Why do we experience so much hardship and so many needs in life? Mainly because we have been incapacitated by our own fear and our pessimism. Consequently, the world around us helps us condition ourselves and we are willing to settle for anything, I mean anything, the cheapest things we can get with minimum effort. Fear is a paralyzing force which, if it is allowed, may encompass any kind of accomplishment that we could realize, great or small.

I want to close this chapter with a true story, but one which may sound funny or ludicrous to a number of you out there. Experiments show that if you take a bear and place it in a cage, say 6 feet wide by 24 feet long, over time the animal will walk that measured length (distance). Having learned and believed (if lower animals have a belief system) that this is the only distance it may travel, you can remove the cage and the bear will continue to walk as far as 24 feet and back to square one. This is what psychology terms automatic or 'classical conditioning' as opposed to 'operant conditioning' (B. F. Skinner) where the individual is actively involved in eliciting a different response from the environment.

We train our mind by playing through the "CANNOT" cassette. Added to that, fear, low self-esteem, lack of motivation and incentive combined keep us in a cage-like mentality, so much so that we seldom play and listen to the "CAN" cassette. Just as David, we need to believe that we in fact can win, we can indeed overcome, and can in truth experience real freedom from the obstacles, but how?

❖ CHAPTER XIII ❖

"Live Free or Die"

Figure 13.1 *The prodigal son and his deplorable encounter with the herd of pigs.*

With both hands, the young religious fellow reaches to the food in the container, but one hand feeds the herd of pigs and the other goes to his mouth. A foolish decision which later causes a lot of grievance! A leap from bad to worse!!! Will his confidence be restored after the damage control?

Before the French social class revolution in 1789, all the way to the Proclamation of the Great American Emancipation in 1863, bondage seemed to have been thought of in a very narrow sense. The inability of any human being to freely move and dispose of himself or herself was considered the only form of enslavement.

This type of physical binding disregarded the rights of the subjects to self-determination and reduced them to mere objects. Wherever slavery was enforced, the master exerted absolute control over the serf. For the slightest violation against the master's order, a slave could face extreme punishment or even death in many cases. In a way, we might conclude that such practice represented the most bestial, most inhumane, and the lowest and even the cruelest form of sacrilege that a human being could be subject to. There was no question of will for a slave. Thank God almighty that these periods are over for many of us.

However, as we come to a fuller understanding of freedom and self determination, we then expand on the definition of slavery beyond just a person's body. It involves every aspect of an individual's existence and well-being: physical, mental, emotional, psychological, spiritual, or economical, and it may be voluntary (self-imposed) or involuntary (by default). In fact, most of the things that human beings fight for have a component that relates to power necessary to control or to dominate other people by reason of discrimination, conflict of interest, dissension, and individual and/or territorial pride. Then, as the parties involved lose the ability to peacefully resolve their conflict, those in the weaker position become subjects of the strong ones or they become the "Governed" hence they are ruled by the dominant class or culture.

Natural law creates the basis for cohabitation of species. From that, scientists develop what is known in biological sciences as the "Food Chain Theory" where the strong learn to live on the weak. You might have heard at one time or another that "the strong survive." In a previous chapter, I have described for you the three main categories of relationships that have been identified, which can exist among different species and between members of the same species. These are: 1-<u>Commensalism</u>, one member or a species lives at the expense of another without causing much harm to the latter. It may also be real or imaginary. 2- <u>Parasitic</u>, one member or a species controls another and causes the latter to go to extinction or to disappear. The third type of relationship is called <u>mutualism</u> (mutual). As the word implies, all the parties involved derive some benefits. We might add that the third type represents a more or less balanced, two way relationship with some mutual respect shared among the inhabitants, more specifically among humans. In this case, a slave master relationship would probably fall between commensalism and parasitic. We usually do not use the following terms when we refer to relationships among humans, but in a more descriptive or dramatic way, we talk about predator and prey to say who chases whom in the jungle. Now, earlier in this chapter, we talked about self-imposed or voluntary slavery versus involuntary (by default) enslavement. Both types have been practiced in human history. In the second one, the strong literally hunted the weak, and in the first instance, some people would sell their rights to someone with greater socio-economic affluence and receive some form of material compensation. Slavery can take many forms or shapes, and it may be real or imaginary. Sometimes, a whole household or a part thereof (just children and at one time that could also include the female spouse), a whole nation, a whole race could become the subject of another nation, race, or what have you! In other instances, only one person may be involved.

From the Bible, we read the interesting story of the "Prodigal Son." There, we are told of an individual who made some difficult choices and had to bear the consequences for a while. We do not know them, and the details are not readily available. So we can only assume what the conditions might have been at his father's home and among his siblings. According to the story, for the first time this young person took upon himself to live an independent life away from all his relatives and old friends.

He requested his share of inheritance from his father and took off to an unknown destination, no relatives involved and no social or moral support of any kind. Soon thereafter, through mismanagement, he found himself broke. He was left without a penny. What that gentleman did not realize or miscalculated was that he was running from someone or from something to someone or something else. And having spent all his fortune in a foreign land, all the friends he had made turned their backs on him. He found himself in the most extraneous situation. When he could no longer pay his rent and eat, he got himself the only job which was made available to him. He begged someone to accommodate him with a place to lay his head and in turn he would feed that person's herd of pigs and hide a portion of the food for himself. The story reported that he was a Jew (St. Luke, Chapter 15, vs. 11-32.) and at that time, for Jewish citizens just the idea of dealing with pigs was a social disgrace. Humiliated enough, this Jewish fellow was not only caring for the pigs, but also he was feeding himself with the same substance that he had to feed them. You can imagine the psychological and the emotional trauma that he brought into his life.

At first, we might attempt to say that by his trying to find a job represented a normal course of action. However, the whole scenario displeased him, and instead of improving his conditions, he deepened further into the crisis. Instead of reconciling with himself after finding food to eat, he came to the verge of suffering from psycho-pathic disorders. These can emerge from different origins, but his presupposed diagnosis revolved around his ideals. In other words, they originated internally when he thought of his previous standard of living, and the conflict between his past and current belief system, all of that tempered with his emotions, thereby inflicting within him a sense of hopelessness.

Emotional stress can wear you down much faster than the physi-cal. When you have no one to confide in, no one that you can share your happiness or sadness with, nobody to display your love and affection to, and of course, no one to reciprocate those sentiments or feelings to you, life is that miserable. Psychologically, we do better in an environment where our basic needs can be met. We also feel good when we are cared for with a sense of pride and dignity, for no one likes to be looked down upon. In a way, whether you are reduced to slavery either by force or out of your own free will, the end results are somewhat the same. Per our working definition of bondage:

That includes conditions that you voluntarily or involuntarily accept to live under despite your dissatisfactions. Sometimes, you may even be in disagreement with a part of yourself over what you do or what happens to you. Your mind and intellect may oppose some actions that your heart (emotion) leads you to take. If you had a chance to read my book on relationships, you might notice that I raised the following questions in it, "The heart or the mind, which one decides?" That's one way conflict of interest may be generated. At that point, there is nobody else involved. We are simply at war with ourselves, but we often come to terms by mediating a conflict resolution process.

Now, the sooner we can resolve the issues at hand, the quicker we will be able to establish balance or some form of internal stability. Therefore, the less stress that we will impose on ourselves, hopefully the less damage will be done to our systems. However, it seems that as we live, obstacles never end. They have a way of getting through to us. After we manage to solve a particular set of problems, we say to ourselves that it is over. Then, we get ready to lean back a little bit and enjoy for a moment the fruits of our labor, and suddenly, we end up with more problems than we ever imagined.

Naturally, life is made as such. Some of these obstacles were in the world even before you and I came into being and they will remain to the end of time. Others are created by us and/or by the environment (other human activities, natural phenomena, and sometimes circumstances which evolve beyond our control), which means that at any given time, depending on reality or our distorted observation, we may perceive problems and obstacles. And I am sorry to say that many of them are a matter of perception, which in fact may be rational or irrational. Nonetheless, too often we do allow these circumstances to steal our happiness and hold us captive or hostage.

A- Focus On The Opportunity Instead of The Obstacles

As we now know, the air is full of different kinds of waves that travel through simultaneously, creating enormous impact and causing various interference. Radio waves, for instance, fill our world. We simply need the appropriate receiver (s) that are equipped to intercept any kind of radio frequencies. And the only reason you and I do not hear all the signals from around the world is because we do not possess the kind of resources that would provide us with such a powerful receiver. By the way, if you are up to date with the world of science and technology, you may know that the US Congress has stopped funding a project aimed at producing the most powerful satellite station based on earth. To be accurate, the device is an 84 foot tall, billion channel radio telescope dish set at Oak Ridge Observatory, Harvard University, Cambridge, Massachusetts. The goal is to detect and pickup the lowest or the farthest signal emitted by any form of extraterrestrial beings from other planets. Now the program is not dead. It simply means that private agencies sponsor it. If E.T. phones home, science is ready. (*The Boston Globe*, Tuesday, Oct. 31, 1995, pp.21,24).

Many people have their minds conditioned to intercept distracting wavelengths. As a result, they can pick up signals that their receivers can **selectively** intercept and play to them all the time. Many situations in life become obstacles simply because we perceive and interpret them as such. Also, we often close our circuit to other frequencies (I mean to say other opportunities) and allow these that we first heard to jam or overpower our minds with all the negative messages. Many of us end up making the wrong choice, traveling the wrong roads, and crossing the wrong bridges in life because of our distorted vision. Let us consider another example. The O.J. Simpson trial followed a distinct toll and the whole world watched it with particular interest. Well, some people argue that the prosecution was solely concerned with evidence that would prove O.J. guilty. On the contrary, there are those who say that the defense looked for any data that would prove his innocence. Whether that is the correct conclusion, I am not sure. What we can argue though, it is very precise that we often condition ourselves and become a single-tracked mind; then we search for evidence that would support whatever arguments we wish to raise. Anything that we look for in this world, we can find it. Such is our frame of mind, such is our thought.

We see what we are up to. We look for obstacles, then we end up seeing plenty of them. The world of obstacles and the world of opportunities co-exist and are super-imposed (back-to-back). Only those who seek diligently, patiently and persistently care to look deeper and farther for these opportunities. Again, just like the examples of catching up the radio waves, some people are only tuned to a few selective channels, as if that's all that ever exists. They become so limited that all the space around them is used up by obstacles, leaving them no room to fully experience life and to grow. They become like the Iraqi President, Sadam Hussein, "hostage in their own backyard" to quote former US President George Bush at the end of "The Desert Storm War".

If you are hooked on a particular kind of receiver, obviously you will keep receiving only one kind of signal. I once heard someone say, "There are three kinds of people in the world, those who watch things happen, those who wonder what happened, and those who make things happen". Which of those three groups are you associated with?

It is interesting that two people may grow up together, one will conceive dreams and see them materialize while the other remains sessile and amorphous. One is motivated toward some form of accomplishment and the other remains passive. One is upbeat and optimistic about life and the other very cynical and pessimistic about everything or distracted by things. While one will focus on ways to thrive beyond the obstacles and try to be part of the solution, the other may feel threatened to make a decisive move and therefore decide to be part of the problem.

Live Free or Die is the motto of the state of New Hampshire, which I take to mean that these citizens have a clear choice, either to strive to maintain their freedom or to die with their dignity. Now, is socio-economic and spiritual freedom achievable by all people?

B- The Fear of The Unknown

The French writer, Voltaire (1694-1778) in the piece entitled *Candide* said, "All is for the best in the best of all possible worlds". It takes tremendous courage to cut off the link between one and the placenta and sever the relationship without any hope to reconnect, should all attempts to live an independent life fail. To me, that is the biggest fear of all. To put it bluntly, this is called fear of insecurity. Even though we all fall beneath it at one time or another, we do not like to admit that phenomenon as such. We are experts at putting on fronts.

We see what we now have but we have no faith and no confidence that we can change things for the better. Therefore, we settle for the status quo. A whole belief system is born from fear to change things, whether it be looking for new opportunities, changing one's behavior and attitude, or moving into a new environment. Sometimes if someone were to be gracious enough to let you walk in his or her shoes, you might have adopted a different attitude and perspective in life, but unfortunately that is rarely the case. More often than not what we observe is "Dieu pour tous, et chacun pour soi" (To each his/her own). Unfortunately so, that's part of the real world. You're on your own baby, that's how it feels many times. I am neither a pessimistic nor a vengeful person but I'd like to set a record straight. You might remember reading this from your world history book or from the Bible. About 13th century B. C., the Egyptians who represented the rich and most powerful kingdom, subdued the destitute Nation of Israel and forced all Jews into slavery. As the story goes, they became Egyptian subjects and were induced into slave labor. They stayed there for over 400 years; then, at the end, the whole country of Egypt became so troubled by the presence of the Israelites that the king of the land felt that it was about time for him to ease the yoke off their necks. He released a decree with this instruction, "You may now leave but your assets ought to stay in Egypt" (Exodus, Ch.10, v. 24 and following). The conclusion to be drawn here is that not everybody really wants his or her neighbor to succeed; that's the disturbing fact, which makes life extra hard sometimes! Some of us had a pretty rough debut and encountered very resistant and troublesome currents, hard enough to make us quit. Nonetheless, that's no reason for us not to look up and go forward. Any muscle or tissue that does not grow atrophies. The fight continues until we die; and the more we invest in life, though it may get harder at times, but in the end it will be better than if we didn't do anything at all.

Despite the fact that scientists never knew what was awaiting them in space, they took a step of faith to invest on a first flight, on a second, on a third, etc. Motivation got them on track and habit keeps them going. It is obvious that many people have made significant progress in their lives and have managed to make the world a better place; these individuals share the basic characteristics, needs, and aspirations of all human beings. Nonetheless, they have realized that who continues nothing gains nothing. They have allowed themselves to take risks and make mistakes (which is okay by the way) but in the process they have come out better men and women. They have matured and reached some degree of interdependence.

C- Whatever Your Bondage, Be Free

Ignorance is at the base of most human suffering. Furthermore, <u>what often hurts us is not too much knowledge but a lack thereof</u>. In order to make any kind of progress in life, we must be willing to take risks and make certain sacrifices. We must invest our resources, develop enough motivation to keep us afloat. Most of all, we need to keep our belief system in check to see where we must make changes; because from the crib to the grave is a lot of trash and garbage that we need to push aside in order to step forth. It is not always important for us to find out how the trash ever got there; however, it may be toxic to our health and well-being. Therefore, we must remove it regardless. Furthermore, along the way, based upon our inadequacies and the inaccuracy of different messages that we intercept (either by sight, by hearing, by touching, by feeling, by tasting, or by our entire sensory track) and record in our database, we will formulate a lot of misconceptions, which in turn will hinder our growth. Are you familiar with the paradigm of the glass being half full or half empty? Which half of the glass do you hold? And even if you were forced by circumstances to hold the latter half while its content is being sipped away from your hand, could you save or recover some of the contents, or fill it with something else, or could the glass itself be useful to you? We live and achieve according to how we perceive the world around us and how we respond to it. The following picture depicts two different groups of people with distinct attitudes in the world: those who only see things getting worse and that there is nothing they can do to improve them and those who believe that they can make an impact.

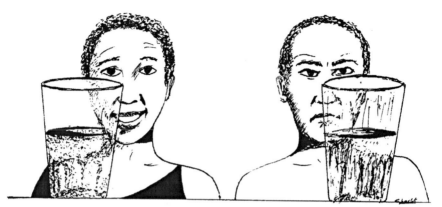

Figure 13.2 *The Glasses*
Optimism = Glass is ½ full   Pessimism = Glass is ½ empty

These individuals who approach life positively or who cultivate that optimistic outlook about themselves will experience less frustration in their lives; many studies confirm such a claim. They will live with less anxiety and stress. And of course, everything else remaining equal, they will tend to live healthier with fewer hospital visits during their life span. It pays to be optimistic. Meanwhile, the rest of the people can only visualize a glass that is draining (half empty). It is a matter of time until it dries out. Some people may get scared of an atheist, a rapist, or a child molester, but I have learned not to let myself be troubled or distracted in the midst of negative folk and habitual procrastinators.

For some of us, nothing ever goes right; they always find reasons to complain. Many of such individuals belong to the "tator family." They are: **imitators**, **agitators**, **irritators**, **intimidators**, all the wrong "...tators". They procrastinate throughout their lives. They always look in one direction and that is the very reason they see obstacles all the time. Unfortunately, the kind of house that we build most often than not becomes our dwelling place. Whatever the architecture, we end up leaving our house. We are actors in our own shows. Sometimes, the expectations may play a narcissistic and a hospitable role of rescuing or seeing the actor come out alive. However, other times the audience is just as passive as dry leaves in autumn that it provides us with no incentive whatsoever. Most of us could do better if only we looked in the right place and flock with the right crowd that will provide the support and encouragement we need to carry on.

Those of us who wish to enjoy the real charm that nature offers must also change or modify our focal lenses and start looking at different and opposite directions. We must be able to take our minds off the valleys for a while and start focusing upward and over the hilltop. Who knows, after climbing the mountains of life, we may discover the beautiful plateaus where the grass is greener.

Before we can make any kind of upward move either socially, economically, politically, spiritually, etc., our minds must be sterilized or cured against any kind of brainwashing. Our spirit or intellect needs to be sharpened so that it can listen to and pick up varied signals of opportunities that are being aired at different wavelengths. Let persistency be your powerful radar or antenna that will help you pass the usual frequencies which you have been intercepting all along. Moreover, whenever the melody becomes too monotonous for your brain, you can hear new and exciting pitches. Just change the station. Only you can limit your growth.

Life can be seen as a sea of obstacles. It all depends on the viewers' perceptions and the kinds of mentality and the environment they live in. They may not always have a choice in the geographic location that they evolve in, but they certainly can change their attitude over the geo-political boundaries that they evolved in. They certainly can change their attitude and their views for the better.

As long as you are not bound in chains physically and your mind is not literally in a vegetative state, you can change your conditions and the environment. Try to have a very limited use of the "cannot" word. I do not recommend that you eliminate it altogether from your vocabulary, then you might get yourself into trouble. Nonetheless, you need to look on any positive role model whom you can possibly identify with. Also, take a close look at yourself. I suggest that if you have pictures of yourself while you were in the crib, look and see how little you were. It took time but you have grown up eventually to become the strong, handsome or the pretty individual that you are now. So, do not be deceived or too concerned; every process requires some time. You have encountered enough obstacles already. We do not control how fast time passes and we cannot reverse the biological clock. However, we can use our time wisely. In addition, we just need to plant within ourselves the right and positive seeds. We ought to stop telling ourselves that we cannot do this, we cannot do that. By the time we finish, there may not be anything left for us to do, except drugs, getting depressed and cutting somebody's throat.

So many people are in jail because they have goal displacements and they end up using the cannot word in the wrong context. They end up being not only a walking obstacle against their own personal growth, but also they serve as a nuisance to society and the environment as a whole. Whatever we do affects others around us. If we are productive then the world expands its beauty. If we are builders, then we may represent an imposing monument, a role model for someone else. On the contrary, if we are stagnant, unproductive, and reluctant about life, even when the opportunities come by, since we have not been careful enough, we may destroy them or they may go by unnoticed.

We must set our receivers for those wavelengths which will help us reach the road leading toward freedom. We can be set free only if we want to pay the price. Lastly, note that some obstacles find us instead of us finding them. In addition, no matter what we do we'll never match up to everybody's expectations of us. Therefore, don't be fooled by the external forces thinking that we can change the world. Each of us first is responsible for his or her own little world and whomever that he/she may be allowed to include in it. In closing, nothing can keep you enslaved: your race, your gender, your age, your nationality, your culture, or your family background. It largely depends on you. Thus, life itself (not just the English Canada, as depicted on the automobile license plates) is yours to discover.

❖ CHAPTER XIV ❖

Reaching Your Potentials

Research indicates that most of us only use ten percent (10%) of our brain potential. Others may use less than that, just as some people virtually employ more than the 10%. Another way to interpret this is that some ninety percent (90%) of our potential or resources is not being utilized properly or is wasted, and that hurts! To me, that is like having at our disposal a power plant which could enlighten every corner in our home but then, we choose to capture just 1/10 or 10/100 of it, barely enough light to clear our path. No wonder that so many people are destitute, living in abject poverty, and barely caring for themselves.

If in fact all human beings are created equal, and if in fact we possess so great a capacity, but yet oftentimes we become incapacitated in front of life's challenges, that is sad, very sad, extremely sad!! Something is wrong somewhere! Either somebody does not tell us the real truth, or we defeat ourselves in the way we live our lives. Point in fact, both statements are correct. For someone like me who takes interests in both natural and social sciences, I can say that I have a good understanding about symbiotic relationships, where we identify at least three different kinds of interactions that influence our socioeconomic well-being, namely: parasitic, commensalism and mutualism (which I briefly eluded to in the previous chapter). A parasitic relationship means that one member of the association benefits at the expense of the other; this represents an extreme side in the interaction because one party is being preyed upon. At the other extreme, we find mutualism and it means that both parties interact or all the parties involved equally benefit from the relationship. Between the two extremes, we identify a third level of relationship, the commensalism. This form of relationship is one-sided; one party benefits while causing no harm to the other but the latter gains nothing. We intend not to plunge too deeply into heavy science here, for I might lose the attention of too many of you out there. However, this stuff is important, and once you all get a grasp on it, you may come to a higher level of truth and as a result, you might realize how to better develop your resources, and your relationships, thereby modifying your belief system and improving your living conditions.

As we talk about interrelationships in general and how they affect our lives, we come to identify some other interesting concepts that influence resource availability and resource accessibility.

1. Food webs, where a number of "eaters and eaten" make a food chain
2. Limited resources
3. Population explosion
4. Migration
5. "Survival of the fittest", competition for the same resources
6. One's belief system and one's motivation to reach higher goals in life

If we were to gather all the living things, namely all the animals, including humans, and if we were to create a system describing how they interact and survive, we would end up with a pyramid with different organisms living from around the bottom all the way to the top. The concept which I am about to describe to you here is adapted from the biological sciences, and I just want to make a point. So don't you worry, be happy. You never have to become a biologist especially if your interests do not lie there.

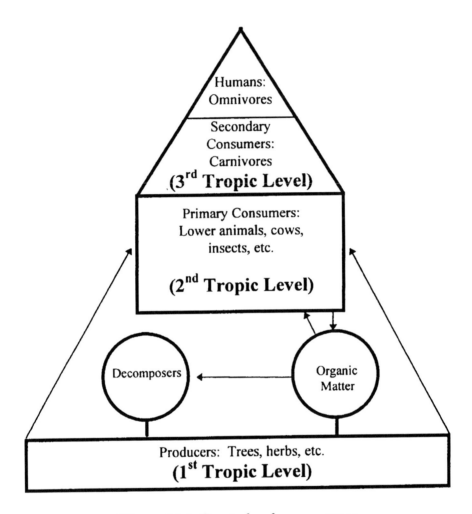

Figure 14.1 *Tropic levels or resource availability and the food chain theory.*

At level 1, plants, bacteria, and other organisms manufacture food and make it available to the next level. Level two represents primary consumers. They are herbivores (herb eaters) such as cattle, sheep, donkeys, etc. which live on the production of or on level one. The third level can be considered the level where carnivores (flesh eaters) are found and they live on the levels below them. Level four, tertiary consumers, some of the groups of species found here are also represented at level three, but it generally includes those organisms that can eat anything. They represent the group that we commonly call omnivores (vores = eat, omni = all). We human beings are supposed to be at the top of the pyramid as part of the tertiary consumers forming the food chain.

From a sociopolitical point of view, we human beings are the most intelligent, most advanced creatures among all. And <u>we are supposed to be producers</u>. Unfortunately, this is not always the case. For one thing, as we study the make-up of a food chain, we discover that we consume more than we produce, at least for many of us. Of course, at the level of the arrangement discussed in the pyramid, we live on (consume) everything that exists in the environment and do not have to produce for anyone else, not even for our own selves sometimes. That is a major problem, I mean a major one!

Obviously, as one moves from the bottom of the pyramid to the top, one will notice that resources become less readily available. If we were to take this idea one step further, we might attempt to conclude that as more people find their way to the top of the social ladder, or the social echelon, the more they will have to compete to survive. While there is some truth to this argument, not all of us will buy into it. To a certain extent, it surfaces some of the ideas of Thomas Malthus, a British economist who said that there are more mouths, or more human beings, than there is food for them. That was eloquently stated in the theory of "The population grows exponentially while resources grow arithmetically."

Taking everything into consideration it seems that a vast majority of people consume but do not care to produce much in many instances, and given that we use approximately 10% of our brain, we are proven to be deficient in some ways. If we consume while we do not produce, then we spend resources that we do not have, which translates that we live in deficit or on credit. And it is not that we cannot do better, for the resources are there. It just requires some effort, thinking, and creativity on our part in order to make them readily available; however, very few of us state or envision higher goals for ourselves and see them materialized.

Every mature or responsible human being needs to have purpose in his or her life. Similarly, every one of us should be aware of the three very important time sequences being identified: the past, which responds to the question where a person started; the present, which helps describe to a great extent how a person lives today; and the future, which makes plans for times that lie ahead.

A. Living With A Vision

Before you can effectively tap into your resources, you need to have a purpose in your life. Also, you want to keep track of these three time frames. The purpose will give you something to live for or to fight for, and the time frames or the awareness of it will help you get situated or will tell you where you are in terms of reaching your goals. Greed does contribute to it, and some of us seem to live to amass or accumulate wealth just so that we have enough to take with us when we leave this place. There is no question that self-centeredness and goal displacement have a direct relationship to resource scarcity. When you look at statistics across each nation and consider the skewed percentage of nationals who own most of the world's assets, you wonder what would happen if we all were that greedy, but at the same time many people perish or live in abject poverty for lack of vision. The behavior of the two groups is in total opposition. I do not want anyone to have the impression that having a lot of money is a goal in itself; you may possess great material wealth and be very shortsighted, not knowing how to use it for the greatest good of society. It's like having children, and many of them too, with no real plan for them or their future, which by the way was a part of poor people's assets and/or mentality. They would have as many offspring so they could be provided for later on, not realizing that these children themselves may not even be able to care for their own needs if they did not receive a good foundation at the beginning. By that I mean proper nurturing, love, care, and most importantly, a good education. As far as I am concerned it's better to have many goals and many visions (a few short range, a couple of medium range, and a few long term range) throughout life than to have none whatsoever, or else you go nowhere.

You know where you came from, hopefully. If you didn't I would be a bit concerned, because the idea that we all have a past is one of the few absolute concepts which we operate under. In addition, those who forget their past or where they came from may not have a firm ground under their feet and may virtually sink as they try to rise and go forward. Someone eloquently said that "Who have no past, have no future". Which I tend to agree with. Just as today may predict how tomorrow will be, so we make plans and we just act on it, and it may so happen. Let me say this: if a group of people woke up one day and said that they had received revelations or visions from God to sit around and just pray for the rest of their lives, I think that would be very stupid and irresponsible on their part. I have faith just as anybody else who believes in a deity, and I also believe that miracles happen; however, that is the very reason that they call them miracles, they do not occur on a regular basis. And while many of us may experience several of them during our lifetime, it still remains our prerogative and our obligation to use our minds and our talents for the pursuit of our happiness while we live in this life. I used to hear the most ridiculous statement ever that people are poor simply because they sin and do not pray enough. Some of these individuals are so heavenly minded to be any earthly good in the first place. Others have the best of everything that you can possibly find on earth, and yet they encourage their fellow brethren to be content or resign themselves in the present state that they are in. I have great concern for people who say to others, "This is how you ought to live, but as for me, I will have it my way!"

Now, with respect to the past, even though that is a part of history, at least we need it for reference, and the experience too. Secondly, as we focus on the present or where we are now socio-economically, that should enable us to evaluate or assess the distance that we have already traveled and how much farther we need to go and how much effort will take us there; and this goes far beyond economic endeavors. Our relationship to the three periods of time: past and present and future, is an indicator which tells us whether or not we need to refocus, develop new strategies, and find in which direction we need to set our compass as we go through the motions of life. Depending on our goals, our itineraries, and the distance that we are from our destination, we may have to reassess our plans for the remainder of the journey and dispose of additional energy and resources to make the final strokes. <u>All that I am trying to say is that if we reach for the stars, we may not always get there</u>. However, we lose more by not making any effort, and that is not God's fault or Jehovah's or Mohammed's or anyone else's but our own. And who knows, even if we never reached our final destination, but by standing on our feet and taking some responsibilities for ourselves, we certainly will not remain stagnant and overly dependent on others.

I have learned some time ago that the shortest distance between two points or two objects is not always a straight path. You may agree with me on this, but if you don't, I'll just pray for you. The pathway to life itself is often twisted, steep, discouraging. That may mean traveling a longer distance, spending more time, and using assets that you do not have. Nonetheless, that should be no reason for us not to develop our talents and make the best of any situation which we might find ourselves in. Despite what happens, thank God, our efforts will never be all wasted. Behind it all, lies a noble cause.

If you have money in your hand and you do not make a plan on how you wish to use it, you might just waste it. Consequently, you cannot maximize your assets or develop your potential if you don't take time to really think and come up with goals, ambitious ones too. Let me add that no dream can be too high to be materialized. If we do not think that it is mandatory that we eat to stay alive, work so that we can meet our expenses, rest in order to keep our bodies in shape, take showers regularly as personal hygiene requires it, do our laundry so that we do not smell nasty, and sleep so we may be re-energized, then we might never see the necessity to set goals either. In which case, we may sit in the pit till Jesus returns or until the time comes for us to die. However, granted that we all try to sustain ourselves by caring for ourselves daily means that we want to be here a bit longer. And as we continue to be, we must make plans for our future, despite the odds. Life is like a race, and sometimes it gets very harsh and complicated. Nonetheless, we must go forward, and no one can really set you free if you do not have eagerness to become free. Reaching your potentials means more power to you, more personal freedom to decide for yourself and live life to its fullest.

B. Rising Up Beyond Your Fear

As you are well aware, it seems as though those of us who survive the calamities of life all the way beyond our 18th or 21st birthday tend to be problem solving-experts. If we live this long we just cannot afford to let our problems overcome us. Somehow, we must rise beyond them. We can be anything, if we would believe in our potential and take actions that promote us.

I have a very dear friend who is afraid of dogs. Just by hearing the animal barking, her legs start clicking. By the time she sees the actual dog, she has already urinated in her underwear and her heart is about to come out of her mouth. I'll make sure that she reads this book and try to encourage her to expose herself more often to the animal that she fears. I should be ashamed telling you that there is a particular animal of which I am fearful, but my fear is nothing like my friend's. Aside from this, I must not tell you which beast that I am fearful of, otherwise you might want to check me out for that one day. Anyway, how do I overcome my fear whenever I bump into that species?

At first, my impulses increase my anxiety to being fearful, getting me ready for a passionate fight-or-flight response. I want you to know exactly how I personally handle it. My immediate reaction is usually to take a few steps away from my source of fear or from the animal. Then, within that distance, I decide whether I want to fight (attack) the organism or flee the scene altogether. I often end up chasing it until I kill it or until I cause it to disappear. Also, by multiple exposure to the animal, I become desensitized or less frightened. That is a method used in psychology to help people overcome fear.

Now, based on the above story, you will tell me that this is different from having fear over not being able to make your next car payment or meet your mortgage or the rent for your apartment, and I could not agree more with you! Nonetheless, the worst that you could do is sit there and keep saying over and over how in the world am I going to meet those expenses! Fear has a way of making us feel powerless, hopeless. It also serves the purpose of keeping us in a resigned mode. This is a venom (poison) against any kind of move toward personal growth. It represents a potent cause of underachievement and poverty. Another determining factor that keeps people from improving their lives has to do with a lack of determination. What happens is that oftentimes many of them will dream or make plans but never follow through with them. In addition, some people seem to be inhibited and/or intimidated by the kind of environment that they grow in, and therefore, they are never able to make decisions on their own. They often look for someone like a mother or a father figure to initiate things for them or they desperately search for the approval of others. If they never get that help, they feel that they must be doing something wrong, ignoring the fact that not everybody will provide the necessary support that they would hope for. We discover several key issues why people do not excel in life or reach their potential. The most common ones include:

-lack of discipline
-eagerness for the approval of others
-the absence of motivation
-low self-esteem
-no guidance
-lack of persistency and perseverance
-lack of vision to see beyond the visible realm
-no sense of priority
-lack of self-confidence
-fear of failure

These are odds that we must all fight and overcome as we look to live a more complete and productive life.

It looks so familiar to many of us to take things for granted that quality time which is often required to fight the odds. We encounter obstacles in all shapes and forms. However, I cannot overemphasize the fact that, as long as we keep living, problems and obstacles will always emerge around us. Obviously, we only solve a set of problems to get ready to face the next set. Some of us just do not want to meet greater challenges in our lives. Others are willing to step forward and take a risk but need an environment that is suitable, which may not come until the end.

Freedom
From Fear to There

There is one thing that I would like to assure you, and that is learning to fly with your own wings. That may prove to be an extremely difficult process; however, there exists no other way. The parent birds will train their young ones only to a point and after that they must develop their own technique of flying. Similarly, for us humans, somebody somewhere may decide one day to give us a lift under his/her wings, but that someone may sooner or later want to use his or her wings to assist another person, or may no longer feel that appropriateness and withdraws his or her support. Sometimes, it is more costly to us trying to fly under other people's wings. I can find so many reasons why that every human being needs to develop their own skills and abilities. I am not saying that one must be skeptical or resent any offer or help that might be extended to him or her. There are but a few genuine individuals out there who really offer their assistance unconditionally or who want to help without ulterior motives. However, until they prove themselves with time, you have no way of knowing that. Therefore, the key word is to try as hard as you can so you may be dependent as little as possible.

Focusing on the problems, yes, you ought to do it. The message here is not that you turn away from your obstacles and forget that they exist. Oh, no! Actually, we all have them, and they constitute part of our excess baggage, but we must learn to sort them out and figure out how to carry them along. There was a family of four, a husband and a wife and two children, and they possessed a small boat. One day, it became necessary for them to cross over to the other side of a river. Now, the problem was that the two adults weighed 100 pounds (lbs.) each and the two children 50 lbs. each. The boat itself could only carry a 100 pound cargo at a time. What was the family to do, sit around and cry over the boat? That's definitely one of their options, a dumb one, but nonetheless, it was one among the many choices. Another one would be to forget about crossing the river altogether. Still another one would be for any one member of the family who knew how to swim to try to cross and let someone else take the vessel across the river. None of these options were selected. They could also ignore the physical law which restrained all four from getting into the boat at once, in which case, they would attempt to overload the small vessel and sink with it.

If you have not done so, at this time, we would like for you to start thinking about how this family of four actually resolved their dilemma. I do not know how many of you who are reading this book have an analytical mind which would enable you to take a particular problem or a part of it and then try to derive a solution (s), passing through varied steps. Sometimes that helps, other times we are not aware of the appropriate steps to take and we just jump over the problem, and what happens occasionally is that we become over-whelmed and get bogged down and finally we give up. Trial and error is a method that we all use at one time or another. So do not be overly concerned with a particular problem that may not lend itself to an easy answer. If you find that the best way is to keep trying, make sure that you learn something each time you try; otherwise, it will be a déjà-vu all over.

Now, the <u>first step</u> the family took was identifying the problem; and may I say that this is the foremost step. If we do not recognize that there are problems, then there is no way we can possibly look for solutions. <u>Step two</u>, they (family members) tried to find out whether there was a similar problem that some other people might have encountered and found a solution for (that is, a little research), and found no readily available solution. They had to come up with their own. Thus, they proceeded to <u>step three</u>, maybe for this particular situation, it might not have been applicable that they dissect the problem in bits and pieces to see how to solve it, which could lead them to cutting up their only boat, their only hope to cross the river. It was small but that is what they had and must use. Then the <u>fourth step</u>, they started raising hypotheses or coming up with questions; what if we do this or that? <u>Step five</u>, they gathered all the facts they humanly could, regarding solving this problem and moved on to the next step, which is <u>step six</u>. At that point, they did a little test to see if one of their hypotheses would work. They walked through it.

With a little arithmetic, they were now ready to take the ultimate step in solving their problem. <u>Step Seven</u>, they decided that the two children would cross first. Upon their arrival on the other side of the river, one of them would stay, the other child would bring the little boat back. When he reached where the parents were, he came out and one of the two parents took the boat alone and crossed. As he got

216

there, he came off and gave the boat to the child who was already there to take back and carry that other sibling ashore. Now, as you can see, at that point, one half (½) of their problem was solved: one parent and the two children have crossed and that is three round trips. Then one of the kids took the boat back to the other parent and stayed there, waiting to be picked up. As the second parent arrived, he passed the boat back to the other kid who went back to the starting trip to meet his sibling and the two made the final trip. So, it took them four (4) round trips and a one way just to get all four of them to the other shore. A great deal of resources: time, and energy just to cross the river. Perhaps, they did not have the money to rent a larger vessel or friends who could lend them a much bigger boat. To every problem there is at least one solution. Sometimes, the amount of patience it requires just to solve one problem is just enough hassle to make one call it quits. However, these people would never make it on that trip, granted the amount of effort they had to deploy. So my admonition to you is <u>don't quit</u>. Use your head (the gray matter), use your skills. Now one of the things that people go through as they try to solve problems is to start over <u>step four</u> all the way to <u>step seven</u>. That usually happens if what they thought would work failed; even then I recommend that you explore all your options, I mean all your legitimate, feasible options. Be determined, and best of luck and may your God carry you through.

C. We Are All Athletes In Our Own Special Way

"Be not discouraged. There is a future for you...The resistance encountered now predicates hope...Only as we rise...do we encounter opposition" (Frederick Douglass, 1892).

The life of an athlete is not fulfilled until he or she wins the prize. However, a lot of groundwork must take place prior to the contest. Also, an undeniable fact for any one contestant who engages in a race is that one must believe that he/she can win and then search for opportunities instead of focusing on the obstacles in the field. As Shelby Steele stated, "Opportunity follows struggle. It follows effort. It follows hard work. It does not come before."

It is true that all athletes go to a race to win prizes, but not all of them generate the enthusiasm, the discipline, the motivation, or undergo the training required to succeed. Note that any athlete who makes it to the top will admit that his or her victory did not incidentally happen on the day that the championship was played. The winners have already won way in advance. They do so by going through constant practice, by imposing rigorous discipline on themselves, and through time management. In fact, Dr. Richard M. Suinn, a sports medicine physician, describes seven different steps that an athlete needs to take before he or she can be competitive enough to win. These are:

> -Relaxation training
> -Stress management
> -Positive thought control
> -Self-regulation, which I call self-discipline
> -Mental rehearsal
> -Concentration, which I term
> -Persistence, and
> -Energy control

Just as an athlete, we need to know how and when to relax. Our body can only tolerate so much tension, and we perform better when we rest our body and treat it right. Stress management will be discussed in subsequent chapters. Positive thought control: not only do we need a positive attitude in life but we also have to see ourselves as competent and as capable as anybody else. So many studies have shown how important it is for us to have a positive self-image and high esteem of ourselves. Discipline is one of the most important characteristics of any successful person. Kids need it to succeed in their schoolwork and we all need to succeed in our endeavors if we want to make any significant contribution in life. Mental rehearsal is a kind of training that focuses on playing the same message to our mind over and over again. Repetition brings familiarity. How many of us learn to concentrate? If we cannot do that and set our minds on a distinct subject for any specific length of time, we probably won't attain various goals that require mind work or constant thinking.

Concentration is linked or related to self-motivation and makes it possible for us to stick to a goal long enough until we bring it to term. And then <u>Energy Control</u> is an important aspect of resource management. To get anywhere in life, we need to have some form of energy or resource. If we waste it, then it may not be available to us when we need it.

Just as it is not easy to be a successful athlete, we cannot rise to our potential without committing ourselves. And it is not somebody else but our own responsibility that we make the best of our life by using and developing our talents and using them and our time wisely. Above all, we must also realize that a life of continuous dependency simply reduces us to a lesser human. That is why I believe in learning and teaching how to catch one's own fish. When you can catch your own fish, no one can tell you how much and when you are supposed to eat. This may seem arrogant, but so be it. I'd rather be arrogant and independent instead of being polite under the rein of humiliation. Too often we trade our dignity for a piece of pie or for peanuts. The human race should not despise us because of our position in life, which we have the power to influence and improve. As far as I am concerned, we are not born geniuses, we become them by making the best of our talents and our time. And it is never too late to set goals for ourselves. Realistically, some of them may not be obtainable at certain times in our lives, but not to have any is just as diminishing and humiliating.

I urge you to reassess your life and set goals that you are going to work on just now in order to experience the fullness of life. Remember, as long as you remain in the cocoon, you will never know the joy of laying out on the beautiful flowers. Moreover, as long as you rely on the umbilical cord to survive, you will only grow to reach the size of the placenta. To everything, there is a season. We must be grateful to the cord, but when the time comes for us to move on, we should generously choose to detach ourselves. Our socio-economic future is in our hands, and the way we live and the choices we make will greatly determine our individual freedom. The morning is still young, just seize the opportunity at once. Your pursuits may not always bring the highest anticipated reward; however, regardless, it is worth the effort.   Otherwise, you cannot but blame yourselves for not achieving any dream that you might have conceived.

❖ CHAPTER XV ❖

"...If You Run You Might, Otherwise..."

As you turn to this chapter, please do not get too aggravated, excited or depressed if exercising is against your principles. I am simply using the term "running" as one of my own athletic activities to illustrate some important concepts or ideas. I promise that I will not make you run. I might, however, get you warmed up just for that; then, at the end of this section, you may find yourself in the best shape to run the race on your own without being dragged by someone or by circumstances.

Note, if you have had difficulty jogging in the past or you feel out of shape, seek your physician's advice before signing up with us for this PE201 (Physical Education) class.

However, if you can or choose to sign up with us, we appreciate your business. It will be good for your psycho-social well-being. Just like anyone who is interested in becoming a professional athlete and who wants to remain competitive, he or she needs practice, discipline, motivation, and a sense of pride, direction and dignity if he or she is to win. Life is as a race, and it demands that you throw away any crutches: drugs, hopelessness, feelings of inadequacy, welfare program, excuses, cultures that promote socio-economic dependency over self-sufficiency, and any religion that advocates resignation which you might have relied on to help you move around. Those are the very devices that kept you back all these years so that you would not reach your potential.

Among other athletic activities, running is considered a sport, and many people engage in it as a career or simply as a form of gymnastics to shape up or maintain their physical fitness. Overall, almost everybody has at least tried to run at one time or another in their lifetime. Those individuals who wish to become professional athletes in it or in any other sport, as far as we are concerned, must undergo rigorous training. They aim at doing well during practice and perform at their best in all eventual competitions, hoping to win the prize.

Others run just for recreational purposes. Still others do so by necessity, as in the case of "Fight or flight", a concept in biology which literally means that any animal, including humans, when threatened by some obstacles tend to fight back or run away. However, whichever category of runner you fall under, you have your own set of experiences and your own ways of perceiving and describing them.

I agree with you thus far, you may need to set your own pace in life, for we are all different in who we are by virtue of personality and individual exposure to the physical environment. Therefore, it is normal for each of us to visualize and conceptualize things in life somewhat differently. Nonetheless, whatever your rationale or your personal opinion, life is what you make of it. As much as possible, as much as it depends on your own personal efforts, you should strive to see the end product of your project and don't just throw your dreams out the window. Set and prioritize your goals and apply yourself to win the final race by keeping your eyes focused on the prize rather than on the obstacles. Having said that, may I add that no victory is forever final in life. Your partial success simply prepares you for the next level fight. Professional athletes know very well that successful completion of one race does not mean automatic victory in subsequent races. In fact, they must continue with their training and whenever necessary change or modify their strategies to some extent to fit or accommodate the actual set of events or circumstances. Remember that we are talking about LIFE being a RACE, and if you do not see it that way now, we do not blame or condemn you except that we fear you might realize that too late.

Taken right from Dr. Richard M. Suinn: "We all differ in what we need, and...Exercise and fitness have taken their rightful place in today's society. There is nothing that compares with the satisfaction of such activities and of knowing that health benefits will also occur". Equally, for almost all of us, (with the exception of a few unusual individuals whose lives shine thereby turning them into bright circumstantial stars without much effort on their part), socio-economic and spiritual (intellectual) benefits and gratification do not come as a giveaway but because of our own diligence, self-determination, self-imposed discipline, and great sacrifices despite our professional pursuit.

Let us go back to unveil an important concept of Dr. Suinn's writing, as he sees all successful people or athletes. He describes seven steps which he believes will peak the performance of a career athlete, and they are: relaxation, stress management, positive thought control, self-regulation (or self-discipline), mental rehearsal, concentration, and energy control (or resource management) (pp.1-5).

For a moment, let us think of any kind of accomplishment that we made in our lives and which did NOT require at least one or a few of these steps we just mentioned above. Did you come up with any? I did not.

Then, you may agree with me that life, in general, may be considered as a race, and by way of repetition, a competitive one. Whatever you wish to accomplish: either dreams, goals, or to simply find a reason why you are here, will require some level of commitment, an understanding and the application of the following steps, which I consider the **ABC's** of social, intellectual, spiritual, and economic growth and development of individuals and communities as well:

- Self-motivation - Know what you want and go after it. Don't sit and wait. Miracles do happen, however, each of us may not get more than one during our lifetime.
- Time to plan and make things happen - Set a timetable for yourself.
- Discipline - You cannot be but in one place at any given time.
- Balance in your life so as to keep your stress level low - work, play, laugh, and meditate.
- Self-awareness - Have a positive self-image.
- Participation - Where do you belong? How are your efforts remembered?
- Self-evaluation - Do this before setting the goal, during the implementation process and at the completion. You need to know your strengths and the

resources that you now have or that you can tap into.
- Some prioritizing - Do first things first.
- Wisdom to seek professional advice whenever necessary.
- Ability to accept the criticism of others. We don't know it all.
- Control of the social pressure - Don't give in to immediate gratification.
- Patience
- Objectivity - It's not always accurate, but it is a great instrument to have.
- Self Sustenance - Aim for independency and not total dependence.

To quote Dr. Suinn one last time: "Mind games don't win events for you..." Put in another context, it means that if you want to appease or satisfy your hunger, you cannot indefinitely play tricks with your mind, hoping that your belly will be filled with food by just thinking about it (without actually feeding yourself). Taken a step further, you cannot experience healthy body and mind and spirit if you do not maintain healthy habits. Maintaining a healthy life-style means that you not only believe in good health but also you find ways to develop practical plans that will keep you healthy.

By the same token, personal growth, whichever way you look at it—psychologically, emotionally, socio-economically, physically (to a great extent), or spiritually requires your own personal efforts and undertaking. President Nelson Mandela of South Africa would have never been elevated to the highest office of that country if he did not have the charisma to first conceive the dream and second, to believe that he could achieve it. Thirdly, he prioritized his goals and perhaps came up with three different categories: short range, medium range, and long range, which I assume he further classified in the order of urgency or significance. Fourth, he must have developed specific objectives (strategies) and identified resources including support necessary to get there. Ultimately, he set his mind and concentrated towards seeing them materialized. It is that simple. Do you want to accomplish anything in life? Do you wish to move forward? Then, set your goals and priorities, and work towards realizing them.

It might have been a wonderful realization if you and I could simply twinkle our eyes or just open our mouths and our wishes could be executed. I realize that some of you out there may feel linked to some mystical or supernatural forces that could do just that. While I do not wish to categorically ignore such powers and their existence, you may possess such a force or it possesses you. In either way, you are accountable to yourself before God and society. If you can get things done that way, more power to you. Also, good luck may seem ideal and may even look real to some people but even if such a thing exists, it is absolutely not a practical way of life. And too many people, including the younger generations, set out for cheap shots and aim at immediate gratification. They get their priorities mixed up and their minds distorted, and in the end they have nothing that is worth living for and fighting for. As Rev. Jackson said, "Down with dope and up with hope. I am somebody. If you want to save or protect any human pride/dignity and experience the fullness of life, you must live responsibly and you definitely have to set up goals and boundaries."

Besides God's providence, if you believe in Him, your own personal input is the most important in shaping your life and making it a success, whichever way you describe success. Even if someone were so generous to deny himself or herself to be with you 99.99% of the time in order to see you succeed, you would still be solely responsible for the 0.01 percent of the time. And other than Christ, the <u>Great Master</u> who unconditionally gave himself, I do not know anybody who claims to love his or her fellow humans so much to the point of denying self for their own sake without demanding anything in return. Now, I am not referring to family settings where this kind of sacrificial living might make sense.

If you are still in possession of all your physical and mental faculties or capacities, it tells me that you have not been abased or reduced to a vegetative stage, a condition which might require constant assistance of another person to care for you. Otherwise your destiny is in your hand, and to be totally dependent on somebody else or allow yourself to become part of a welfare state is dehumanizing. See, some of the attributes of being humans include the capacity to freely move or to change location without the aid of another person. Another such attribute is freedom of choice. A third one is the intellect or the capacity to think rationally. With these three characteristics at our disposal, we are well on our way to caring for ourselves. At times, we may all require a helping hand, but overall, we have the capacity to become self-sufficient. That is the reason that no victory is ever final but to keep on living literally means constant effort. Just as we say in English, "Keep on keeping on". Success does not come automatically. Even though that is the reality or the fate of the majority of people in our society, but life was not meant to be mere survivorship. The fact is that so few of us actually believe in ourselves and are determined or willing to pay the price to change things around.

Sadly enough, many people started on the right foot in life but for some reason shortchanged themselves. They become overwhelmed, and get discouraged or sidetracked by the events that are constantly happening around them. Let us think about it for a moment, at any given time, there are more obstacles taking place in our surroundings than we can actually account for. Therefore, we do not have the luxury of pursuing our dreams in an environment free from distractions and disturbances.

Arthur Godfrey, a US radio host in the 50's and the 60's said, "Even if you are on the right track, you will get run over if you just sit there." For one thing, everything else but you will be moving; therefore, it would be suicidal on your part to sit still. Secondly, many people make the mistake of not following through with their visions and dreams, which is unfortunate because life does not often give us partial credit for our incomplete tasks. Thirdly, by not moving forward you are most likely to deny yourself further opportunities which may lie ahead and that you might unravel simply by reaching higher up. Consequently, you automatically disqualify yourself. Fourthly, by remaining sessile (bound to one place), you prevent access to someone else who could either use the passageway or benefit from your own realization or discovery! Fifthly, life is just too short for us to stay still, wandering around and wasting time and resources. Time well spent is money. And I could go on and on describing reasons why we ought not sit and take life for granted and not even attempt to make something from it, but even that would not be so productive. Furthermore, it would not be the best use of our time and resources.

Because the vast majority of people never move up on the socio-economic ladder or reach higher up in life, we need to address some of the real issues as well as some of the perceived problems associated with that. We could endlessly talk about all the injustices and loopholes in our social system: uneven distribution of wealth, discrimination of whatever kind, selfishness, ignorance, lack of opportunities, etc. And while many individuals before us have addressed the issues and succeeded in bringing some changes, we would not want, however, to spend our resources into fruitless pursuits or exercises. Instead, we are writing this developmental guide to every person out there regardless of who they are, where they live or come from, what they believe in, and what they may look like.

Let us focus on the individual's achievement. I am certain that you will agree with me, just as life proves it, that social progress is not an accidental phenomenon but a process, meaning that we must be constantly nurturing it or continuously working at it. If it happens that you did not work at it one day, then the next day you should increase your effort. Just like an athlete does not succeed unless he/she works hard and applies himself or herself. Therefore, running or moving upward/forward for us is not an option but rather a must or else we will contribute to our own genocide (destruction). A little help/support from friends and loved ones, whenever that is available, can give us an upward push. I am not the one to deny that it can make life somewhat easier for us, but that's not all. Many times, community organizations are encouraged to write proposals requesting funding to develop projects only to find out that they are not qualified or that the assistance given is just a tease. So where does help come from for the poor and the disadvantaged?

We have to take charge of our destiny or we will be on somebody else's roll as destitute. Now, how do we do that? The ABC steps given on a previous page will take us a long way. I wished that you and I took every minute and every moment of our time to think, act, and engage in ways that would elevate us beyond everyday obstacles. As a result, we would become more creative in our imagination and probably more productive. It takes much more energy to pity over the possibility of not making it. Let us just run; let's forget about the likelihood that we might not reach the end of our journey. The thought alone is a self-fulfilling prophecy. In other words, what you expect is what happens. Put bluntly, thinking you may not reach the end is suicidal. Let us concentrate on running the race successfully. Eventually, we will get somewhere or even reach our final destination.

Give yourself a chance; make some sacrifice now and get more for your time, effort, and energy, at the end. Postpone some of the immediate gratification. I am not saying to just live in the future, forgetting life here and now. By the same token, you may short change yourself by simply focusing on the present. My suggestions are to plan your life a little bit better, set priorities for yourself, and be more engaged and focused. As much as possible, flee passivity and a nonchalant attitude.

Next, if it is available and if you are qualified (say you don't have your own source of funding), take a loan to go to business/vocational school or college, learn some trades and acquire a few more skills. If for whatever reason a loan is not available to you, then find the cheapest ways you can get an education and sharpen some of the skills that you already have so you may maximize your job options, thereby making yourself more marketable and more industrious. **The worst that could happen to any of us is not so much being overqualified for a job but the challenge of not being qualified for anything**.

For that matter, we have been, throughout this chapter, comparing life in general to that of an athlete. Because being an athlete, and remaining competitive in one's own field requires continuous effort, we are all athletes in our own special way. During the 1996 US Presidential election, I remember that some of the democratic contenders said that they would seek to make former Senate Majority Leader and Former Republican Presidential nominee, Senator Robert Dole retire permanently. Too many of us retire before our life even begins. Fortunately most of us can still get on track and run the race successfully. Life is a process and every individual who wishes to improve his or her skills and living conditions can do so by starting here and now. Do not compare yourself to anyone else. There are not any identical human beings like you. You have your own merit and capability. Many people feel inadequate and deploy that timid look on their face as they try to imitate or walk in someone else's shoes. You may become all that you want to be by first tapping into your own resources and your own intrinsic values. I must also add, don't be overly confident or you might fall and be unable to rise. Do not underestimate your potential; you have a lot more in you than you can actually use in your lifetime. Tap into your own resources, and other than to strengthen yourself or give a word of encouragement to somebody, you should resist the temptation of being shut in by other people's great accomplishments and avoid being intimidated by them. Who you are has already been predetermined in the genes of your parents (unless you are a clone), but fortunately what you become is on you.

In addition, networking!!! This is an invaluable commodity that too many of you out there so often overlook and/or underestimate. Have you ever heard the expression, *"It's not what you know but who you know?* I will say though, in many respects, it is just as important, who you know and what you know. Imagine that you and many other applicants are submitting resumes for the same job, which you are all equally qualified for! Besides personal style, presentation, neatness, and tact (which, by the way are not what I consider networking) during the interview, could you think of any factors that would stand out for you and enhance your chance of getting that position over the other candidates? A well-written letter of recommendation from someone that the hiring committee may easily relate to? Your personal encounter with the boss or the person interviewing you, maybe? Many times, jobs are filled not so much on professional merit and technical skills but on interpersonal relationships as well. Hence, you want all the qualifications before you can run a successful race.

In recapitulation, or to go over one last time, Dr. Suinn lays out for us some seven steps necessary to achieve peak performance and I quoted them at the beginning of the chapter for your own personal fulfillment. In a way, I am giving you a shorter version that includes six (6) steps, which you might call the *Eno Mondésir's Principles to Personal Growth and Achievement*:

— First: Start with a goal or goals for yourself. (Hint: not all goals can be achieved here and now.)
— Second: Set your priorities.
— Third: Keep your motivation high and your eyes on the goal.
— Fourth: Discipline yourself.
— Fifth: Be patient. Give yourself time to go through the process.
— Sixth: Prepare yourself to receive appropriate training and if at all possible, keep sharpening your skills.

I would like to focus your attention a bit more on the word 'motivation'. By that I mean to keep your vision alive and to keep your eyes focused on the goal you have set out to accomplish. While you are working towards it, you may experience some level of anxiety at times. You need some of that to keep the flame burning inside of you, hoping that it will not exceed the level of pressure or stress that you can handle.

According to the American Heritage dictionary, to motivate means *to move to action, to impel*. Motivation will help you keep focused on whatever task you aim at accomplishing. Self-discipline is a concept whereby people display behavior patterns consistent with higher and inner human expectations. Self-discipline is almost the same as self-control; it is not only the ability to prioritize or be constantly minded of one's time, but it also involves the use of one's energy and talents (resources) in the most efficient way. You carry yourself in a certain fashion that would not only make others proud of you and respect you, but that would also be self-gratifying in the end. That includes setting priorities and taking steps that lead towards their fulfillment. Appropriate training for the Goal setting. Practice makes perfect, so they say. If you get into the habit of training or setting your mind on higher goals, you may not be able to lift up the world onto your shoulder or change it, but you will definitely succeed in reaching to the stars in the firmament, or you may bring them down to your feet. You will never, ever know what you are capable of until you actually try. I could not agree more with Reverend Jesse Jackson when he says,

"IF YOU RUN, YOU MIGHT WIN, BUT IF YOU DON'T, YOU ARE GUARANTEED TO LOSE".

Sharpening your skills. If there is a time where we really don't need just skills, but proper skills, such time has come. Thirty, forty or fifty years ago, you and I may not know it and perhaps one reason is that we are not old enough. However, we can hear people say that back then, for many positions in the job industry you did not even need a high school degree to be hired. On the contrary, today, not only are we required to have college degree (s) but masters and doctorates if we want decent, prestigious, and relatively good paying jobs which also offer reasonable benefits plus other opportunities. In addition to the academic achievements, it is expected of us to acquire a lifelong experience before we can secure or be considered for these same positions that others could have entered then with minimum preparation skills. The more you can learn, the better it will work to your advantage. You cannot and should not fathom that your current training or skills will take you through the twenty-first (21st) century intact. Much less, you cannot and should not gamble with your life or waste it. It is your life which God gave you, and you are the one to nurture and care for it. If you don't ask yourself why you are in this place, somebody else will assign you a role (whether you like it or not), or they could care less! If you don't take time to define yourself and which directions your life ought to follow, somehow, someone, somewhere will gladly but yet drastically assume that task and affix his/her own price tag on your person.

Run, and you might win! Remember, who ventures nothing gains nothing! This could be interpreted to mean that you are a marathon runner, and it depends on you, how far you wish to run. It may also mean that you are willing to take risks (chances) or make certain decisions for yourself when you don't know for sure what the final outcome will be as is often the case in life's pursuits. Bear in mind

231

that only those who make it the farthest possible distance receive <u>the medal of honor</u>. I am not saying that you will be appropriately rewarded or compensated by your peers every time you make an accomplishment in life. In fact, you may never see it and you should not expect that either. While scores of people who make contributions (great or small) to society but have not been credited, rightly so for those in minority groups especially, the self-satisfaction, realizing that they did something for themselves and humankind, makes their lives worth living. That is a major difference between living a passive life or one that is very engaged, creative, and fulfilling.

My heart aches when I see so many young people fooling around (hanging) on the streets and messing up around the neighborhood, wasting their time and talents. Something is definitely wrong in our society, and there is an absence of leadership and authority or a lack thereof. Not only are these individuals destroying their own lives but they are causing problems for other folks and tearing down the environment. They have no sense of accomplishment and of course no ambition to postpone gratification until later. By delaying immediate gratification, they might not be able to drive the top notch or the ideal car now, however, when they have acquired the necessary skills, not only will they be able to do so, but they will have the privilege of developing and keeping sufficient resources to change that car for the latest and best model as deemed appropriate. Time is of the essence, and the minute we are born we start getting old; plus there is no rewinding of the clock for neither *women nor men* (neither genders nor even the others in between). Time well-spent is worth a lot, and there is a time for everything under heaven: a time to conceive or be conceived, a time to be born, a time to love and be loved (if one isn't under or over age, obviously) and a time to refrain from such love, a time to rest and a time to labor and make good use of one's talents, a time to grow and a time to die. A time to sow or invest and a time to reap what was sown or invested. There is no question about that. Sometimes one doesn't even seem to be rewarded for one's labor. Can one imagine just sitting around and not really working at anything, or how can anyone expect to reap without first investing?

This constitutes one of the greatest challenges of our time. Too many people do not learn or bother to learn when to invest and when to reap. Perhaps up until now, they have never been told of the fundamental differences between a producer and a consumer or between lifelong investment and quick fix, which I consider a tentative or temporary solution to a problem or a crisis, but that requires continuous and assiduous work or until the situation has changed for the better. An example of a quick fix would be getting you a job mopping the floor, which of course will put a little bit of food on the table while you acquire more needed skills for more sustainable work. Also, sometimes some people plant or try to harvest in the wrong season (at the wrong time). Not to mention the fact that many have tried to reap where they had not sown or collect that which they have not labored for, but this is another area that we discuss in another section of this book. Nonetheless, we all need a lesson on how to plan our future strategically and live a life that is more efficient. We also do not want to wear ourselves out in the process. Therefore, take time to enjoy your life's achievement as you go forward.

Another concept that is worth mentioning here is that life is a road, a two-way street shared by all <u>marathoners</u> or drivers so to speak. Sometimes, selfishness and ignorance may prevent us from extending a courteous gesture to the next runner or driver as he or she sways through life's journeys in an attempt to reach the mark. I talk about running and running more strategically, just a simple physics rule for your personal good. Two bodies cannot occupy the exact same space at the same time. This implies that as a runner or a driver, you may not willingly want to let someone else take a turn before you. However, that could work to your best advantage to consider it. As often taught, we are competitors and the only way you and I can succeed in life is by bringing the person next to us down or by blocking his or her access. That is the individualism and an archaic notion, but what we oftentimes fail to remember is that we live and function better in communities. We cohabit the earth, meaning we share the resources, and we are co-facilitators of whatever common goal we may be able to achieve together. Consequently, we don't always have to chase the other fellow away just like dogs behave when they eat and another dog comes along.

In your own endeavors sometimes, you may feel like slowing down; that's normal and legitimate. You may even consider running at a pace which does not correspond to anyone else. Nonetheless, the worst that you could do, which is also a disservice not only to you but to the entire human race, is choosing not to run at all! You might as well be dead if you carry yourself like a disabled body just taking up space! Stagnation is not a way to live, and it brings a soul much faster to its grave. I understand that stability may be your concern, as it is mine; however, living a successful life requires a lot of gymnastics and wisdom. We cannot afford not to run, and we might even win if we do run. You have everything lined up for you to stand on your feet and get in the race, if you are not a vegetable. It's about time that you start doing something constructive with your life. Consider the contents of this book as a mentor and a coach to help you through. There is no time for more complaints. And other than you, who ever pays attention to them anyway?

❖ CHAPTER XVI ❖

Living is a Risk.
You Might as Well Take One!

Every human being has the capacity to give and receive love and affection. The extent to which each of us responds to such feelings may have a great deal to do with the process of socialization and culture. For example, you may want to feel physically close to someone you love all the time, or you may like to express your emotions in a certain way as a result of your upbringing and based upon your own personal beliefs and instincts also (we cannot forget that). However, the point to the matter is, we all feel attracted to someone at some point in time. Adam experienced such strong impulses for Eve that he could not contain himself and said, "This is flesh of my flesh and bone of my bones" (as it relates to the Biblical accounts found in the book of Genesis, Chapter 2). Some of us go even further to say to the person that we feel attracted to, "I will climb the highest mountain and walk through the deepest valley for you, given that it does not rain at the time"! What you and I often do not realize is that there exists a direct relationship between love and risks, the very act of turning over the key to your heart to someone that you barely know. I am sure that there are many reasons why we do not always think of it, one of which is vibration. During the encounter with that person, the heart beats stronger and stronger, then it becomes almost uncontrollable.

For one thing, in our perception, we might be led to believe that we can win the other person's heart. If and only reason allowed us to be so naive, then we could go through life with the idea that we can always walk up to someone and say, "I love you" and expect that person to reply in the affirmative, "I love you too". Unfortunately, some of us have found out the hard way. Experience tells us that while we express our love and sentiments to another person, there are risks involved. The same feelings do not always reciprocate themselves in the other person's heart. In turn, we may feel hurt or rejected. That is a great challenge to all of us or a risk to those who ever walked down the aisle and made the love confession, but we keep doing it. Strangely enough, we can't live with them and we cannot live without them; that's just another paradox of life.

While we cannot be all romantic about taking risks, every day brings its new set of challenges. And if we do not want to be consumed by the day-to-day events or circumstances, we have to choose and take action (s) in order to diffuse those challenges which may mean taking risks. Having said this, we might add that the fact of not choosing is already a choice in itself. Therefore, do not be fooled! For example, in election time, when people are running for public office, you may disagree with the stands of many candidates on many issues. You are entitled to have your opinion, absolutely. However, when you choose not to vote for whatever reason (s), then somebody you do not like and you would never trust with the power to act on your behalf will automatically decide for you by casting a ballot for the wrong individual. Then, we will all live with the consequences, good or bad. Life is hard, and most of us would agree to that, but it proves to be harder when we are forced to live with strenuous circumstances just because we did not make the choices ourselves.

Let me stop here and say that our purpose in this chapter and throughout this book is not to raise your anxiety level any higher than it already has been. Instead, we aim to increase your consciousness and raise your level of awareness on matters relating to your own life. We want to help you explore your environment (the world around you) and find out how you can change adverse conditions in your own life by using your energy, time and effort more positively and more effectively to become more productive. No one else but you have the obligation to make your life a success. Perhaps no one ever told you that, but if you go to the grocery store not knowing what you want, do not expect someone else to know that for you. I am not preaching narcissism, and you do not always have to put yourself first to lead a productive, successful life. In fact, the word of wisdom is not to always put yourself as the number one, or the Mr./Ms. Special. However, besides God, you are the co-facilitator of your own destiny, which you may get tired of hearing me say. Where we are in life is often a result of our own choice and the kind of philosophy or belief that we buy into.

Let me use an expression and ask you the following question. Do you ever get cold feet about anything? Have you ever had an idea or a dream but chose to never follow it through? I can hear your affirmative answer. Indecision, indecision and uncertainty! In fact, some people are great talkers, others are great dreamers that only dream for the sake of dreaming. Others are great imitators. Still others are great spectators. Others are great agitators and intimidators. However, few of us, thank God, are great doers, great leaders, great optimists, who can take ideas and turn them into actions. Then there are the blind followers, and you alone know which category that I just mentioned you fall under.

I accept the fact that we do not always have the right experience to match the situation at hand. Maybe if we did, life might be boring for one thing. This makes life complex and challenging for us, and we always find ourselves at the apprenticeship of some sort. Now the great question is whether we want the experience or not!

Principle # One - No more cheap shots!
Many of us too often like to set for the cheap shots. Instead of taking the risk to endure some hardship and become more refined and equipped for life, we look for immediate gratification and forfeit long term benefits, which is one of the major components of the C.O.P. (the existing Culture of Poverty), and a major setback for young people today. They want things and want them now! A distorted view of reality makes our young people want to gamble with their lives, not realizing the heavy penalty that awaits them ahead. What a great shame of our time! Whether we act wrong or right there are consequences, and the price associated with the wrong kind of action always weighs adversely upon us.

For instance, driving under the influence of alcohol is known to cause problems. Some people decide to take the wheel while intoxicated, not realizing that they not only place their own lives in danger but they run the risk of jeopardizing other people's lives and property. Therefore, this is NOT the kind of risk that I am encouraging anyone to take. When people use illegal drugs, they cause harm to themselves and others. This, too does not reflect the kind of risk that we are talking about. Therefore, try as best you can to avoid such involvement.

Principle # Two - Work on minimizing the costs and be entrepreneurs.

In everything we do, in every action that you and I take, there are risks involved. Thus the question is how do we minimize risks or casualties?

We talk about "calculated risks". By that, we mean making the best possible choice and taking the right course of action (s) after evaluating the pros and cons. It would be a very serious mistake to stick our hand in a burning flame or place our fingers in a very hot pan to see what result we would get, contrary to life's situations and events which we may be often driven into.

Principle # Three - Look where others have failed and take heed!

Sometimes other people who lived before us faced the exact same dilemmas and had to decide right from scratch, and their experience becomes a legacy. Therefore, we do not have to repeat the same mistakes they did. Other times, we have to become our own sacrificial lamb or our own guinea pig. After all, that is what life is all about, unless we decide to remain stagnant. In which case we not only resist changes by keeping the status quo, but also we do not allow ourselves to experience any kind of growth. This ties people to the existing Culture of Poverty (the C.O.P.). Don't be shy, you might be the next inventor whose name will pass on in history.

Principle # Four - Work on your belief system.

Our state of well being and welfare is tampered by our belief system, what we feed our mind on, and of course by the environment in which we live. Some people feed their minds with lies and the notions that they cannot do anything to improve their present conditions. They look around themselves and they can identify with all impossibilities and obstacles. They have a very limited perception about themselves and life in general. They believe that either everything evolving around them was called upon by God and that all is set, or that in their short-sightedness, what is to happen simply will happen by itself. Therefore, they don't have to do a thing to promote themselves. Lies, lies, and more lies. Let's get down to basics. Everything that you want in life you have to go after and create it or else you will never, never, never get it. It's like being hungry and waiting for someone to actually place food in your mouth or put it in your stomach in some strange way. Not that everything can happen at once or will happen in your lifetime; it would be like believing in Santa Claus. However, you can cause many things to happen if you take time to pursue them relentlessly, wholeheartedly, and not halfway or with cold feet! There are limitless possibilities in life. Focus on the opportunities and go after them. There is a difference between chasing them away and going after them, and in most instances, they will not come to you. You have to go to them. And you sit there, thinking that you are the king, they'll come to you. Believe me, you have a very long way to go! I wish that I could be more sympathetic to your current belief.

Principle # Five - Don't make anymore scapegoats; set your own goals and priorities.
Oftentimes we hear people who blame everybody else but themselves for their miseries. They feel that because other people succeed that's why they find themselves in the situation that they are in. We need to set goals. We cannot go through life without even setting some kind of purpose for ourselves.

Principle # Six - Self-accountability
Lack of discipline prevents many of us from reaching high. We must force ourselves to set small tasks for ourselves and give us time to fulfill them.

Principle # Seven - Overcoming lack of self-motivation and determination.
We need to reach within ourselves and into the supreme being (The Higher One) for that sense of power.

Principle # Eight - Overcoming self-defeated prophecy and self-distracted spirit. We usually set ourselves up for failure when we don't believe that we can bring ourselves out of a situation. Moreover, we create our own source of distraction that in turn defeats or destroys our plan. A certain behavior or lifestyle does not lead to personal growth or socio-economic progress. Sometimes we need to be alone with our goals in the dark or the upper room where there is very little interaction between other people and us or things so that new inspiration may unfold.

SOBER is an acronym which stands for Slow On the Bottle and Enjoy the Road, that is if you want to be a responsible or designated driver. So too frivolous, childish, and pleasure-seeking behaviors are not conducive to any kind of significant achievement in life. By assuming the role of responsible individuals, you have to let go of certain manners.

Principle # Nine - Work on improving your self-esteem and bring out your potentials.

Low self-worth represents one of the greatest obstacles to personal growth and higher power. All of us are beautifully and bountifully made (which David, king of Israel, could not comprehend: Psalms 139, v.14) and carry our very unique set of resources.

We can think of countless situations where people put their lives at stake just to see if they might change things around; for when people stand up to address injustice, bigotry, racial discrimination, and the like, they take tough stands. And definitely, not every road that we take in life will make us proud in the end or will necessarily lead to prosperity or personal and socio-economic growth. Oftentimes, just thinking about what we need to do to succeed in life can be torturing.

I remember talking to a friend of mine recently and she quoted her sister in this well stated comment. She was having her first child and as you (ladies) know, labor pains do not resemble anything like making love or like the pleasure of reaching the sexual plateau or the point of having an orgasm. As she was experiencing the pain, her sister said, "That's the way it is, very sweet when going in but painful to come out". I even wonder what thoughts crossed the mind of the first human female species after several months of being pregnant. Perhaps, one such thought might have been, "Gee, amazing! That very smooth and gentle instrument penetrated me and dropped a tiny bomb inside, which I could only feel but not big enough to be seen with my bare (naked) eyes. Now, look at my belly; how in the world am I going to get it out!" You're thinking about risk. I still believe that getting pregnant or bearing a child is a very big one. Besides all other implications (social, emotional, physiological, economical, psychological, moral, etc.), this is another reason why we should not let ourselves be driven by our sexual drives to just get involved in the act without ever thinking of the responsibilities associated with it.

Slightly less but still another significant risk was the first human mission landing on the moon in 1969 by Neil Armstrong. We don't need to shop far at all to discover how risky (fatal) life can be; you can find out how many of us take risks every single day. There is such a thing as foolish risks. We do not want to embarrass ourselves; however, every time we make choices, we expose ourselves to be criticized. In the process, a great number of us try to take calculated risks. And as we grow in maturity and become smarter, hopefully we will weigh our ideas before we decide which bridge to cross and which one to burn. Needless to say that even then, some of our choices lead us to dead end venues thus resulting in heavy penalties or severe consequences to us, our relatives, friends, and to the environment. Therefore, the question is why do we take risks and how much should it be? Instead of answering it for you, let me ask another one, "How big and how important is your dream to you? How brave a soul are you?"

A- Moving From Crisis to Crisis.

From a religious perspective, some people truly believe that life was not meant to be so hard; however, it has become an art that we all try to learn and excel as we go along, doing better than mere survival. And as the psychologist Abraham Maslow explains in his scheme on the Hierarchy of Needs, as long as we live, we will continue to have needs (see figure below)

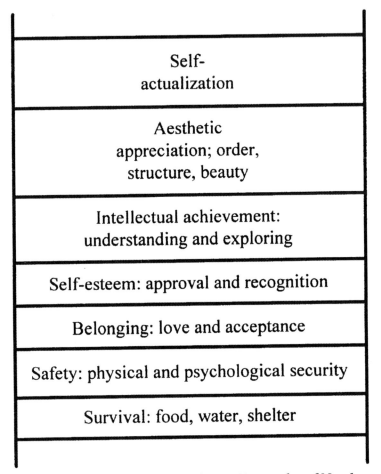

Figure 16.1 *Abraham Maslow's Hierarchy of Needs*

Some of our needs are very basic, for they are essential in keeping us alive. And as we look to satisfying some of them, we often engage in risky behaviors. Furthermore, as free agents, meaning being responsible for our acts and providing for our own needs, we always have to make choices, take risks, and be willing to live with the consequences, whether good or deceptive, encouraging or painful. I should also mention that we do not engage in risk taking activities just for survival purposes (what some people refer to at times as "survival of the fittest"). Some risks are simply to satisfy our egos, make us feel good or give us control over the environment including other human beings. In which case, we would differentiate between the latter and former aspects of needs as wants and needs respectively. All that we need to do to remain alive and function as individuals are in fact needs and everything else that we do to necessarily embellish our social image, advance our selfish gain, and dominate over the environment become or tend to be secondary and therefore satisfy our wants. Truthfully, we can get ourselves into just as much trouble trying to satisfy those wants as we normally would to have our needs met.

Unfortunately, for many people, life no longer brings that enjoyment and satisfaction that they once dreamed of; and it seems as though they keep moving from crisis to crisis, little and big. They never finish solving the same basic problems. Although perception has a lot to do with this, every person knows when there is a crisis at hand. Potentially, we all have the capacity to solve most of our problems except that sometimes we are afraid of doing what is required. Oftentimes, our vision is too narrow, and too limited. It looks as though we put ourselves in a box, thereby preventing ourselves from seeing anything beyond! Additionally, I might say that we do not get anywhere because of our fear of success. As someone put it, "The majority of fears that we have are not life-and-death fears, and yet we give them more power than they deserve and permit them to govern our lives" (Les Brown. Live Your Dreams. William Morrow and Co., Inc. NY., 1992. pp.145-150).

Fears sometimes give us the perception that we are in the middle of a crisis and instead of taking steps to remedy the situation, we become so powerless and the problems deepen and turn so complex. By not getting our feet wet, we live and roll in crises.

Being able to take risks is part of our growing up, and that also means looking for possible answers beyond the usual places. Moreover, as we expand our knowledge and acquire more experiences, we should automatically attain a certain level of maturity which would enable us to face the challenges and come out on top. We oftentimes succumb, give up, or try but do not come out from under. Our social and cultural upbringing as well as our own inadequacy and ignorance may have helped to maintain it that way. Nonetheless, I am telling you right now that you cannot live without taking risks. Parents sometimes teach their children not to take risks. Relatives and friends are excellent people, and had not it been for their support, life would be unbearable, but they too can make us afraid of taking risks, which could be good for our growth. To our demise, sometimes we realize that far too late. Risk taking is a part of human existence and can be quite beneficial when taken wisely and appropriately.

B- Learned Helplessness

That's right! We are trained to become helpless and give up using our minds. We are all good at learning different concepts. Those individuals who excel in engineering are not necessarily good at law. Those who perform well as athletes could very well experience great difficulty mastering a math or a chemistry concept. Equally, people can be trained to become hopeless and resigned. **I was born in this situation, I grew up in it. Therefore, I solemnly declare myself handicapped in solving any of my problems**. We have discovered through psychology that kids who have been taught early on that they are dumb, incapable of learning, and stupid usually accept that as hard fact. Teachers and parents are supposed to know better. So when children turn to them for answers, if the answers they receive make them feel inadequate and incompetent, they could either throw the wrong information out of the window or digest it, which more often than not the latter is what they end up doing. Then, they (kids) become the product of what they consume or what they are taught and grow up believing. I am more than certain that you have heard people say that we are the product of our environment.

It is almost impossible to develop the genius that is in you while you are part of a group, a culture which is so negative and stagnant. It is almost like trying to reap tomatoes from an orange tree. Let us consider this particular case. If you were to catch a fly and place it in a jar, what specific behavior or behaviors would you expect to see it display? Perhaps, if you have never done such observation, you can make it your next project after completing this hands-on experiment with us.

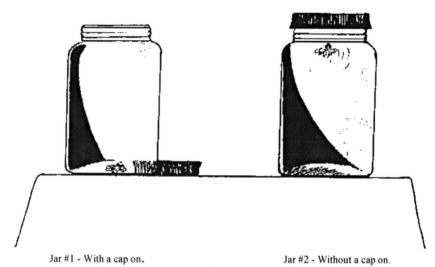

Jar #1 - With a cap on.   Jar #2 - Without a cap on.

Figure 16.2 *Jar of Learned Helplessness*

After we place the fly in Jar #1 we seal it with the cap and let the whole thing rest somewhere. Now notice what is happening in Jar #1. For a pretty good while the fly is going to turn around the top of the container and even hit the cap in an attempt to escape. 20-30 minutes have elapsed, and what happens? The fly is still trying to come out of the jar, and it will probably continue to do so until it becomes tired. Then, it will give up. Now let us see what is taking place in Jar #2. As you can see, there isn't much action going on. The fly is at rest at the very bottom of the jar. If nothing else, the fly has already learned a very damaging lesson. After it has tried unsuccessfully to leave the jar with the cap on and could not, it resigns itself to remain at the bottom of Jar #2 even with the seal being removed. The fly already convinced itself that there is no chance to escape. It has been conditioned to accept adverse situations even though the conditions favor a way out or the boundaries no longer exist!

Learned helplessness! That is the saddest condition to be in! It is like standing still and not being able to move although at some point the conditions were favorable to do so. We might argue that the fly has tried and spent its energy to help itself, and that was some risk taking, and therefore it deserves some credit for trying. I absolutely agree with you. What is sad about the whole situation is that the fly has reached a point of resignation and has given up. No more effort to come out of the jar. Many of us have done just that by not taking risks. Consequently, we never fully experience the beauty of achieving new knowledge and reaching our potentials.

In case you did not know it or someone might not have informed you, people who achieve high and obtain a better share in this life are usually the ones who are willing to take risks. Let us consider, for instance, the idea of believing in God. If you look at it, the very act of believing is a risk in itself. From the start, it compels the adepts to exercise faith which is often hard to prove but you still do, or you believe in your parents and never question whether they truly are believable.

C- Living and Taking a Risk

Whenever you are ready to retire after a day of hard work, you have no way of knowing that you will definitely wake up to see the next day. It is all by faith that you take the risk of going to bed. I hope that you are not paranoid about dying (eschatology) or you will probably sequester yourself in cloister for fear of getting into an accident if you go out. And whether you choose to take risks or not, the consequences can still be harsh. Therefore, you might just take another one. The sad thing about it is that you do not always know the safe passage, nor can you always predict the outcomes. That is a challenge, however, that makes life what it is. Moreover, either way you have a choice to make. For example, you can simply sit there, doing nothing to improve the conditions of your contaminated drinking H_2O (water), wishing the downfall and death of all politicians while you, as an individual or a citizen simply sit there doing nothing constructive to help improve the quality of that water or to change for the better any adverse conditions with which you are faced, be it lack of education, lack of productivity and therefore a lack of buying power.

In conclusion, I know you may be saying that it is deluding to think that you too can aspire to some position where you might influence the decision-making apparatus, meaning those people who influence politics and even decide on the quality of air that you and I will breathe. Nonetheless, any great idea originates in somebody's mind. As Rev. Jesse Jackson says, "If your mind can conceive it, you can accomplish it". You just need some impulses to ignite your motivation and keep the flame burning, for it is the only way I know of to take risks or dream and follow through. Again, it is not always pleasant not to be able to predict the future, but if you wish to get anywhere in life you might have to just accept that fact and work with it. All the big names in human history and all the great accomplishments that the world has known thus far came from men and women who accepted the challenges, worked through the dynamics, sacrificed their lives and the good time they might have had in order to bring a new dimension in the life of humankind.

As I bring this chapter to a close, I would like to reinforce the notion that risks are to be taken. However, not only they may not all be worth your energy and time but also they may lead you astray. In essence, you ought to know the amount of risk that you are willing to take. For example, if you have money and you are looking for ways that you can invest it and get a return, unless you possess some real skills in money management, you will need some expert or professional assistance. Occasionally, when my eyes would catch 'Jeopardy' and 'Wheel of Fortune', I would notice players who bet foolishly. Also, there are others who make calculated moves, and even though they acquire the sum while gambling, if it comes to a question whose answer they are not so sure of, they only invest or bet a portion of their assets. Note that I am not advocating gambling as a way of life. I am simply making an analogy between taking risks and intelligently investing in your fortune. For example, I consider it a far more exceeding risk to take by introducing your body to narcotics or to illegal drugs and alcohol. Such deeds simply bring you down to your knees. Such risks I do not recommend, and to quote Jesse Jackson, "Down with dope, and high with hope". Your situations may be such that you lose all hope and are about to resign yourself to hopelessness. Let me tell you, use the power that you have. To all those who live, there is hope (Eccl. 9:4), and wait till you read the very next chapter.

❖ CHAPTER XVII ❖

The Lesson From a Spider

I am almost certain that at some point in your life, you have used or heard someone else utilize this English idiomatic expression: "To each his own". It sounds just like this one: "Different things (stimuli) arouse different folks".

It goes without saying that many of us won't waste our time dealing with trivial or petty things, using the concept that time well spent is money. From this same vein, sometimes some people look or act so foolishly and so awkward that they make you wonder if there is anything one can possibly learn from them! Now it is not surprising at all to discover that no matter how ridiculous people may be, they attract some folk. After all, let us not forget the notion that birds of a feather flock together. This is how prejudice, and racial and ethnic biases emerge. One individual or a group of individuals did not like some people who look or act differently than they. As a result, they develop hostile behavior and show intolerance toward that particular group.

However, preconceived feelings or ideas toward other members of society are usually baseless. They may be reformulated. That's one reason why if you spend enough time around people you were once uncomfortable with, you might end up liking them and find that they are not as bad as they look or as you once thought.

This idea of opening up to what was once perceived as foreign or bizarre derives from a law called *the law of proximity*. The more time we spend in an environment and the closer we get to it, the more we identify with it and the more uniform it becomes to us. Nonetheless, these two forces exist regardless. One is called repulsive, and the other is called attractive.

Figure 17.1 *The Patience of the spider relieved the desperate fighter*

Oftentimes our own limitations and biases prevent us from seeing the world around us with an open mind. They also keep us from developing an appreciation for things or creatures which may look simple or repulsive to us. However, our best lessons may come from objects, things or people that we place so little value on. What can we learn from a spider? Can it help us in any way to shape our lives?

The spider is a very common species. There exists different kinds (genera) and they are ubiquitous (meaning they're everywhere). And if you study biological science or more specifically entomology (a field that studies just insects), you may develop a much better appreciation for these creatures.

I remember when I was doing my undergraduate studies, I chose biology as my major. At some point, I needed to take a course in ecology (study of the environment and different forms of life interacting within it) to fulfill the school requirements so I could graduate. I signed up for the class. Several times during the semester, I had to go on field trips and collect insects for experiments. It was for the first time in my life that I had such a close contact with some of these species (animals).

Having said that, let me rephrase the earlier question to you personally. Can you learn anything from a spider? In other words, would you allow a spider to be at best a temporary teacher to you? Say yes! Should your answer differ, I will make sure that I bring one such species along for our magnificent exploration so that I may convince you.

Let us get to the core of our discussion. Each battle that we fight and win in life gives us something to rejoice about, and it should also help us acquire new strategies for subsequent battles, since victory is never final in this place (you fight until you die).

Those of you who are familiar with the story of Israel as a nation may be better able to relate to what I am about to say. After all the battles that Israel had won in ancient times, it came a time where the entire nation was on the verge of being defeated. And none of its well-trained warriors could face the enemy. Not only were they at their very low point but also they gave into fear and developed a culture of helplessness. They felt as though it was a lost cause with those giant Philistines. And no one on the Israeli side had the courage to stand up and confront Goliath. All the Israeli soldiers gave into intimidation, not only looking at the height but the whole physical structure of Goliath. He also had a reputation of being an agile man of war. All of his adversaries could easily give up except little David who later became the powerful King of Israel. When we look at it, these Israelis were not alone in their despair. So many times in our lives, you and I face warriors like Goliath and before long if we are not vigilant enough, it may seem as if we run out of options and strategies to launch a successful battle, especially when we allow fear to control our minds and distort our vision from the truth. And if we dare try, the very minute our plan is aborted, we drop our weapon and surrender to the enemy. Moreover, we defect to the enemy's camp where we become prisoners at will for life.

I do not know what Goliath you now face and I do not care how many times you have given up. Gird yourself and put on your motivational garment. You can defeat almost any enemy if you want to: violent temper, addictive behaviors, helplessness, low self-esteem, negativism, procrastination, the existing culture of poverty (the C.O.P.), and any others that have made you their prisoners. Easier said than done? It could be. However, if you feel that you are defeated, then you are. No one can do anything for you. Self-assurance, self-confidence, determination, and persistence are some of several weapons that you and I need to lead and succeed in our warfare. How do you think that Bill Clinton defeated George Bush in the 1992 presidential race; that Jacques Chirac, the actual French President fought Edouard Balladur and all of his other opponents in 1995 and took over the French leadership; that Nelson Mandela survived the odds that he had against him to fight apartheid and become the first Black South African president.

Life is made up of little wars, both internal and external. Internally, many times, we are at war with ourselves. Wars that we create in our concept of things, in our ideology versus reality, in our needs versus wants, from our belief system versus life's forces. To be successful, we have to first overcome all these internal conflicts, uncertainty, and wars. Externally, destabilizing forces outside ourselves so often demoralize us, thereby contributing to our misfortune and influence how we go about caring for ourselves and our loved ones. These forces are greed, injustice, lack of access to the social welfare and existing resources, lack of buying power, poor family background, limited skills, etc. It is just as important to overcome the external forces as it is to conquer the internal ones if we really want to bring out the best of ourselves. I am not encouraging you to become another fanatic of religion, but you may find it a comforting idea to focus on your Creator or God and reconcile with Him as you try to make your way in this world. Now, let's move on.

I hope that by now you are all fired up; the spider is closer than ever. Be not afraid, it is not a dangerous one. Even if it were, I would not let it hurt you, especially you, my honored guest. We are talking about a relatively small and often neglected insect but a great teacher in practice.

During my childhood, I was led to read the story of a man who received a fascinating lesson on self- determination from a spider. They called that man Robert Bruce. And his latest conquest remains engraved in my memory, and I wish to keep it until I die.

Robert Bruce learned a lesson from a spider and that changed his entire life. He used that experience as a milestone to revolutionize his thinking, his belief system, and hence his entire existence. See, Bob had been at war for quite some time. And to his disappointment, lately none of his battles had ended in his favor. In life, we can face a single war, just as we may encounter several ones simultaneously. However, in each war several battles may develop. What we hope though is not so much to win so many battles and lose the war at the end. Eventually, we must all learn this lesson. Planning is critical if we want to win any of the wars of life. We also need to realize that no one will fight for us or stand at our side until we decide what we want and be willing to make some commitment ourselves. After all, why should anyone follow us if we don't even know where we are going? I know that I wouldn't, would you?

I am not implying that Robert Bruce was the kind of person who entered those war (s) carelessly or that he was not committed or did not know where he was heading. Maybe he needed to learn it the hard way like many of us. He accentuated his winning, but somehow, was prevented from doing just that, and it became a real challenge for him. Like many of us, at one point Bruce simply reacted to crises but never took the time to plan his life, reassess his tactics, and develop new strategies. By the way, not all crises have to end up in a war; there exists peaceful ways to solve most if not all of them. However, one factor that we ought to recognize is that when crises are of external origin, the person or persons causing them may decline all pacific means to resolve them. Thus, inevitably you are drawn into war. Now you talk about legitimate war, acting in self-defense, so on and so forth. Let's move on with Bruce's story.

When Bruce first responded to a situation that broke up into a seemingly endless war, he fought a **first** battle and lost it. Nonetheless, he is my type of character, in that he did not give up so easily. He confronted his adversary for a **second** time and lost again. Robert Bruce, or Bob, conducted character research and found that it just did not make any sense to surrender to an enemy that will reduce him to a serf and a captive. He got up a **third** time and went to the battlefield. Again, he did not know what victory smelled like. For a third consecutive time, how many of you out there would say, "The hell with it. There is no way for me to win", and therefore concede victory to the enemy and count your losses? That is probably the last battle you were going to lose. By giving up half way in, you will never smell the fragrance of success. Do not give up. If you must take a pause in order that you may regroup, by all means do so, but keep on keeping on. Keep the fire burning. Do not let anybody or circumstances quench the flame. The victor has many friends, but the loser, on the contrary, is despised by all.

Then what did Bob do? Well, as long as the obstacle existed, he could not find peace; therefore, he had no other alternative but to keep fighting until he could win. By that time, Bob entered and concluded his **fourth** battle in heavy casualties and losses. Nonetheless, he still possessed his mind. That's the bottom line, try not to lose your mind; if it must go, so be it, but let it go last. How many times did Bob have to lose before turning himself in as a POW (Prisoner Of War)? In fact, he never had to, and you too don't have to give in. You are allowed to fail as many times as you need to. You can win as long as you believe in your mind that you can. See, a great flaw in our society is that it calls us to build from success but not from our failure. Neither does it have patience to teach us that life is made of both successes and failures and that one represents the converse (reverse) of the other. Not everybody, or not every team can win at the same time. Today it might be the Patriots' or the Giants' turn and tomorrow it might be the Celtics or the Toronto Blue Jays. We just have to learn how to turn failure around. If everybody hugs you, kisses you, and applauds you only when you win, then you really have no one to count on, for all they can see is your success; and I even question their intent. Listen, you absolutely do not need a bunch of people around you who can elevate you at your high point when you can win. Life is such that none of us will be winners in every field and in every situation; therefore, you definitely want those individuals around you who can cheer you up in times of loss and who can really help build you up for the next time around. As long as you can believe it, you can win.

Again, how many times do you have to lose before giving up? You never have to. Remember, life is a battle; you can't simply give up. I can understand if you are caught in a competition where someone just looks to attribute success to one party and failure to the other, in which case, you are not on your own. For you have been evaluated. Consequently, you might win or lose twenty-five million ($25,000,000) dollars in 89 seconds, just like Mike Tyson. Please note: Number one, not all fights are so short in time and so lucrative. Number two, you do not win your competition while on the stage, you do so while you force yourself to practice for long hours, and weeks and months and years of rigorous discipline and training. If you believe in cheap shots, you might as well become an amateur and bet at random. Then, if such thing as chance exists, you may be the winner some day, and number three, let's face life's reality. Humanly speaking, the reality is: when push comes to shove (as it often occurs), we are all on our own down here; therefore, it requires our individual effort to get somewhere in life or at least the first steps. We may have our parents, friends and loved ones next to us, but there are times where none of them will be there; so we all might learn not just how to defend ourselves but also how to be better stewards of the assets and resources which we have been entrusted with.

May I ask you the question again? Did you know that you could learn so much from a spider? Don't worry, there is more to come. Robert Bruce had the stamina to sustain himself all the way up to his sixth battle which he also lost, unfortunately. Let's face it. All that time, he had been expending energy and perhaps had lost most of his allies or friends by then. He must have felt drained. But remember, I said earlier that it is not over until you say that it is. Bruce became resigned to failure, apathetic to his own cause. After **losing six battles**, it appeared as if he had lost the war. I do not know how many times in your life you have felt deceived. Hold on tight; the worst may be behind you!

Bruce gathered the rest of his ammunition left from the war and went to sit under a tree in a remote area. No money, no friends whose shoulders he could lean on, no wife or girlfriend. Seemingly, the time it took him to fight the war left him with clothes on his back and a perplexed but intact mind.

<u>A sixth time loser is about to turn things around and be named a hero, not because he was a genius but just because of his focus and tenacity</u>. While Bob was resting in a reclined position under the tree, something came up. He was lying down with his face up looking toward heaven (refer to the picture above, if you need to). As time went on, the poor soul noticed that he was not alone and desperate as he once thought. A spider had joined him and he exerted great interest watching the insect (creature). Bruce was about to learn the most significant lesson ever. His eyes remained focused solely on the spider. He watched every move it made. Soon he realized that not just human beings have to put up with battles and wars but apparently every living creature does. Someone may want to call it "survival of the fittest", a scenario which resembles Bob's. Just as he did, the spider got up there six consecutive times and consistently fell off. Meanwhile, Bob's eyes remained on the animal. For the seventh time, the spider tried and succeeded in reaching the web site.

Obviously, the lesson could have been taught to Robert by any other species, however, the spider became the great instructor by which the man learned not to give up and that he too could succeed. Bob arose and returned to the battlefield for a seventh time. With no surprise, he took the offensive this time and conquered the war which made him a warrior. He lost six battles and won the last one which also made him the victor of the war. Isn't that great? Had he given up, he would have never known such success. Someone said one time that those individuals who succeed in life are not the smartest but those who are persistent. It takes determination for anyone to fail six consecutive times and have the nerve or the courage to carry on. That is what this book is all about. Do you believe that you can win the battle which you are involved in now? Why or why not?

❖ CHAPTER XVIII ❖

The Bill Cosby Way:
"Don't Know the Key to Success, But…"

When looking at the life of Mr. Cosby, one would argue that socio-economically he has well succeeded. By all standards, one might conclude that he has financially made it to the top of the ladder, which is in part the definition of success by contemporary ideologists or by capitalistic standards. In fact, there are but very few successful blacks in America, or for that matter a minute number of individuals in any race who are financially secure enough to donate $20 million to charity. And I wish that more affluent people were as generous! At any rate, it is their fortune which they have amassed; they do as they please with it: sleep on it, bathe in it, make friends or enemies with it, or they may even choose to leave a will with special orders to have a coffin big enough so they may take their money to the grave with them. I am not convinced though that this is their right! Perhaps, at the point of death they will realize that "naked they came into this world, naked they will return to the dust. Thus, they may decide to be a bit wiser using the resources of the world."

The point of the matter is that:

Rule #1: We live and make decisions for ourselves, and I partially acknowledge that freedom because we function within an established culture or in a system that pervades some form of social norms and values. These social constructs strongly influence how we might be expected to behave individually or even as an ethnic minority.

Rule #2: to make any kind of advances, we need to use our individual liberty to choose self-determination, or self-awareness and self-assertiveness.

Rule #3: Our individual freedom is being compromised by several factors such as territory or sphere of personal influence, conformity to existing social norms, constraints, or traditions, interdependence, circumstances, natural selection (some of us are more adapted or are born in a milieu that offers more to some and less to others). *Therefore, some of us need to constantly be reminded that as individuals, we do have the power to change our present state; however, we have to push ourselves, which is the reason I am writing this personal letter to each of you out there. Without personal offense to anyone, for too long, some of us either by personal choice or by default have decided to sit on our "Gluteus Maximus" (our rear end), thinking that our conditions will necessarily improve on their own.*

Rule #4: When we do not choose, someone else will be more than happy to make choices on our behalf and tell when to run or to stop, when to work, and when we may rest.

Rule #5: Imitation represents a track that many of us choose to travel on, but creativity which may be a much better road is being inhibited. While we have the freedom to seek and create opportunities, we become so used to being thought for. What happens? As they do the thinking, they take away our freedom.

Rule #6: Freedom is not a license to do as one pleases, for it bears consequences. We should not use our freedom to terrorize our neighbors or destabilize their strength to self-determination. Mutual respect is the vase that holds freedom, without which we perpetuate a villainous society, one filled with predators, and human parasites.

Rule #7: Self confidence! If you do not let yourself become intimidated by the Goliath (see previous chapter), you would not be forever defeated, giving rise to more unscrupulous, ruthless rulers over you! For there is but one master; and if only you care to search out for Him, you will find that your world of opportunities is limitless just as He is omnipotent and omniscient or as small as you portray Him to be, be it God or Jehovah, or whatever other name your culture recognizes.

Having laid out the ground rules, may I say that the purpose of the current chapter is self-awareness or self-identity. Far too often, so many of us live our life passively and we walk in the shadow of somebody else. Until we die, we never know who we truly are and never develop that self-worth!

During the human life cycle, several stages are recognized by researchers. Briefly, we would like to lay them out. It all starts with the menstrual cycle of the woman. Every 28 days or every lunar month, as we know it, women of the reproductive age and who are normal have their period. For those women who regularly menstruate every 28 days, they usually ovulate around 14 days beginning with the first day of the menstrual cycle. Women who are not regulated every 28 days have irregular cycles and can ovulate as early as 9 days or as late as 19 days counting from the first menstruation day. Ovulation refers to the release of a mature egg (ovum) into the uterus (womb). If there is sexual intercourse during or around that period and the man's ejaculates contain trillions of viable sperm cells deposited within the woman's vagina, they will travel toward the fallopian tube and fertilize the egg. Thus the woman will become pregnant. May we add that after ejaculation, the sperm can remain alive and fertile in the female reproductive tract for over 48 hours before disintegrating. Similarly, the ovum can remain alive and fertile for 24 hours which basically means that a woman with a regular 28-day cycle can get pregnant between 12 and 16 days from the first day of her period. In other words, pregnancy may result from sexual intercourse which took place 3 days prior to ovulation or 3 days after (Guyton, A. C. 1985; Villee, CA, et al 1989.) After fertilization has taken place, the stages of human development are technically referred to as:

Stages

1. Zygote
2. Embryo
3. Fetus

4. Neonate
5. Infant

6. Child
7. Adolescent
8. Young adult
9. Middle-age
10. Old Age
   Time Period

Up to 24 hours after fertilization
From 24 hours from fertilization to 8 weeks
From the 9th week till birth or depending on where one starts counting (Villee p.1221). Pregnancy is usually 9 lunar months but may vary from 266 to 280 days
From birth to 4 weeks old
From 4 weeks to two years or until ability to walk is acquired
Two years of age to puberty
Puberty between 9-14 or up to about age 16
End of adolescence to about 40
Between 40 and 65
Age 65 and above, or until death

Table 18.1 Human developmental stages

The above stages represent different biological cycles being identified in human development. There is one form of development that we will escape here. Child development, which is a fascinating field that Swiss psychologist Jean Piaget and many others have contributed to, has little relevance to this particular chapter. However, we will consider the emotional and social (psycho-social) developmental stages of human beings as explained in the theory of Eric Eriksson, a psychologist who specialized in the field of personal and social development. According to Eriksson, we should go through eight (8) different stages during our lifetime:

Relative Age	**Psycho-social Stages**
1. From birth to about 1 year old (Infancy)	The level of trust vs. mistrust
2. From 1 to two years old (Toddler)	Level of autonomy vs. shame and doubt
3. From 2 to about 6 years old (Early childhood)	Level of initiative vs. guilt
4. Between 6-12 years old (Pre-adolescence)	Level of Industrious vs. feelings of inferiority
5. From 13 to about 19 years old (Adolescence)	Level of Identity vs. role confusion
	Level of Intimacy vs. isolation
6. Between 20 and mid 30's	Level of Generativity (creativity) vs. stagnation
7. Mid 30's to middle-age	
8. From middle-age up	Level of Integrity vs. despair

Table 18.2 Psycho-social Development

(References: *Education Psych.* pp. 79-115; *Sociology*: Intro. pp. 105-126; *Social Psych. On Social, Cultural Influences and Confor-mity* by David G. Myers, pp. 164-273.)

As we compare the human developmental stages with their psycho-social corresponding age, we discover an extraordinary amount of information about ourselves. The depth of these stages expand much beyond the scope of our discussion in this book. However, as we talk about self-identity and self-actualizing, most of us will eventually acquire physical development and maturity. It is not so much a problem to physically and chronologically grow from the neonate to old age even though environmental factors such as poor nutrition, lack of caring by other humans, diseases, etc. exist.

Once we are physically fed and nurtured, this kind of growth occurs automatically because the process could also be altered by some genetic factors, natural phenomenon, (internal or external) or early death. Sometimes, we look at people and we argue that they act either more mature or immature for their age. That conclusion is often based upon the psycho-social (emotional, personal, and social) development of the individual. Which leads us to say that self-identity crises persists throughout the lives of many people. Eriksson links identity with adolescence in stage #5, just as he talks about autonomy in stage #2, initiative and industriousness in stages #3 and #4, creativity vs. stagnation and integrity vs. despair in stages #7 and #8.

There are many reasons why people do not attain psycho-social maturity. Sometimes, they evolve in a culture that does not stimulate them to self-actualization but instead encourages total dependency. Other times, the process of socialization deindividualizes people, reducing them to a distinct category with no real identity. In addition, those individuals who suffer traumatic experiences early on or throughout their lives have difficulty adjusting to the next psycho-social stage. Acculturation or people becoming part of a new culture can face inability to cope and adapt. We might also add that too many changes too fast could prevent individual maturity, hence inhibiting self-identity. Other factors which can contribute to an identity crisis have to do with one's perception, creation of one's belief system, fear of growth and resistance to role reversal, role playing, passiveness, and nonchalance.

A great many people never really grow past stage four of the psycho-social development which corresponds to pre-adolescence. The feelings of inferiority and incompetence prevail in them indefinitely. As a result, they either resign themselves to whatever the wind of life may blow their way (God is good. I know that I am His child and He will just take care of me. I don't have to do anything), or they spend their lifetime trying to imitate somebody whose shoes they may never fit.

It is no surprise that Bill Cosby said: **"I don't know the key to success, but the key to failure is trying to please everybody"**. This statement covers one side of the equation. A great number of people don't always deploy their own imagination but rather they look to adapt to whatever social influence dictates. In relation to that, many parents usually want their kids to be something that they themselves could not be or to choose an occupation that will help perpetuate (keep) the family tradition. That may not be wrong in itself but our children may not have the aptitude for that discipline. On the other side of the equation, where people do not develop their identity and potential to become more independent, there are real barriers; however, much of the underdevelopment has to do with personal choice. In many situations in this life, we have the opportunity or the freedom to choose. Whichever way we choose, there are risks or responsibilities involved. And there is no such thing as abstention (not choosing any side). The fact of not choosing is already a choice in itself. When we do not choose, guess what! The choice will be made for us by those who least care about our welfare. For one thing, they do not know us. Secondly, when it comes to the idea of the "survival of the fittest", those who possess the best weapons or who are better equipped will make better strikes and survive longer. Thirdly, if we don't know what we want for ourselves, and we have no incentive and no motivation, why should anybody else? After all, what you look for in life is often what you get, and sometimes even much less.

For instance, if you want to get rich quick or settle for immediate gratification, you go on drugs, prostitution, or you rob people. Or if you are satisfied with working for $4.88 per hour, then you resign yourself to live on that or combine two or three such jobs to make ends meet, then you live from hand to mouth. However, time passes you by and you attain the age where your strength is gone and you can no longer run between jobs. Could you have done better? How you use your freedom and your time now will greatly impact your life later! The more knowledge you gain and skills you learn, the more options you have to choose from.

❖ CHAPTER XIX ❖

Who Stands for Nothing Falls for Anything

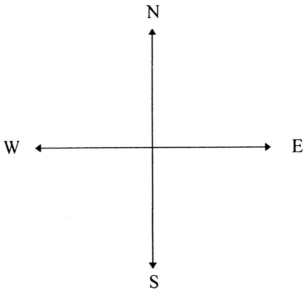

Figure 19.1 *The pole and the wind*

From which direction does the wind blow? And which direction does it follow? Or does it have one? Do you have any? Several years ago, I was told the story of a fellow who left his country for the Bahamas. Upon his arrival, he was warmly greeted by his relatives, who preceded him to the foreign land. These immigrants left their home country in search of better economic opportunities. Therefore, when they reached the Bahamas, their destination land, they looked for a job. It happened that the last gentleman took some time to get himself something to do.

As you know, such phenomenon as people with different cultural backgrounds and language migrating to other parts of the world to look for economic mieux-être (opportunities) is quite common. A similar case has come up here. This guy who just got there spoke no

English and perhaps possessed very limited skills for the jobs that were available. As a result, he had to remain in the house alone while his relatives would go to work. Since he was homebound, he was entrusted the task of cooking for the household. Well, the other folks left for work in the morning. They made it clear to him that they would like to have a feast of pork tail in the evening upon their return from work. Since he did not yet know where to get that product and how to ask for it in the English language, they spontaneously opened an ESL (English as a Second Language) Class 101 just for him so they could teach him how to specifically say "pork tail."

He progressed well in the class and showed signs of an excellent student, needless to say that it did not take him much time to get his certificate on how to say "pork tail". Now, he is ready to become the best chef at least for the day. However, by the time the gentleman arrived to the meat market, his memory had already failed. He just could not remember what the word was in English (by the way, if you read my brief autobiography, you may be wondering by now. I sure was there but it was not me.)

Two problems arose in the gentleman's mind; he could lose his English certificate, and secondly he might lose his chances to be decorated as an outstanding chef. So in order for him to purchase that exact part of the pork, he took a few minutes and shaped himself up into a pig like morphology. How did he do that? Give me a minute and I'll tell you. He simply imagined that he was a pig with a long mouth and tail, and he made sure that he could replicate the exact sound of the actual animal. Then he walked up to one of the employees in the meat area, held his long imaginary mouth with one hand as he pulled his tail with his other hand. In his nasopharynx membrane or pipe (commonly known as throat), he artistically reproduced the sound of a pig going like this: gweh, gweh, gweh, gweh. The worker seemingly understood the man's needs and showed him where the pork tails were located!

How does this story fit into our discussion? See, many people nowadays just take off, go to a mall or any marketplace and start shopping. They do not really know what they want. Some of them even make it a pastime or hobby, spending hours after hours shopping, not having any vivid description in their mind as to what they want. As they walk around, if they happen to find a so-called sale, they may have a need for a certain item and perhaps they have no cash on hand, but they will get it. Some people use plastic money (credit cards) as if they will never have to pay it back, and they end up burying themselves in debts for the rest of their lives.

This gentleman could not use the English language aesthetically or adequately to clearly state what he needed to buy, for that matter no one will deny that he had very limited knowledge. At any rate, he did not settle for second best or any other product that he did not want. Through acoustic signs, he was able to convince somebody and have his need met. Not only did he know in his right mind what he was looking for, but also his determination got him to the proper place, and with some action, he succeeded. In spite of solid education and degrees that you might have (which is extremely important), each of us needs to have: **a) a goal, b) strategies or plans for how to achieve that goal, and c) the need to be persistent.**

In addition, at times every one of us needs guidance and/or direction. Sometimes, in order to carry our dream to completion, it may take someone else to help us focus. Not a baby sitter but someone who has heard, the experience and who is sympathetic to your cause, or else they will not only kill your idea but also you. You are the driving force behind your dreams, and you were not made to constantly fail; it is a matter of when and how you turn failure around. Another analogy, let's see! A car is made to be moved in either the forward or the backward direction. However, since most vehicles which we now have for our daily use are robots, they cannot move by themselves. For that matter, if we wish to make use of the technology, we actually have to sit in the car and do all the thinking for it. You operate the vehicle and tell it (by pressing the button) which direction you want to go, at what speed or how fast to move, when you want to switch lanes, when to slow down, stop and turn, etc. The car has an engine which could be viewed as an analog to a human's brain or mind, but cannot think or make any decisions for itself. Without you, the operator, a car is useless no matter how expensive it may be. You are the one to turn the ignition of that car and start the engine, then you USE this great man-made locomotive to make life easier for yourself. Your life cannot go on successfully without directions.

When you have no focus or goals in life, you just go along with whatever comes your way. Consequently, other people can easily take you for a ride. Picture a car with a driver and someone in the back seat. I am not saying that we use other human beings although it is sometimes the case.

You have a mind of your own, and when you choose to use it, you won't necessarily have to follow other people's agendas <u>ALL</u> the time or let them decide for you in everything, like you never mature to become responsible for yourself. You were made in the image of your creator which gives you the freedom to think for yourself, have rational ideas, freely move around and make decisions that are in your best interest (especially as a mature adult). Moreover, if you can and are willing to contribute to the trip that others wish to take you through, then you will not be a passive or a blind follower like someone who is being assigned a permanent seat in the rear of the bus. They will ask for your input and may even buy your ideas. However, when you do not have any aspiration in life, no goal except to being a dead weight or a homebound body, you just sit there like an amoeba, taking up space in whatever form or shape.

Even the wind has an origin and blows in specific directions. Even so, human beings cannot afford being taken for rides all their lives. That is to say, we are all capable of using our judgment to build initiatives. We have the faculties which, when we tap into them, will enable us to set goals for ourselves and establish priorities. We will be able to make plans and follow through with them. If you look at the picture at the beginning of this chapter, you will notice two lines that are drawn perpendicular. In mathematical language, we would call the vertical line the Y axis, and the horizontal line the X axis and they give rise to form 90 degree angles, also called right angles. However, you need not bother with all that detail for now, and I solemnly promise that I won't trick you. We are simply concerned with the figure as far as direction goes. There are an infinite number of directions that could be drawn, but since we want to keep it simple for everyone (which is different from keeping it simple, stupid or

K.I.S.S.), we only chose four directions which we designate as North (N), South (S), East (E), and West (W).

It is unfortunate that the more we reach higher civilizations, it seems as though we tend to put less and less emphasis on human values (just like the thought which says we use people and love things). We manage to displace our goals and become a more materialistic society. We spend less and less time teaching our kids the proper values and savior-faire. Our level of tolerance for disguise has lowered and we observe a mentality of laissez-faire among the younger generation. Many cannot value their own lives, nor will they value someone else's. They display a passive attitude and show no ambition whatsoever for higher goals. They are willing to do anything to get a buck. That is what happens when people grow up making no goals for themselves. As dogs that follow their master, they tend to follow after people who may not even have their own goals or direction in life. Worse than that, they may feel that this person or that person's idea sounds great and they start chasing them all over. To paraphrase this or put it in a nicer fashion, their personal vision becomes impaired and distorted and they start walking in everyone else's shadow. Today's generation needs more focus on values, goals, and a sense of direction.

Kids, young people, and you adults, you cannot resign yourselves by choosing to stand for nothing. You all possess great many talents. If you take the opportunity to concentrate on making something good of your lives, you will stop choosing the second best in life or falling for anything. Like a young woman who has been brainwashed by socio-cultural taboos, she watched her biological clock spinning and passing her by without a man in her life, then she decides to take a chance with whomever comes her way. Moreover, she comes up with all the right reasons that give her incentive to bend over backwards and get pregnant just for the sake of it or as a strategy to hold on to the man, not having a sense yet where that man is from and where he is heading. Honey, if a man loves you, believes in you, and it is the right timing in his life, he will stay with you. Otherwise, you may become pregnant for every man on earth and still end up without one in your life. Just because the clock is passing, you do not give in to peer pressure. Around 25, you just started life, and if you decide to focus on your potential, you can accomplish great things, then men will want to stay and live with you; you become a woman with real substance, not flesh but a thinking mind. I don't mean to sound paternalistic, after all it is your life but I would suggest that you be more concerned about shaping up your life and sharpening up your brain. These last few words apply to both men and women equally.

Have you ever heard of a concept called delayed gratification? It means that you put certain things on the back burner for a moment. For now is the time to go to school, to acquire basic skills, and to learn a profession, and there is no age limit on the way to do this. Now is the time to focus on your education or to work and save money until you can afford to buy what you want or care for a spouse. That way, you won't give in to the temptation of having all the wrong ideas, selling your body, doing drugs, or attacking other people to possess what they have earned through hard work and sweat. All of us, including kids, need to hear this gospel once in a while.

King Solomon, in his wisdom, made such a remarkable, philosophical and poetic statement about timing. And there is an artist _n_a_m_e_d_ "Ecclesiastes", who arranged the words found from the King's statement into partitions and wrote a song that you might have heard once upon a time. It goes as follows, and you are welcome to sing along: "To everything under the sun, there is a season; a time to be born and a time to die, a time to laugh and a time to weep, a time to sow and a time to reap what is being sown, a time to be a child and a time to become adult with all the rights and privileges apportioned thereto; a time to make plans or have goals, and a time to fulfill them." (Eccl. Ch. 3; verses 1-8)

Every human being has some talent. No one can excel in every domain or discipline, but there is no such thing as non-talented people. If you recall the story of the three stewards and the banker, you remember that the one that was treated as a useless vagabond and who was also thrown in jail by the investor (banker) got such a penalty by being so lazy that he did not even consider using the little amount of money which was disbursed to him. For the complete story, I suggest that you read Saint Matthew 25:15-30.

Are you familiar with the saying, "Whoever does not work should not eat"? In case your memory has failed you, it may sound like a

Republican or Democrat's idea at one time or another. However, it applies to neither one of them. It is found in the second letter of St. Paul to the Thessalonians, Chapter 3 verse 10.

In life, there are duties and privileges or rights and responsibilities. To put that in an eloquent way for the more intellectually challenging mind: for every action there exists an equal or opposite action (Isaac Newton's third law of motion). The central notion or idea that I wish to relate to you here refers to the fact that we, human beings, are exceptional animals. And part of our characteristics or features is the ability to care for and respond to our needs.

While someone may make assumptions about my needs, I alone decisively know what those are if in fact I am in touch with my true self. Seemingly, I cannot be in touch with myself if I do not know what I aim for in life. And just as **the pork tail man** whom I described at the opening of this chapter, even though you might be limited in vocabulary to fully express your feelings and sentiments, aspirations and wants, you still do not have to resign yourself to whatever comes your way. You reap what you invest in life; if you invest nothing then the outcome is nothing. Zero minus zero is still zero (0-0=0). No wonder why so many people do not harvest and perhaps never will.

I am sad to say this, however, even in church we find people who have been brainwashed, thereby becoming conditioned. They have come to develop a particular belief system, in that if they only pray then all their problems will be automatically solved, ignoring that the very God that they try to serve and who called everything into being gave specific instructions to Adam and Eve regarding the use of their time in the garden. Unfortunately in churches or Kingdom Halls or elsewhere, many people are blind followers. They do not know who they worship, much less what is required or expected of them. If we believe in any kind of Supreme Being, God or whatever your own religion calls Him, He also gives intelligence and power to everyone to do greater than any other person has accomplished. We just need to be focused and have a sense of direction and purpose in life.

We cannot afford living day after day without any kind of initiative of our own. A farmer cannot expect to harvest corn if he or she did not sow any seed. How can anyone spend money that they do not have unless they borrow, which they have to pay back, steal and run the risk of being thrown in jail, or sodomize their life to drugs and prostitution and jeopardize their health! Life is necessarily what we make of it. As human beings, our responsibilities began the instant we came apart from the placenta and the umbilical cord (think about taking in O_2). Perhaps many of us grownups believe that we are still being cared for in a womb-type environment. Wrong!

Certainly, we all have a sense of belongingness, either to our family, our community, or our nation, which is fine. Nonetheless, there comes a time where we have to sit and develop our own goals that will not only benefit us as individuals but also as a collective body. If that time never comes, however, by all human standards we are essentially handicapped and therefore useless.

If you never had an agenda of your own and you are never determined to see one materialize, then you resemble a fetus that is being washed in an intoxicated fluid in the woman's womb. Sooner or later you will die; a danger that pregnant women who use narcotics or illegal drugs (including alcohol and smoking) often expose their newborn babies to.

I realize that independent living is hard, however for us not to set short-term goals and long-term goals makes it even harder. Everyone who has been on his/her own for some time, except those who have inherited a fortune, can testify to the hardship of being out here. For that matter, it is imperative for us to continue to have goals as long as we live, no matter how young, how old. Regardless of our race, our nationality, our gender and our religious beliefs, living is a constant battle; and we can make the best of life only by investing our time and energy and by developing our talent along constructive paths.

Special Note: Parents, we need to be firm with our children. We also need to provide them with guidance and leadership, so that they may be able to grow, mature, and assume responsibility for their own lives. Otherwise, they will just give in to whatever they happen to be fed on out there. Sometimes, circumstances of life may not allow both parents to be present under the same roof at all times. However, that should not stop one or the other or both to do their best for their offspring. You do your best, then the rest is up to God and them.

Kids: drugs won't do it! Gangs won't bring you closer to your goals either. Immediate gratification does not always help either. Sometimes, you need to postpone having a new toy, new car, new sneakers, new clothes, etc. Know what you stand for and not what your friends out there want or tell you to stand for. Note that many people are happy when you take up their ways. Identify your own strengths and build on them so you do not become too vulnerable and give into peer pressure and end up practicing deviant behaviors that may cost you more than you ever imagined. Remember, who stands for nothing ends up falling for anything that comes his or her way. Your success in this life depends largely on you, how you live and how you use your time and talents.

❖ CHAPTER XX ❖

Culture of Poverty

It has never been an easy task to try to bring together a group of individuals and sell them all one particular idea. The fact that every person is unique, raised in a different milieu, being exposed to different circumstances and values. Consequently, they are able to formulate their own personal opinions about themselves and life in general. That makes it a challenge quite often for people to tolerate or stand each other and work and live together. However, we all learn or witness how cumbersome it can get, trying to be self-sufficient by working alone all the time or living alone apart from other human beings. It is just not possible.

There are certain activities or tasks that we undertake individually and which may be more rewarding than if we were to share the labor within a group. By the same token, we cannot underestimate the benefits of group efforts. We do not have to collaborate with anyone, but it is better sometimes, if we do. For in so doing, it exposes one person's strong points and his/her shortcomings alike. Conflict of interests may arise as the group looks to create an organization or society where everyone would share similar goals. It takes a lot of discipline and flexibility to actually belong to a fraternity or a social activity. Occasionally, before joining a group, one has to review his or her socio-cultural values. What one does not want to do is to live in contradiction with one's beliefs for the rest of one's life. There-fore, it should not come to anyone's surprise that "Birds of a feather flock together". In other words, people with similar beliefs, aspira-tions, and opinions tend to inter-relate much better. This brings us to the level of culture. What is that anyway?

Culture is the total sum of one's beliefs, tastes, and values. Through culture, traditions are passed from one generation down to the next. We share those elements with other people who hold similar cultural convictions as ourselves. Also, you can have a culture that develops within another culture. Technically, the one that gathers less adepts, believers, or members is called a subculture or culture of the minority. You may not belong to a sub-culture, but you necessarily and intimately associate with a distinct demographic group either through biology or natural birth, or through legal procedures or by individual consent where you agree to abide by or follow the principles of that said group or culture. That's when sociology talks about the process of socialization, adaptation, conformity, and all that sort of thing. Only God does not identify with a culture and you can figure out why (He does not have to); the rest of us will carry that trademark until we substitute another culture of our choice which implies that, as a function of time, we can actually dissociate or distance ourselves from and embrace values or principles of another culture or a subculture instead. Subculture itself can be considered as a circle in a bigger circle or as described below:

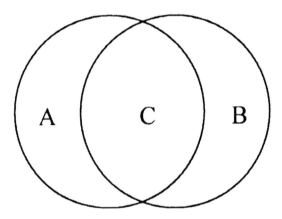

Figure 20.1 depicts a culture within another culture. The larger circles represent the conglomerate or the more established cultures. On the contrary, the smaller circle stands for the newer, less accept-able culture. Usually the less represented culture, the sub or smaller circle, comes about in retaliation to values being imposed by the larger circle or through the infiltration of a more influential culture. As you can see in **figure 20.1** you have either two separate groups or nations growing side by side thereby influencing the elements which compose the identities of each other. The scheme (**20.1**) shows three

areas which I identify as A, B & C. Areas A & B stand for the cultural values that remain somewhat unaffected during interaction. No acculturation is taking place. The C area represents points of identical beliefs and values as a result of infiltration or acculturation. You have two separate groups interacting, and for a period of time they go through a transitional phase where they lower their resistance and increase their level of tolerance of each other. During invasion, what takes place is acculturation. The captive group or culture submits to the will and culture of the invaders, which is the reason why many of us speak a different language other than the one our ancestors spoke before being "civilized" or invaded.

In the relationships among different populations or nations, if mutual respect exists, one can actually acknowledge the culture of the other without being consumed by or becoming a part of it. In conjunction with that there is no such thing as the right or the perfect culture. You cannot have perfect principles and values brought forth by imperfect people.

As a matter of fact, each culture conveys standards which present a set of positive values and another set made of negative models, impacting its members adversely or negatively. As cross-cultural influence occurs laterally, subjects are capable of and should be free to choose among the elements of the cultures which they have been exposed to. Thus they would show preference in one area of one culture and preference in another area of another culture. But/inadvertently, let me remind you that we are referring to a totally different animal when we talk about a **Culture Of Poverty**. And just before I elaborate on that, let me briefly say something about **Figure 20.1.**

It is an area which we do not want to spend too much time talking about at the moment. That has to do with several ethnic groups evolving simultaneously or they coexist in the same physical environment.

As demonstrated in the same diagram, you have a bigger circle which all the ethnic groups that constitute the general population identify with. Also, each of which displays some forms of beliefs or values of its own that other groups do not necessarily share. Please note that if this process emerges as a result of distinct groups of

275

individuals with different cultural origins coming together to form what we might be tempted to call cultural pluralism, the interaction may be conducive to both community development as well as individual growth. However, as the inner circle (C), which represents the developing or the inner culture evolves from the other two cultures (A & B), it will eventually adopt its own set of values in the process, thereby creating some sort of tension in the environment. As a result, that may cause a certain destabilization in the already established population or cultures. This takes us right back to the first scheme or figure 20.1 which is our main focus in this chapter.

In essence, a <u>culture of poverty</u> is one in which members of a group or nation adapt to values and beliefs that do not reflect those of the main culture. More often these (beliefs and values) are looked upon by main stream society as a demoralizing force on the pre-existing system. Such culture is usually fought by non-members without much consideration as to why the group develops such behaviors in the first place. In other words, they're often not concerned with causes and when they are, the approaches that they take usually run through a discriminatory and hostile vein, not regarding scientific methods that would bring effective results.

Looking into the root causes of <u>culture of poverty</u>, we discover some internalized patterns. <u>First</u> of all, there is a problem of population growth. The English economist Thomas Malthus argued that when the world experiences difficulty in feeding its people, that has to do with the population growing exponentially or so rapidly while resources are being exploited rather arithmetically or at a rate much slower than the population expansion. Malthus' idea is that the world suffers from population explosion while sufficient resources to care for it are not readily available. Many people and world organizations buy into that claim. While we may argue over that statement as being true, there is evidence that some people live in extreme or abject poverty because of reason number <u>two</u>: some of us are too greedy, and reason number <u>three</u>: many of us are so lazy. <u>Fourth</u>, we find the impact of wars on poverty. It destroys resources and preparation for the war itself displaces or misuses resources at times. In addition, after a war, you have to evaluate not only how much destruction is done to the physical environment but also, you have to look at how many great minds are lost as a result of that.

Fifth. Some people do not set goals or priorities for themselves. Whatever happens, happens. No motivation or determination to mutate from or come out of the socioeconomic abyss where they are at.

Sixth. In some ways, parents or custodians with an arsenal of children do not have enough resources to properly equip them for life in this world. Therefore, for lack of guidance, these kids may have difficulties making it.

Seventh. Besides famine, natural disaster, and the unfavorable side of migration, there exists an extremely large number of people in every nation and every culture who have been brainwashed to simply resign themselves to the conditions that they presently live in. On another vein, this particular demographic will most probably expect manna to fall from the heavens. They rely on some mystical power to take care of them. They will most likely become welfare recipients generation after generation. Never a decisive concern and enough motivation on their part to become self supportive, many will convert themselves into mercenaries, having dozens of weapons and all kinds of dangerous and violent behaviors. They also will attack and destroy people in order that they might make a living. Lastly but not least, eighth: others have been too tired to make something of their lives, however either the system has failed or more precisely they did not have the guts to pick up the pieces and keep moving on, and so they QUIT in the middle of their efforts.

These eight categories of people and any other which you may come up with create two groups: the haves and the have nots. Of the latter group emerge those people who were from the culture of poverty. A segment of that population will blame other people for their situation. Others will develop an incentive to try to turn things around and still others will instead resign themselves to literally doing nothing to promote or elevate themselves. Sometimes, some of them will look for the easiest way out and turn themselves into drug busters, and be in default with the rest of the society by becoming a public nuisance.

I realize that there exist forces in nature that prevent many individuals from reaching high; however to blame it on a system which we voluntarily or individually help create is not so smart. When we study the degree to which many people resign and the amount of abuse that they are willing to take, we will also find the amount of misery that they are willing to tolerate.

A- Learned Helplessness

As someone said, if you feel that you are defeated, then you are. When you resign yourself to say, "I cannot do anything to change my conditions. I am doomed to where I am", then you force yourself into the culture of all these people out there who already sent the same message to themselves.

Learned helplessness is a mentality, a belief system which makes you feel like you have no hope and you cannot help yourself. There is nothing you can do to reverse the course of actions. Your fate has already been pre-determined for you. Along social class, racial divide, and gender differences, people often make their own bed by accepting that they are inferior and cannot accomplish anything of value to themselves and society. Your perception counts a great deal in this issue of learned helplessness. It is only as you perceive yourself and situations around you that you will be able to act on things and make an impact. Learned helplessness is very easy. It simply takes several steps. Just like a child who is being told that he is inadequate and incompetent. After listening to the same note over and over, especially coming from somebody in authority and whom the child could picture as a role model. Then, the message will be stored in a tape in the brain to be played conveniently. Once that message is internalized, it becomes part of that child's belief system. From this point on, the child has already accepted that he/she is inadequate, and this will reflect on his/her attitude and work performance.

If you let the obstacles consume you, you will be paralyzed and reduced from your present state to a lower one. If you preach resignation, then you live on resignation, and nothing will change for you. If the only messages that you send to your brain are negative in content, then you become a negative atom, a stagnant personality and you can only affect things negatively. The longer you live in the neighborhood of those who are hopeless, the more likely you will become a hopeless case yourself. It is an absolute truth, you are what you eat and practice. Once you become part of the culture of poverty, and believe in your mind that you are incapable, inadequate, and incompetent to help yourself, then you pretty much settle to pursue hopelessness. However, no matter what or how long you have identified yourself with such an environment, there is hope. You can still come out. Culture of Poverty is an epidemic that is contagious and people need to learn how to rid that or they will be eternally doomed to misery.

B- Poverty Is a Habit Which We Must Fight

In the French language, we encounter an idiom that says, "Habitude est une seconde nature." Without my input, you probably understand the meaning; but in case your French forgot you, it literally means that when you get used to doing things in a certain way, they become an integral part of you.

In my book about relationships, I received a few comments, good ones though, from readers regarding my calling marriage a career. Perhaps you have questions or comments about poverty being a habit. I welcome them and please, do not hesitate to contact me especially if you would have me rewrite this book to your liking. In the meantime, imagine this. Even if you do not own a car or do not even know how to drive one, we will help you in between your readings to get the skills. We won't be able to give you a car, except if we sell enough copies of this work to make us millionaires; then, we might consider the idea. Anyway, imagine that you have learned how to drive a vehicle and you become a skillful driver (hopefully no bad records) over time. After that, you get so used to driving that almost every move you make with the vehicle becomes automatic. You open your car door, turn on the ignition, and shift to the gear that you want to drive. As you drive, you look for traffic signals. All that comes with repetition. What do they say, repetition makes perfect? So even if you did not pass the driving test, you can look in your life and pick some skills that you have mastered well, and you no longer need anyone to tell you what to do. <u>You know that you know what you know.</u> That's knowledge, a wonderful asset for people to have (although certain knowledge may not be appropriate for someone to have at a certain time), but overall, when you have it you can use it to your advantage. You can actually use knowledge constructively and progressively to reduce suffering and poverty in your world.

People who are born in poverty and who later on develop the mentality of helplessness in the course of life circumstances often eat poverty, grow in poverty, sleep in poverty, dream poverty, and talk poverty all the time. Those who meditate on poverty, train themselves on poverty and most of all believe in poverty as a virtue, educate themselves on how to be poor by sitting there doing nothing uplifting. They become graduates of and belong to the Culture of Poverty. Members become part of such a fraternity; they talk alike, their beliefs are alike, they live almost alike and behave almost alike. That pretty much makes a sub-group belonging to a sub-culture evolving parallel to a bigger culture where the two coexist.

When you observe the two cultures of the two groups, it is as though you are looking at two separate nations in one society or two people but one nation. The two groups are identifiable through the naked eyes. You just have to hear them talk, observe them for some time, find what they believe in and how they behave. It is like separating two teams of athletes by dressing one in green and the other in red.

The two groups have a mentality of their own, and that is what distinguishes them, not so much what house they live in, what car they drive, the clothes they wear or the neighborhood that they live in, even though society has criteria that categorize rich from poor. We do not want you to read this book thinking that I am separating people who have money, plenty of it from those who do not have any. It does not quite work that way with respect to Culture of Poverty.

I come from a very poor family. I lived through the hardships and, using the standardized dichotomy of wealthy versus poor people, I still consider myself in the category of poor people. I do not have any money; I have not even purchased my own home yet. However, I can tell you that I do not belong to the Culture of Poverty. I have dreams and aspirations that I am pursuing.

Behind the Culture of Poverty and underachieving lie a whole mentality, a mindset, if you will. Some people learn through life experiences and use that to reach higher. Others acquired the same experiences but instead they use it to destroy themselves. It is like somebody who holds a gun or any other weapon to defend himself/herself and turns around, and pulls it toward himself/herself.

People in Culture of Poverty (C.O.P.) are self destructive. They turn all that they ever had against themselves. Individuals who live under the slavery of sub-culture or Culture of Poverty (C.O.P.) fit the following profile:

1. They are negative or pessimistic about life.
2. They do not have higher goals.
3. They do not reach far in life because they never gave themselves a chance to or developed any efforts towards that goal.
4. They are monotonous, hard to be around.
5. They probably complain all the time about things going wrong, which is a bit depressing.
6. They have low self-esteem.
7. They could be nosy because they have all the time in the world to stick their noses in other peoples' business.
8. Their personal hygiene is questionable.
9. They accept being poor as a fate which was designed for them.
10. They tell themselves they cannot do anything to turn things around.
11. They resign themselves to whatever their good luck might bring their way. No personal effort.
12. They develop what is commonly called LEARNED HELPLESSNESS.
13. They become dependent on everybody else.

I could fit right there had I not motivated myself to do something about my original socioeconomic status. I could lament for the rest of my life trying to blame the whole world and never taking any responsibility for myself.

For many people who live in poverty, it is a choice. You may be born in poverty or under the culture of poverty, but you don't have to adopt it as a lifestyle. You can change things. To recapitulate or repeat myself:

C- Rising Above The Challenges

C.O.P. is a disease that is highly contagious and people need to learn how to come out of it or they will be eternally doomed to misery.

If you are poor, you have the option to change whatever conditions that you now live in. God already gave you the power. If you believe in somebody or something else, so be it, I am not writing to make you what you do not want to be or do not want to do. In fact, nobody, not even God can force you to do anything. Use your free will. Use your talents. Find ways to train yourself so that you maintain an optimistic view or a positive attitude about life. You should not confuse self-confidence with arrogance, just as you should not get the word humility mixed up with humiliation. Self-confidence is bringing the positive image out of you. That's not a sin, at least not a mortal one; but humiliation...! That's the right one baby. Not only can you do it to yourself, but also certain folk will volunteer to feed you so they may humiliate you.

Think a lot about the message that you play to yourself. If after watching violent films people tend to deploy behavior that expresses threat, and if prolonged exposure to an oppressive and depressive environment has adverse effect on us, then you better believe that negative message does influence us in a negative way, too. Do yourself a favor by not putting yourself down. Also don't do it to your child or to anybody else, because what goes around comes around. Teach yourself to be content, jovial, and courageous in the situations that you are in now and work towards changing those that you may. You won't be able to change everything but you can actually change a lot of things. Just as that poet says:

"God grant me the serenity to accept things that I cannot change, the courage to change those that I can, and the wisdom to know the difference" (The Serenity Prayer).

Make sacrifices wherever and whenever it is necessary. It is possible to become a better person by learning some new skills every day. You can also offer to help others around you who find themselves embedded in the e-C.O.P. (the existing culture of poverty). Plan and develop some form of discipline for your life: some work habit, some play or distraction (exercise), some sleep, some meditation, and some reading every day. Apply yourself to live with your head high. You cannot see where you are going or what lies ahead if you never take some steps forward. Set some goals for yourself now and be determined to bring them to completion. The mountains will not come down for you; in fact they don't need you. However, you need to be up there or on the other side; and if you are afraid of falling, you will not climb any height. And God alone knows how many of those mountains that you and I will face. Therefore, you stand a better chance learning to rise above the challenges of life. You may not be able to design a perfect plan which will get you there instantly or as fast as you would, but you have to determine which move to make. You may need advice from relatives and friends who have been there and who show deep interest in you and your success.

Next, it remains your job to work on your perception. The way you perceive yourself is how you will act in life and present yourself to others. Remember, every time you are in the midst of other people, there are messages (spoken and unspoken) being communicated in both directions or between you and others involved. It is very important as to what you are conveying. If you show a sad face, then people see you as a sad person or think that you are. If you always present yourself in a depressed mood, others will tend to call you "DEPRESSED personality" as your nickname. Whatever you convey or project outwardly may count for or against you. As you try to move out of the abyss of poverty, you need to not only relate positive messages to you but to others as well. Pay a compliment to someone as you would want done to you. They will be the judge around you as you interact with them. It is hard if not impossible to succeed alone in every step of the way.

Your interrelationships will greatly count when you need a good word or a letter of recommendation to apply for a new job. Treat others with courtesy and be willing to go out of your way to help another fellow human being. You will be surprised even in this life, as to how much you get for helping others. I also recommend that you go back a few pages behind and read the profile of people under C.O.P. and just do the opposite.

If you are on a trip and you find yourself lost and you know for sure that you are lost, stop, find where you are and if that is what you have to do, try to retrieve your path. Try to go back to the same place you started. Usually, upon returning, you will find the right way, whereas if you are lost and you keep on going, you simply bury yourself deeper and deeper. One group of people that I have a hard time tolerating are those who perfect themselves in quitting. They have all kinds of degrees in that field: B. S.; B. A.; Masters; Doctorate; and all the certificates, you name it. My friend is afraid of dogs; I am scared being in the same room with those people for a long period of time!!! You look at them and all that you are able to see written all over them is the *I quit, I quit, I quit!* And the funny part is that **they quit all the wrong things**. They will even threaten to get you converted to their religion. You can understand why I am scared! Nothing to be wanted.

Instead, you need all the motivation you can get to overcome the e-C.O.P. and move forward. If you cannot motivate yourself enough, start by changing the pace at which you do things. Maybe you need to make some changes and slow down in some areas while you increase in others. Be willing to try new ideas. Don't be a coward, thinking about failure. If you never failed, perhaps you never tried to stand and probably you never gave yourself a chance to grow. When things do not go your way the first time, do not quit. Discipline yourself, force yourself into learning new concepts and be willing to experiment. Be persistent and keep your eyes focused on what you are doing. Don't let motivation leave you one minute. Walk with it side by side, and you will do just fine in your new tasks. Best of all, remember it all relates to your perception and belief. You can improve your life and make your world brighter, happier, and healthier by taking the first step in the positive direction today. It is never too late to start changing your life toward what you want it to look like.

❖ CHAPTER XXI ❖

Catch Your Own Fish or Risk
Being Fed on Intoxicated Food

Food and water intake fulfills one of the most basic physiological requirements of animals, including humans. Somehow, all living creatures ought to meet these needs if they are to survive. There is no maybe, or I am too young, too old to eat. One can't even say: well, I'll eat next month or next week when conditions permit. We all respond to it as a constant need, and of course it is. Are there any others? Do we live to eat or do we simply eat so we may have enough energy to go fulfilling other obligations; how about food for one's mind?

Abraham H. Maslow, a well known humanistic psychologist, came up with a triangle where he specifically described human needs and aspirations, going from basic necessities to more selective or sophisticated commodities. Actually, this whole idea is based on motivation which, in turn, emphasizes personal freedom, choice, self-determination, and an eagerness for personal growth or self-actualization (*Ed. Psy.* pp. 305-315).

In simple terms, self-actualization means fulfilling your potential, something that is limitless. No one human being can really exhaust his or her resources in a lifetime. It is only due to lack of creativity, self-imposed limitations, and poor perception that we are pushed to a wall with no more options, no alternatives, or with no room to grow.

Based on day-to-day observations, Maslow was able to construct a triangle and place all that we would hope for inside of it. See diagram below.

Maslow's Hierarchy of Needs

❖ CHAPTER XXII ❖

What About It:
Your Self-image, Self-esteem?

Why do people profess poor self-esteem rituals, practice lack of self confidence, or put themselves down in the first place? Does this sound incomprehensible to any of you readers or are you caught up in it too? We might even ask Why some people are shy? Last but not least, where (in which direction) do they look or focus their attention?

Those individuals who are critical of others tend to function on two separate indices as they try to elevate themselves as Mr. Smart or Ms. Cute over the rest of the world. As they pronounce the sentence against their fellow humans, they point to the weakness of others rather than to their strengths. Then, they attribute the failure of those they are judging to internal factors. Whereas, when they attempt to explain their own fall or shortcoming, they attribute the cause (s) to outside sources. For example, Bill looks at John and makes a comment like this: John lived rent free in the home of his supporters. Therefore, John must have an ethical or character flaw; something inside of John causes him to behave that way. On the other hand, if Bill is allegedly confronted for a similar act, he will defend himself saying something like: he had every intention to pay the rent. It is the fault of the landlord for not accepting or asking for the rent money. See, by bringing a judgment against John, the ground for convicting him is definitely John himself, but by being his own judge, Bill casts the blame on the environment rather than on himself. This kind of intervention often takes place on legal ground, in the court of law or whenever a case is brought to the judicial system opposing the plaintiff (accuser) against the defendant (the accused).

Some people are fortunate enough to grow up in a healthy and stimulating environment where they learn early on about self-worth. Others spend a lifetime and they never discover who they truly are and the infinite amount of wealth they possess in the form of potential. There exist a number of factors that contribute to that. One might be that they never received a compliment after completing a task. They then convince themselves that they must have done terribly. Another factor is verbal messages that negate people's ability to do well which place them at risk of developing later on a sense of poor self-esteem, a lack of self-confidence.

Also, those who grow up in extremely protective or authoritarian homes are either never allowed to be on their own and to take risks or are punished for their mistakes and tend to become less assertive. They always look to get the approval of others. When they don't receive it, they blame themselves for being so inadequate or incompetent. Similarly, people who are raised in rigid homes with perfectionist attitude parents always compare themselves with others to see if they match up. They constantly look for and imitate heroes who will become their idols. They may have many such heroes whose shadows they try to walk in but never equate. After a while they focus on their inability to meet their own expectations and they begin to feel worthless. Another factor could be some kind of traumatic experiences early on that leave the individual petrified or in a state of shock. Consequently, they become withdrawn, timid, introverted, or even anti-social.

One way that some people deal with or compensate for low self-esteem is by overeating (which may lead to bulimia) or by starving themselves (leading to anorexia.) Furthermore, children or young adolescents whose psycho-social development have been impaired tend to fall behind in acquiring full maturity as they get older. As a result, they either experience a sense of fear of coming forth which may lead to their avoidance of public gatherings or speaking in public, or their personality is never asserted which can be viewed as a form of psycho-social disorder or retardation.

The list could grow much longer but we will just relate to this last possible cause of poor self-esteem and lack of assertiveness. Whether or not we fully understand how learning takes place, what we see and observe greatly influences us. Therefore, it is not necessarily inaccurate to say that we are in some ways the product of the environment. Just as you have read about learned helplessness and the culture of poverty in previous chapters, our personality and temperament is a combination of innate characteristics, hence genetic on one hand. And on the other hand, the way in which we allow ourselves to interact with the environment produces in us a lasting impression and it gives us the perception that we eventually use to build our belief system.

At this time, I would like to deviate slightly to address a little bit the issue of temperament, personality, and then come back to conclude on our current topic which is poor self-esteem or self-image and lack of self-confidence. At the end I hope to be able to at least help you modify your perception of yourself if need be.

A- What Does Temperament Have to Do With It?

Had not it been for our enlightenment or our higher intellectual and spiritual superiority, we probably would not be able to explain and understand how to interact effectively with each other (human beings). We often refer to it as the process of socialization and it is a way of life which all of us learn in order to fit in this world and have our needs met.

Generally speaking, we, human beings, experience or create and identify a great number of needs, which by the way could be named in three (3) basic areas or categories. They are:

1) Physical needs: Ex. food, clothing, shelter, etc.
2) Emotional needs: The need to love and to be loved, to express ourselves and share our feelings with those around us.
3) Spiritual needs: The desire to commune, relate or fellowship with a higher human being. Among all living species, human beings alone share this great aspiration.

Before we go on to having these needs met, we practice the rules of the game. We form or adapt to socio-cultural demands.

Many times, we experience difficulty in trying to get along with others because, generally, we haven't the slightest idea about the temperament of these individuals or in many instances, we could care less. Nonetheless, family relations, race relations, public relations or for that matter, human relations, all work only to the extent that we allow ourselves to first know who we really are and learn about the others. Then and only then can we start to co-habit or live together while having our needs met.

Some people tend to believe that temperament is 100% inborn and that is all there is to it! Others think that it is all learned through the process of socialization, in which case we are all born the same and shaped by our environment. This school of thought falls short in explaining why even two identical twins (developed from one ovum or precisely from one egg) who grow up in the exact same environment yet have distinct temperaments and different personalities and behave differently.

There is a third school of thought, which I am apart of, that considers temperament as the sum of heredity (+) plus one's culture, environment, and personal attributes (experiences and maturity). Based on these ideas, temperament cannot be explained by heredity alone. You will understand it beyond all the shadows of doubt. We all have what are termed dominant and recessive genes. The recessive genes or the hereditary materials which we acquire from our parents do not express themselves significantly. They are part of our total makeup but they play a secondary role. The dominant genes, on the other hand, carry the expressions or whatever characteristics are pronounced in us.

For instance, we do know that there exists a special gene for every trait: curly hair, blond hair, blue eyes, brown eyes, big ears, small ears, short stature, tall stature, to name a few. However, the gene that determines how tall or how short we will be does not act independently from the ecological or environmental factors. In other words, the actual height of any individual is not only influenced by the parental make-up but also by the milieu. While a woman is pregnant, how she carries herself and what she eats and puts in her body greatly determines how her baby will come out. That is why many babies are born abnormal or with congenital malformation and many others have difficulty developing into adulthood. If a child does not receive proper nutrition, all the genes for tallness in the world will not make that individual tall, but instead he or she will be subject to suffer from kwashiorkor (an advanced form of nutritional deficiency usually associated with diet poor in protein in children) and even rickets (a condition which results from lack of vitamin D, an essential element in bone formation). Hence tallness cannot be understood or explained from the point of view of heredity, as simple as that. Consequently, we must also understand temperament from the point of view of heredity and environment. Now another test is how do we define temperament? What does it mean to have a bad or a short temper?

It has to do with who is defining what. Specialists from different disciplines always have a definition that is convenient for them. That in no way means that some definitions are wrong; this simply makes it hard to agree upon a particular one. For instance, "Le Petit Robert", a well known French dictionary, defines temperament as a set of innate characteristics in a person, which are psycho-physiologically complex. These characteristics determine the behavior or personality type of individuals in light of his/her general congenital traits as originally explained in the four humors by Hippocrates. Our dear old friend *Webster's* says that temperament is 1) the peculiar or the distinguished mental or physical character determined by the relative proportions of the humors (based on medieval physiology) 2) characteristic or habitual inclination (disposition) or mode of emotional response.

Considering *Webster's* definitions, we cannot but underline two important words here: humor and emotional responses. Both humor and emotions have to do with or are affected by the physiological and the mental well-being of an individual, as well as his or her psychological state. Each of us responds differently to different situations and at different times. The physiological response is how our body works and is affected by the hormones. Males and females are both under such influence, however, with menstruation, females or women go through frequent mood changes every month. The mental well-being deals with the mind or the brain at any given time. Are we mentally healthy or balanced? How rational or coherent are we? Can we really make sound decisions at all times? The psychological response focuses on or is concerned with how we behave which is part of our development process and maturity.

Now, the more appropriate definition of temperament we will adopt is a working one. In other words, we plan to embrace a definition which will enable us to talk about the subject in a more concrete way. <u>Temperament is the personal identity that distinguishes one individual human being from everyone else</u>. Just like a fingerprint, there is no such thing as two individuals with exactly the same personality traits or temperaments. That is to say: we are all different. We have our own way of perceiving and interpreting life's events. Temperament tells who we are and how we go about having our needs met or how we interact (respond) to the environment as we are stimulated.

There exist many ways of introducing what I am about to, however, I will focus mainly on a format layout by the National Christian Counseling Association of America. It is indicated that we have three different areas of needs as it relates to our interaction with the environment be it animate or inanimate, and that shapes our behaviors and attitudes in life. The first area we find has to do with <u>INCLUSION</u>. According to the National Christian Counseling Association (NCCA) literature, this area does not involve deep emotions but rather surface relationships which we portray in our daily social interactions. The way we deal with intellectual processing of information links to the inclusion area.

The second area of interest is <u>CONTROL</u>. This area dictates how domineering we will be once we are involved in a relationship. Do we look to establish ourselves as a dominant (domineering) force or as equal players and partners in a relationship? Who makes all the decisions? The third area is <u>AFFECTION</u>, and it expresses how emotionally involved we are in the relationship. Furthermore, are we close or distant?

Sigmund Freud may help us answer this question. His work in psychoanalysis tells us that we human beings carry three faces: a) a social face, b) an ideal face, and c) a real face (the real us). These components dictate how much we will disclose and in what environment. They affect our:

Personality
Character
Behavior
Temperament

Three areas of needs

The types of temperaments

I find that the three faces influence the three areas of needs mentioned above. Hence our temperaments to some extent. Therefore, temperament is neither 100% innate nor 100% learned.

Just as you have seen earlier in my explanation, a child may inherit genes for tallness but if such individual does not receive the proper stimuli from the environment, there is no way the child will be tall. Environment plays an important role in the life of the individual. A child does not grow tall simply because the gene or the genetic materials of the parents carry such characteristics. One has to take into account the kind of environment in which the child developed as a fetus as well as the environment beyond the birth canal. Beyond birth or early on, our parents and guardians are responsible for providing our basic needs; however, as we grow older and become mature and independent, we have a vital responsibility to identify who we are and...

B- Be Proud of Ourselves

In this present manual I am not referring to personality and temperament as some psychiatric literature relates to them as deviance and disorder or necessarily the unhealthy personality. Psychiatrists, mental health and other health care professionals, in an attempt to establish the diagnosis of a client, often refer to the famous book called *DSM III, IV* or as the case may be. DSM stands for *Diagnostic and Statistical Manual of Mental Health*. We are simply talking about personality as it relates to temperament but nothing to do with disorder or mental problems.

See, there are as many temperaments as there are individual human beings. When we talk about different personalities and different temperaments, we are not implying that some are necessarily bad and others are necessarily good. This varies from one individual to the next, so much that not even two identical twins are 100% compatible. For that matter we could simply add that some could improve in some areas and others could in other areas. However, one premise that holds true is that people with low self-worth and lack of assertiveness who constantly put themselves down need a lesson on personality growth. No matter how painful the transition may seem, for us to rise and evolve beyond mere survival, we must be assertive. We must work to improve our self-esteem and promote a positive self-image; for no one can really do it for us. That may come about only when we start believing in ourselves, seeing ourselves as competent and as adequate as anyone else. We promote self-worth when we stop putting ourselves down and begin to focus on our inner abilities and talents.

How you look and present yourself to others tends to be a major expression of who you are and what your belief system is. You may be among the most talented individuals in the whole world, and you may have a long track record of achievements which is commendable; however, usually that does not show on your face. What am I driving at?

Sometimes, the outer appearance may seem to work against us, even though we may be very articulate and possess the right credentials or the proper knowledge that a potential employer is looking for, but we fall short somehow of his or her expectations. I don't know your personal experience, your work skills, and how many job interviews you have had in your lifetime. Nonetheless, if you live long enough or talk to enough people with the "right kind of knowledge" about fashion designs and its affect in promoting or in selling yourself, you already have a good sense of what I mean. You may be the rare kind who does not believe in or who cares less about psychology and its significance in our daily life. However, if you already do and have a personal friend (perhaps you know someone) in this particular field, that person can tell you how much of a role your self-esteem plays on your personality and your outward look. That individual can also tell you how other people see and accept you as part of their clan. This is important stuff in your interpersonal relationships and if you value the opinion that others will have of you.

You may not care, but that is your life and your personal decision. You are entitled to have your own taste, that is what makes us unique. But we, as human beings, long for the approval of other people around us; also, we often value their opinion and rely on their acceptance.

Deep down I know that some of you may think that I am being ridiculous, but I am not and I don't mean to be funny at all. When I went to college and applied for a degree in that discipline, I was told by the school administrators that I was a minority and on top of that, their 'funny degrees' have been conferred strictly on a specific group of 'gifted individuals' which I was not considered a part of! Anyhow, let's see if you don't care or if looks (appearance) does not matter.

Let's presume that you submitted a job application to a prestigious firm and you are called for an interview. You could dress in red socks, white pants, black shoes, yellow shirt or blouse, and a gray jacket. You probably would get the degree that I mentioned in the last paragraph, but I really question whether the people giving you the interview would run away or call an ambulance for you. My guess is that they would call the ambulance with specific instructions to have psychiatrists on board and that the team be ready for possible casualties. Perhaps all that was not needed but you certainly gave the people reason to be alarmed; so wear that outfit in your closet at home. The way you present yourself to the interviewer (s) or the interview committee will greatly influence their decision to hire you. I don't want anyone to miss my point; I am referring to your outer appearance (how neat or presentable you look). Most often than not, that represents a determining factor for whether an employer will continue interviewing you much further. We cannot or should not judge anyone based on his/her appearance, but that is not the real world. Therefore, no matter how proud and how unique you wish to be, there is a code which people utilize as they mingle with us.

Now, it is unfortunate that some of us don't have that individual pride, but instead try to be the clone of another human being. We must once and for all stop that game of comparing ourselves with other people. We were not made to be somebody else but ourselves. Taking this into the intimate/romantic world, what does it mean, how do you relate to somebody with different tastes from yours? Where does your individual pride or want kick in? That's another topic and we need another book for it. Maybe I will translate my book on intimate and family relationship for the English audience. However, let me answer this way. You will always find your match if you are patient and persistent enough. It is true that birds of the same feather flock together. Nonetheless, whomever you want to meet, Mr. or Ms. Right, you still have to face the reality, which is your self-image. You cannot force anyone to love and accept you if you don't love yourself, don't know yourself (who you truly are) and if you have not developed an intimate relationship with yourself. It is no coincidence that when Jesus spoke to His followers, He instructed them to love their neighbors as they love themselves. This is something which you have to experience firsthand before you can talk about it or share it with someone else. And if you don't have it you cannot show it; that is the bottom line. Once you start seeing yourself as a product of God's love and start feeling good about yourself, you will also begin to believe in yourself. Consequently, you will eventually take pride in your accomplishments. You need not wait until you become a renowned rocket scientist to praise yourself. As you know, not everybody can be everything. Therefore, your personal achievement may not withstand someone else's, nonetheless, it is yours. And who knows, success is built on success. Your initial dream might be to accomplish a small goal which may become the foundation or the cornerstone of a greater dream. Self-incrimination is synonymous or the same as self-destruction. You don't build yourself up by cutting grass under your own field. That is suicidal.

I want you to repeat this pledge with me: <u>I will never, ever put myself down again. In order for others to believe in me, I must first start believing in myself; and no one can give that which one does not have.</u> You may think that I am a narcissist but I do not believe for one minute that King David of Israel had that in mind when he said that he was fearfully and wonderfully made…(Psalm 139:14).

Assertiveness & Aggression

"The aggressive part of human nature is not only a safeguard against predatory attack, it is also the basis of intellectual achievement, of the attainment of independence and even that of proper pride which enables a man to hold his head high amongst his fellows". (Storr, A.: Human Aggression, New York, Atheneum Pub., 1968, p. III In: Eleanor C. Hein and M. Jean Nicholson, *Complementary Leadership Behavior*, J.B. Lippincott Company. Philadelphia. 1994.[4th Ed., pp. 123-127]). The assumption is that assertiveness is constructive aggression, to the authors. We might say that being assertive represents a constructive form of aggression, which in a way reflects the "fight or flight response", or it typifies an attempt to resolve a conflict either by acting directly on the perceived problem (in which case, one fights back), or by moving away from the obstacles (in this case, one flies away).

Fight or Flight Response

"Fight or flight responses indicate an attempt to resolve a conflict either by acting directly on the perceived problem (fight) or by moving away from the difficulty (flight) (Hein & Nicholson, p.123).

Six A's of Assertiveness, according to the above author:

1. Authority
2. Anxiety
3. Anger
4. Constructive Aggression
5. Accountability
6. Autonomy

We will never be somebody else, don't even waste your money trying to clone yourself; you will simply be another Dolly (the sheep made in Sweden, the first successful product of animal cloning in history). Neither can you make a copy of yourself, even if you had all the dominant genes in the world, because you cannot reproduce personality; for that is a set of distinct traits and characteristics which result from both genetics and the environment over time. The best you can do is to constantly work on improving what you have in you. Don't put yourself down, but make every effort that is humanly possible to grow daily and attain that sense of self-worth. Also, don't be intimidated if you do not seem to have it all; no one that I know of does. Everyone of us represents a complement of the next person. However, you can make yourself look attractive, starting from the outside in (great look and great mind) or from the inside out (the refining of spiritual and the inner substance and a little beauty). One will complement the other; just don't fool around with dangerous substances!

❖ CHAPTER XXIII ❖

Whatever Your Addiction:
It May Be Dangerous to Your
Health and Growth!

A great number of people are addicted but may hardly ever acknowledge it; they either don't know it or they are in denial. Just as it
is possible for someone to live with cancer cells or the AIDS virus in
his or her body for years and never know it, chances are that people
may live with crutches throughout their lives but are inhibited from
seeing them as such. It's not because that does no harm to them to be
moving around on crutches all the time, but their perception, culture,
sub-culture, interpretation of that, or their private logic may prevent
them from acknowledging it. I might also add that somehow
addiction has been so narrowly or marginally defined that it makes
provisions which automatically exclude a lot of addicts. That is a
disservice not only to the person, but also to society.

The widely acceptable form of addiction to date embraces the use
of drugs, illicit chemicals such as heroin, marijuana, cocaine, and
other major substances. As we know it, a great number of substances
that people are hooked on and a lot of poor habits that tend to destroy
people's lives are in fact overlooked by society. Only in recent times
has our definition of drugs extended to include alcohol and nicotine
(from tobacco) dependence.

Earlier reports released in 1987 by the *US News and World Report*
confirm that some 5.2 million Americans actively use cocaine. The
same report indicates that the price per kilo in Miami as of 1987 was
$19,000, down from $50,000 three years ago (*US News and World
Report*, June 22, 1987). Nine years later, different reports find that
more drugs have been pumped to the American market and that more
people are using them. Illegal drugs may be classified into different
categories depending on the type and how they affect the individual's

neurological pathway or the way the body responds to them. The following groups have been recognized:

Narcotics	Depressants	Stimulants	Hallucinogens	Cannabis
Ex. Opium	Barbiturates	Cocaine	LSD	Marijuana
Heroin	Benzodiazapines	Amphetamines	Amphetamines	Hashish

Table 23-1 Chemical Dependency Chart

Drugs are not a problem in the United States alone. Each country in the world has its share, though some of these countries have hardly been affected in terms of the amount of any substance being distributed on the local market and the number of people using that specific drug locally. Every year alcohol/chemical dependence destroys many lives. From drunk driving to violent crimes committed under the influence of some sort of drugs, hundreds of thousands of innocent men and women, including children lose their lives while others end up spending a good part of their existence serving time in jail. In addition, hospitals or medical care facilities are constantly flooded with people seeking help as a result of substance abuse and substance dependence.

Addiction in itself is not a disease but the consequences that it brings are immeasurable. HIV, for instance, the virus which causes AIDS, strikes a significant percentage of its victims through different kinds of risky behaviors associated with drugs. And the results are suffering, misery, and premature deaths.

Many people who do not have an alcohol or drug problem don't see themselves as addicts. Whereas, the behavior that they display partially or fully demonstrates their true characteristics as people who are addicted. Addiction can cover an array of habits which often attack the morale of an individual thereby making his or her spirit dull and reducing one's ability to excel in life. For that matter, I want to make the term more inclusive.

A- From Denial to Acknowledging Your Addiction

Addiction is mainly a behavior-directed habit that a person develops at times to an object of love or of attraction or to a substance which he/she becomes dependent upon and which also places the person at greater risk for some physical, mental, psychological or emotional harm or complications, compared to the rest of the population. Based upon this definition, most of us may be surprised at how addicted we are. However, we usually do not want to hear about it or deal with it, and for a long time we may keep blaming it on anybody else until things get out of hand, but that does not take away our individual responsibility. Blame it on the dog, on our friends, on our spouses, on our relatives, on the system, or on whomever or whatever if we simply want to feel good or make believe that things are all right. Nonetheless, in the end that puts excess weight on our personal baggage, plus we are still accountable for our actions and we feel heavy at times, unable to operate or function properly because of the nuisance created by our addictive behaviors. It is true that some people are more strongly addicted and therefore cause more harm to themselves and the environment. We develop vices which give way to addiction as part of our socialization process or as a form of a coping mechanism because of our unreadiness and unwillingness sometimes to address the real issues, or we simply do not know of any effective way to handle them. It is fair to say that most forms of addictions are neither innate nor associated with any genetic predisposing factors, but rather they kick in as a process that we learn and perfect over time which might make it much easier to recover. And the longer we wait to look for help, the more dramatic things can become!

As we already said, some individuals are addicted to chemical substances (drugs) and/or sex, or food. Others choose hatred and a violent temper as their drug of choice. Others are addicted to material wealth (where their entire existence revolves around money) and power to rule everyone else's life, and still others hang on tight to poverty, or what have you, as their source of addiction. Many people are in chains or cages, based on their belief system and their lifestyle. When you allow anything to enter your system and take control of your person, and it turns you into its subject, you become an addict indeed. Jean Jacques Rousseau, French philosopher, said, "Man is born free, and everywhere he is in irons". Our addictions put us in chains, and we oftentimes develop them in response to other underlining issues which we try to avoid. We do not become addicts spontaneously. Think of The Foot in-the-Door-Technique in that we walk our way into them gradually by taking a first step, and a second, and a third, so on and so forth. And while addictions cost a lot to maintain, we usually beat around the bush and deal with the symptoms instead. Then, we: individuals, humanitarian organizations, and governments, turn around and ask why things are not getting better, when in reality we are not really doing anything to make a difference! What works and what doesn't?

For some people, 'Just Say No' may work; however, for the rest of us who might need an alternative or a good substitute to hopefully replace the bad one (s) that we've cherished for so long, professional intervention may be necessary. In other words, a quick fix does not usually cut it. So I am greatly concerned by the fact that human beings continue to live a life of desperation and hopelessness. They are constantly liquidating their needed assets including the power to do for themselves what nobody else can do for them. While making sound choices is an inherent attribute of ours, we don't always spend quality time exploring our environment to unveil all the different possibilities.

That may not always hold, however the more options that we have, the greater the probability or the chance of us making better choices. This is where the idea of community finds its place. A community may be big or small but it's made up of individuals who may share similar values and belief system. The composition of such a group of people may encompass several biologically-related family members, just as it can include the citizens of a whole nation or the entire human race. Within those boundaries, we identify different subgroups or entities such as fraternities, sororities, church, government, the state or society at large which individuals belong to. When men and women are unable to deal with the reality of their own lives and keep their individual addictions in check, it becomes the duty of the community in which they live to create the means and offer alternatives to them. Sometimes, given the opportunity, many people would have chosen otherwise. Then they could really say NO to potentially distracting forces. I believe that's where elected officials, community leaders, clergy and organizations that focus on individual and community development must concentrate. Their effort can also offer today's young people better alternatives to really say no to substances, especially alcohol, drugs and tobacco and to brighten their future. Nonetheless, the final decision remains with the individual himself in making sure that he seeks what will help enhance and promote growth.

B- Beside God, You Are the Ultimate Architect of Your Destiny

Obstacles may come. In fact, they always do. And our responsibility is not necessarily to avert them. Oftentimes, they are unpredictable, so we are not always prepared to effectively deal with them. Moreover, sometimes they reach us just like a stormy wind or a hurricane that lands ashore and tries to uproot everything that it finds in its way. In those circumstances we need to lay low, letting the current sail off. No obstacle is permanent as far as our experience has proven. And if you try to face every situation head on you probably won't live long, since they are so many, and they are so vigorous. Sometimes they come your way for that very reason, to destroy you. That's when you need your mind free from any addiction so you will be able to think clearly and rationally.

Now, let's face it. Do you see yourself a loser or has anyone ever called you a loser? It does not really matter what people call you. What you respond to is what matters. Do you know that no one is born a loser? However, if you are addicted, then you are a prime candidate to become one! And as long as you remain addicted, you not only enslave yourself, but you associate yourself with losers, people who have nothing good to offer you.

It is up to you though. You can break any pattern or cycle which you have developed and which continues to haunt you. You can break the chain if you are willing to. You need to 1) acknowledge your addiction 2) seek professional help or advice if need be 3) set goals for yourself 4) be motivated toward these goals you have set for yourself 5) make an initial move and take one step at a time instead of none at all 6) set a timetable for reaching these goals 7) take pride in your accomplishments 8) seek guidance from the great master.

Your resources are limitless, and you can accomplish anything that you set your mind to. Modern technology allows us to invent the great tool which we call the computer. It is an archetype or a representation of the human brain. We possess great capacity, limitless megabytes, and RAM. We need not replace our model for it is one of a kind provided that we do not waste it or allow it to atrophy (or degenerate) or let it fill with toxic garbage. Let's use this brain of ours which God gave us and we will do well. The following is a letter sent from a lover to a long time concubine. I am reproducing it here as an instrument that I hope will help set you free from your particular addiction. You may have to draft yours specifically to your particular case. At any rate, this should serve as a guideline. Here it is:

The Love Affair is Over

"My Dearest, Dearest Love:

This is a very difficult letter for me to write, very difficult. I've started this letter several times, but the words just wouldn't come. I just couldn't get it right, but then I realized it's something that has to be done, my life depends on it. You know, you have almost destroyed me. You took the clothes off my back, you've taken the food out of my mouth and made me lie down with you in deserted houses, in filth. You've caused my family to disown me, made my brothers hate me; my sister ashamed of me; my children have left me; and the last person in this world that truly loved me has turned her back on me...

You've made my life so unbearable that I have thought of ending my existence. I have committed crime for you and gone to jail for you several times. Nothing else mattered as long as I had you, nothing! I walked all night in the snow just so I could have you. I didn't care what happened to me. I didn't care about how I look, whether I was clean or dirty, not at all. Often I didn't bathe, wash my hair or brush my teeth. I just wanted you at all cost. I even gave up my God for you! I sold my body for you, for any price, to anyone who wanted. I didn't care about protecting myself, AIDS didn't matter, getting pregnant didn't matter, who cared? I sold myself again and again, just for you. You were my pimp, I was your whore. I was whatever you wanted me to be! You see, I loved you with all my heart and my soul and what did I get in return for loving you? Misery and despair, humiliation and shame, loneliness and poverty.

I sometimes think about you and the joy you used to bring. How happy and secure you made me feel, if only for a little while. You were great at first and then you began to beat me down, use me and abuse me, physically, emotionally, spiritually, and financially. Regardless of the joy you use to bring, there is nothing in this world that can block out the pain, the humiliation and shame; the memories of misery, the sleepless nights, the guilt, the days of loneliness, the craving...You. You made me your slave. Now, I hate you for all that you were and all that you are. I don't need you anymore, I don't want you, there's more to life than you. I was willing to go to any length for you; now I am willing to go to any length to be without you. I've found someone else, someone who can help me regain all that I've lost. I have found myself and I have found recovery...I love recovery more. I hate you!!"

Source: From a recovering addict

❖ CHAPTER XXIV ❖

From the Welfare Roll to Apprenticeship

The first part of this chapter comprises a series of case reports from individuals who for different reasons have been on the welfare roll and some who still are. Since they represent past and actual recipients who have participated in the system, I thought that by listening to them and by incorporating their own testimony in the debate might in some way contribute to a deeper insight into some of the impact of current welfare changes by the U. S. Congress.

I extend my sincere gratitude to each one of these people who allowed me to hear their side of the story. Their actual names will not be used and personal references will be omitted. The overall approach will focus on: **1**) the need of a nation or a government to establish social services to help care for its underprivileged citizens **2**) the efficiency of these programs and **3**) life beyond the "welfarism" or the attitude and beliefs of beneficiaries to either remain on the roll or to move on. First, let's hear the case reports.

To start with, we have **Attle,** 26 years old, mother of four, born and raised in the U. S. At 16, she became pregnant, and as a result she dropped out of high school after the 10th grade while her teenage boyfriend stayed in school trying to finish. She then conceived her first child and joined the welfare roll. Her children are 9, 5 ½, 3 ½, and 2 years old. Attle managed to live with her mom and four (4) siblings during her first pregnancy up until she became pregnant the second time. Then she moved out and split a two bedroom apartment with a girlfriend of hers. For the first child, Attle used to receive about $385.00 monthly from welfare for all her expenses. During that time, she didn't have to pay rent because the home that she lived in was a government subsidized housing project provided to her mother. After giving birth to her second child, she and her boyfriend and father of her two kids now have decided to move in together. Her man managed to get a job working for a supermarket, but made barely enough to support a family of four. So, they were qualified as "the working poor", which entitled them to receive food stamps. All that time, Mom never worked, and during the year, the plan fell apart when Attle's boyfriend lost his job. That sort of put an end to the relationship.

While receiving under $600.00 for her two children, she got involved with another man by whom she became pregnant shortly thereafter. After five months into the pregnancy, she already had several fights with this man and they decided to split while she went on with her life. For the next four months, Attle had the worst time of her life; she moved from place to place trying to find a way to avoid paying rent while keeping her welfare money. Meanwhile, her diagnosis revealed that she has a severe case of herpes, which seems to have provoked some complications with the pregnancy leading to a few short hospitalizations. Thank God, she gave birth to a normal baby a little bit on the low birth weight side. As we can see, there are many issues with this mother of four. She became pregnant while she was underage and never got a chance to finish high school. She never held a job, and there seems to be very little incentive for her to do so, not because she could not or can't, but aside from having a load of children to care for, the whole picture looks rather somber. Attle has minimal job skills, very little education, and more importantly, she does not have much expectations of herself. No self-assurance! She thinks that the only way for her to make it is by remaining dependent on welfare for the rest of her life, which suggests very low self-esteem. Very sad, isn't it?

Second case. This time it involves 32 year old **Amanda**, a third generation welfare recipient with four (4) live children and three (3) miscarriages. The oldest is fifteen (15), whom she gave birth to at the age of 17; then, she just completed 10th grade. The other three children are 7, 4, and 3 years old.

Amanda grew up being part of an extended family, with three siblings, her mother and her grandparents. She evolved in an environment that gave her very little stimulation to accomplish something great or significant in her life. Amanda herself indicated that at one time she wanted to become a professional athlete and a sportscaster with a major news media organization. However, what happened to all her dreams seems to be similar to what happens to so many people; a trade off for something less, a past or a heritage that does not create much room for socio-economic and spiritual uplifting, a person that procrastinates a lot in her life and who has difficulty following through with dreams, which results in nothing being done.

Despite her unfortunate start in life, with some inspiration and with a little help from her relatives, Amanda managed to graduate from high school and completed one year of college at a community institution. She became the first one in her family to attend college; however, her socio-economic background, poor academic perform- ance, and her passionate romantic involvement at least with the wrong man and at the wrong time threw her off balance! Fortunately, with all the changes that are taking place, at 32 Amanda has also decided to make changes in her own life. She is back in college trying to get her bachelor's degree in Communications.

<u>Third Case.</u> Sylvia is 30 years old, a first generation immigrant who arrived in the U. S. a few months after her 20th birthday. Back home, she finished high school and worked for two years as an office manager for a beauty parlor until she emigrated to the States.

As the youngest child from a family of three, Sylvia described herself as a bit pampered in that though her parents did not have much of anything, she got her needs met and did not feel obligated to do a lot.

She arrived here alone and lived for two and a half years with a distant cousin who came to America as a nurse four to five (4-5) years prior to Sylvia's arrival. As a professional, the cousin managed to save her money and after being here for four years, she fell in love with a man, got married and they had enough in their savings to put down on a house where Sylvia stayed when she arrived. Contrary to her cousin who had a profession, Sylvia taught herself that, if she could find a man, someone to father her child or children, maybe that man would marry her and buy her a house. So, she started dating various men and ended up with one fatherless child, never mind a husband. Immediately, she started having problems with her cousin and husband about her lifestyle and family values. Sylvia, instead of shaping up, shipped out of her cousin's and applied for social welfare for her one year old child. While on welfare, she became exposed to illegal drugs by going out with the wrong crowd; however, she indicated that she experienced nightmares every time she used these chemical substances. Consequently, she withdrew since the morning was still young for her and she did not develop a chemical dependency as yet.

She tried to join the workforce, but with a small child and not enough work experience, all she could find was part-time minimum wage job offers which she declined on the grounds that she won't have enough to live on, and she would lose her welfare benefits. So what happened after that? Sylvia who was very attractive physically seemed at times to have a lot going for her in terms of romantic relationships, except that her mind followed her body instead of the other way around. She attracted men just as fast as they left her; the guys who were serious about her usually ended up leaving because of her limited skills! At the age of 25, she already felt that the biological clock was going against her, not being married; so she got adventurous and went on some blind dates with the help of several dating services. In less than six months, Sylvia ended up being pregnant with twins by a lover who was convicted for grand larceny and possession of illegal weapons. In her seventh month of pregnancy, the father to be is incarcerated, and Sylvia is left alone with $458.00, no job, no health insurance, no education, no husband, and no family support. After giving birth to the twins, she went back on welfare and got a total of $819.00 per month for herself and her three children.

As much as I would like to elaborate on other cases, I do not want to take too much time and space talking about situations that probably you are already familiar with in some shape or form. So, why don't we discuss and extrapolate from these three cases and then after that make some recommendations?

We have opened up the chapter by delegating some responsibilities to government and State officials to provide social assistance to their needy citizens. And I believe that this is where a lot of the currently existing programs find their applications or become necessary. There are many different kinds which exist under specific names with distinct criteria for eligibility. Some of which are federally funded, some are joint programs of Federal and State governments, and others represent just State sponsored social services. We will not take time to name every existing program and go over their specific requirements for eligibility, but the main ones include: **a**) SSI (Supplemental Security Income) which through general tax revenues pays disability benefits to people with disabilities (physical and/or mental) or who do not own much or have a lot of income, **b**) Social Security or Social Security disability insurance which is different from SSI. This program is administered by the US Government but is paid for by workers, employers, and the self-employed with their own social security taxes. According to Social Security Administration, this program pays monthly benefits to some 30 million workers and their families. The age for eligibility is presently 65 but is expected to increase to 67 in the year "2027 for people born in 1960 or later". Then, there are Medicaid and Medicare which usually cover medical care needs and services. For example, Medicare represents part of the taxes that workers, self-employed, and employers pay over the years and on the US employees' pay stubs they call it FICA (Federal Insurance Contributions Act). So far, for every dollar that United States workers pay to Social Security and Medicare,

$0.69 goes to a trust fund which pays retirement and survivors benefits,

$0.19 goes into another trust fund that covers Medicare benefits, and

the remaining 12 cents goes to a third trust fund which pays disability benefits.

In addition to these programs, there is EAEDC (Emergency Aid to Elders, Disabled and Children) formerly known as AFDC. This plan also provides Food Stamps to qualified U. S. citizens or eligible immigrants. One of the eligibility criteria as the name implies is that the applicants must have dependent children or children under 18 years of age, which is one of the reasons I present three cases of only women, since existing laws mainly favor women as legal guardians of minors in single family homes in the United States. Another broad category name that covers a range of these programs is better known to many, at least to Social Security Administration workers, as OASDI, which stands for Old-Age, Survivors, and Disability

Insurance. Now, these reflect social programs provided by the US Government to its citizens and other eligible people such as refugees living in the US and legal immigrants (which may disappear in the years to come, depending upon how Congress decides on these issues and how much pressure they get from varied interest groups and advocates). Social services per se go beyond the scope of this manual, and I would hope that each government in every country has some form of social programs to assist the needy.

We also believe that many people have legitimate claims to obtain such services; for example, those with known disabilities, physical and or mental. Apart from this category, there are elderly individuals with limited financial means who deserve to be cared for. Society should not neglect the elderly or just place them somewhere like old cars and without any kind of assistance. Third, we recognize that there exist unusual circumstances beyond people's control that may require the government, churches, or other humanitarian organizations to intervene socio-economically to help their fellow citizens defray the costs of living. Whether or not the above agencies will always have the means or will always be willing to continue providing assistance, these kinds of services will always be in demand.

We further believe in individual responsibilities which we could learn on our own or that could be required of us when we fail to live up to our tasks. I am of the opinion that social programs should not be designed so as to promote and encourage total dependency of the beneficiaries. There should be an arm of those interventions that not only teaches people about independent living but that also sets aside a percentage (%) of their resources and educates the recipients as to how to achieve that. Many people who become dependent can learn how to function on their own and be more productive members of society, given the opportunity, especially those who are young and simply have socio-economic disabilities which I consider to be temporary and reversible circumstances in one's life. Let us look at some statistics and facts from some of the welfare programs in the United States.

The following reflects US Federal Government standard for SSI payments for 1996:

Amount per individual = $470.00/month
Amount per a couple = $705.00/month

Amounts paid from SSI to individuals living below poverty thresholds:

Family unit	1993 (actual)	1994 (actual)	1995 (preliminary)
Aged individual	$ 6,960.00	$ 7,108.00	$ 7,309.00
Family of two, aged head	$ 8,487.00	$ 8,967.00	$ 9,221.00
Family of four	$14,335.00	$15,141.00	$15,570.00

Figures from the US Census Bureau

These numbers provide a rather simplistic version of eligibility to receive aid from the US Government under the old welfare guidelines. All figures reflect the US Government. Statistics from social services in other countries will not be provided in this book.

Programs like AFDC (now EAEDC) were created by the United States Administration following the Great Depression of the 1930's to provide temporary relief or Aid to Families with Dependent Children. This is commendable and every government should look to develop or create opportunities for their citizens, especially the poor and needy. However, what government should try to avoid is creating an unnecessary dependent community. Any agency that puts itself in the position to take care of or provide for someone who is not physically or mentally impaired and not emotionally or even psychologically disturbed should make it its obligation to engage the recipients in becoming self-sufficient, by educating them and helping them develop a healthy belief system. Anyone who really cares about helping people fight poverty should do more than just handing them fish, so that one day they will be in the position to provide for their own needs; otherwise you just teach them how to become dependent and that's no help! In a sense, doing that just contributes to making the world poorer. If all we could do for our kids is teach them how to be totally dependent on us or on anybody else, it would be much better that we never had them in the first place. This is where I believe that people should be cautious about having so many children. How will I care for them? How am I going to provide for their education? If I were dependent myself and know what that meant to me, I should avoid putting those that I love in the same predicament!

First, for the elderly whose conditions are likely to worsen over time and for other citizens or people with somewhat permanent disabilities such as physical or mental/psychological, special programs designed to help meet their specific needs on a permanent basis may be relevant. **Second**, contrary to the above category, physically, mentally/psychologically able bodies who have the ability to work to support themselves but simply have socio-economic constraints may receive temporary economic aid or welfare assistance to help them make ends meet. Similarly, those individuals who face emergency situations and who require additional or extra help to respond to their immediate needs, governmental agencies, humanitarian relief services, and philanthropic organizations together or individually could design short-term plans or programs that would provide socio-economic services to those affected. These programs can offer cash assistance, food, shelter, stipends, and other forms of help necessary to see the victims through the emergency. After the crisis is over, or after normalcy has been restored in the lives of those people for whom the short-term interventions were created in the first place, the emergency plan should end. Should there be a need for services to go on indefinitely and for the same group of individuals, namely for categories two and three, then something is definitely wrong, and the program ought to assess its original goals and perhaps redesign new plans which will include medium range as well as long-term goals or interventions. Therefore, we are suggesting the following service plans: **A** = short-term plans, **B** = medium-range plans, and **C** = long-range plans or goals. And each of which should include at least some of the following components or specific area of assistance:

A

Basic needs: food, shelter, clothing

A safe environment

Moral support

Civic Activity

Family-oriented services

Control over credit

B

Needs assessment
Some form of counseling

Training on self-esteem and positive self-image

Budgeting/money savings

Time management/self-discipline

Stress management

Limit # of credit cards to 1 or 2

C

Job training

Education

Career planning

Skills enhancement

Financial aid to study

Small low interest loans to develop business

Help promote healthier belief systems

Use them only when absolutely necessary

This list is simply a suggestion, and it does not include every kind of intervention that social programs or individual plans should include. Neither does the government have to provide these services or be directly involved. It could initiate some of them or it could sponsor them, or it might encourage employers or the private sector to do so and give them some form of incentive to design and implement such programs. Then, more people would work and provide for their own needs. The industries would benefit from helping to build stronger, healthier communities. Government would collect more taxes from working people, and it wouldn't have to bother so much about the bad guys trying to beat the system, because for one thing they would not be collecting indefinitely. They would receive temporary assistance, plus training if necessary so that they can learn how to be independent.

Many people rely on other folks only due to circumstances. As soon as they are able to make changes, they go on their own. Others live in a transitional environment, waiting for the right opportunity to come by. Still others have not been offered the opportunity or they are conditioned to remain dependent upon somebody else.

Underprivileged, disenfranchised citizens of every country should be helped to some extent by their own government. They should be encouraged and/or offered the same opportunity like everyone else to make use of their hands and their brains in whichever capacity. Then, they should be appropriately compensated for their service. <u>Giving a fish to someone all the time is not only humiliating but also it helps create a dependent society</u>! Every human being is created with so much potential that they cannot use it in their lifetime. However, as they grow up, they often fall for the wrong idea or pick up the wrong baggage that ends up weighing so heavily on their shoulders, or they simply do not give themselves the chance to fully mature. Sometimes, they become confused with different ideologies, and different unhealthy concepts. I hope that the following chapter, especially, will assist them in making the appropriate changes.

❖ CHAPTER XXV ❖

The Road Traveled by the New Immigrants!

Life in the ideal world tends to be stable and everyone lives happily, no disturbance and no migration; except that only a few individuals ever made it there and perhaps, no one knows of them.

On the contrary, life in the real world is tainted with joy and sadness, a period of tranquillity followed by a period of great disturbances and war, a period of stability and a period of migration. Paradoxically, in the best possible world, even some of today's celebrities, the famous, and the haves will be among the have nots of tomorrow and the opposite is also true, so that no one, no one should boast.

Migration for many reasons is oftentimes inevitable. The war on ethnic cleansing in Bosnia-Herzegovina, with the blessings from their western allies, has just ended. Now, the trend shifts from Europe (the Eastern Block) to the African continent, where we start seeing a new flow of exodus, namely the Hutu refugees, as the Tutsi go on the offensive into the Zairian territory (*Boston Globe*, Monday, October 28, 1996, p. A6). Meanwhile, 67,000 immigrants who illegally entered the United States to look for gold have been repatriated or deported by years end (*Boston Globe*, Monday, October 28, 1996, p. A6). Whether it is in Central Africa, Iraq, the Middle East, the Soviet bloc countries, Europe, Asia, America or wherever, migration presents a threat to the socio-economic stability of those who are directly affected by it. Sometimes, that gives rise to conflict between those who have long established themselves and the newcomers where the latter often get blamed and prosecuted as well as persecuted for everything that goes wrong in the host country. This represents a particular situation where Thomas Malthus' (English economist) theory of too many people and too few resources tends to become an enigma or a problem.

It is true that to some extent the influx of people migrating into a new area can outgrow resources that are readily available, which natural population growth may also do; however this is not the whole truth. We will not get too much into that but let me ask you: have you ever heard that "the rich get richer and the poor get poorer"? Does it also mean that the poor get "less creative or lazier" (if they ever were in the first place) while the rich become smarter and greedier, or is it all mere coincidence? When people migrate, where do they go, why, and what do they bring as assets?

How can they become an important force and make their voice heard in this new environment? Is there a sense of belongingness (do they belong here); or are they involved politically (*"If they don't vote, they do not count..."* that's a famous saying from different interest groups), economically, intellectually, religiously, and how much of a role do they play in community activities? The answers to these questions to a great extent explain why people, especially migrants, usually face socio-economic stagnation for they (the immigrants) often have no buying power which they either give up striving for or they end up resisting changes and continuing in their trivial pursuit which is making careers out of jobs with no future, a wrong investment of their time and energy.

A- The Two Types of Migration

Migration (immigration and emigration) may be internal or it could be external. When people move from one town or province to another or from one state to the next within the same national geographical area, we often call this internal migration. This involves no border crossing into another country. In fact, this kind of mobility is quite frequent in places or countries where resources and opportunities are not readily available, or everything is centralized to a main location and citizens do not have access to them unless they relocate themselves. Usually, people migrate from the rural to the metropolitan areas, looking for better opportunities, or for places to live, and where they can work, receive better training and education for themselves and also to raise and educate their children.

The other type of migration, which we call external, and it focuses on people leaving a country, usually their native land, to go and live in another one. In either case (internal or external), the process may be voluntary or involuntary. Relocation of relatives can drag other family members against their own free will. War and natural disasters often force people to vacate places where lives of the inhabitants feel threatened. To date, the most common reasons why people migrate have to do with economics, political disturbances, and famine. Usually what the migrant has in mind or perceives before leaving his or her homeland is quite different from the reality that awaits him or her in the new land.

B- The Uncertainty of Migration

Let's start by asking the following questions: does migration ensure a better life? In other words, are migrants always better off? What do they leave home with, and what do they get upon their arrival in the new land? Are they always welcome? Sometimes yes, and sometimes no! That depends on a lot of factors such as: who they are in terms race and gender, their country of origin, the raw resources (capitals, skills, etc…) that they bring with them, and the need for them in the local market economy. Now, another important question is the following: do these new migrants have what it requires for them to adjust to this new life? Are they willing, able to make certain changes in their lifestyle, or do they really know how to adjust/adapt in order to promote themselves in a world where competition and survival of the fittest is the name of the game?

If I may, I would like to open this segment of our discussion with my own personal experience on migration. I will rather focus on an earlier migration in my life.

It was in November, 1972 that I had my first external migrant experience. Up to that time, I was living with my parents, but I went to boarding school and lived with an older cousin from my mother's side, which I consider internal migration. At any rate, in June, 1972, having successfully completed my first year of high school in Haiti, there was no prospect that I could continue in October. My parents had two children: myself and my sister who is deceased as of 1992. However, resources were very scarce.

I could remain home with Mom and Dad and my younger sister but to me the idea of not attending school in the next academic year was so devastating. By early November of 1992, an older friend and classmate who had previously left the country and landed in the Bahamas was on the brink of leaving Haiti for Nassau by boat. Now the whole trip did not sound too savvy; however, it presented a choice between two evils and I thought that I chose the lesser one!

By mid November, it looked like the trip would occur. I forget, but I think that the price per person was between $500 and $800 U. S. dollars. Nonetheless, the captain of the boat would accept partial payment till passengers arrived and found a paying job. Both my father and I envisioned that going to the Bahamas might create some opportunities for the future of the family. Except that we later discovered that although our goals could be reached, they were not so realistic at that particular juncture in our lives. The boat finally set sail for Nassau around November 23, 1972 with about 60 men, women, and perhaps some children. I myself was just in my teenage years.

The boat had no engine. It sailed under the natural force, wind power. Food, water, and clothing were limited. In fact, we were advised not to carry more than one extra pair of garments and the reason being that upon landing we did not want to have too much in our hands to hinder us and make us look like new immigrants.

Looking back on this atrocious trip, I probably would not do it that way again. That first experience had little merit, if any. My father, who was a renown cabinet maker in our hometown, could not make a living in that profession. Now, he was on his way to the Bahamas with no legal papers, not one word of English to converse with people should he ever make it to his final destination. I myself, a teenager with one year of high school, and no profession, limited to a few English sentences which I picked up from earlier English classes, managed to remain in the Bahamas for a year and a half, thanks to a fervent Haitian minister, a man of God who was very instrumental in helping the newcomers. A few weeks after my arrival, arrangements were made for me to fly to Marsh Harbor, Abaco, another one of the many Bahamian islands, where I was supposed to harvest produce from farms, and which were to be exported. I never asked my father where he went upon his descent from the boat but he was interrupted by an Immigration Agency and expatriated later on.

I lived for a year and a half in solitude with no one in my immediate family, nobody at all. I had no prior knowledge of the culture, nor did I have the skills necessary to find a job. I cannot say a decent job, because generally there was none available to a "Just Come", a term used in the Bahamas to differentiate newcomers from those who have been there.

There was no more school for me while I lived there. Jobs were quite sporadic; a month or two of work followed by a month or so without anything to do. I just spent whatever I was able to save earlier. There was not a real, balanced interaction between people of the two cultures. Also, there prevailed a great sense of mistrust, hatred for immigrants on the part of many Nationals who saw us, the new comers, as intruders, coming in to take away their jobs. In that same vein, life for many immigrants was rather cheap there with not much respect from many government officials or from private citizens. We lived there under constant fear of deportation. By May, 1974, I had had just about enough. I made a plane reservation and I returned to Haiti by the end of June with $60 U. S. dollars.

C- The Fate of New Immigrants

Accepting the realities of life while we try to bring positive changes or living under false pretense through times are two opposing views that do not always spare the newcomers. Oftentimes, the flaws or the paradox in the thinking of the new migrants and the day-to-day reality often do not match. Anywhere around the world, when migrants are moving into an already well-established society, only a few of them with financial resources to invest, political clout, and/or who possess the job skills that are in demand will find a better reception. Everyone else, except for those who have relatives that preceded them, must make it on their own, in isolation or loneliness or what have you. They must face the frustration of acculturation which involves making all kinds of adaptations: overcoming language barriers, learning to function in the culture, acquiring new job skills to even find work, observing changes in the weather, or in a social structure, living alone, trying to be self-sufficient in every sense of the word and no family member to share any task with (be all in all). Sometimes, the individual must work several low paying jobs that provide no benefits, and the revenue earned must be split in two in order to provide for family members living here and support for the relatives that are left behind. Also, there's a noticeable difference in the ages of the migrants. The younger ones have more energy, perhaps lots of dreams to fulfill. Though it should not be the only group to try to take advantage of the following opportunities, in the same setting it might be easier for much younger migrant members of a family to make a sacrifice to go to school and learn the language, some trades, or a profession and become better equipped to sustain their survivorship.

Due to issues ranging from socio-cultural, psychological, legal, etc., many times immigrants have to work harder than the citizens (the Nationals). Because, oftentimes they end up entering the workforce doing menial jobs that do not provide any kind of security. When times come for them to get a promotion, they may be told that they lack real experience, which can be the case; but at the same time the people (we might say employees) receive no practical assistance that would empower them and help them prepare for a better, brighter future. Those positions are usually dead end streets or temporary placements which offer no alternatives. Not all immigrants really discover the gold mine that they have dreamed of. For many of them, the gold mine was back home. In other words, socio-economically, many migrants become less able. Sometimes the pressure coming from the process of acculturation and the expectations of other relatives is enough to cause them to have a nervous breakdown. Psychosis, a mental disorder where people who suffer from it often lose contact with reality depending on its stage and severity, can be very detrimental among immigrant populations.

Please, do not get me wrong. Some newcomers who either worked hard or were favorably grafted into the new culture are able to adjust comfortably. However, among the odds that new immigrants often have to fight is prejudice. In many instances, they are blamed for all the things that go wrong within the internal affairs of the nation that hosts them. It is like a handshake with the right hand and a slap on the cheek with the left hand. Immigrants are so often perceived as scapegoats on whom the citizens cast their blame for a stagnant economy, lack of jobs, violence, germs, etc. But let me say this, some people forget their past so soon that they have problems seeing where they are going. Too often they become distracted and allow their dreams to evaporate or go up in the air.

I would like to leave the following message with the immigrants in particular. No matter where you are, you have to try to make the best of life. Sometimes, as immigrants, you work several jobs in an attempt to support two households. I think that is commendable. Nonetheless, I just have a suggestion for you. You may be young now and feel very strong, strong enough to carry the world on your shoulders. I do not know if cutting your working hours will help you survive economically. I am not even sure that going to trade schools will bring lasting stability that we all search for. Whatever the case may be, that's no reason for you not to put some new skills in your head. Anyone who wishes to remain competitive in the job market must always look for ways that will help upgrade or sharpen one's skills. Above all things, every human being, particularly new immigrants for our discussion purposes, must learn how to allocate readily existing resources or create their own. Nowadays, it is not uncommon to find people with skills and who cannot get a job. My philosophy is this: I better be more qualified for a position than have too little qualifications. After all, there is no limit as to what you can become or how far you can reach in life. If you set your mind to it and believe that you can, you will!

Note: Parents of immigrants in particular, whether you never went to school back home or here, whether you are economically unable or not, you are legally bound before the law for the actions of your under-age children. Reprimand them whenever and wherever necessary. Set good examples for them, be loving, tender, and kind to them. Like you, they try to fit in and as a result they face many challenges which you, adults, may not be sensitive to. Therefore, communicate with them as your friends, without letting let them take over before it is time. They will if you allow them to, but the outcomes may not be pleasant. Somebody needs to be in charge. I am neither diminishing their humanity and their self-worth nor underestimating what they can do. In fact, ask for their input on matters regarding the family; however until they are old and mature enough to take over, you are in command. Also, you need to know where they are at different times during the day and how their school work is coming along! Give them some freedom but not a license, for when they fail, you fail; freedom is good but too much of it may do harm sometimes. They are underage and live in your house. If the police comes looking for them, you bet that you have some explanation to give.

❖ CHAPTER XXVI ❖

Sustaining Your Energy Bank
(Energy Source)

Coming from the United Negro College Fund (a U. S. based organization), is a slogan that reads as follows:

"The Mind is a Terrible Thing to Waste."

Obviously, that is a true statement, for out of one's mind comes all sorts of input: emotional, psychological, intellectual, philosophical. Equally important is the brain. Whatever movement we want to operate with our body or part thereof (conscious or unconscious) through one of our five senses, a signal must travel with specific messages all the way to the brain which will then communicate back to that part and coordinate the desired action. In that sense, the brain serves as a relay station; but how can one reconcile or relate brain to mind? In other words, how do they fit together?

Anatomically, they are not two mutually exclusive entities. Using strict scientific jargon, the mind is to the psyche as the brain is to our nervous system. Sometimes, we refer to our mind as being inside our skull, which is in essence the protective cage of our brain. Biologically, the brain represents a segment or a part of our nervous system which consists of:

1) The brain
2) The brain stem, and
3) The spinal cord

If you will, the mind, according to *Webster's Dictionary*, represents the seat of our consciousness, our thoughts, feelings, will, and intellect. Somehow, when <u>WE</u> choose or make decisions (especially sound decisions), we engage our mind in the process. Let's take this a step further. Contrary to reacting just during the excitement of the moment, if WE are truly concerned about our personal growth, or want to develop our potential, then our decisions ought to be rooted in our own mind, the motor of our soul. Therefore, we have every reason under the sun to say that the mind is the most powerful instrument we ever possess. As a computer, we can program our mind to carry on any function or task which we want it to; and only you, as an individual, can limit what your brain or your mind is capable of. The weakest mind has more potential than any computer or robot that mankind will ever create. Within this context, we may relate to the mind as the most powerful energy bank. For that matter, energy bank, energy source, and powerful instrument are all synonymous terms in this book. Can you use that power to build yourself up?

That will demand a certain amount of critical thinking which I will describe as the ability of the individual to raise sound questions, research, and collect accurate information before making decisions or jumping to conclusions. This represents a superior level of thought, which is really where I would like to engage you as you visualize new ideas and concepts or face a new set of problems/challenges. You may be able to dissect them in their smallest components by raising the kind of questions which will eventually lead to the right kind of answer (s). However, I realize how important it is for us to lay the groundwork effectively before we can help stimulate your mind thereby raising it to the operational level where you may become an independent thinker and a sharper problem solver. I do not wish to sound cute, and neither do I mean to convey an eccentric or egotistical, selfish message by saying this, but think for a moment of your problems being yours and nobody else's. Now, let me ask you, if you could think smart enough to the extent of arriving at the right solutions to these problems, wouldn't it look kind of self-deceiving for you to just sit there and wait two (200) hundred years for someone to come help you? As I get you to think about that, I'd like to address the next sub-heading of this chapter.

A- Potential Energy

As the most powerful instrument, the mind is equipped and may be <u>positively</u> stimulated to help promote ourselves, build the environment in which we live, strengthen the society, the culture, the nation or the world of which we are a part. On the contrary, that very same mind can help us accomplish the opposite effect: to tear ourselves down and destroy our neighbors, the environment, etc.

Even though I do not wish to have you work hard to comprehend this, let us consider for a moment some basic chemistry. There are two opposite charges which exist in nature: the positive (+) and the negative (-). The refrigerator in your house or the electrical appliances that you own, your heart, your kidneys, to name a few, are all dipolar or electrically charged with both positive and negative poles. Do you remember feeling too hot or too cool or getting an electrical shock (static) by touching something that has a different temperature from your body? In these instances and in many others, we do not refer to the plus (+) as good or to the minus (-) as bad. That is simply how nature works to bring together many different ions (e.g. Calcium or Ca^{++}, major components of animal bones), atoms (Hydrogen or H, Oxygen or O_2, gas which keeps us alive), compounds like Sodium Chloride (NaCl) or HCl (hydrochloric acid, a gastric juice also found in the stomach which if it is allowed to sit in high concentration for too long can create problems). All of it is POTENTIAL at the start; however, when these small parts are brought together, they have the capability to build themselves up into gigantic structures. That's also how nature keeps a certain order or balance. For instance, every cell in our body proportionately needs both charges (+ and -) in order to function and maintain homeostasis, another big word, meaning: keeping balance. That way, our body is kept in check, so we do not undergo too much variation too quickly. Do you imagine what it would feel like to be extremely hot one minute, and then extremely cool the next minute? In other words, too much change in any one direction is no good; it would actually lead to the extremes and chaos.

The main reason for bringing this last piece into our discussion is because we do not want you to be caught up in the notion of positive and negative poles or influence out of the proper context. When you receive a lab result from your physician, for example, the idea of a positive or a negative test result can be good or bad. Now for the next few moments, I would like to invite you into an exciting exploration, do you mind? By the way, fasten your seat belt please!

And as we get the engine warmed up for takeoff, let me ask you two more questions. First, if your mind is a powerful energy source, how do you use such power? Secondly, can you use it to build yourself up? You need not search too far for the answers; we will walk you through in a stepwise manner. Just have your paper and pencil ready.

A bit earlier, before we started talking about that chemistry business, we used the expression: the mind being "equipped or potentially charged". Once we get you to understand this concept, you will be all fired up to answer the preceding questions.

In technical terms or in college physics, POTENTIAL means:

TO EXIST BUT NOT FULLY DEVELOPED OR EXPLOITED. So, when we talk about potential change or potential energy, we mean energy stored in our body due to or in relation to its position, or simply an energy that is sitting there waiting to do work for us. Now, let us read the questions to you once more. If your mind is a powerful source of energy, how can you use such power? Two, can you use it to actually build yourself up, or in what way have you been able to? Please, write down your answers.

1)_____

2)_____

Then, follow attentively.

A house can be in total darkness, even though there may be energy of some sort flowing in or stored in it. If the power line and the electrical circuits have been placed, and if that work is complete, someone still has to turn the light switch on or there will be no light, there is power in the house but it has not been used. If it is a lamp or a candle that you use as your source of illumination, you or someone in your home must light it up or else there will never be light inside that house. Obviously, you are next to or surrounded by potential light switches that have not been utilized. Again, how can you use this power plant, your mind, to actually build yourself and open up the gates of opportunities for yourself? There is something called Energy Conservation and what that means is simply this: the total energy in a system remains constant (the same) even though that energy may be converted from one form to another.

Almost in every home in this world, there exists some form of a device or a system which can generate fire or heat. Moreover, there is fuel stored in tanks in almost every country where modern technology is used. All of which are sources of energy and can be used to carry on constructive works or destructive missions. Our mind has the capability to engage in the building up of mass destructive weapons, while at the same time we can use it to bring about innovative works that human eyes have not yet seen and our imagination has yet to discover.

B- Exploration: Use Your Mind/Brain Positively and Constructively

Figure 26.1 An Enslaved Mind

You can decide for yourself who you want to be or what you wish to accomplish in life as you continue to attain maturity. However, until you identify your power outlet, in this case your mind, and how it functions, you may be viewed as someone who holds a car key without knowing how to drive. We've seen this phenomenon every day, rich folks living like paupers. They have contributed to having their own wealth confiscated. Many people have voluntarily given their consent for their mind to be locked under maximum security, thereby limiting their upward or forward move. If you cannot think clearly or rationally, you are not involved in any kind of decision-making regarding yourself (assuming you are not a child or medically disabled) and your imagination is blank, while it may seem that you are free, you are a prisoner indeed.

All that I am trying to say to you is this: just as an athlete trains himself or herself, you've got to do the same. As you train your brain/mind to develop higher thinking power, you may actually access an enormous source of strength that will help you function on a different level. **Consider these steps:** 1) Take a little time every day to be alone 2) Meditate 3) Try to free your mind by not focusing on current event (s) in your life, especially the sad ones since they have the potential to keep your spirit down 4) Close your eyes and concentrate on a phrase, any phrase or word, a particular song, a distinct piece of music that relaxes and relieves you of your stress; and if need be, repeat it several times until you feel that renewal 5) Then make a pledge to yourself, starting with a small one. Set a small goal, give yourself a time limit to complete it; for instance it could be attending an exercise class a couple of times weekly 6) Look for someone you might consider a mentor whose life exemplifies a success in some way. After completing this first task, if you have to rest and get recharged, please do so but do not make it your final project, set the next goal (and you may repeat the steps as often as you feel like). Again give yourself a timetable and move on with it. Do not tarry forever. Ask the questions that you dared not; you may even ask why is the sky blue, why is the sun steady, or why are your parents married to each other.

You not only need to feel energetic, but you also have to channel that energy in such a way that it is not wasted. Don't wait until tomorrow to ask the question what if; do as much as you can today because you cannot go back and do or undo what you could have done yesterday! How often do we hear very young, not too young, and older people complain about lack of energy to do their work?

Sometimes, there may be underlying issues such as personal, emotional, or psychological stressors that make a person feel that way. Also after a long day of strenuous activities, it is actually normal to feel energy drained, Even after being in bed all night may not provide you with sufficient energy to carry on through the day. Sometimes we become restless and wrestle with different situations to the extent that we bring our physical being to bed but our mind remains unsettled. Maybe we need to take an inventory of the situation to find out what causes such a problem. Also, take notice that a lack of incentive or motivation can cause us to feel very lazy and dry to the point that we do not want to do anything but just sit down in one spot. Just a kindly reminder, and you may put a check in the mail for me as I make this announcement: nothing ventured, nothing gained.

Each of us needs to find appropriate activities which stimulate our minds and thinking. Otherwise, we run the risk of letting other people think on our behalf. Then, we end up being distracted followers with no clear direction where we ought to go or what we are to do. Every one of us that has a brain ought to think for himself or herself. Don't allow your energy to go to waste and not live up to your potential. Instead, train your mind to meditate on higher power that you have been given by your creator so that you may succeed in all your undertaking. Avoid the company of those individuals who practice filthy behavior like laziness, procrastination, most forms of addiction, drunkenness, gossip, backbiting, violence, socializing for the sake of it, and pleasure at all times. Having a keen mind will help you travel a very long way in life. If you have not done it yet, add a little bit of aggressiveness to your personal characteristics.

❖ CHAPTER XXVII ❖

Which Should You Change:
Your Skin Color, Your Belief, or Both?

A- Racially Speaking: The Socio-Economic and The Political Framework of Color

Besides other traits and characteristics that we humans use to categorize, congregate, segregate, discriminate, and isolate people, race represents such a substantial element. And it goes without saying that no matter how homogeneous or similar all of us look, we tend to create all the time a new breed of individuals that will not only be different from us but also inferior to us; per reinforcement, either by fear, ignorance or by sheer incompetence/inadequacy the person being discriminated against is never equal or superior to those passing the judgment. We should be looking into racial diversity for all that it is worth and welcoming its beauty; instead we use it as a tool to hate, exploit, and repress, at least those of us who provide the medium that nurtures and transports racism throughout our circulatory system! To further promote our own selfish agenda, we develop an egomaniacal (from egomania) attitude vis-à-vis our own ethnic identity while dehumanizing and demonizing others. We consistently hold onto our vivid imagination when it comes to establishing situational differences which will necessarily confirm how we view and present ourselves in relation to other races and ethnic groups. Again, the interesting thing is that the way we select those situations and how we go about validating them are both arbitrary and suggestive at the same time; there is very little scientific evidence or facts to support all of our claims, especially racism (racial differences).

Consciously, based upon whatever criteria we deem suitable, we make determinations as to how different people, objects, and different things ought to be classified. So, cognitively it seems to make sense for us to create a distinct category for all the differences which we can possibly come up with. For instance, all the people who have big noses, flat noses, or straight noses each fall under a separate category of their own. And we do the same for them with respect to their eye color, hair texture, so on and so forth. We even group them in terms of the types of cars they drive, the kinds of houses they live in, the colors of socks that they wear: black, blue, gray, pink, white, and red, as in the Boston Red Sox. Once we complete our nomenclature, we legislate our beliefs by ratifying our socio-political constructs which will help protect and justify whatever rationale we will later formulate toward these groups. Then, to whomever we attach a label or labels, those individuals or those groups of people become our target or the stereotype that we can at will pick on, discriminate against, and whenever we feel like it we can dispose of. Although differences do not mean unequal or inferior to, for our convenience, we implicitly equate the two terms to just that. And if you will, the context in which we often refer to race has lots more to do with control than anything else; and except for few biological differences, gender gap follows almost the same pattern, and that is the reality in which we live.

Our socio-economic and political agendas, to a large scale, help explain why race is such a major issue in society in general. At least, on a structural level, socio-economic standards greatly determine the power relations across distinct races, ethnic groups, and social classes. Throughout human civilization, social existence seems to almost always be interpreted in the confines of economic might and socio-political superiority of one nation or an ethnic group versus another, which of course relates to geo-political expansion and/or military strength. Thus, the like come together and after they agree on certain criteria which identify them as one, they formulate their objectives, and then set their locomotives in motion. You better believe that these objectives for the most part are discriminatory and represent self-serving bias or tools in the hands of the group that designs them, in that people who do not fit their criteria are excluded from drawing any benefits. The end may not always justify the means for the group or the country that discriminates against members of a different ethnic group; however, social dynamics focus on these premises which give way to all forms of prejudice. Racism is one form of prejudice that transcends different ethnic compositions. In other words, although racist practices may be enforced as a retaliatory measure toward members of another group, they are not directed only from white against black. Obviously, whites discriminate against blacks, blacks discriminate against whites, white against white, and black against black. For example, Caribbean blacks, African-Americans, and blacks in the African mainland do not consider themselves equal, just as not all Latinos/Latinas see themselves equal; earlier fighting which came to be known among Bosnian-Serbs as ethnic cleansing is another such example. Conversely, when a prejudicial attitude is pointed back towards those who initiated it, it is called reverse discrimination, meaning an eye for an eye, and a tooth for a tooth; or your treatment of me determines my treatment of you! You can tell that with this kind of attitude, prejudice will never end; it will keep going in circles. We might ask the following questions: Number one, why does racism prevail even in a civilized, law-abiding society? Number two, what are the bases for it, and three, is there a color that constitutes success? In other words, can we find scientific grounds for racial discrimination, and where does that lead us?

B- Green Melanin: The Color of Success

Dr. David G. Myers, a respected professor of Psychology and well known writer in this field, in his book entitled: "Social Psychology", when referring to prejudice in general suggests three distinct sources, which he identifies as: Social, Emotional, and Cognitive (Myers. Social Psych. pp. 483-530.)

1- The social root of prejudice. According to Myers, first, we lay the ground work which will serve as forces to be used by us to validate social inequalities that we ourselves create. Once we have that in place, "prejudice can be used to justify the economic and social superiority of those who have wealth and power. Thus, discrimination breeds prejudice, and prejudice legitimizes discrimination...").

2- The emotional context of prejudice. As different groups of individuals compete every day for the same resources, the frustration that virtually arises from it is often directed towards their competitors, whomever they might be. Therefore, as explained in Myers' work: "prejudice springs not only from intellectual justifications but also from passionate emotions".

3- The cognitive source of prejudice. Before going any further, let me divert for a moment to give a working definition of the word cognitive. It refers to our thinking process, and it includes perception, awareness, and the way we make judgments. This provides a base to not only help us simplify the world but also to justify the decisions that emerge as an end result of our thinking process, including stereotypes. Therefore, social thinking which goes hand in hand with each group's ideology and culture, the political climate, and self-identity become a driving force in establishing social inequalities.

There exist other forces supporting racial discrimination such as personal bias, ignorance, religious beliefs, and ethnic/national pride; however, most of which fall under one of these three sources mentioned above. Hence, justification for slavery and the legitimization of any other forms of repression and suppressive rights against folks that we perceive as different from us becomes real. Thus, injustice, racial discrimination, and other forms of social inequalities follow basically the same formula, each of which may be covered under different names, and we may use different tactics to enforce each form of prejudice, but the base remains almost the same.

In order that we might justify our own hostility and discriminatory opinions, we design different laws and create institutions that enforce them. We had laws in place to validate slavery; we continue to develop mandates that control who may be able to move up and around the socio-economic ladder and how they go about doing that and to put it bluntly, we do have guns to make sure that they comply, especially when we do not want those people over there to benefit from the same privileges as we because they don't look like us. In many instances, that is how social tension gets started. You have one group that controls the advantageous end of the spectrum and who wants to keep it that way. At the other end, the disadvantageous one, congregate those groups of people who are striving to distance themselves from the stereotypes that they have been associated with for so long. One of the oldest stereotypes relates to physical appearances. Under this umbrella falls an array of traits and characteristics, including skin pigment or simply color. Different pigments have been recognized but in scientific jargon, we use MELANIN, a general term which embraces them all. Somehow, human civilizations have almost always associated a certain ethnicity and/or a certain pigment to wealth and power. Now, it is not accidental that the two (W & P) oftentimes go together for one helps secure the other; and in turn, they largely control the environment under color codes.

With respect to some preconceived notions, some colors are more legitimate and have superior birthrights over others. These colors or pigments identify with real human beings. At some point in their existence, there are people who wished that they fit the criteria of the color associated with one of the pigments for success! "Greenback" seems to be a universal color that governs the world; please note that the term is used here in a broader sense to include not just the American dollar (which many people have referred to by that name due to the original tint or dye on the back of the money), but material wealth in general. The expression GREEN MELANIN which I refer to in the subheading of this section so derives from the connotation within the parentheses. When this "Green Melanin" intertwines with political power, the two then help redefine racial identities and/or boundaries. The World Bank (WB), just like any other major world bodies, as well as individual nations, recognize at least three different depths of this pigment alone. Searching in the World Bank data, you will not find the word pigment. What you will see instead are:

1- Low-income economies, which refers to countries with a GNP per capita (Gross National Product) or the number of dollars per year for each citizen in a particular nation in a specific geographical region. The figure here is $ 725.00 or less, based on WB 1994 report.

2- Middle-income economies represent countries in a particular region with a GNP between $725.00 and $8,955.00 per capita for the same period of time, 1994.

3- High-income economies. This refers to a GNP per capita going from $8,956 to infinity, still for 1994 (The World Bank. World Development Report, 1996. pp. 180-182.)

Depending on which country you live in, these different economic brackets or pigments can have extreme repercussions on you, your family, and your nation in general. That can affect your well-being in many ways, namely in the area of basic necessities like food, shelter, and clothing, health care availability, the quality of education, etc. I don't think you mean to tell me that the deeper your pigment (in this sense, we might as well say pocket deep), the better you look socio-economically and the more acceptable/tolerable you become in the eyes of the world. Therefore, our behaviors and attitudes are greatly influenced by societal norms and values. This is one of the reasons why in any society where material assets seem to be the end of it all, corruption prevails so much. We use ethnic/racial diversity to build ourselves up and flip it over to tear or keep others down. What we often witness is that the oppressed of today become tomorrow's oppressors. Another behavior that we usually display along the racial and ethnic lines is the following: we condition ourselves to see our mishaps as the work of someone out there always making sure that we do not succeed in our search for the right color or the right pigment. You know just as well as I do that some people don't wish you well, and different cultures express it differently. Some might call it racism, while others call it political sphere of influence (that's their territory, you keep away from it), and they use force to impose that if need be. Still others tend to rely on voodoo while others take drugs to try to prove themselves. As a result, when things go right for us (strong economy, low unemployment, perfect health), we attribute the success to our own intelligencia and give ourselves a pat on the back; however, as things become sour, as they often have a tendency to do, we look for somebody else to cast the blame on. This is also the reality when we are frustrated and we do not seem to be able to find the right answer to our problems or the right color that will confer upon us material wealth and power.

C- In Search of the Right Color

Every human being that lives to be a certain age becomes confronted by the need of self-identity or self-actualization. Consequently, most of us more often than not, voluntarily execute the role that society sets for and expect of us. That's not necessarily wrong morally, for besides other things it provides a sense of belongingness. It also helps shape our personality and characters and serves as a medium that promotes individual growth and all the other good stuff. Through self-identity, we can go on to create an environment where we may see ourselves as equal and as competent as our peers, or we can take different avenues and view ourselves as superior or as inferior to other human beings. Sometimes, society calls the shots and we simply respond; other times, we call them ourselves and respond to our own shots. A superiority or inferiority complex can come about in these two ways. Someone who is being told this or that and who believes it tends to act accordingly, feeling above everyone else or less than anyone else. A person who has suffered some kind of trauma or who has never believed in himself or herself can display the same attitude. Why is this important here? It helps explain the root of prejudice to a great extent, and many of us never grow past that point. We either receive the notion in our childhood or we develop it during our adult life and subscribe to it. Groups like the KKK (Ku Klux Klan), the Skin Heads, or any such supremacist groups are examples of that. Anti-Black, anti-White, anti-Semitism, anti-women, anti-rich, anti-poor people, anti-intellectuals are also a few examples of the manifestation of discrimination.

Conversely, I remember one of my former job supervisors who used to say, "the oppressed becomes the oppressor". When someone hates somebody else that first hated him or her, that person practices what is called "reverse discrimination" which is just as bad as the one directed at him or her. Both forms have to be reprimanded if we want to solve the problem of prejudice. Nowadays, if you want to be politically correct you use words like racial tolerance or empowering of the poor. For reasons that we mentioned before, skin pigment or color does favor inequalities in the advantages of the "Superior Race". Therefore, those who are economically deprived and politically underrepresented and who have no significant input in the decision-making machine need a helping hand just as anyone else, at some point in time. From a secular point of view, wealth and political power represent two very significant tools that people need if they are to reach racial equality. They also cannot underestimate the self-identity issues; just as they must dissociate themselves from the Survival Mentality. They need the whole four to successfully make it to the right color. A fifth component to be added to the equation is a sense of spiritual bonding. Even secular scientists are now looking into the role that prayer plays in healing. Also, it is equally important that those individuals don't depend totally on the system. They must not see themselves as total victims of capitalism, liberalism, dictatorship, communism, or whatever system they are under, but rather as able bodies, capable to participate at all levels of decision-making in their respective communities.

President Clinton made talks on racial equality a priority series of his domestic agenda after he officially delivered a presidential apology to blacks who have been treated wrongfully in the Tuskegee experiment where during the mid century black men with syphilis were denied proper treatment. I believe that is a real place to start because trust represents a major component in establishing better race relations here in America and anywhere else where the rights of one group might have been violated by another. Somebody must stand against what is wrong. And it should not be one institution like the NAACP (National Association for the Advancement of Colored People) or the American Civil Liberties Union that is fighting to end racial discrimination. Beginning with equal access to education, every institution in the nation ought to sponsor programs that aim to close the racial gap. The same message goes to any countries where racial discrimination is practiced. What is considered wrong socially and morally should be settled once and for all. It takes great courage to accept one's wrong; however, it shows a sign of strength and maturity to not just acknowledge wrong but to want to correct it. Both sides, whites and blacks, have been wounded, more so blacks with respect to slavery; nonetheless, once this old account starts closing itself up, America may gain more strength than it ever had in its history. There is **strength in unity.** Forgive and forget may not be the right lyric; however, blacks in America can take pride in building the nation. And every ethnic, every individual that lives and works here or in whatever country they identify with (African-Americans, Haitian-Americans, Spanish-Americans, Native Americans, etc.) has a social, as well as a moral obligation, to mend the social fabric. More sincere dialogue that brings back trust is needed. Greater tolerance for and sensitivity to ethnic diversity must be addressed on all sides. We were never the same to start with, and never will be; therefore, only respect for each other and collaborative effort can help us find a lasting solution. America can no longer be looked at as the "White man's property". All of us who have lived here for a generation or more invest in it; if we feel that we do not belong here, no one should force us to feel that way. But I believe that it makes more sense that all of us either retrieve our path or come to an agreement with ourselves as to where we belong and start working at it to make a difference. No country is good or bad in itself; it all depends on the people who live in it. Don't live in a place and take no real pride in it either as individuals or as a group and still expect your rights to freedom and self-determination to be guaranteed. No way Jose; whatever you want to see in your home, your neighborhood, your community, or your country, take your share of responsibility. Then, if it does not work you may start complaining. Otherwise, you have no right to say anything bad, if you feel that it is none of your business. Many folks from many countries like to complain about what goes wrong around them, yet they sit still as if somebody, somewhere, was predestined by God of heavens, or Allah, or Mohammed or any other deity to fix the problems so they can enjoy life. In this way, I might add that patriotism must prevail. Lastly, if someone cannot run his/her own life or home efficiently, there is no way that he/she will able to run a whole nation. Prejudice would not survive had it not been pushed by one side and accepted by the other, and violence represents the worst tool that anyone could use to fight violence. To fight racism, what exactly do we need?

D- The Right Genetic Stuff But Still The Wrong Color

It is more important that we change our belief system rather than our skin color? In fact, whereas the latter may prove to be a useless task for among other things it is deeply rooted on our genetic makeup and does not say anything about how we go on living our lives, the former can be looked at as a great indicator by which we may be able to determine the quality of life here on earth. Our belief system and our perception often distort day to day reality. We must arduously and continuously revisit our thinking process which fosters our belief and reshape our knowledge bank whenever necessary. Otherwise, we will not only lag behind and feel destitute but we run the risk of keeping ourselves second or even third class citizens.

❖ CHAPTER XXVIII ❖

Education is the Gateway

EDUCATION = ECONOMIC SECURITY

The equation of Honorable Thomas M. Menino, Mayor of Boston, Massachusetts

The Mayor gave this equation during his State of the City Address at The Jeremiah E. Burke High School, Dorchester, Mass, on January 17, 1997. I reserve my comments for later in the chapter; for now, I'll simply say that I hope that Education is made more accessible to every child in every country.

In the present chapter, we would like to emphasize the importance of education, but we do not want to leave in the mind of anyone the vague notion that education alone is necessarily associated with higher pay or will open every door in life. It certainly will unlock a great many doors, and while it remains the best tool that anyone could have to make improvements for oneself, it works more effectively when it is combined with a couple of other variables (such as entrepreneurship spirit, better stewardship of our resources/money, improvement in our public/human relations or the art of networking, etc.), which we have been discussing all along. And since it is so critical that our audience is enlightened, before getting too deep into the subject matter, we wish to define these two terms: Education and Knowledge.

According to *Webster's Dictionary*, education means dealing with methods of teaching and learning in school (life itself is a school.) Knowledge itself emphasizes the fact or condition of knowing something, the acquaintance with or the understanding of a science, an art or a technique. To educate, based upon the same defining source, denotes the following meanings: to lead forth, to rear, to provide schooling for, to train by formal instruction.

Traditionally, education was viewed as a formal approach to rearing children and young people. Then parents and those versed in pedagogy or the art of teaching would design a specific curriculum that was to be followed through grade schools and universities. Sometimes, socio-culturally speaking, an age limit was perceived for pupils or students to complete a certain level of study. We do not want to refer to this strict sense of education, because it might convey the wrong message. First, we believe in thorough education of the individual: spirit, mind, and body. Secondly, we advocate for education with no time/age limit or just classroom exposure. Our philosophy is for all people to acquire whatever knowledge they can, whenever they can, and wherever they can. An educated person has a fortune to carry with him/her wherever he or she goes.

A- The Politics of Education vs. Education & Politics

In the old politics of education, only a certain category of individuals with noble birth could attend school and get educated. Traditionally, female children were discouraged from going to school. Next, under the savage and atrocious policies of the masters, slaves were considered half-humans. Therefore, an education was automatically denied them or their children. This practice was carried out through the years, and even to this very day many higher education institutions accept just a select few students from minority groups, as a favor to them. We hope that such a practice can be boycotted wherever and against whomever it is being held because it violates basic human rights as stipulated in the United Nations chart on The Declaration of Human Rights. Based on the 1996 report published by The International Bank for Reconstruction and Development/The World Bank, and taking into consideration the Menino Equation, if education represents the best predictor in determining a person's socio-economic success, then something is definitely wrong with our society. When we take a look at the report, there are countries where enrollment in tertiary (superior or higher/beyond secondary) education is as low as 1%, as of 1993. Here is what the report says: "The tertiary enrollment ratio is calculated by dividing the number of pupils enrolled in **ALL** post-secondary schools and universities by the population in the twenty to twenty-four age group. Pupils attending vocational schools, adult education programs, two-year community colleges, and distant education centers (correspondence schools) are included." (World Development Report 1996. Pp.228-30.)

With respect to education and politics, human beings have different levels of needs as described by Abraham Maslow and elaborated on in previous chapters of this book. Chances are that people will be operating at different levels of needs. At times, they may need expert advice to guide them through stages of their lives, even though the final decision should be theirs and no one else's! In addition, the well-known Greek philosopher, Aristotle (who lived 384-322 B.C.) said that human beings are political animals. He meant that we need to interact with each other, just as Genesis Chapter 2 previously indicated. It is not good that man should live alone…(Ch. 2, V.18). Therefore, we may conclude that education not only represents a medium for personal growth and interaction but also it is a means to facilitate better communications and exchange among humans. Once you are educated or trained, you become knowledgeable; and knowledge itself is power, which is what we are advocating here.

Most of the time, people perish for lack of knowledge. On the contrary, as you become knowledgeable, hopefully you will be better able to act rationally and decisively on issues that will create greater opportunities for you, your family and your community.

B- Knowledge Will Set You Free

President Nelson Mandela of South Africa said, "Education is the most powerful weapon which we can use to change the world." For instance, when your friends or foes are up against you, if you know their motives and how to get under their skin, you could possibly win their sympathy a lot quicker and help them identify and diffuse the source of their anger and frustration. An education that goes beyond the mere classroom setting will elevate people beyond the animal instinct, guide them through their human relations, and facilitate their involvement in activities that promote growth and self-awareness. You may have all the education in the world, but if you lack knowledge of how to use it, that is just as useless as you holding the key to a very beautiful car but not knowing how to drive.

Getting the Right Job, Reaching the Right People

As adults, you need the knowledge that fits your particular dream or aspirations. Again, while traditional classroom knowledge is in no way to be neglected it can be further modified so that it provides relevant, necessary information to help one grow. As one increases his/her knowledge through specific job training, regular classroom education, and/or trade or vocational school, one automatically raises his or her assets.

Get your education validated or else you may be out of commission. Your involvement with other folks in the community and different communities is as important as a good education, and that's what people refer to as 'networking'. In this society, most people I know value education very highly and so do I. It is supposed to open doors for us, but I've got news for you. While many positions are being advertised in the media daily, there are some high profile jobs that are not advertised, and the people who often get those positions don't always have the best qualifications. But still that's no reason for you to neglect getting the best education. To make it in this world, you need all the qualifications; the most eloquent way that I can say it is, "It is not just what you know but also who you know." Don't think that I am making this up so as to impress you or to talk you into buying my book; wherever you go you will find that someone got ahead of you just simply because of an old acquaintance.

When looking for opportunities, those individuals in the minorities especially usually end up getting a bigger slap in the face. They may be relying on what they know alone, whereas other people with a lesser education but with the right contact will make headways before them. Therefore, you need as much education as possible. Also in your network, you need as many contacts as possible. And when you walk in a place, you have to be assertive, as though you belong there. You are not intimidating to or intimidated by other people, at least not intentionally. If they feel threatened or intimidated by who you are and by your appearance, of if they have a problem with you being assertive, let them deal with it, and you go on with what you need to accomplish very politely and diplomatically but firmly. In a way, a college education is a fruitbearing tree where you may find fruits in and out of season, and as long as you have that tree there is hope. And frankly, to be educated, there is no age limit and while your body may be wasting away with old age and perhaps by disease, you can rely on your mind which will keep you going.

You probably have learned by now that no human being is indispensable. You may be well-needed for a particular task. Perhaps, for a moment you might see yourself as the right candidate. However, as time goes on, eventually more people will match up with your qualifications, making your future less stable. Hopefully by then, you may be ready for a promotion within your company or you'll move to accept a post that is more gratifying elsewhere. Be careful to keep your knowledge bank updated and your networks active or else your training will soon be invalid or obsolete.

Entrepreneurship! To start with, I am sorry to say that certain college or university degrees are a waste of your time and resources, because not only do too many people have the same ones but they do not carry any weight beyond the issuing institution. I will let you find out yourself; however, may I say that some diplomas are only recognized locally. If you want to remain competitive, you'd better go for something better than that. In addition, be creative, use your imagination to the maximum. You may have enough resources to develop your own corporation or business, and I wish that as we move to a new era more institutions would open new curricula (curriculum, singular) towards teaching trades such as vocational subjects at the high school level and for adults who did not have the chance to acquire a formal education. I also wish that educational institutions took more time to teach people effective principles of entrepreneurship! Maybe as individuals, all you need is a partner to start your own agency, a family business, or a community-based trade. Take some risks; sometimes partnership works, and sometimes it doesn't. Learn more about investments, any kind of investments. You may still work for someone while managing your own business on the side. Nonetheless, you do need the education and so do your children. You can excel in your career, whatever that may be.

1. Our Kids and Their Future

An education is the second most valuable tool that you could give to your children if they are to succeed in life. Per comparison, in order for a tree to grow it needs the following: 1)fertile soil 2) water 3) sun or light and 4) proper nutrients.

Kids need more than that. First and foremost, a child has to have a loving home, safe from violence and all other potential hazards. Next, it needs food and water. The child also requires social interactions with other members of the human race. Furthermore, as children grow up, they need guidance and a sense of leadership toward social norms and mores in order to become responsible citizens. One of the principles that children must learn early on is respect for authority, who is in charge, who do they report to! Too often these days do we see young people who clash with authority. They have no concept of law and order as though nobody ever taught them.

Looking at the current trend in the world, some reform is definitely needed within the traditional model of education. Grammar school may do with minor changes; however, from high school on, the curriculum somehow should be to accomplish two things for young people:

1) Offer them an education that responds to some of their immediate, critical needs
2) Prepare them for the future.

In other words, such a curriculum should be designed in a way that provides young people with better alternatives: some basic skills, technical or vocational training, or even trades, which we have mentioned a minute ago. That way, they have something to hold on to as they try to make their way into the real world. If for whatever reason they drop out of high school, for instance, and/or do not go beyond high school, they possess some real basic skills and tools necessary to sustain themselves independently.

2. Hint

It is true that everybody cannot learn a similar profession or many of us would never get a job. For one thing the job market would be saturated, resulting in no more room for other people to join the workforce. However, I must warn you. Despite the fact that you should make the learning environment as much fun as possible, too often, so many young people and adults choose the easiest, cheapest courses in the school curriculum or in life in general. They do not want to work hard and sacrifice a little bit more to get some good courses under their belts.

I am not downplaying any kind of profession, but can you imagine a world where 80% of the people who attend colleges or universities train to become clerks or secretaries. Again, there is nothing wrong with being a secretary. However, if you went to school and spent all that money, time, and energy, I suspect that you would want to get a job that offers a better package and some security. And guess what, some people don't even have to go to college or technical schools to really study some of those cheap career paths. Put in another way, you can still earn your degree but do not get a job. Let me be plain, you can become the top barber in town, just learn the art well.

Other than that, the more competitive or selective your educational background, the better are your chances of securing a job where you can last for a while. Going to school to acquire an education requires some sacrifice, some discipline in setting goals, prioritizing, and following them through. That also means choosing delayed gratification. In other words, the question is really whether to buy an expensive car now and incur a huge debt or postpone going on a cruise and use that money to pay a semester of school.

Once you have your training, you can get the job that you want and that pays more. Then you may start getting the things that you always wanted. It often pays to be patient.

Another setback that prevents some people from signing up for certain courses is the fear of not succeeding. Some of us obviously have long developed that phobia of such topics as math, biology, mechanics, or simply science. Perhaps we have been told that these fields are not for us. Still another determining factor for not choosing these subjects is that not everyone can be good at everything. To respond to that: many schools provide tutoring. So, if any student has a problem with a particular subject, he or she can request such assistance. If you do not wish to seek help from school, you can look for help among your circle of friends, siblings or other family members who are good at that topic which you have problems with. In terms of paying for your schooling, don't just jump on the wagon and pay the high cost of any school. At some places, you have to pay for the brand name. Secondly, find the most appropriate living arrangements you can make which will not add to your stress level. If you have an understanding and supportive spouse, that will make your life easier. If you don't have one yet, think twice before making a move towards having one; he/she may be on a different mission than you. Your parents may be good resources in supporting you: morally, financially (living arrangements) and otherwise. You may have to sacrifice a lot of "good times" to get to where you want to be, but it will be worth it in the end. If you are looking to save for your kids schooling you may open an account just for that purpose or put savings in a safe where you don't have easy access to it. When you have a good education, you can refuse to take somebody's back seat all the time, at any time.

C- Training, An Adult Business

Here, I take the word adult to include anyone who no longer depends on his or her parents to survive. Along with this definition, I'd like to elaborate a little bit on what I mean by training. That can be the pursuit of a degree from an academic institution, a vocational or trade school, or it could be any training which qualifies the individual to either take on a new task or perform his or her old task better.

No one can be too old to learn as long as the desire is there. Let's pick on the new immigrants for a moment. I believe that it is imperative that they learn the language of the country to where they migrate. Even though many countries do not validate a degree earned from a foreign country, if the immigrant speaks the language, maybe he or she can study and pass the required boards or tests. Sometimes the foreign graduate may have to go for a little more schooling before receiving accreditation to practice in his/her field, which oftentimes is just formality and politics. Other times, he or she may end up in a position lesser than what he or she was originally trained for. Migration does not always guarantee a better life.

Training! That's for everyone who is concerned about staying on top in his or her field or who just wants to remain necessary and make an independent living. Hence, that person may do it on his/her own (self-trained) or seek professional advice to determine what might best qualify him/her for the job market.

After taking office in 1993, President Clinton made a comment in one of his speeches. He said that every five years one needs to be retrained or learn different job skills. Well, he is not far from being right. For the most part, many people who remain socio-economically stagnant were never qualified for anything in the first place. Secondly, with many companies downsizing nowadays, a lot of people are losing their jobs and need to reassess their qualifications and options. For instance, the more advanced we become technologically, the more sophisticated and more complex the world gets. As a result, human labor (manpower) is being replaced by robots and/or computers, and it seems that for profit corporations are much more concerned with maximizing their assets than helping families/communities grow. It requires more and more skills to remain competitive in the job industry. Some of us view higher education as a necessary tool; and if you are contemplating going back to school to take some courses, it may be a hard undertaking but I salute you. Unfortunately, you may do so just on your own and not expect your friends to always stand by your side. Many of them won't understand and may characterize you as crazy or someone who does not have anything better to do. And as much as they might have liked to support you before, now you have set a tone; your company may be hazardous (dangerous) to their health. Don't give up; life in general is a test; had not it been a test, you wouldn't be born just the way your mom and dad conceived you. It was a mere test for them, but please, no more comment on that.

Now, when you're done studying and get yourself in a better socio-economic position, they may follow in your footsteps. So be it. However, just as people can be at a greater risk to develop certain conditions that may be caused by secondhand smoking, by you making it a habit of quitting may inhibit the growth of your loved ones and any motivation which they might have later. Do what you have to and be an example.

Lastly, an American idiom says that you shoot for the stars. In fact, we can all shoot for the stars; however, for a lot of reasons that I have eluded to, not all of us will reach. Nevertheless, if you try, you might get there, and even if you did not, you will definitely land somewhere higher than where you once were. Don't let anyone tell you that you can't do this or you can't be that. Be your own judge and do not deceive yourself. Sometimes by being too modest, we do not give ourselves credit. We need to start taking pride at our own accomplishments. Lift up your head from down below, look up where you need to be. Stop procrastinating; instead start walking while the morning is still young and you have some strength left. Always remember the foot-in-the-door technique. As you take the first step, all the rest will be made easier, for you already facilitated them on your first initiation. Also, note that different sets of circumstances will create different sets of opportunities and challenges. It is up to you to find ways to handle them as adequately and as efficiently as possible. Otherwise, you may not be able to either overcome any perceived obstacle or live long enough to reap and enjoy the fruit of your labor. Thus, I would like to provide you with the next chapter as a tool to: 1) help you identify stressors in your life 2) guide you in developing some effective techniques for stress management.

❖ CHAPTER XXIX ❖

Overcoming Your Stress

Almost everything that we think of and do in this life will bring some level of stress in our lives. In fact, no one can say that he or she experiences no stress whatsoever in his or her everyday dealings. Some of it may even be physiological by nature so that one can simply react to it. Consider for instance that you are traveling. Your bladder is full and you find yourself in a place where there is no toilet facility or you have just a couple of minutes to make it to a very important interview. You look at the clock and realize that if you stop, you will be late and you do not want that. Perhaps you just sit there in a traffic jam, and your bowel keeps sending you signals that it can no longer wait. That can be stressful. I bet that each of you can recall at least one such example.

Even though stress may be based on our perception of the events taking place in our lives and our ability to deal with them as rationally and as effectively as possible, it is important for us to mention two distinct categories: internal and external. Any stress that has to do with our physiology or the way that our body functions may be seen as an internal source. Anytime a factor outside our body causes the stress, then we focus on an external source and the environment is responsible. Sometimes, these two sources can combine together to produce stress within us. Let's consider, for instance, someone who has just been diagnosed with HIV (Human Immunodeficiency Virus), the virus that causes AIDS (Acquired Immuno Deficiency Syndrome). The person has to deal with the reality of possible changes within his/her body over time. Also, right then he or she may start focusing on the kind of reception that she will get as he/she discloses the diagnosis to relatives and friends: full acceptance, total rejection, or partial support with quarantine. In addition, the person may even perceive more stress coming into his/her life, as he/she thinks about lack of resources to care for himself/herself.

A- Stress and the Stressors

As we think of stress, we can conceptualize the many ways in which it may affect us. It may impact us physically, mentally, psychologically, emotionally, and otherwise, thereby causing significant damage to our health. Technically, we may present stress as a major contributing factor to many of the health problems, and unless it is properly dealt with and in a timely fashion, it may even increase our risk of dying much sooner than we would expect. However, before we get into great lengths discussing the issue, we would like to ask the following questions: What is stress and what do we call stressors? What is the reality about the topic? What role does our perception play in it? Who gets stressed out? For how long can we survive stressful events?

1. Definition of Stress, Stressor (s)

As you may already realize, there is not just one definition given for stress. Even professionals in the same field tend to differ on how they perceive and define stress.

> A) *Webster's* defines stress as the deformation caused in a body by such forces as physical, chemical, or emotional factors resulting in bodily or mental tension.
> B) Miller and Keane (both from the medical field) describe stress as: any condition that causes strain or tension (*Journal of Clinical Epidemiology*. 1993. 46 <1>.; *Canadian Journal of Public Health*. 1992. 83 <1>, 42-46.;)
> C) From the *Medical Advisor* (a guide to disease and treatment) stress is defined as a reaction of our bodies and minds to something that upsets their normal balance.
> D) Catherine Heaney (Assistant Professor of Medicine at Ohio State) describes stress as a process by which objective physical and social conditions are ap-

praised and are reacted to by individuals (Mottaz, P. et al., 1991; Kasaba, SC., 1979.)

Despite variations in the definitions of stress, it is well documented by health care professionals and allied health disciplines that stress has the potential to cause extensive damage to and even the death of an individual. In a while, we will focus on different aspects of the subject matter. For now, we want to adopt a more inclusive definition, a working one:

E. Stress is an event that causes change or demands re-adjustment in the life of the 'average' person. Now, a stressor can be any such event that causes an individual to experience stress in his or her life.

2. The Rule of Perception in Stress-related Events

Epictetus, a Greek philosopher, once said, "Men (humans) are not disturbed by things but by the views which they take about them". An American idiom says, "Different strokes for different folks". This is not to say that people fake the situations causing them to in turn experience stress. What happens is that every day we are faced with various circumstances and events in which we (as individuals) often react differently. And even the same person can respond to the same event differently at different times. Many reasons account for such variations. First of all, we all differ in personalities. This makes us see and interpret our world somewhat differently. Secondly, as we reason logically or we so judge. Therefore, we have a judgment call here. Thirdly, to a large extent personal experience accounts for many ways in which we behave when we are faced with new situations. On familiar grounds, we tend to react in a pattern. Fourth, age and maturity also dictate how we perceive and respond to each situation. Ultimately, as emotional beings, our mood fluctuates so that our overall reactions cannot always be predicted. We could include other factors that influence our perceptions, but one of my commitments in writing this book is to keep my statements short and simple whenever possible. That way, we may be able to entertain you much longer and maintain high interest. Now, let's consider life's general events and their relationships to stress that you and I experience.

3. Stress As a Day-to-Day Phenomenon

People get married, and they feel some kind of stress. They go through a divorce (a separation), and they complain about stress. They lose a loved one through death, and they are saddened and stressed out. They receive a promotion on their jobs, and they experience a period of anxiety, joy, and a series of adjustments which in turn bring a certain amount of stress in their lives. Some people prepare for an exam and undergo periodic episodes of stress. Individuals who are shy become shaky and sweaty when asked to perform a task in public.

In general, each phenomenon or life event strikes every one of us in a particular way so that we go through our own set of stresses on our own terms. Going for a job interview, dating for the first time, becoming pregnant, approaching menopause, or approaching puberty can all be stressful experiences. Exposure of our body to environmental changes such as extreme weather (hot or cold) causes internal adjustment thereby increasing our stress level. Fighting our way through life and trying to make ends meet are different types of stressors. In fact, stress plays an important part in our daily lives, and it is partially involved in our success. In an article published in the Virginia Pilot, the news reporter, Livi S. Kadasa, quoted Anderson, a health care consultant saying: "…But you take away stress, you take away vitality". And the title of the article says: "Maybe a Little Stress Isn't So Bad After All" (Virginia Pilot. Oct. 2, 1995. P. E6).

Yes, a little stress may not be that bad; however, too many of us try to function for too long under very stressful situations which are detrimental to our health and well- being.

B- The Adverse Health Consequences Associated With Stress

Obviously, many health problems have more than just one cause. If one contributing factor is strong enough, it can illicit a response all by itself. Other times several factors may combine to produce a synergetic effect, meaning that they all play a role in the overall impact. A brief example can be obesity which results from genetic disposition, eating disorders, sedentary lifestyle, metabolic problems, aging, and/or lack of exercise.

Similarly, stress is not the only risk factor associated with the following health problems which I am about to highlight. However, many studies support the evidence or the link between stress and these symptoms. Excessive stress may put someone at risk of developing very serious disorders such as: gastritis, peptic ulcer, cancer, high blood pressure, diabetes, immune problems, asthma, migraine headaches, heart disease, and post traumatic stress disorder. Prolonged stress may eventually reduce the body's ability to cope and produce chronic fatigue, lack of energy, burnout, loss of appetite, headaches, frequent colds, insomnia, fatigue, digestive changes, indigestion, overeating, neck or back pain, sadness, anxiety, anger, irritability or inability to concentrate or to perform at optimum levels (*American Journal of Health Promotion*, 1990, 5(6),413-420; *The Medical Advisor*, 1996. When our coping capabilities diminish, feelings of insecurity, inadequacy, and depression might occur. We can tolerate only so much stress for any extended periods of time.

When we live under stressful situations for too long, the body's immune system is thrown off balance and vulnerability to illness and diseases might increase. There is a very elaborate process of how different organs and body parts become affected. We will not go through each step involving every organ, given the scope of the writing in this book. However, we would like to touch on a few organs which are directly involved in stress-related events.

1. Heading Towards Possible Disasters

Hans Selye, a world renowned expert on stress, emphasizes three possible steps that people may go through. They are: 1) Alarm Reaction 2) Resistance Reaction 3) Exhaustion.

During extreme, prolonged stressful situations, a wide range of bodily changes occur, which Selye refers to as G.A.S. or General Adaptation Syndrome.

a. Alarm Reaction

We have a pair of glands called adrenal glands, each of which sits on top of our kidneys. Each gland consists of two parts, a central portion called adrenal medulla (or emergency gland) and an outer portion named adrenal cortex. During the alarm reaction, stress stimulates a specialized area of the brain known as the hypothalamus (commonly called the body's watchdog). From there, a message is sent to the adrenal medulla for it to start secreting (pumping) epinephrine (adrenaline) and norepinephrine (noradrenaline) into the bloodstream. The person begins to think faster, fight, or run harder. Meanwhile, the gland secretions reach the heart, causing it to work harder, hence raising the blood pressure, increasing the heart pulse and rate, and forming the concentration of glucose (sugar) in the blood. On the other hand, the cortex produces another kind of hormone called cortisol (hydrocortisone) which helps reinforce the actions of adrenaline and noradrenaline by making nutrients available for sugar transport from the bloodstream to other parts of the body. An overall response to this activity results in increased circulation, building up of energy (catabolism), and a reduction in non-essential body functions. This sequence of events continues until the situation is corrected or the stress is no longer felt. If the condition is not brought under control in a timely fashion, the hypothalamus (the brain) causes other hormones to be secreted for long-term reactions (Raygada, M. et al., 1992; Wickizer, TM. Et al., 1993.; Zimmerman, T.C. et al., 1993).

b. Resistance Reaction

During this time, different hormones may be secreted in order to bring the stress under control. Among such hormones (regulators) we find:

CRF = Corticotropin Releasing Factor which controls secretions in the cortex

TRF = Thyrotropin Releasing Factor which controls secretions in the medulla. For more details, refer to the chart thereafter.

As this stage persists, it allows the body to continue to fight the stressor and re-establish stability (homeostasis) long after the alarm reaction has ceased. At this level, blood pressure usually returns to about normal pending further accumulation and an excess of hydrogen ions. If everything goes well, the body functions return to normal. However, should the resistance level fail, the body goes into the third stage.

c. Exhaustion

The ability of the body to protect us against adverse situations depends on many factors, such as our general health, our effectiveness in correcting the problem in a timely manner, the extent of changes over time, and so forth.

When we are unsuccessful in eliminating the stressor or bringing the situation under control in the first two steps, we approach this final stage of the game. At this point, a common sign which may be felt is fatigue. The main reason for it has to do with an imbalance in the ions. During this process, too many potassium and hydrogen ions are lost as a trade-off for sodium and as they are secreted in the urine.

God forbid, as cells continue to lose more potassium, they become less effective in sustaining life. Then, they start dying. At this stage it is no joke. If the condition is not immediately brought under control, vital organs may stop functioning as they get weaker and weaker. The person will eventually die. (Tortora et al., pp.420-430; Villee et al., pp.1163-65). The following is a list of possible stressful life events given with a number. The higher the number, the higher your risk of developing some stress-related illness. Check the list below.

Different Stressors and Their Strength in Points

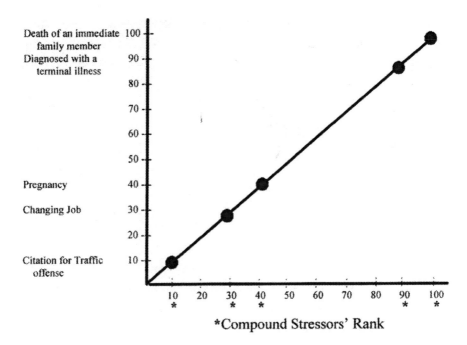

Figure 30.1 *Stress-Related Diagram*
(also called Social Adjustment Rating)

C- Stress Management
1. Prevention

"One pound of prevention is better than 100 pounds of cure". No one may claim absolute immunity from life experiences which bring stress in one's existence. By definition, stress is a part of life, and it has a positive and a negative side to it. More and more we find ourselves dealing with prolonged, strenuously stressful events, and sooner or later we might lose our ability to successfully compete in this life. One major factor that each of us should try to enhance is our perception. As stated earlier in this chapter, we are not so much disturbed by things, but by our views about them. Two persons can survive an accident but as they both come to think of what happened and try to relive it, one may lose his or her ability to cope and subsequently succumb while the other totally recovers. Every time we have the opportunity, we should try to reshape our perceptions, for they are such inaccurate instruments. Perceptions can cause just as much harm to us as good. I would do you a disservice had I closed this book without talking about stresses in this life and ways that you and I may prevent them!

As we have seen, from a physical standpoint, stress can affect our physiological systems, thereby contributing to many diseases including cardiovascular diseases, peptic ulcers, diabetes, mental blocks, strokes, etc. Mentally speaking, once a woman lost control over her person and was placed in a nursing home. As she lost power and self- esteem, she then resigned herself to her situation. Soon thereafter, she became unable to cope and died (Breznitz, S. et al. 1982.; Graham, N. 1988.) From a social perspective, individuals who are under continued stressful situations may show difficulty relating to other people. They may be snappy (short-tempered), withdrawn, and aggressive. No matter how cumbersome or tedious it may seem, you ought to do everything within your power to retain an optimistic point of view of life, a keen mind, and self-determination to pursue your dreams with endurance while maintaining your stress level at its optimum. Now let us look into different ways to keep our stress levels low.

⇒ Not all sources of stress can be eliminated, but you may do without some of them. If you are a type A personality, hardworking, competitive, risk-taking:
- Whenever possible, avoid situations that you cannot stand
- Manage your time better
- Reduce type A activities and exchange them with calmer events
- Take a break from work
- Try not to live beyond your means or struggle with credit here and there
⇒ Create boundaries where you can increase your buffer zone and feel comfortable working.

⇒ Develop a lifestyle that has some aerobic exercises which can help reduce the heart rate. Find activities that you can perform without putting your body in increased danger.

⇒ If you are a musician, perform more often. If you are not, you may listen to soothing music more regularly and sing more often.

⇒ Relax your tense muscles through body massage. That also helps circulation and provides stimulation for the mind.

⇒ Laugh, laugh at yourself more often.

⇒ Plan events that will help you overcome monotonous habits.

⇒ If you can get plenty of rest during the course of a 24 hour period, do it. Develop a sleep pattern.

⇒ Avoid heated debates or constant quarreling with your mate.

⇒ Take time to get in touch with your feelings and make sure that you maintain some control over yourself.

⇒ When things do not go your way, do not get upset. Try to find out why they did not. Seek help.

⇒ Practice stress-reduction techniques. For example, there is a technique known as yoga. Lie on your back with your legs open up to about 2 feet wide and turned toward the side. Place your palm up with the back resting down. Close your eyes and breathe slowly and deeply through your abdomen as opposed to your shoulder and diaphragm. Do this exercise for 12 to 15 minutes once or twice a day or as needed.

⇒ Visualization. Try to visualize a pleasant situation and combine it with soothing music.

⇒ Find a pond, a lake, or elsewhere where the water and the environment are calm and peaceful.

⇒ Have a balanced diet. Reduce your fat, cholesterol, and sodium intake. Increase your vegetable and fruit consumption. Do not drink or eat large quantities of caffeine (tea, chocolate, or coffee).

⇒ Meditation. You may find a comfortable position, pref-
erably one sitting down, and with your eyes closed, you
focus on a specific object.

⇒ Be content with the material assets you have.

⇒ When you face stressful situations, don't become over-
whelmed or consumed by them. Instead, try to see if you
can break the problem down and solve it piece by piece.

⇒ If you are comfortable with it, have a mental list or a written one on things which you have difficulty with. Then try
to predict the likelihood that any of them may surface and
see if you could come up with possible solutions beforehand or even avoid them altogether.

⇒ Change the pace at which you work, slow down a little.

⇒ If you face any kind of problem at home, at work or elsewhere, try to address it with the person or persons causing
it. You need not be offensive or confrontational. If the
two of you cannot handle it, find a mutual third party to
help you out. And if you feel that there is potential for a
bitter argument, stop for a moment, take a walk, and return
to it later. If you and the other parties involved still cannot
find a solution and things are getting ugly or out of hand,
look for professional help.

2. Treatment

We hope that you do not have to go past the level of exhaustion.
As you can tell, there are conditions that require hospitalization and
even prescriptions. You may need to seek professional help such as
medical or psychological assistance, depending how chronic the
situation is.

◊ If you feel tired, fatigued, or have headaches, some of the
relaxation techniques will help you. As for me, I can lie
peacefully and comfortably, or I can take a shower first, then
rest.

◊ Therapy for stress largely depends on you. Practice a low-risk
lifestyle and exercise.

◊ Some treatment involves anti-depressants and psychotic medications for mental disorders that require professional assistance.

◊ Counseling is another form of therapy.

◊ Also, aromatherapy (the use of essential oil called lavender) is suggested. I am not familiar with it, but you are supposed to either put several drops in your bath water or place a few drops on a piece of cloth and inhale from time to time. (*The Medical Advisor*, Time Life, Inc., 1996).

3. Conclusion

Stress, given our current definition, may not be altogether avoidable. It represents an integral part of life. In fact, we need an optimum amount to maintain balance, both physically and psychologically.

For example, if we say that any kind of stress is bad or disturbing, perhaps we should not look for a job promotion or reach out to make new friends, or better yet, when a pathogen invades our system, our body should not react. However, since these are not ideal goals that one may necessarily look to set in life, then we come to develop an appreciation for Selye's idea on different stages of stress. Thus, we can never eliminate all the stressors or control one hundred percent exposure to them. Sometimes, the best that we can do is to increase the buffer zone (safe area where we can function more effectively) and enhance our coping mechanisms. Furthermore, we cannot pertinently establish causality between a stressor and a particular illness or disease. Different contributing factors may have to be accounted for; whether they be genetics, behavioral, psychological, social, or environmental in nature.

We hope that by introducing this particular component, it will help you reduce the amount of stress that you may be about to experience. Thus, by creating and adopting several models suitable for your own personal needs, you may be able to effectively cope and improve your quality of life. And if it works for you, why not offer your newly gained knowledge to help someone else?

Eno Mondesir

To be successful in becoming free, we sometimes need to put up with a lot of adverse conditions and strenuous situations. Only as we are able to cope adequately and effectively can we rise to our potentials. It requires that we shape up or else…

❖ CHAPTER XXX ❖

"Straight Talk": Shape Up
or Else Ship Out

As I was thinking of a chapter to end this book, I tried to place a collect call to Attorney Johnny Cochran to get his opinion on the political correctness and the legally sound wording only to find out that once I am connected to his line I would have to pay in Japanese currency (the yen) for clearance to use the air space. Of course, this not only means flying over Japan first to lay out the power lines but I would also need permission from the U. S. Chairman of the Foreign Relations Committee, Senator Jesse Helms of North Carolina, before I can leave the country, and the irony is that he might be more comfortable giving me a male earring instead of a hearing, which may also be the case for all those seeking diplomatic posts but are not of "Ambassadorship Quality". Except that for me personally, another problem has just emerged, and that is, as a male what would be my purpose for wearing earrings? Therefore, I conclude that a wonderful way to end this work is by entitling the chapter **Straight Talk: "SHAPE UP or Else SHIP OUT"**. For those of you who did not know or forgot, the first part of the above phrase stands for:

Shift to

Higher

Altitude through the

Power of

Education, and

Unleash your

Potential

or

Stay
Handicapped,
Immersed in
Poverty, powerlessness and

Overtaken by
Uncanny
Tyrants

As you already know and as we have emphasized throughout this book, our belief system is not genetically tuned; instead, it is the offspring of years of socialization, expectations, and our urge to feel that we belong somewhere. Tentatively, some of us do more or pay an exorbitant price for that.

It goes without saying that it is okay for us to shape our social beliefs by putting in place healthier ones as we grow up and become more mature. This, in turn, will help shape our attitude toward ourselves and life in general; and the ultimate purpose is to become better individuals who are more understanding and more responsible for ourselves so we may be more self-supportive and be able to live with dignity.

"Shape up or ship out" means all of the above, including my eloquent acrostic arrangement, even though its literal meaning varies minimally. It has been used in the following ways: "Do your job or you will be fired", "get your act together or else here is the doorway", if you don't behave appropriately or change your ways of doing business, you better move elsewhere, for you will no longer be coming here".

Whether we like it or not or whether or not we think about it, our individual conduct has a direct impact on our own lives and exerts some influence on everyone else who lives around us. So that we may end up exercising our rights and living up to our responsibilities, every civilized (human) society that ever existed has adopted its own set of ideals or values and established laws. And the fact that we may choose not to exercise these rights or live up to these responsibilities, however, does not exempt us from being accountable or make us less liable. Just like me, you must know that the fact of our not choosing one or the other when we are presented with different alternatives also represents a choice in itself. Let's consider a couple of examples. For the sake of argument, suppose you have been wrongfully summoned by a law enforcement officer to pay a fine presumably for some violation. You may be given the options to contest the fine, pay it, or go to jail; but you could also choose to ignore it and that is another option, not a healthy or legally sound one because chances are that the fine may increase over time to a point where you might even be stripped of the very rights that you once had. Then, you have no more choices. The same thing happens to us, our family, our neighborhood, or even our country when people around us are engaged in destructive behaviors and we just sit there, taking no action whatsoever. We observe this phenomenon repeat itself so many times. And I am not about to convert anyone of you out there into a "Professional" politician seeking elected office, for example. However, I become overly concerned when I hear people complain about a corrupt system, yet they are not willing to do anything to remedy the existing situation. Also, I am equally concerned when I see well and able bodies wasting their time and their potential for whatever reason or reasons.

From the crib to the grave, all of us humans ought to live with a mission, which stands as a mark of distinction, differentiating us from the rest of the animals! And God sure did NOT create us inferior or equal to them. They are born, they eat, they (sexually) reproduce, and then die. Having a purpose is the very least of their concerns or what they have accomplished during their lifetime. They can even care less about what contributions they have made to society or what they may leave behind when they are gone. If we are to claim superiority over them, we must do beyond what they are capable of doing. We must be able to identify and overcome the opposing forces which prevent us from reaching our potential and become more productive members of our own society. To help those of you who are concerned or who might be interested in shaping up your lives, I propose that you pay special attention as you read each chapter of this book. Try not to use this last chapter as a substitute for reading the entire manual. You may instead see it as an addendum (an addition) or reinforcement to what is being written here. Having said that, I would like to recapitulate or highlight and synthesize the previous chapters, and then draw a final conclusion.

31
"Straight
Talk": Shape
Up or Else
Ship Out!!!
30 - Overcoming
Your Stress
29 - How Many
College/University
Degree (s) Will Get You There?
28 - Education is the Gateway
27 - Which Should You Change:
Your Skin Color, Your Belief, or Both?
26 - Sustaining Your Energy Bank
25 - The Road Traveled by the New Immigrants
24 - From the Welfare Roll to Apprenticeship
23 - Whatever Your Addiction: It May Be Dangerous to Your Health and Growth!
22 - What About It: Your Self-image, Self-esteem?
21 - Catch Your Own Fish or Risk Being Fed on Intoxicated Food!
19 - Who Stands for Nothing Falls for Anything **20** - Culture of Poverty
17 - The Lesson From a Spider **18** - The Bill Cosby Way: "Don't Know the Key to Success, But."
15 - "…If You Run You Might Otherwise…" **16** - Living is a Risk. You Might as Well Take One!
12 - What Do You Perceive Your Goliath to Be, Defiant? **13** - "Live Free or Die" **14** - Reaching Your
Potentials
9 - Fear of Shedding One's Shell **10** - Nelson Mandela's Recipe **11** - A Mind Held Captive
7 - Conflict Resolution: Improve Your Negotiating Skills **8** - Fear of Rejection
5 - Freedom From Self-incriminating and Dangerous Behaviors **6** - Socio-cultural Intolerance/Hostility
3 - Freedom: An Expression of Independence and Maturity **4** - Freedom of Self-determination, Self-
actualization
1 - Fear: Its Roots and Consequences **2** - Are Bondage and Freedom Two Sides of the Same Coin?

Table 31-1 All the Chapters at a Glance

Chapter I Fear: Roots and Consequences!

Fear may be described as an emotional state of apprehension and anxiety that a person experiences or perceives over the course of either an abrupt or prolonged chain of events. It could come about as a result of certain external or environmental conditions or by internal changes that the person has not yet adapted to. We have talked about positive (healthy) or negative (unhealthy) fear. And if the situation giving rise to the fear persists over an extended period of time and it is being internalized by the subject, it may be transcribed into a paralyzing phobia (specific type of fear) in which case the individual experiences outbursts of demoralizing emotions which in turn may throw him or her off balance. The condition that generates the fear may be either real or perceived. However, in both cases, it may produce the same reaction and similar results if it is not properly dealt with.

Observations made when watching different animals, including humans has allowed researchers to come up with the most common form of reaction known as the "Fight-or-Flight Theory". When a person or another animal feels threatened, the basic tendency for that subject is to fight the source that produces the fear or to run (fly) away from it. Another kind of reaction is the cowardliness of the person to either accept or resign himself/herself to the perceived condition which usually follows a period of desperation where an individual perceives himself/herself as powerless to do anything to remedy the situation or to overcome whatever created that fear in him or her. By learning what is called "Learned Helplessness", many people who are low achievers in life or who do not stand up for themselves fall in the latter category. I hope that by reading the chapter, such individuals will come to a better understanding of their own fear and start seeing themselves as active agents of change instead of passive characters or victims of circumstances in the hands of chance. That will be a determining factor as to whether they will work to free themselves or remain bound for the rest of their lives!

Chapters II-IV   From Bondage to Freedom

By definition, we hold the two words, *freedom* and *bondage*, to be different or opposite in meaning. Whereas freedom literally describes the quality or the state of an individual not being under the control or the domination of another person, bondage or slavery implies that someone is being subdued under the power of somebody else. There is a vague notion of freedom that some misguided people tend to associate with the word license whenever they talk about individual rights, and they think that they can do as they please regardless. In practicality, freedom seems to mean different things to different people depending on their perceptions, their places in society, the cultures that they identify with, and the social dynamics. In social psychology, we find the expression, Private Logic, which basically means that we individually have our own hidden ways of seeing and defining things in order to support our own deeds.

Sometimes, there seems to be even a disillusion of what is really meant by being free, especially from the point of view of power and control. This makes it look as though we are not necessarily as free as we may think so that we don't always take time to reflect strategically and rationally to the extent that we oftentimes run from one situation to another or from the influence of one master to the dominion of another. And sometimes the very thing for which we fight becomes our new master. Anyhow, however relative it may be, freedom does exist and it is constantly being sought by individuals, different ethnic groups, and communities.

In other words, people may lose their freedom to become enslaved to their own thoughts and ideas (i.e. pessimism, negative attitudes, ill-beliefs, etc.), to things that they have allowed to control their lives (i.e. cars, a beautiful house, money, etc.), or to other individuals who have moved in and taken over (i.e. peers, parents, children, a spouse, a boss, any charismatic leader, society, etc.). On this note, it is worth mentioning that while bondage can be either voluntary (self-imposed) or involuntary (forced), it exists in different forms depending upon the setting wherewith it is being enforced. Nonetheless, individuals as well as bodies of people strive for freedom. People take time to educate themselves, force themselves to pursue a career, and increase their productivity rather than just focusing on their reproductive capabilities. They look to find new meanings for their lives all the time and to live with a sense of pride and dignity. Nations engage themselves in endless wars and their citizens commit their lives fighting for and if need be dying in the pursuit of freedom. Among these individuals who value freedom and who know what it is worth, many end up giving their own lives in order that they might set others free.

In the history of humankind, we find very little evidence to show that the entire world has ever been at peace for any extended period of time with complete absence of some kind of war going on. For example, a country constantly either is invaded or invades another thereby infringing upon the freedom and the rights of the citizens of that nation. The need to self-rule and or the urge to control everyone else often leads to power struggles and a lot of bloodshed among different individuals and groups.

The amazing thing is that while some people are willing to do whatever it takes to set themselves free, many others are afraid, too afraid of having in their own hand the power to govern their lives or to even fathom the idea of becoming free. I don't know if you've ever heard of the idea that some people are afraid of success; it's basically the same phenomenon that we try to explain here. So many people develop a whole mentality based on that notion and they dare not take the chance of moving one inch beyond the self imposed boundaries, or dreaming anything else other than the ordinary day to day stuff! This category of individuals is usually contented with the little bit that they have done or accomplished in their lives. They do not see the need to make additional improvements in their lives, nor do they have any incentive to expand their efforts over and beyond a world with limited resources and explore the one that has endless opportunities.

Therefore, their lives become stagnant early and remain that way until they die or become entrapped either by certain events which cause them to make changes, or by someone else who exerts some strong influence over them, forcing them to consider further possibilities. Sometimes, others who have set sail for the pursuit of freedom started on the right foot but later they became entangled in the complexities of life; they forfeit their noble cause altogether. It is very common for this segment of people to end up being too busy chasing the wrong rabbits and fighting the wrong battles or the wrong causes. Lastly, we oftentimes come across certain individuals who could care less whether they are free or not, for they don't know the difference. I would not go as far as saying that some people will never get it. However, fear, bondage, and freedom, while interrelated, each has its own formula, and unless the free-spirited individuals are willing not only to learn about them but to also commit themselves to apply these formulas constantly, they will never discover that liberty of which we speak.

Out of fear, we may disclose to our enemy the very secrets or the very tools which we could use to liberate ourselves. In this case, fear is linked to bondage. Or we may have not been watchful and powerful enough to protect our freedom against outside invaders; thus as they take control over us, we lose our freedom. Then, if our new status of being bound gives way to fear, we first comply with the demands of our master (s). As time goes on, we may develop belief systems which will create in us a sense of hopelessness and helplessness so that we resign ourselves to our fate and later accept it as divine. And that works the same way with us being our own enemy or our own barrier to our freedom and personal growth as it does with the outside invaders or intruders trying to overpower us. The only difference is that we can control our mood and our feelings by reconciling with ourselves through self-monitoring and by constantly educating ourselves and thus adjusting our perceptions with each glimpse of light that we allow to shed through us. In other words, if we want to free ourselves from any domineering powers, we must first conquer our own weaknesses.

Freedom is not just an abstract word. Of course, in its deepest sense it does bring a lot of restrictions and even confusion sometimes in terms of where it begins and ends for each of us. Also, it imposes individual responsibilities and mutual respect among different members that form each community.

We need freedom to be able to exercise our individuals rights and pursue our destinies. We cannot rely on the environment to provide it to us either, since it represents a commodity to many of us. That is why we not only hardly offer it to other people, we often try to deprive them from it or measure the amount that they may be able to use. And may I add that even if you were to have all the money in the world, and no education, it would not make much difference in helping you maintain your freedom. In fact, if you have a lot of money and are still stupid, it may even be dangerous to your health and your well-being. What I want to say is that you need some of both, an education and material wealth to sustain your freedom. You may even have a large amount of them which you can use while you travel this world. However, if you really care about making a difference in your own life and the lives of other people, first getting an education might be a much better way to help yourself achieve the freedom that will last. In my personal observation, there seems to be at least three (3) fundamental elements that join together to provide individual freedom. They are the acknowledgment of one's creator, an unbiased, broad-based education, and material wealth! To me, they're all very critical and everything else is derived from them.

The person who achieves all three elements not only seems to be better able to establish some sort of balance and maintain some degree of freedom in his/her life but also has great potentials to develop interpersonal relationships that are positively influential. However, having only one seems to be so inadequate! Education, for instance, plays such a pivotal role in helping us shape our lives that we cannot afford to neglect it. Many people with low self-esteem and compulsive/destructive behaviors who have some sort of difficulty in establishing their own identity go through their adult lives displaying certain social mal-adaptive personalities which may be rooted in their upbringing. Chapter five has in part addressed this issue, and I would recommend that you refer to it and other sections of this book for your own information. Nonetheless, we will continue with our work and we believe that freedom must be won from all sides.

Chapter V   Freedom vs. Mal-adaptive Behaviors

I am sorry to say that to a great extent our society wastes so many resources putting emphasis on treating symptoms that we have allowed many of our social diseases to become chronic and almost irreversible! Just like diabetes (Types I and II) and High Blood Pressure which have multiple causes and may require multiple approaches, many of our social ills exacerbate either by misdiagnosis/mismanagement, our refusal to effectively deal with them once and for all, and by unattended psychological problems.

Freedom from destructive behaviors cannot be overemphasized. Such dealing is no less an individual handicap than it is a social abnormality. From juvenile delinquency to domestic violence to rape to manslaughter, none of us seems to be immune in one form or another, either as potential victims or as overt/covert perpetrators! There seems to be no place to hide; our suburbs just as our cities and towns are constantly being plundered and torn apart by violence from individuals or organized gangs. At times, these people become so powerful that they act in ways which defy constitutional authority.

Chapters VI-VII Socio-cultural Intolerance

When you find two individuals who look identical from head to toe and who show the same personality, you may have a problem with your sight or with your perception/ judgment. Otherwise, you may need to conduct an investigation and make sure you identify the real person from the clone. That's the only way you can have two people who share all characteristics or demonstrate the exact same physical and personality traits in every sense of the word. Even then, if such similarities were obvious to the naked eye in the vivid imagination of both individuals, the real and the clone, they would necessarily create some diverging elements to quickly dismiss their commonality!

It is not accidental that the cutest and most powerful woman who sweeps a man off his feet and brings him to his knees now, or the gentleman who has all the right qualifications to be treated as a sweetheart or a prince in the highest regard now is turned into a little bit less than a devil with tail, claws, and horns by that same person! The whole world would have a far different atmosphere or climate had not it been for our biased, divisive attitude and our tendency to categorize, and disdain/repudiate all those individuals who look and behave different from us. Often, we marginalize people on the basis of their appearances and hastily act to demystifying them for not looking or coming across the way we would like them to!

Our reasons for finding differences among ourselves and other people may vary significantly. As we perceive, we judge whether our motives are right, wrong, or unfounded in the first place. In addition, our limitations, ignorance, and our selfish interests often help us create the need to promote those differences which we will further use to support the way we choose to treat our fellow human beings. What remains peculiar in the whole gimmick of categorizing/stereotyping others is the process for how we decide who we want to look different and when! In so doing, we often cover ourselves under the blanket of social ideals/norms and culture. While our social upbringing and culture certainly play a decisive role on our perception and in ways that you and I reason sometimes, those views and ideals which they help us formulate do not escape the influence of sheer ignorance, political maneuvering, and self-interests that dictate and/or shape our individual/collective behavior.

If we consider varied instances where people are being viciously attacked or discriminated against, we can often relate the incident to one or several motives, as mentioned above. There may be occasions where we have to take these differences into consideration and process them as fact. Of course, we behave, talk, walk, act, react differently; and we all have different styles and tastes. However, that does not make one person superior to another or reduce someone's inherent rights to live freely and seek one's own destiny. Sometimes, we do not respect those differences and when we come close to each other we clash. Oftentimes, our own temperament gets on the way, creating an unprecedented hostile environment. Then, to justify our own ignorance we exchange names (profanity) with other people around us by calling them hostile. Lastly, I would like to add that the mere fact that we have different personalities and grow up in different environments, we will always have disagreements. The bottom line is how we treat each other because of these dissimilarities. Despite our degree of disagreement, we should always look for those elements which unite us and relate to each other in the most civilized manner. We should never, ever close the windows of opportunity by completely blocking from our lives those who may have pronounced differences.

Conflict Resolution

This subheading may sound like a big word to some of you; however, by no means am I offering an apology. Conflicts, problems, misunderstandings, and even disagreements mean almost the same thing; we experience conflict with others just as we do with ourselves. Then, resolution, taking care of business, or finding ways to solve the existing problem give us the ability to develop different coping techniques so we may go past those not too pleasant situations and enjoy life for what it is.

Every time there is more than one person present in an environment, the potential for conflict increases, adding to the already existing disagreement within self. It requires special skills, and it takes some growth toward a higher level of maturity and tolerance to first know and/or conquer self and then, live, treat others with respect they deserve. There exist many ways in which we approach a particular problem and come up with the appropriate solution. Several techniques have been recommended throughout chapter VII. I wish that you take the time to read and become more familiar with them.

Negotiation is necessarily the name of the game. And again how do we do that and with whom? With oneself, a term most commonly used is reconciliation. To reconcile with self or with others, either way. Negotiation, a more savvy, sophisticated word, means that the parties involved in an existing conflict engage in good faith to find common ground, a solution that each of them can live with. It further means that no one party should corner the other (s) to the point where they feel like a loser in the end.

At the start or around the negotiation table, the parties should engage in some elementary level of discussion which will lead toward the setting some ground rules that they will all agree to abide by, especially in the area of mutual respect and trust. Then, they can move toward a more focused agenda deciding what they want to accomplish and forming a timetable conducive to the realization of their mutual plan. We constantly do resolve certain issues; nonetheless, negotiation is an art in itself and it goes into levels. Therefore, aside from the persona, it requires very good communications skills. Equally important, each party must listen attentively to what its counterpart is saying, otherwise the conversation tends to shift toward more gridlock. Sometimes, parties may seem to be so close in an agreement; yet they are so far apart.

Again, the debate is not one party's agenda, but ought to reflect the will of different groups involved. In some instances, a neutral party is brought in as an intermediary to see that all sides are heard and given a fair chance.

When negotiating, it is a courtesy and a good practice to acknowl-edge the opponent's feeling. That way, you make it somewhat difficult for them to become resistant and defensive. While your disagreements may be sound, you must go beyond your own selfish interests to make sure that your opponent's interests are given equal weight at the negotiating table. If during talks you feel angry and are about to explode on your opponent, it may be time to call for an intermission. You will **not** make good impression on him/her if you cannot control your emotions! If need be, leave the room for a while, walk outside, go to the bathroom, talk to yourself or drink some fluid.

Reflecting on your opponent, don't expect him/her to be soft. Sometimes, you come across those people who love to play hardball. Your best bet is to keep your calm, and as often as it deems necessary, bring the discussion around the objectives for which you met in the first place. If you feel compelled enough to have the discussion, don't be intimidated as so many of us do during a job interview process, for instance, or at times when we face a very challenging issue or an intimidating personality. Most likely you will have something to offer which the other party may need. It is up to you how much value you place on it. It could simply be your strength or your style of negotiating.

Keep the negotiations focused around the topic of discussion and refrain from triviality or side issues which seem unrelated to the subject matter. In the end, even if you did not accomplish your mission, congratulate your opponent for agreeing to meet with you. And in your eyes, if the negotiations failed, together with your counterpart (s), try to assess why it has and look for a commitment from them for you to meet soon. I wish you all the best. Don't be overly concerned to let your opponent know that you are willing to go the extra mile in playing your part until a consensus or an agreement is reached. However, try not to hastily settle for some evasive accord that will eventually fall apart. If there is a fear in you as to how you should prepare to enter into the negotiations, get some expert advice or call on a neutral party, a professional who has the reputation in the field.

Chapters VIII-IX   The Fear of: Rejection, Shedding Off the Shell

Freedom will help you overcome all the barriers and tear down the walls of separation that have prevented you from becoming forthcoming or self-assertive if you let it. Fear of rejection is a symptom of a much deeper problem and many of the people who suffer from it won't even acknowledge it. Some people can remain in denial for a long time.

The problem is rooted in early psycho-social development. It is more of a learned experience and it touches the emotional leverage of the individual thereby causing some imbalance.

In childhood, a person might have been abused or put down by adults. Also, during his/her teenage years he/she might have experienced some trauma in his/her life. As a result, emotional and psychological growth remains stagnant. Lack of social exposure may attribute to some of the malaise or the uneasy feelings that the person has. *In its mildest form*, it can make a person feel unprepared to express himself/herself even in a small crowd regardless of how much preparation the individual has done prior to getting ready to say something. Someone who is in between can still go out and meet new people but will find it very hard. The person is very reserved and withdrawn for the most part because of unwillingness to be hurt or rejected. In general, no one likes to feel unwanted, which is the main preoccupation with the person. Because of lack of self-assertiveness and low self-esteem, these individuals are just as concerned about how they will be judged or evaluated by their peers. Consequently, instead of focusing their attention on their audience, they constantly reflect on themselves as to how inefficient they are compared to other people. For that matter, they can become very devoted followers once someone wins their trust. On the upper end of the scale, they can be quite manipulative in their relationships. They may try to overcompensate for all the other relationships that they would like to have; so one of their trademarks is control of other people's lives. That could be either unconscious or overt.

To overcome fear of rejection and shyness, one must first acknowledge that the problem exists as is the case with any other issue or obstacle. The next thing you want to do is find out how that fear kicks in and the ways in which it manifests itself, meaning your reaction. Now, you need to contain your emotions. Visualize being in the actual situation; at that time your body will probably start tingling or you will feel nervous. Then, quietly or intimately talk to yourself by saying something like, "I am not afraid", or "I know that I can overcome my fear". You may want to identify some people in your surroundings who might serve as moral support. You need to bear in mind that the very thing that you are afraid of is what you must do. If you are afraid of talking to a large audience, find every opportunity you can and do it. By becoming more exposed to the object of your fear, you'll definitely get rid of it. If you want a piece of the pie, but are afraid of expressing your need or claiming that piece to be yours, you are most likely to be ignored. Having applied all the advice that we gave you here, you are well on your way to becoming one of the most talented and most assertive in the whole world. Just don't forget to read each chapter in its entirety for your personal edification because any attempt to rely just on this synopsis will certainly deprive you of key concepts devoted to guide you as you initiate your individual journey towards FREEDOM, the highest mission ever.

Freedom is a powerful track to strive for throughout our lives until our hearts stop their voluntary functions and our brains discontinue all of their ordinary activities. At which point we slip into a vegetative state, if you will, and can no longer operate on our own.

I oftentimes try to emphasize throughout this book the transitional stages of a human being's life. Obviously, the uterus (placenta), or the womb of a woman, represents the safest environment to have our debut. At that early age, or even within the first trimester post-conception the human fetus has already met all the biological requirements that qualify it as a human species, life is best sustained through the aid of another person. The woman, besides all the physiological and emotional roles and functions that she assumes, also provides maximum protection, oxygen, and all the necessary nutrients to make certain that the "child" lives. However, despite all, that full dependency can only go on for a brief or limited period of time; then, from the crib to the grave many of us may often attempt to hold tightly to or keep looking for that umbilical cord whose role has long ago ended!

Sometimes, some parents do their children a disservice by being overly protective of them. And other times, a lot of individuals themselves do not seem to want to let go of their benefactors who may even be debilitated themselves and can no longer provide the support or simply are not interested any longer in helping. Bear in mind that the parents-children relationship and the umbilical cord are analogies drawn here to set the stage as we talk about fear that many people have vis-à-vis growth, maturity, and becoming independent. Therefore, life which was intended to be an enjoyable journey is reduced to mere survivorship. Every time we fail to fulfill a mission, we deny ourselves some important benefits and contribute to the misery of the world in which we live. Some levels of growth may have been predetermined by the genetic materials which we inherit from our parents but still require our input. Moreover, think about it, growth is everything. It encompasses mere physical or emotional development and goes on until we die and return to the dust. Until then, we have a universe in which to grow and explore. The choice is ours as to how far we want to travel. Lastly, as soon as you decide to grow, you will be surprised how much space is available; nonetheless, do not think of it as a gift.

Chapters X-XI   Freedom From the Bondage of One's Mind!

It is amazing how fast we develop the ability to learn the assigned roles or fit the model set for us by society. I find, even more amazing, the degree of effectiveness with which we allow ourselves to become conditioned. I mean, we literally buy into the idea of restricting or limiting ourselves and our potential. More directly, we constantly tell ourselves that we prefer bondage to freedom and that's how we want to live.

Take for instance a young man in New York City, specifically Manhattan, who made headline news in 1995 as he told his story to the court and to the media. After going to superb area restaurants and treating himself to delicious food that he could not afford, he would get arrested and locked up in jail. After a while, he would be released then simply try to eat for free again. His line of reasoning was that he would get arrested and sent to prison. Then he would be cared for while incarcerated.

People with great ability and who could invent the unimaginable turn out to be underachievers, dependent on a system that is already bankrupt. They are constantly putting locks on their potentials. They have not released the power stored in their minds. In fact, it should come as no surprise to us that many studies indicate that most people only use ten percent (10%) of their brain power! What happens to the remaining ninety percent? If we were to tabulate data from various surveys, then we would not only have ample information to document every percentage point where that brain power has gone, but we could also answer "why" to every other question about our wasted resources.

Children who have been told all the time that they are no good and that they won't amount to anything end up believing just it, especially when they hear it from adults whose authority they value! That has a negative impact on their self worth and their overall achievement in life. Secondly, many of us grow in an environment with no or very little incentive to push ourselves. Our social belief can be a positive force in helping us develop dreams and fulfill them. At the same time it represents a major drawback for almost all of us.

Belief affects every aspect of our existence and has everything to with who and where we are in life. It influences our social, spiritual, and romantic life as well in terms of who we affiliate with, and it greatly dictates how industrious a people we have become. Belief is one hundred percent (100%) learned, which means that it can be pretty suggestive and taboo. Aside from that, our inconsistency, fear and ignorance take a toll on us, which inherently limits our vision. Therefore, with all these as obstacles, we lose control of our minds and eventually lose the power which ultimately leads to the loss of our freedom.

Both our body and mind may be controlled by people and circumstances, as well as by different things and objects. Sometimes, that can happen against our own free will especially with us humans who already have that great affinity to control other people's lives! The worst case scenario is for us to become enslaved in both areas, body and mind, and, on top of it all, to believe that we can't do anything to reverse the situation.

Fortunately, bondage can be a temporary situation; you may regain control at any time during your life. And no matter how complicated things get, try to keep your sanity and entertain your mind by doing different activities that can increase your ability to think rationally and objectively in order to be content in the present state while pressing on to higher ground. Remain motivated and optimistic, constantly mindful. President Nelson Mandela gives us a perfect example of how we may be able to reach our goals if we do the above and remain focused.

Chapters XII-XIII   Your Goliath May Seem to Be a Defiant Foe, But You Still Have Options

I promise that I will not retrieve the story of Goliath in the synopsis because you probably will have a better appreciation for the work that I've set forth in the chapter. Therefore, I invite you to take a short trip back and read chapter XII, if you have not done so!

Remain focused, with your vision (s) and plan (s) right at the center of your very existence. That way, you will always be reminded of your objectives, and your move will be strategically and systematically planned. The reasons you need to do that are plentiful and you do want to come to the point where you will ask yourself if it's too late. Your adversaries and all the odds are moving right along with you and towards you; it's up to you whether you want to be defeated, walked over, or taken hostage, or whether you want to maintain or gain enough ground to lead your fights.

Every day in our lives we face obstacles from every side, and if we are not prepared and trained to move meticulously and conspicuously and sort them out in rank of their significance and their priority to us, we have a big problem. Life is an uphill battle that ends only when we give up breathing, and too often we are not properly equipped to meet challenges. Sometimes, you feel that you have just completed or you are about to round up a fight and you say that it's all over. Now, you say that you're tired and drained. So, it's time to sit and relax and forget about everything else! I've got news for you. The little joy that you now have may be taken away from you because of your sitting and relaxing for too long. The next wave of challenges are just around the corner, and you never know what you will face.

In America, the blacks talk a lot about the American emancipation and the feminists elaborate on continued violations of women rights. In spite of all the progress being made to improve and help raise the living standards of every citizen or human being, the fight goes on, and even more intensely! This is not a talk against America or anybody specific; we are talking about everyone, for that matter, who would like to keep their dreams alive and pursue them.

See, the story of Goliath is a real one. When the Israelites were freed from their "captivity" in Egypt, they had some preconceived notions of life afterwards. Many had different perceptions about things, as you and I do. And virtually all of them, except for David, had given up hope in the face of a new challenge which you discovered in chapter XII. I frankly do not know what you are faced with, perhaps failure upon failure, and now you are about to lose your most valuable (cherished) asset, your freedom.

When Haiti gained its independence from France at the turn of the 18th century, all the citizens who gathered around the Haitian emancipators cried with a loud voice pledging to "Vivre libre ou mourir". In the motto of the State of New Hampshire (USA), we find the same phrase but this time in a comprehensible language, at least for our English speaking only readers and that is: "Live free or die."

In life, many people die just because of their fear of dying. They did not want to stand up for themselves because of fear of losing out. Others die on the battlefield fighting to maintain their freedom. Eventually, both groups end up dying, but one group chooses to die with dignity and pride. Put in the context of personal growth and development, many of us forfeit our vision while focusing on the obstacles, just as some of us never had any to start with. Some of us too often feel the burnout or find it too cumbersome to continue the fight; however, they may lose the best opportunity by giving up too early. Also, many of us do not fulfill our dreams or missions in life simply because of our perceptions. The way we perceive things can be so much further away from reality, and that may interfere with how we approach a particular situation or problem. Oftentimes, our real enemy or our most defiant adversary is usually ourselves, our own beliefs. All that can change. Actually, there are very few situations in our lives which we cannot change. All of us can accomplish more in life than we have, and we all dispose of countless resources which we have not tapped into.

Chapter XIV Reaching, Unlocking Your Potential

In case you have not made the discovery, I am a strong believer in the Supreme Creator of all things. Therefore, I find it fair to say that I believe in Divine Providence, but that does not take away my responsibilities of being accountable for the way that I choose to live and how I use my time as well as my talents. I know who I am and believe that I have been given the tools and ammunition to go through life making the best of it and become all that I can.

Some people believe that it is just chance or magic that certain individuals succeed so well and in so many things. If this kind of magic exists, I am not convinced. However, one thing that I am sure of has to do with each of us keeping up the momentum.

Our parents, our predecessors, or society at large, barely mention how to really prepare ourselves for life's different events, and we can come up with many reasons as to why that is. So, apart from a few mentors who sometimes come our way and share with us their personal experiences, we usually learn the tactics on the battlefield or as we move up and down and through the motions of life. Due to different reasons including a lack of guidance, motivation, and discipline, very few of us are led to think rationally and make decisions that are in our best interest. Consequently, what ends up taking place is that our essential resources go to waste; our relay station literally atrophies. Our thinking shifts from dealing with reality to serving our biases. We neither set priorities nor abide by a plan that carries weight or that has substance to it. If we were to turn the clock back or start our lives over, would we have done things differently? Do we think that certain people work their way through by facing various challenges courageously to become successful or powerful? Or do we most likely envision that nature just works wonder in the lives of some lucky individuals? Perhaps, someone out there so loving and so caring just decided to promote them? While there exist very few instances in life where certain conditions may seem to have been moved by mere chance, most often than not our distorted perceptions cause us to avoid seeing the realities and deal with them as such. We baffle ourselves a lot! When we already possess the necessary equipment to make things happen, it is suicidal to leave them in the hands of chance. Any human beings who can breathe on their own and who are not children, and not bedridden due to some severe medical, and psychosomatic (involving body and mind) debilitations do not need to be provided for indefinitely but have enough potential to make improvements in their lives.

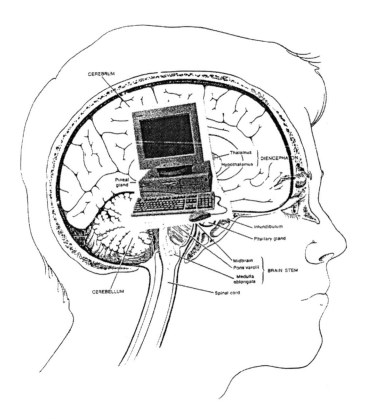

Figure 31.1 The Brain Capacity vs. a Robot

Despite all the technological advances that we have made, we still have not developed a computer that can operate as fast and efficient as the human mind. As you know, a computer is an imitation of how the human brain works and it performs many of the same functions that only human intellect has been able to prior to this invention.

The superhighway or the Internet, which represents the latest scientific wonder, is the most powerful medium (The Worldwide Web, or as it is abbreviated: WWW) ever created that connects different cells across the globe at once and that relays information back and forth so efficiently. In spite of all of these advances, a computer remains a robot and depends on somebody to set it up; otherwise it is useless in itself. And I suspect that it will remain that way if not indefinitely, but at least for a very good while. We on the other hand, do not require any additional touch to perform whatever tasks we set out to do. We have our own circuit, and we never experience any shortage of power.

Some of us manage at times to let our brain go for too long a period without using it, causing it to slow down. Memory deficit and the inability to think quickly, and take command of any situation that we are in largely results from our lack of motivation, training, and discipline to entertain brand new ideas all the time; therefore, the responses are not forthcoming. Does our brain fail us or do we fail our brain?

What actually happens is that we try to turn on the switch and our brain does not respond as fast as it should, or it just does not fire up period. After we have allowed it to vegetate for so long, it atrophies or is reduced in its capacity to carry the order effectively! Nonetheless, it is being programmed once and for all and holds that capability long after we hit old age and start getting senile. Before that, anytime we want to use it, we simply have to take control of our emotions, discipline ourselves, or do some mental/intellectual exercise (meditation, reading, music, dance, sports, etc.) In order to get into the right frame of mind, it is a must that we set our priorities. I would also like to warn you that certain environments are just too distracting to provide you with the appropriate stimulation. You need to choose who you are going to side with; in other words, pick your friends carefully. I really want you to grasp what I am trying to convey. You want to develop your potential; that means you want to make your way to the mountaintop although some people near you may not be interested in getting there themselves. They are just comfortable being at the bottom where they'll probably stay for the rest of their lives. Thus, with respect to your goals and aspirations, this is a perfect example of incompatibility. It's not a nurturing environment!

Remember, we are all unique and we all have the capabilities of performing far more efficiently than we can fathom. Our lives do not have to be so limited to the point where we resign ourselves to whatever comes our way and live within extraneous socio-economic hardships or in dire poverty. We all can do better; we just need to activate the gray matter (our brain cells) and walk on. And if you find that walking is not getting you there fast enough, just run. You do not have to be on similar wavelengths with everybody else; you may set your own pace. Just don't sit there while everything else is engaged in constant motion.

Chapter XV-XVII   Don't Be Passive in Life, Take Some Risks: Learn From a Spider

Arthur Godfrey has made the following statement which I have previously cited in this work. He says, "<u>Even if you are on the right track, you will get run over if you just sit there</u>". I don't think that we need to comment on the statement, for it is so clear, direct, and self-explanatory.

Nature automatically does engage us several ways in life, whether we want or not. We human beings go through many different stages in our development; however, the overall process brings us all to the end point of our journey. So, no matter who we are, what we become, in what family we're born, our social status, etc., we start from the crib and walk towards the grave. Some of us reach there very slowly (at a very old age), others make it at a relatively young age, and still others, unfortunately, run and get there so fast that they barely leave a footprint for anyone to see. Lots of people go through life without ever realizing that they have been given a **Torch** which they ought to light, lift on high, carry around all the time, and shine bright, before it fades away to never reappear. That torch represents our very lives. The following analogy is the story that I was told, and I tend to believe that it might have a particular meaning to many of you who will read this book. Here it is!

It has to do with a man who was offered the opportunity to amass a treasure. However, based on his miscalculation, he won the prize but lost it all in the end. The man met a very wealthy inhabitant who owned an exceedingly large quantity of land. He told the man, "You see this vast expansion of land, it all belongs to me. I will make a deal with you. Any portion of it that you can run over and touch with your feet in one day will be yours, granted that you return to me before the sun sets that very same day." Great deal! The man who had a wonderful opportunity to make some real estate development with that land, agreed to take up the offer. So, the very next day, very early in the morning, he started running over the land. He kept on going and going and the further he went, the more attractive the land seemed to him. When he finally lifted his head and looked up, he realized that time was against him and the sun was about to go down. He then turned around and ran at such an accelerated speed that he overtook the sun but succumbed to cardio-pulmonary arrest because of running too fast. It is a story with a rather sad ending. He won the prize but did not live one minute beyond to enjoy it!!!

It is not really one of our tasks to go around and conquer the world and subdue everyone else under our command (as it may seem in the above story). Nonetheless, we do have the responsibilities to move forward and make our time, as well as our lives, worthwhile. In life, no matter what choices we make, there are always some risks involved, and that is a dilemma for many people who are afraid of taking risks. Whenever possible, we have to calculate or measure the amount of risks which we can take that will result in a higher turnover with a minimal number of casualties. Once we do that then our future looks a bit brighter already. Our success however, depends on several factors:

1)- our general health
2)- our vision/mission
3)- our motivation
4)- our tenacity
5)- our ability to keep reevaluating our progress, and to set new guidelines for ourselves if need be
6)- our willingness to view obstacles as stairways that offer us the advantage of climbing to the next level.

I would like to underline one thing. Godfrey stated that it would be self defeating for you to think that just because you are on the right track, you can sit and foul around. Before you know it all your efforts will amount to nothing: economically, socially, politically, spiritually, academically, and otherwise. A simple reason is that everything else keeps on moving. So, for anyone to consider any amount of progress that he or she has made as final, he or she is dead wrong, which is a phenomenon that we see happening now at an accelerated rate more than ever before to people who did not bother to acquire any job skills or who have minimal qualifications. That's going to be even more threatening in the next millennium, if people don't improve their skills.

RUNNING here, as you can see, is used as a figure of speech. Otherwise stated, it means that we have to be diligent, constantly on the lookout, trying to do something to improve our humanity, whatever that something may be. The man in the land story got the message but was not meticulous or watchful enough. Another way to interpret his move is that he was trying to accomplish far too much, given all the restrictions that he had. It could happen sometimes that some people try to carry more than they possibly can. The opposite is also true. When you look where everybody is in life, how they live (in abject poverty, with a survival mentality) the majority of them barely take it upon themselves to accomplish any significant achievement other than consuming oxygen and other life- sustaining products.

Just like athletes playing any particular sports, we all start at the same place in life, some of us with fewer opportunities; however, the way we use them usually determines how successful we become. Some individuals for lack of patience, get frustrated too fast and concede losses prematurely. For them, I cannot think of a better lesson than the one from a spider. I am sure that you already read the story. It does not hurt to review any part of this book as deemed necessary. In fact, I hope that as you continue to make use of it, you will find sufficient inspirations to pursue and fulfill some of your old dreams. Don't allow a spider to be more patient and smarter than you. The beauty of life lies between thin lines separating success from failure. There is not just one general recipe for everyone to strictly follow in order to succeed; however, sitting still, and not carrying on any vision is by all means counterproductive. Having a human model around may provide greater incentive for us at a cost.

Chapters XVIII-XIX   How Much a Conformer/Imitator Are You?

No human ever lived and shaped his or her life after his or her own self one hundred (100%) percent. This is even more so for those who have developed a high affinity or constant need to socialize. We survive best in the company of other people. We make friends and interact with them; we look for mates so that we may give and receive love, even though the paradox indicates that we cannot live with him/her just as we cannot live without them. In many ways, our successes depend on people in our lives. If we are satisfied with them, we do things certain ways so that we may have their company for much longer periods of time. As it stands, the process of sociali-zation is a very complex one; it diminishes our individuality to the benefits of a collective body. At the same time, it provides many advantages to us as individuals at the expense of the group. Given the opportunity to choose between living in complete isolation versus limited chances to socialize, I would go for the latter.

What often creates a problem in everything that we do is a lack of balance in between, too much of one thing, too little of another. The TV entertainer, Mr. Bill Cosby, indicates, "I don't know the key to success, but the key to failure is trying to please everybody." Social interactions, intimate relationships, and social interdependence can help nurture the individual thereby promoting personal growth, emotional well-being, psychological balance (wellness), and the facilitating of one's goals and ambitions. However, the experiences can be the total opposite. As much as we need other people and as much as they need us, we cannot dissolve our personality to fit into someone else's which imitators try to do. We can neither live nor mature if those relationships do not provide room for our personalities to express themselves. First, may I say that there will never be a person who will meet all of your ideals or who will respond perfectly to your personal tastes. Because you are born with different charac-teristics, raised in different environments and become exposed to different circumstances which shape each of us in a unique way, you have to make that person your ideal mate or your ideal friend. Some personalities will never match and shouldn't try to force to either please the other person or think that you can change that person. It is best that you find someone whose personal characteristics and traits match your personal tastes. If you have strong doubts and reservations, and you find it hard to accept all that person's personal baggage and tastes, chances are that the doubts and reservations will come back later. Some of us have personal baggage that we cannot grow with, never mind someone else trying to get along with us!

Chapters XX-XXI   Learn to Catch Your Own Fish and Declare Warfare Against the C.O.P.

The C.O.P. or the Culture of Poverty, is the expression used to describe people of very low socio-economic status or those who live in abject poverty as it relates to the mentality or to the social belief that nurtures it.

In other words, those who use the term are not trying to divert attention from all the other causes of poverty; but what they are actually saying is that some people develop a mentality or a particular belief system in which they perceive themselves as incapable of doing anything that will help them improve their present conditions. Put otherwise, over time some people have been conditioned to see no way out of an existing situation, so they in turn develop what is called "learned helplessness". Just like the fly which was left in the jar with the cap on, after so many times that it tried but did not succeed in escaping, it later gives up all the hope trying to free itself. It then goes to the bottom of the jar and resides there indefinitely, even though the cap which prevented it from escaping has been removed!

Having this kind of attitude makes it hard for people to transform their lives. If they ever did in the first place, they no longer believe in themselves, and their self-esteem tends to be quite low. Also, they have low educational backgrounds and lack basic job skills.

To bring about any significant changes in their lives, they have to do some work themselves. They may need mentors who could help them embellish their self-image and raise their expectations. In order for them to do these things, they must modify some of their previous belief systems. The negative messages (all the cannots, the self-pitying, the pessimism, etc.) that they used to play to themselves must gradually be substituted by positive ones. At that point, a person is about ready to engage in the battle to become self-empowered. People should not become frustrated and give up because this is not working as fast as they would expect. There exist many forces which one must overcome in order to change total dependency to interdependency. It means that instead of blaming everyone else for your misfortune and rather than waiting for a fish to be dropped on your plate, you remove yourself from being part of the problem to becoming part of the solution. Instead of seeing yourself as victims, you take some responsibility and give yourself credit where you need to. Note, many agencies and organizations are not really in the business of helping people achieve self-empowerment. In fact, many of them prefer to give a fish to those in need rather than to teach them how to catch their own fish so that they may become self-sufficient. Sometimes, people are forced into dependency by the socio-political system in which they live; other times, they just impose it upon themselves. However, either way it does not really matter because the fact is that you are faced with a reality that you must do something about.

The whole world may want to volunteer to help you, but you have to be involved yourself. You have to make some decisions for yourself, regarding your life. It is so unfortunate that many people don't even know who they are and what they want in life! They just go with the flow. Every man and every woman, every child and all young people have to learn about their socio-cultural roots and develop a sense of pride and dignity within themselves. We mentioned this in the chapter "Reaching your Potential". To do so, a person must know who he or she is and begin by making positive changes in his/her life through building self-confidence.

Chapters XXII-XXIII Self-esteem, Individual Temperament, and Addictive Behaviors

Biologically or anatomically and physiologically (body buildup and body function respectively), humans very much resemble the other animals and in a likewise manner, they display somewhat similar features that allow a comparative study of conduct. To function, humans and the lower species need to meet almost the same basic requirements in order to survive. These are food, water and shelter (for security against potential threat). Within this category of needs, humans have an additional need for clothing, which no other animals require. These are typical needs that all living things share in common. However, given that we human beings function at a much higher level compared to everything else, we have other legitimate demands that are just as important if we are to sustain life and live it fuller.

Abraham Maslow, the father of a subdivision in psychology called behaviorism, described three or four other levels of needs for us. We did mention them in previous chapters but it does not hurt to briefly review the list. In his diagram on hierarchy of needs, Maslow points to some significant concepts about self and self-determination/ actualization.

As you saw earlier, self-esteem or self-actualization is very big on his list. Just as we are confronted by healthy and unhealthy belief systems, we can do damage to our personal growth and emotion in the way that we perceive and feel about ourselves.

Self-esteem is not narcissism or infatuation with self-love at whatever cost. Instead it has to do with self-awareness, who we are, how much confidence we have in ourselves, and how much pride we take in ourselves. This is very critical to our self-worth and our overall well-being. People do strange things to themselves when they don't know who they are or they don't have self-esteem. There is a marked difference between humility and humiliation. The first word describes someone with a humble spirit while he or she still maintains a high degree of self-worth. The second expression works against our self- esteem. The way we carry ourselves or allow other people to treat us can help determine whether we take any pride in who we are.

Before we may be able to mature and experience personal growth, we have to keep improving our self-image. It is not communicable, and each of us needs his or her own concept of self-worth. Now, as you know, too little of something can be a problem and too much of anything can also be lethal. Low self-esteem is detrimental to anyone's emotional and psychological well-being. This may even be a major setback in trying to build up relationships where you don't know yourselves. Consequently, instead of loving others and receiving their love, you try to control and own them. You become extremely jealous of them and make it almost impossible to establish a balanced relationship. The other extreme of too much self-esteem sounds like narcissism, a compulsive type personality. You almost become too stubborn and no one can stand you for long. You need a balance and you can do it yourself by giving yourself some credit and accepting compliments. Stop putting yourself down all the time. Children, especially, need an environment in which they can hear that they are somebody. They need adults who trust and demonstrate pride in their accomplishments.

Many people allow substances and drugs to control their lives in search of some identities not necessarily their own but ones that they have been trying to imitate or copy their lives after. There exist many different forms of addictions, and you know better than anyone else what you are addicted to. Some people are addicted to different kinds of substances, including nicotine and alcohol, and others have been hooked on many vices which literally claim their lives. I do not know how long you have been possessed; you may even need professional assistance. But the first step is on you, and the sooner you take it, the sooner you will be able to start working towards promoting yourself. Last, but not least, this book has everything to do with freedom and self-empowerment. Therefore, I feel that I need to say something about the social welfare programs and the danger of people becoming totally dependent on them.

Chapter XXIV   Where do the Welfare Recipients Go from Here?

Whose responsibility is it to provide for those people who are socio-economically at a disadvantage or who find themselves at the bottom of the socio-economic ladder? Should they be on the government welfare roll, should the private sector or the wealthy intervene and be the "Good Samaritan", or should the church make it its task? Will the poor/needy even be able to swim upstream and help themselves through self-empowerment? How long should they be provided for? Perhaps, a better question might be, who is providing what to whom and at what cost?

Almost every person, once in a while, needs a caring hand, someone who might help make one's life easier. In fact, no human being can really live a life that is one hundred percent independent from the rest of the world; we all do a lot better with someone around us and with whom we may interact and rely on. For that matter, I believe that the word interdependence conveys a much more realistic view of the world at large. The latter portrays a healthy type of relationship regardless of the contribution that one is able to make in society. There is also the idea of mutualism being expressed in interdependency. In other words, it resembles a two-way street. People reciprocate, or whatever they receive they put something back into the system. The best illustration that I can think of when referring to interrelationship or interdependency relates to the way that our heart actually functions. The heart keeps pumping blood 24 hours a day, 365¼ days per year; but it does not take in newly made blood after supplying each organ. It operates on an extremely efficient two-way system which allows it to keep recycling the same blood. In other words, the heart does not just receive the blood and keep it. <u>Without the blood flowing in our body, we are dead. And even though in the average adult individual, the total blood volume is approximately five liters. However, the heart, being such an efficient apparatus, pumps this much blood in about one minute, collects it, and pumps it out again. The process goes on and on. Therefore, simple math can tell us how many liters of blood go through the heart every day. To sustain life, it works on an input-output system.</u>

When we take a deeper look at any welfare system in general, we underline two major flaws which relate to people's social belief systems and the socio-economic and political structures of the world. Some individuals would like to exert total control of the wealth of the world. The opposite of that is people who have allowed themselves to be conditioned to the point where they do not mind being recipients. Sometimes, you wonder what kind of people society is made of! It seems as though some people are quite comfortable with the idea of being predators; they prey on others to help them lead glamorous lives, while some others sit around and constantly wait for somebody to hand things to them.

Social programs targeting different groups of individuals should and must exist. What I personally have difficulty dealing with is the following: if all that governments, social programs, and some so-called humanitarian organizations do is provide the people that they serve with a piece of bread every now and then, they do no more than create a welfare state. Furthermore, if we do not help our young people and the socio-economically disenfranchised of society get the education/training they need and if we do not encourage them to make use of their resources, should they alone be held accountable or should we all take responsibility for their failure? Nowadays, we talk a lot about helping the needy empower themselves; however, most of what is taking place is the opposite. In many cases, we simply offer Band-Aids to cover the symptoms that come out of social ills. And in so doing we help perpetuate the vicious cycle. We need concrete solutions to socio-economic problems that are endemic in the world.

Chapter XXV   Migration: Should You or should You Not?

Yes! Should you or should you not? You probably recall the quotation from Arthur Godfrey that says, "Even if you are on the right track, you'll get run over if you just sit there". I agree with Arthur. However, I would disagree with you if you tried to convince me that one must migrate anytime, anywhere. There is a question of context that must be considered here if we wish to answer the above inquisition in light of Godfrey's statement.

Some people see jumping out of the ship as the way to save their sinking ship, but there are those who do not really see it that way. Actually, there are countries where almost entire generations try to envision their future based on their tentative migration to another country or another continent! This is considered external migration. We also encounter internal migration where citizens move inside their own country from one town to another, from the country to the city sometimes without a clue as to the repercussions, whether or not they're trying to run from a situation that is relatively bad or chaotic to one that may be suicidal.

I am for any move or any action that can have a positive net effect on changing things for the better. Just like making any other major decisions, moving to another country or to another environment, there are risks involved. One needs to weigh the pros and cons. Migration causes a breakdown within the family unit and among friends, thereby creating a void and leaving scars that even time is unable to heal!

A lot of people, in their eagerness to migrate, end up trading many of their old values in order to try to conform to the norms of their new home or their new culture.

Besides having to undergo additional training in order to be qualified for a job that they were well accustomed to do back home, migration is not always a positive experience where the newly arrived migrants necessarily are welcomed to their new homes. Certainly, brand new opportunities will open for some immigrants; however, in some instances the blessing is mixed. Just a brief example, many people who follow world news might have read in the *Boston Globe* a very sensitive article which was published about the inhumane conditions of Haitian immigrants living in the Dominican Republic. The article said, "The Haitian migrants who harvest Dominican sugar cane arrive each year in overcrowded school buses and live in fetid dorms. From 5:00 AM to 5:00 PM, they hack 12-foot cane stalks until their clothes are drenched with sweat and dust, but at day's end they have nowhere to bathe. Paid 42 pesos, or about $3.00 for every ton of sugar cane they cut…An experienced worker may cut one and a half tons per day…" (*The Boston Globe*, "Sugar Season's Bitter End", by Steve Fainaru, Wednesday, August 20, 1997,. pp.1 & 12 A.)

When everything is going well for the citizens of the host country (strong economy, low inflation rate, lots of available jobs, overall upscale health conditions) the immigrant population is safe. Otherwise, they get blamed for all the wrong that hits their neighbors. That often occurs as some skillful politicians try to stir public opinion and divert attention from the real issues.

Relocation or migration is not a bad idea; one can learn so many new things about other people, places, different cultures, and life itself. However, it can be a very lonesome, frustrating, and disappointing road. Some people think that moving to another country or to another culture will solve all their problems. From my very own experience, living in the Bahamas and in the United States of America, I will tell you that is a major flaw. For one thing, human beings are the same everywhere. Therefore, you face almost the same situations wherever you go, and sometimes even more. The socio-economic and the political systems may vary with respect to a particular country. Your needs may be ecologically different, but you still have to put up with the social dynamics. In other words, you need to learn about the elements that constitute each and every community that you look to interact with. Your perception and your belief system tends to follow you wherever you go, and if you can live and function successfully in one place, you may be able to do the same elsewhere.

The take home message for immigrants is:

1) There are risks involved in migration (internal or external).

2) You always have to give up something that you already have for a prospect.

3) Once you decide to move, be a little bit flexible in order to become acquainted with and learn from the new environment. Culturally, you will have to make a judgment call and choose between your old traditions and those that you transcend to. On both sides, you should be able to see positive and negatives elements.

4) Don't lock yourself in a gear like this is the only way things can be done. Always try to be innovative and creative wherever and whenever you can.

5) Wherever you choose to live you will meet people. Make sure to build a support system that will help you grow.

6) Learn how to make the best of every situation in which you find yourself. "If life gives you lemons, you make lemonade."

7) With respect to your personal growth, where you end is more important than where you started.

Chapter XXVI   Energy Conservation (Don't Waste Your Energy Foolishly)

Energy is something very valuable that we can all appreciate, for without it, we probably would not get out of bed and do what we have to in order to remain alive. Everything that we have to accomplish requires some expenditure in the form of energy.

There comes a point in life where we all wished that we could go the extra mile nonstop. Usually, kids dispose of a great amount of energy. Many of them play and release some of that energy. Youths are at that age where they feel so energetic and strong that many of them at times think that they are immune from any kind of problem and can defeat the whole world. Hence, they go through different adventures and sometimes put their lives in danger by taking very high risks. When people start feeling old or getting old, as the case may be, the general tendency is to settle down and try to concentrate on one mission, if any. Somewhere along the line, they tend to become more focused or more stubborn; they do what they want to do the way that they wish.

I'd like to make a couple of statements: 1) Some people have no discipline when it comes to spending or no concept concerning saving. Money comes in one of their hands and goes out in the other. 2) It is a kind of "mind thing" to feel a certain way. Many of us move just by feelings and are affected or disturbed by the least change or variation in our world so that oftentimes we feel down. We stay down and act as though we are on the last leg of our journey!

Even age is not necessarily a deterrent to power and to feeling energetic. Sometimes the mentality that we grow up with shapes our lives in such a way that we are hardly ever open to other ideas and suggestions. However, if you ever had a problem and went to see a medical doctor or a healer, most likely you ended up listening and doing what you were told. If you go to see a financial planner or an economist, he or she will probably tell you what to do to get or to keep your financial situations in order. I say this because most of us have problems saving enough money, and perhaps that has to do with the fact that we hardly ever made enough to start with. Even the millionaires have difficulty accumulating enough!

Our journey would not be worthwhile if we had all the right dreams and no power or energy to execute them in the end. In plain financial terms, you run into bankruptcy or you run into a deficit depending on the severity of the case.

People say that they run low on or out of energy sometimes. How accurate is that statement or what could attribute to that? Although we are not necessarily seeking to establish causality or the reason (s) why that is so, we may be able to nonetheless associate certain factors that will shed light on the situation.

Based upon data gathered from research, it is indicated that on the average, most of us only use ten percent (10%) of our brain capacity. Ninety percent has not been used which leads us to believe that the amount of power or energy that we expend is not always in proportion to our total volume. We need to be accountable to ourselves for the unused portion by looking for different ways to stimulate our minds so that energy is available to us. Secondly, through life's many trials and snares, it is normal for us to lose some momentum. Sometimes, we have to learn to slow down, recuperate, and reenergize. Thirdly, too often a great number of us are distracted. As a result, we experience difficulty putting it together again. By that I mean that we lose incentive, we get into a careless mode, we become bitter, cynical, and even pessimistic about everything. Fourth, some of us make it a habit chasing the wrong rabbit or going after too many of them, not realizing that sometimes in life we have to take a deaf ear. Many wars may come our way, but we don't have to fight them all. Learn to prioritize options. Some choices are always better than others. During the second World War, remember how beneficial it was to America not getting drawn in until later? We should learn about our strengths and pick our battles carefully. Now, I invite you for a ride to the jungle to get away a little bit from civilization. I know that this is an enormous task to ask anyone of you, especially those who hold so dearly to the wonderful idea of being "racially superior" or "racially inferior."

Chapter XXVII Which Should You Change: Your Skin Color or Your Belief System?

Welcome to the world of "Ethnic Cleansing" and <u>Improper Race/Gene</u>. Whether or not you are interested, every now and then, a race, color, and nationality different from yours will be shown on your radar system or on your environmental screen. Some may look just like foreign invaders from outer space. Should you be alarmed, I am not sure! You may experience some shortness of breath, you may be intimidated, and you may even be attacked depending where on planet earth you are located at that particular point in time.

Here is what I want you to do, don't panic; just take a deep breath, and for a moment think of yourself as the invader! Then, compare your skin color with your belief system to see which one might not only help you tear down any hostility coming from the other creature but also increase your chances of survival. Where exactly was the hostility coming from? Did you experience any coming directly from you? What can you do?

Change in any form or shape is not a phenomenon that we, human beings, like to make. We are just like particles or atoms in that we enjoy the comfort of being at rest and not having to keep making adjustments all our lives. But guess what? Life is just that. Sometimes, we are forced to change, and sometimes, it seems just the right thing to do. Overall, we like to make changes only when it appears convenient to us.

One of the biggest problems that we human beings have is the need to control everything around us (resources, land, people, nature). The best way to go through those changes is by creating systems that foster compartmentalization or categorization. In one way these systems help us better understand and master the environment. Then, in another way, we use such classifications to discriminate against those individuals who look different, talk differently, dress differently, act differently, and live differently from us. This whole business gives way to varied social classes and social status.

As a result, gender, ethnic origin, religious conviction, family background, national linkage, intellectual baggage, physical appearance, and race are allowed to become tools to segregate everyone who does not fit our mold. As we achieve this level of organization, we move on to the next level and create an elite or a super class of people with all the rights and privileges appertaining to us.

The fact that there are diverse groups of people around gives a rich mixture. While diversity may be viewed as different, in no way does it mean or suggest that any one group is inferior to another in any form or shape. Therefore, any one group of people that you look at is as capable and competent as any other one. The foremost factor which really makes a difference is the belief system of individuals in each group and how they perceive themselves. It turns out that our skin color has nothing whatsoever to do with our degree of success nor our level of intelligence.

Referring to racial discrimination earlier in this work, I remember saying that the power is not found on the skin but rather in the brain/mind. Some people may have a lot of adipose tissue (fat) underneath their dermis which can obviously release a considerable amount of calories. If you want, you may think of your own skin otherwise, but according to science it is a protective layer against foreign agents. The skin also provides support for internal organs and helps maintain body temperature. Our color is genetically determined by the level of melanin (skin pigment) which is found in each of us and which gives our skin its distinct complexion. It is a simple biological expression as any other specific feature that we have and it does not say anything about a particular race being more intelligent or smarter than another one. In other words, it is not an indicator for someone's I.Q.

However, some of us may have been brainwashed to believe that indeed the color business about a certain race being superior or inferior compared to another holds infallible truth given by some deity. However, science has yet to invent the theory to prove that belief. What I can guarantee you in all confidence, is that each of us, every now and then has to take inventory of our belief systems to find where we have faults and thus delete from our memory bank all erroneous information that may have prevented us from reaching our freedom. You do not need your skin to get there from where you are and if you did, it would not be made with the kind of material that it has. Your brain or your mind is the power and not the skin. Please, refer to this specific chapter for complete details. Thank you! We have made a great deal of advances and scientific discoveries during the century; however, so many of us are still blind and ignorant, and we carry on certain myths for ever. Once we make them a part of our belief systems, they become like cancerous cells that invade our body or like poisonous substances that keep eroding our society. The only antidote or remedy against such ills is education.

Chapters XXVIII-XXIX   Education, More Education, and College Degreessssss!

A few moments after post-partum activities a baby starts using all of its five senses to learn from and to communicate with the environment. Then, education has already begun. That process necessarily ends as the grave opens and literally swallows the individual. The amount of information that the person will have gathered during his or her lifetime is directly related to or is in proportion to: a) the level of stimulation received from the environment; b) the normal function of the brain; (For various reasons such as genetics, congenital, drugs and alcohol intake during pregnancy, insufficient nutrition during pregnancy, premature birth, and the early stages in a child's development, a person may have difficulty assimilating information at a certain rate.) c) the aptitude of the individual for a particular topic; d) a person's motivation and interest toward learning in general; e) discipline; (Some of us develop ways to keep a high interest in learning.) f) the lifespan of the individual; (There is no question that someone who dies in the childhood years has relatively less time to acquire more education compared to an adult.) g) some kind of trauma; (Trauma may interfere with the individual's normal learning ability, thereby causing problems with retention or creating memory deficit.)

As technology advances, we become more equipped to assist those individuals who require special attention. Why am I saying all this? There exist two forms of education:

1- life experience
2- classroom setting (modern)

In ancient times and up to the Dark Ages, people relied heavily on life's learning experiences. The daily activities for the most part seem to have occurred by chance. The position of the moon and the sun in the sky was a way to tell the time. Many other asteroids not only served as a kind of timekeeping device, but they were also used as a modern era compass to help navigators find their way. It took months and months to travel from one part of the world to another that we can now cover in a matter of hours. Besides contemplating nature and following its course, there was very little for humans to do that required extensive learning or formal, classroom education. Most work activities relied on a lot of manpower and very little intellectual activity. Since that did not exist as yet, there was no need for a diploma/degree in order to set sail, to ride on the donkey's back, to work the land and maximize its produce to feed more people. Every home served as a bank where each family managed to keep its own assets or resources. Then, as the system developed, it became a separate branch of industry to have banking facilities just for financial transactions and as a means of exchange. During the early unfolding of the industry, some common sense could help one secure a job in a bank. Then, as time passed, people who wanted to work at this institution could get by with some grade school education.

Presently, most of those positions are being transformed and applicants are required to have one, two, or even more graduate degrees to perform the same job. As we evolve to higher civilization, our society becomes more and more sophisticated so that if you want to be informed, and competitive, or on top of things, you have to explore all the options that are available to you. What are they? Is life experience still helpful? Can you acquire sufficient training skills without actually going through standard college and university programs? What are the other alternatives? Is it important to have degreessssssssssssssss? Can they alone make you reach your goals?

First of all, I hope that I can convince you to agree with me that as it now stands, everyone should know how to read and write. For example, if someone holds a couple of prescriptions in his or her hand, for instance, one of which says "external use only" but the person is not able to read the label, he or she may end up killing himself/herself.

It is unfortunate that education is not made accessible to everyone. Moreover, some of us don't take education too seriously. However, as we evolve in this society, it is important that we keep evaluating ourselves in terms of how to make our lives more productive and how to be the best at what we do for the good of ourselves and our fellow human beings. Using every moment of our time, we all should learn a profession or new skills as the world changes.

An academic degree will not give you a decent personality if you don't have one. It may not even get you to *"heaven" or "purgatory"*, as some schools of theology imply, but it will certainly have a great impact on you, how you live, and how you make decisions as a citizen of this world and a productive member of your respective communities. All of us should strive to gain some superior form of knowledge in every possible way and excel in whatever discipline that we choose to practice. Some of us can excel in more than one area. That may be called multi-talented. It is all right! One should get as many academic degreessss as one can; hoping that each one of them will help shape you into a better person. In addition, it depends on how you use them. They carry the potential to help you live life fuller and bountifully by raising your state of mind towards excellence and by giving you some level of control over your socio-economic conditions. A degree can actually assist you in making the transition from being totally dependent on others to being an interdependent and productive member of your community. Academic degrees in formal settings, trade schools, and any other forms of institutions (including home schooling) that can provide special skills to individuals are to be considered of vital importance to society and should be elevated over those places that serve to incarcerate people's minds and bodies, thereby preventing them from being their best.

Not to be the devil's advocate or place myself in the position of condemning anybody's religion or personal belief; some people are so heavenly-minded that degrees don't mean anything to them. Degrees/knowledge should not be antagonistic to religions, but again personal opinion sometimes substitutes for religious beliefs and ignorance. You make the personal decision. You decide what is important to you: a degree, a profession, or a passive attendance on this earth.

Even if you possess a lot of money, you still need an education. Regardless of who you are and where you live, you have to have an education in whatever form or shape. You may be young or old, but you need an education. You are a man or a woman. It does not matter. You need an education. You are Black, White, Red, Yellow, whatever your skin complexion; you may even be Christian, Muslim, Orthodox Jewish, Roman Catholic, Hindu, it still does not matter. You need an education. It will help you to better understand yourself and will provide you with the opportunity to participate in your own personal growth which will eventually impact your future. Also, by educating yourself, you become more efficient in drawing your lines of logic and reasoning. Last but not least, it may improve your ability to interact with your fellow human beings in a more civilized manner. And if you ever become concerned about being competent in what you do in life, education will provide you with the necessary tools which will keep you on the cutting edge in a competitive world. There is virtually no substitute for a good education.

There are those of us who hopefully know how to appreciate education. It helps open eyes and minds; and without being cynical, we come to a greater understanding as to why it makes some folks uncomfortable having educated people around them. Among other things, when you are educated, others cannot exert control over you as they please. As history teaches us, not too long ago that same attitude guided the line of reasoning in many people to deny (higher) education to the slaves, any subservants, and also women. Even today, some form of education and training is still being controlled or guided. Whereas it is difficult to secure admission to some academic institutions, some of them even make it hard for students to survive while they are there. For many of us, it requires a great deal of motivation and dedication to get ourselves in school and complete the cycle, especially in higher education. To further complicate matters, the cost of acquiring an education may be quite exorbitant. The comment that makes me very nervous is when I hear people say, "Is it worth spending so much time and money?" To them I will say to take heed that they do not disqualify themselves and become disabled or unfit to finish the race.

Pertaining to cost, few socialist countries still manage to offer a relatively free or low-cost education to those who can get in. In other places like the United States, in terms of cost effectiveness, the institutions where one pays lower tuition rates are the government subsidized and community schools. Private institutions, despite grants available from many sectors, are still unattainable to the majority of people. Along with the high cost, however, lie great opportunities.

I have one suggestion. If you are limited in finances, but can work to support yourself in school without really jeopardizing your health and your grades, avoid borrowing too much money. It is hard and takes time to pay back; however, I would be the last person to want you to miss the opportunity later on in life. If that's the only resort which is at your disposal, by all means, borrow enough to carry you through your studies. It is also worth the delay in satisfying some of your wants to get yourself a darn good education. Put otherwise, you will do better by postponing some of your pursuits for immediate gratification for the sake of getting an education. That could mean not buying a new car for the time being or not becoming sexually involved and struggling every step of the way with a pregnancy. Experience shows that we do not do well when we act under the influence of emotions alone or on the spur of the moment without some thinking, planning, and strategizing.

In the final analysis, as it relates to paying for your schooling, you may be able to find one of those excellent offers where you don't have to spend a cent of your own money. Someone or some institution sponsors you! Otherwise, there exist different organizations out there that offer stipends and/or conditional scholarships to qualified applicants. Criteria for eligibility usually vary from one institution to the next. You may need to research the field that you are interested in to see what your options may be. Remember, where there is a will there is a way. Also, bear in mind that knowledge is never complete. You may acquire a degree and some limited training required to fulfill the school's expectations; however, learning continues. So, don't fool yourself thinking that when you graduate you know everything, otherwise your degree won't be worth much after a while. And above all, staying healthy is also our prerogative. Be all you can be while keeping your stress level at a minimum.

Chapter XXX   Overcoming Your Stress Level

First, let me say that I would like to be brief in this section, not because we are running out of words or concepts but because of the length which we have already presented the subject matter.

Stress is real and can be overwhelming to anyone. Stress may affect our general health and reduce our ability to effectively cope with different situations which we would otherwise be able to handle. Sometimes, just our inability to find the solution to a simple, everyday problem can frustrate us to the point of creating disturbances in our lives. Even minor situations, if they are left unresolved over extended periods of time can turn our lives into disasters, which can be translated into an elevated level of stress in our bodies. Many studies have documented how stress may impair our performance by causing an imbalance in our emotional, psychological, and physical well-being. Needless to say that exposure to stressful circumstances which we are unable to control in a timely fashion may increase our risk of developing adverse cardiovascular (heart and all the blood vessels included) conditions. Therefore, we need to maintain the capacity to keep our stress level in check. Guidelines for handling stress are laid out in Chapter XXX.

The faster we are able to identify the source (s) of our stress and do something about it, the healthier we can live and the more rational we can behave as everything else remains equal. My immediate recommendation to you is not to allow your stress to overcome you. By then, it will probably be too late to reverse the diagnosis. You may not be able to personally identify all the signs and symptoms of stress, but you will have signals which should raise a flag. And medicine at its best is the ability to prevent rather than to cure, if there'll ever be a cure!

Some of us experience a much tougher time managing our stress and keeping it under control partly because of a mal-adaptive personality. At some point, you must have heard about "obsessive-compulsive" personality type. In diagnosing different mental and emotional clinical manifestations, health care professionals have come up with the terminology, which is also called *borderline personality.* The reason that I mention it here is because individuals with this type of personality can be very demanding and obsessed with things sometimes. At times they either worry too much over a world of wants or when they'll have their desires satisfied. This is but one of the many enabling factors leading toward frequent or constant elevated stress levels.

Other people are just too emotional in their response to life's different events which leave them vulnerable to emotional stress off and on. We all have our strength and weakness levels, and not only that, we find ourselves at different stages at times, which in part explains why some of us do better under certain circumstances. Also, some people train themselves in ways that make them more resilient to stress. Among this group, you may find many professionals working in fields that are very demanding. Many executives and entrepreneurs identify themselves within this category.

Selye, one of the leading researchers on stress, has identified three levels that we may go through: 1) the alarm reaction or stage 2) the resistance stage 3) the exhaustion stage (read Chapter XXX for details). Also, a list has been generated by Holmes and his colleagues indicating different circumstances and the level of stress associated with each of them. For instance, they assign the highest level of stress in points (100) to the survivor of a deceased spouse. To someone who is getting fired from a job, they give that person a stress level equivalent to 47 points. They mention the holiday season and traffic violations as somewhat minor stressors and assign only a small number to them (12 and 11 respectively.)

All kinds of situations can increase a person's stress level, depending on the state and the perception of that person. Accumulation of debts, meeting new people, breaking of an existing relationship, changing jobs, working in an unpleasant environment, preparing to take an exam, sickness, and inability to provide for one's family are different situations that may cause our stress levels to climb. When that happens, our blood pressure usually increases also and many other phenomena take place simultaneously. Stress can be a contributing factor leading to one's death.

The ability of an individual to relax more often and not be consumed by different circumstances is the key to maintaining emotional balance and well-being. Sometimes, we need to take life less seriously and not look at the obstacles that we face as insurmountable. Besides various techniques which are recommended in this book and others to help you deal with stress more effectively, an optimistic look at life increases one's hope and ability to cope more successfully. Your glass can be half empty or half full, and it is not being unrealistic to approach life with a positive attitude and at the same time to work toward changing things. If you are down and stressed out, it is harder for you to rise up, and even if you have no one to hold on to you have no business staying down there.

In your search toward freedom, a great deal depends on you and you alone. The Good Lord may send a good Samaritan your way but even when He does, you must manage to retain a balanced life. In order for us to live and positively affect the quality of our lives, freedom and stress must be indirectly related, in that one must expand while the other decreases. All the work that you and I have to accomplish in order to make this world a better place requires that we maintain good health. If our blood pressure is often running high with no known causes, we have difficulty concentrating/sleeping, we are usually upset or short-tempered, we feel tired all the time, we experience fatigue and/or unexplained headaches, chances are that we live under too much stress. If after reading the chapter on stress, we still find ourselves fighting to maintain our emotional balance, professional help is available. Some of it is free, especially from the church's parish and trained clergy.

As John Carlhoun said, "It is harder to preserve than to obtain liberty." You can set yourself free, even from the stress which might otherwise leave you powerless, as long as you follow some of our advice and are willing to make the sacrifices wherever necessary. This book will assist you a great deal in achieving almost whatever goals you set for yourself.

My anticipation is that somehow you will become exposed to this life-changing manual either on your own, on a classroom assignment during the semester, or through a friend. Whichever way it happens, I hope that you develop an appreciation for the work. And our intent is that it brings you to a higher level of self-awareness and self-realization where you will be able to unlock your potentials to become the best you can. It also aims at helping you develop and maintain a healthier lifestyle.

This book is not written by accident. It has begun and ended with the specific aim to see that you succeed. Whether it be an assignment or mere curiosity that introduces you to this work, we hope you take the time to explore the contents of each chapter. You may use it as a guide to lead a more disciplined life. You are welcome to make this part of your diary and read (instead of write) a chapter each day (31 days of reading). You may even go back and reread special sections of interest to you.

Remember, all of us have the potential to become whatever we want if only we would be persistent enough in our pursuit and look beyond the horizons for new enlightening. The obstacles that we often face are but pseudo hills and mountains which we need to climb in order to reach the plateaus where we are supposed to be. We were never made to drag through the valleys permanently or sit at the bottom of the hill wondering hopelessly. Start each day with a fresh new breath and bear in mind that only those who dare try succeed. "If you stand for nothing, you fall for anything." Lastly, as I bring this work to completion, I certainly trust that your interest in reading these pages will grow past mere intellectual exercise. Instead, you will apply some of the concepts that are discussed in this book to empower yourself, reach a higher level in your personal growth and wellness, and achieve the goals which you are about to set for yourself. I am also interested in knowing whether this book has helped you. Won't you write me today? You may reach me at:

P. O. Box 200040
Boston, Massachusetts 02120-0001
United States of America (USA)
Telephone: (617) 298-2976
email: mondesir@channel1.com

Best of luck!!!

Eno Mondesir

❖ APPENDIX ❖

Eno Mondesir

Table 1

Arrest rates (per 100,000 inhabitants)

By offense, 1971-94

(Rate per 100,000 inhabitants)

	Total Crime Index[a]	Violent crime[b]	Property crime[c]	Murder and non-negligent manslaughter	Forcible rape	Robbery	Aggravated assault	Burglary	Larceny-theft	Motor vehicle theft	Arson
1971	897.1	175.8	721.4	9.4	10.7	65.4	90.3	202.9	434.2	84.2	X
1972	881.5	165.5	695.0	9.4	12.1	68.1	97.0	196.0	423.1	76.0	X
1973	883.4	187.3	696.1	9.3	12.4	65.7	99.9	204.1	415.6	76.4	X
1974	1,098.0	219.7	878.3	10.3	13.3	80.9	115.2	254.1	544.2	80.0	X
1975	1,059.6	206.7	852.9	9.2	13.3	72.4	112.8	250.7	535.1	67.1	X
1976	1,016.8	193.1	823.7	8.0	12.4	62.8	109.8	231.8	528.8	63.1	X
1977	1,039.4	202.7	836.7	9.0	13.5	64.2	116.0	238.1	527.8	70.9	X
1978	1,047.6	215.5	832.2	9.1	13.6	68.3	124.4	234.6	523.6	74.0	X
1979	1,057.2	212.5	844.7	8.9	14.3	63.9	125.4	228.8	536.8	70.2	9.0
1980	1,055.8	214.4	841.4	9.0	14.1	67.0	124.3	230.4	539.8	62.3	8.9
1981	1,070.0	216.8	853.2	9.5	14.0	68.8	124.5	228.4	558.8	57.0	9.0
1982	1,148.9	236.9	912.0	9.9	15.1	73.7	138.2	232.9	612.1	58.0	9.0
1983	1,071.9	221.1	850.8	9.0	15.0	66.8	130.3	207.1	582.5	52.6	8.6
1984	1,019.8	212.5	807.3	7.6	15.8	60.4	128.8	185.9	561.4	51.9	8.2
1985	1,046.5	212.4	834.0	7.8	15.7	59.3	129.6	188.1	580.7	56.9	8.3
1986	1,091.8	234.5	857.3	8.1	15.7	62.6	148.1	189.2	595.6	64.7	7.8
1987	1,120.1	233.8	886.4	8.3	15.5	60.9	149.1	185.3	621.0	72.5	7.5
1988	1,123.5	243.8	879.7	8.6	15.1	58.9	161.2	175.6	615.4	81.0	7.7
1989	1,173.1	268.6	904.4	9.0	15.3	66.9	177.4	178.4	627.3	81.0	7.7
1990	1,203.2	290.7	912.5	9.5	16.0	70.4	194.8	176.3	641.4	87.0	7.3
1991	1,198.8	293.0	905.8	9.8	16.0	73.3	194.0	173.1	639.8	85.1	7.9
1992	1,162.4	300.5	861.9	9.1	15.6	71.9	203.8	168.6	605.5	80.3	7.6
1993	1,131.6	302.9	828.8	9.5	15.2	71.7	206.0	158.0	584.4	78.8	7.5
1994	1,148.4	310.7	837.7	8.9	14.3	70.8	216.6	154.1	595.5	80.1	8.1

[a] Includes arson beginning in 1979.

[b] Violent crimes are offenses of murder and nonnegligent manslaughter, forcible rape, robbery, and aggravated assault.

[c] Property crimes are offenses of burglary, larceny-theft, motor vehicle theft, and arson.

The number of agencies reporting and the populations represented vary from year to year. Due to National Incident-Based Reporting System conversion efforts beginning in 1991, complete arrest data were not available for a small number of States for certain years. See Appendix 3 for a list of States omitted. Arson was designated an Index property crime in October 1978. Data collection began in 1979. For definitions of offenses, see Appendix 3.

Source: U.S. Department of Justice, Federal Bureau of Investigation, *Crime in the United States, 1971*, p. 116; *1972*, p. 120; *1973*, p. 122; *1974*, p. 180; *1975*, p. 180; *1976*, p. 173; *1977*, p. 172; *1978*, p. 186; *1979*, p. 188; *1980*, p. 192; *1981*, p. 163; *1982*, p. 168; *1983*, p. 171; *1984*, p. 164; *1985*, p. 165; *1986*, p. 165; *1987*, p. 165; *1988*, p. 169; *1989*, p. 173; *1990*, p. 175; *1991*, p. 214; *1992*, p. 218; *1993*, p. 218; *1994*, p. 218 (Washington, DC: USGPO). Table adapted by SOURCEBOOK staff.

Table 2

Percent changes in Total Crime Index rates and violent crime rates

United States, 1960-1994

	Total Crime Index[a]	Violent crime				
		Total	Murder and nonnegligent manslaughter	Forcible rape	Robbery	Aggravated assault
1960 to 1961	1.0%	-1.7%	-6.0%	-1.8%	-3.1%	-0.5%
1961 to 1962	6.0	2.6	-3.9	0.4	2.4	3.4
1962 to 1963	7.9	3.6	-0.2	-0.9	3.5	4.3
1963 to 1964	9.5	13.3	6.8	19.7	10.4	14.9
1964 to 1965	2.5	5.1	5.1	7.9	5.1	4.7
1965 to 1966	9.1	9.9	9.7	9.1	12.7	8.1
1966 to 1967	11.9	15.1	9.8	6.0	27.2	8.2
1967 to 1968	12.7	17.9	11.6	13.5	28.3	10.4
1968 to 1969	9.2	10.1	5.9	16.2	12.6	7.4
1969 to 1970	8.3	10.6	7.4	1.3	16.0	6.7
1970 to 1971	4.5	8.9	9.5	9.6	9.2	8.5
1971 to 1972	-4.9	1.3	4.0	9.8	-3.9	5.6
1972 to 1973	4.9	4.1	4.4	8.9	1.3	6.2
1973 to 1974	16.8	10.5	4.7	7.0	14.3	7.7
1974 to 1975	9.2	5.8	-1.8	0.4	5.5	7.1
1975 to 1976	-0.2	-4.1	-9.1	1.0	-9.7	0.9
1976 to 1977	-4.0	1.7	1.0	10.4	-4.3	5.9
1977 to 1978	1.2	4.6	1.5	5.6	2.7	6.1
1978 to 1979	8.3	10.3	8.7	11.9	11.6	9.1
1979 to 1980	6.9	8.7	4.9	6.1	15.0	4.4
1980 to 1981	-1.5	-0.4	-3.9	-2.2	3.0	-2.9
1981 to 1982	-4.3	-3.9	-7.7	-5.5	-7.7	-0.2
1982 to 1983	-7.6	-5.9	-9.1	-0.9	-9.4	-3.4
1983 to 1984	-2.8	0.3	-4.1	5.7	-5.1	3.9
1984 to 1985	3.5	3.2	0.5	4.1	1.5	4.4
1985 to 1986	5.2	11.0	7.5	2.1	8.0	14.2
1986 to 1987	1.3	-1.3	-3.4	-1.3	-5.5	1.5
1987 to 1988	2.1	4.5	1.9	0.5	3.9	5.4
1988 to 1989	1.4	4.1	2.9	1.2	5.5	3.5
1989 to 1990	1.4	10.4	8.8	8.3	10.3	10.6
1990 to 1991	1.3	3.6	3.9	2.5	6.1	2.2
1991 to 1992	-4.0	-0.1	-4.9	1.2	-3.3	2.0
1992 to 1993	-3.1	-1.5	2.1	-4.9	-3.0	-0.4
1993 to 1994	-2.0	-4.0	-5.9	-3.5	-7.1	-2.3
1960 to 1994	184.8	345.1	76.2	309.1	295.3	399.9
1970 to 1994	34.9	97.0	13.7	109.8	38.1	161.0
1980 to 1994	-9.7	20.0	-12.4	6.5	-5.3	44.1
1990 to 1994	-7.7	-2.2	-5.0	-4.9	-7.5	1.4

Crime rates are the number of offenses known to police per 100,000 population. These numbers represent percent changes in crime rates from one year to the next.

[a]Includes the violent crimes of murder and nonnegligent manslaughter, forcible rape, robbery, and aggravated assault, and the property crimes of burglary, larceny-theft, and motor vehicle theft.

Source: Table provided to SOURCEBOOK staff by the National Rifle Association of America, Institute for Legislative Action; data were made available through the Federal Bureau of Investigation's Uniform Crime Reporting Program.

Table 3

Estimated number of arrests[a]

By offense charged United States, 1994

Offense charged	
Total[b]	14,648,700
Murder and nonnegligent manslaughter	22,100
Forcible rape	36,610
Robbery	172,290
Aggravated assault	547,760
Burglary	396,100
Larceny-theft	1,514,500
Motor vehicle theft	200,200
Arson	20,900
Violent crime[c]	778,730
Property crime[d]	2,131,700
Total Crime Index[e]	2,910,400
Other assaults	1,223,600
Forgery and counterfeiting	115,300
Fraud	419,800
Embezzlement	14,300
Stolen property: buying, receiving, possessing	164,700
Vandalism	323,300
Weapons: carrying, possessing, etc	259,400
Prostitution and commercialized vice	98,800
Sex offenses (except forcible rape and prostitution)	100,700
Drug abuse violations	1,351,400
Gambling	18,500
Offenses against family and children	117,200
Driving under the influence	1,384,600
Liquor laws	541,800
Drunkenness	713,200
Disorderly conduct	746,200
Vagrancy	25,300
All other offenses (except traffic)	3,743,200
Suspicion (not included in total)	14,000
Curfew and loitering law violations	128,400
Runaways	248,800

Note: These data were compiled by the Federal Bureau of Investigation through the Uniform Crime Reporting Program. On a monthly basis, law enforcement agencies report the number of offenses that become known to them in the following crime categories: murder and non-negligent manslaughter, manslaughter by negligence, forcible rape, robbery, aggravated assault, burglary, larceny-theft, motor vehicle theft, and arson. All of these crime categories, except manslaughter by negligence, are used to establish a crime index in order to measure the trend and distribution of crime in the United States. The "Total Crime Index" is a simple sum of the index offenses. Arson was designated a Part I Index offense in October 1979. Data collection began in 1979. Unlike the tables from *Crime in the United States* presented in Section 3, arrest statistics for the crime of arson are complete and appear in the "Total Crime Index" and "Property crime" total.

Arrest statistics are compiled as part of this monthly data collection effort. Participating law enforcement agencies are instructed to count one arrest each time a person is taken into custody, notified, or cited for criminal infractions other than traffic violations. Annual arrest figures do not measure the number of individuals taken into custody because one person may be arrested several times during the year for the same type of offense or for different offenses. A juvenile is counted as a person arrested when he/she commits an act that would be a criminal offense if committed by an adult. Two offense categories, "curfew and loitering" and "runaway," are tabulated only for juveniles. Violations of local juvenile acts other than runaway and curfew and loitering law violations are included in the "all other offenses" classification (U.S. Department of Justice, Federal Bureau of Investigation. *Uniform Crime Reporting Handbook* (Washington, DC: USGPO. 1984), p. 60).

Data in this table are estimates based on arrest statistics for all law enforcement agencies in the Uniform Crime Reporting Program, including those submitting reports for less than 12 months in 1994 (Source, p. 381). Due to National Incident-Based Reporting System (NIBRS) conversion efforts, no arrest data for Kansas, Montana, and most Illinois law enforcement agencies were available for 1994. Arrest totals for these States were estimated by the Source for inclusion in the above table. Subsequent tables, displaying detailed breakdowns of persons arrested, contain limited or no data for these States.

For definitions of offenses, see Appendix 3.

[a] Arrest totals based on all reporting agencies and estimates for unreported areas.

[b] Because of rounding, figures may not add to total.

[c] Violent crimes are offenses of murder and nonnegligent manslaughter, forcible rape, robbery, and aggravated assault.

[d] Property crimes are offenses of burglary, larceny-theft, motor vehicle theft, and arson.

[e] Includes arson.

Source: U.S. Department of Justice, Federal Bureau of Investigation. *Crime in the United States, 1994* (Washington, DC: USGPO, 1995), p. 217.

Table 4

Estimated number and rate (per 100,000 inhabitants) of offenses known to police

By offense and extent of urbanization, 1994

Area	Population[a]	Total Crime Index	Violent crime[b]	Property crime[b]	Murder and non-negligent man-slaughter	Forcible rape	Robbery	Aggra-vated assault	Burglary	Larceny-theft	Motor vehicle theft
United States, total	260,341,000	13,991,675	1,864,168	12,127,507	23,305	102,096	618,817	111,950	2,712,156	7,876,254	1,539,097
Rate per 100,000 inhabitants	X	5,374.4	716.0	4,658.3	9.0	39.2	237.7	430.2	1,041.8	3,025.4	591.2
Metropolitan Statistical Area	207,136,441										
Area actually reporting[c]	97.4%	12,032,121	1,665,643	10,366,478	20,543	83,997	594,474	966,629	2,272,607	6,656,460	1,437,411
Estimated totals	100.0%	12,209,050	1,682,021	10,527,029	20,629	85,326	597,567	978,436	2,304,742	6,770,254	1,452,033
Rate per 100,000 inhabitants	X	5,894.2	812.0	5,082.2	10.0	41.2	288.5	472.4	1,112.7	3,268.5	701.0
Other cities	21,329,287										
Area actually reporting[c]	90.6%	1,025,262	95,885	929,377	912	7,548	14,268	73,157	188,430	696,849	44,098
Estimated totals	100.0%	1,134,269	106,719	1,027,550	1,021	8,385	15,903	81,410	205,841	772,728	48,981
Rate per 100,000 inhabitants	X	5,317.9	500.3	4,817.6	4.8	39.3	74.6	381.7	965.1	3,622.8	229.6
Rural	31,875,272										
Area actually reporting[c]	87.8%	584,341	67,372	516,969	1,360	7,619	4,785	53,608	180,512	302,439	34,018
Estimated totals	100.0%	648,356	75,428	572,928	1,592	8,385	5,347	60,104	201,573	333,272	38,083
Rate per 100,000 inhabitants	X	2,034.0	236.6	1,797.4	5.0	26.3	16.8	188.6	632.4	1,045.6	119.5

These figures are aggregated from individual State statistics presented in table 3.111. These data include estimated offense totals for agencies submitting less than 12 months of offense reports (Source, p. 379). Complete data for 1994 were not available for Illinois, Kansas, and Montana; crime counts for these States were estimated by the Source. For definitions of offenses and areas, see Appendix 3.

[a]Populations are U.S. Bureau of the Census provisional estimates as of July 1, 1994 and are subject to change.

[b]Violent crimes are offenses of murder and nonnegligent manslaughter, forcible rape, robbery, and aggravated assault. Property crimes are offenses of burglary, larceny-theft, and motor vehicle theft. Data are not included for the property crime of arson.

[c]The percentage representing area actually reporting will not coincide with the ratio between reported and estimated crime totals, since these data represent the sum of the calculations for individual States that have varying populations, portions reporting, and crime rates.

Source: U.S. Department of Justice, Federal Bureau of Investigation, *Crime in the United States, 1994* (Washington, DC: USGPO, 1995), p. 59, Table 2. Table adapted by SOURCE-BOOK staff.

Table 5

Percent distribution of total U.S. population and persons arrested for all offenses

By age group, United States, 1994

Age group	U.S. resident population	Persons arrested
Age 12 and younger	19.2%	1.8%
13 to 15	4.2	8.4
16 to 18	4.0	12.8
19 to 21	4.1	11.8
22 to 24	4.4	10.5
25 to 29	7.4	14.8
30 to 34	8.5	14.4
35 to 39	8.4	10.9
40 to 44	7.6	6.7
45 to 49	6.4	3.7
50 to 54	5.1	1.9
55 to 59	4.2	1.0
60 to 64	3.9	0.6
Age 65 and older	12.7	0.7

This table presents data from all law enforcement agencies submitting complete reports for 12 months in 1994 (Source, U.S. Department of Justice, p. 381). Because of rounding, percents may not add to 100.

Source: U.S. Department of Justice, Federal Bureau of Investigation, *Crime in the United States, 1994* (Washington, DC: USGPO, 1995), pp. 227, 228; and U.S. Department of Commerce, Bureau of the Census, "U.S. Population Estimates. by Age, Sex, Race, and Hispanic Origin: 1990 to 1994," Washington, DC: U.S. Department of Commerce, March 1995. (Mimeographed.) Table 1. Table constructed by SOURCEBOOK staff.

Table 6

Arrests

By offense charged, age group, and race. United States, 1994

(10,648 agencies; 1994 estimated population 207,569,000)

	Total arrests					Percent[a]				
Offense charged	Total	White	Black	American Indian or Alaskan Native	Asian or Pacific Islander	Total	White	Black	American Indian or Alaskan Native	Asian or Pacific Islander
Total	11,846,833	7,894,414	3,705,713	126,503	120,203	100.0%	66.6%	31.3%	1.1%	1.0%
Murder and nonnegligent manslaughter	18,475	7,705	10,420	126	224	100.0	41.7	56.4	0.7	1.2
Forcible rape	29,759	16,683	12,419	327	330	100.0	56.1	41.7	1.1	1.1
Robbery	146,793	55,055	89,232	737	1,769	100.0	37.5	60.8	0.5	1.2
Aggravated assault	449,179	264,466	176,062	4,063	4,588	100.0	58.9	39.2	0.9	1.0
Burglary	319,466	215,363	97,867	2,844	3,392	100.0	67.4	30.6	0.9	1.1
Larceny-theft	1,235,016	796,212	407,231	12,803	18,770	100.0	64.5	33.0	1.0	1.5
Motor vehicle theft	166,119	95,216	66,544	1,562	2,797	100.0	57.3	40.1	0.9	1.7
Arson	16,727	12,555	3,853	168	151	100.0	75.1	23.0	1.0	0.9
Violent crime[b]	644,206	343,909	288,133	5,253	6,911	100.0	53.4	44.7	0.8	1.1
Property crime[c]	1,737,328	1,119,345	575,495	17,377	25,110	100.0	64.4	33.1	1.0	1.4
Total Crime Index[d]	2,381,534	1,463,255	863,628	22,630	32,021	100.0	61.4	36.3	1.0	1.3
Other assaults	989,654	625,689	341,941	11,991	10,033	100.0	63.2	34.6	1.2	1.0
Forgery and counterfeiting	92,946	59,127	32,001	531	1,287	100.0	63.6	34.4	0.6	1.4
Fraud	330,305	205,362	120,640	1,563	2,740	100.0	62.2	36.5	0.5	0.8
Embezzlement	11,609	7,600	3,816	46	147	100.0	65.5	32.9	0.4	1.3
Stolen property; buying, receiving, possessing	134,694	77,709	54,601	925	1,459	100.0	57.7	40.5	0.7	1.1
Vandalism	259,060	193,538	59,083	2,950	3,489	100.0	74.7	22.8	1.1	1.3
Weapons, carrying, possessing, etc.	213,079	121,834	87,531	1,304	2,410	100.0	57.2	41.1	0.6	1.1
Prostitution and commercialized vice	86,733	53,819	30,860	498	1,556	100.0	62.1	35.6	0.6	1.8
Sex offenses (except forcible rape and prostitution)	81,750	62,300	17,637	897	916	100.0	76.2	21.6	1.1	1.1
Drug abuse violations	1,117,323	677,025	429,479	4,623	6,196	100.0	60.6	38.4	0.4	0.6
Gambling	15,843	7,845	7,247	44	707	100.0	49.5	45.7	0.3	4.5
Offenses against family and children	91,530	58,427	30,242	1,183	1,678	100.0	63.8	33.0	1.3	1.8
Driving under the influence	1,063,491	932,802	107,347	14,655	8,687	100.0	87.7	10.1	1.4	0.8
Liquor laws	423,624	352,683	57,575	10,328	3,038	100.0	83.3	13.6	2.4	0.7
Drunkenness	571,004	460,300	96,200	12,632	1,872	100.0	80.6	16.8	2.2	0.3
Disorderly conduct	600,345	390,326	199,094	7,552	3,373	100.0	65.0	33.2	1.3	0.6
Vagrancy	21,407	12,298	8,635	374	100	100.0	57.4	40.3	1.7	0.5
All other offenses (except traffic)	3,042,887	1,891,312	1,092,034	28,838	30,703	100.0	62.2	35.9	0.9	1.0
Suspicion	11,371	5,643	5,635	63	30	100.0	49.6	49.6	0.6	0.3
Curfew and loitering law violations	105,781	80,319	22,177	1,203	2,082	100.0	75.9	21.0	1.1	2.0
Runaways	200,863	155,201	38,310	1,673	5,679	100.0	77.3	19.1	0.8	2.8

See notes at end of table.

Table 7

Rank order of States according to rates (per 100,000 population) of violent crime, murder and non-negligent manslaughter, robbery, aggravated assault, and rape

1994

Rank	Violent crime[a] State	Rate	Murder and nonnegligent manslaughter State	Rate	Robbery State	Rate	Aggravated assault State	Rate	Rape State	Rate
United States: total		716.0		9.0		237.7		430.2		39.2
1	District of Columbia[b]	2,662.6	District of Columbia	70.0	District of Columbia	1,107.2	District of Columbia	1,441.8	Delaware	75.6
2	Florida	1,146.8	Louisiana	19.8	New York	476.7	South Carolina	780.4	Michigan	70.8
3	South Carolina	1,030.5	Mississippi	15.3	Maryland	402.5	Florida	757.4	Alaska	69.0
4	California	1,013.0	Arkansas	12.0	Illinois	372.6	New Mexico	685.4	Nevada	68.7
5	Nevada	1,001.9	Alabama	11.9	California	356.8	Louisiana	650.3	Washington	60.5
6	Louisiana	981.9	California	11.8	Nevada	352.4	California	609.4	Minnesota	59.7
7	New York	965.6	Illinois	11.7	Florida	328.8	Nevada	569.1	South Carolina	54.3
8	Illinois	960.9	Florida	11.7	New Jersey	288.0	Alaska	544.9	New Mexico	52.4
9	Maryland	948.0	Nevada	11.7	Louisiana	267.2	Illinois	543.3	Florida	52.3
10	New Mexico	889.2	Maryland	11.6	Missouri	230.7	Massachusetts	505.7	Oklahoma	49.6
11	Alaska	766.3	New York	11.1	Michigan	228.9	Arizona	494.7	Texas	48.5
12	Michigan	786.1	North Carolina	10.9	Georgia	222.6	Maryland	493.3	Tennessee	49.2
13	Tennessee	747.9	New Mexico	10.7	Tennessee	207.4	Tennessee	482.0	Ohio	47.1
14	Missouri	743.5	Missouri	10.5	Texas	204.8	Kentucky	469.7	Mississippi	45.4
15	Massachusetts	707.6	Arizona	10.5	Connecticut	187.8	Oklahoma	466.8	Louisiana	44.6
16	Texas	706.5	Georgia	10.0	Ohio	187.5	Alabama	465.3	District of Columbia	43.7
17	Arizona	703.1	Michigan	9.8	Pennsylvania	186.7	Missouri	465.2	Oregon	43.2
18	Alabama	683.7	South Carolina	9.6	South Carolina	186.1	Michigan	456.7	Colorado	43.2
19	Georgia	667.7	Tennessee	9.3	North Carolina	181.2	New York	451.9	Utah	42.2
20	North Carolina	655.0	Virginia	8.7	Alabama	171.2	Texas	441.1	South Dakota	42.0
21	Oklahoma	651.5	Florida	8.3	Massachusetts	168.2	North Carolina	429.9	Arkansas	41.9
22	New Jersey	614.2	Indiana	7.9	Mississippi	162.5	Arkansas	412.5	Maryland	40.7
23	Kentucky	605.3	Oklahoma	6.9	Arizona	162.0	Georgia	400.4	Kansas	37.1
24	Arkansas	595.1	Connecticut	6.6	Alaska	146.2	Delaware	354.8	Missouri	37.0
25	Delaware	561.0	Kentucky	6.4	New Mexico	140.8	Colorado	354.0	Arizona	36.0
26	Indiana	525.1	Alaska	6.3	Washington	139.7	Indiana	351.5	New Hampshire	35.8
27	Oregon	520.6	Ohio	6.1	Oregon	138.2	Oregon	334.4	Indiana	35.6
28	Washington	511.3	Pennsylvania	5.9	Virginia	132.8	Kansas	316.0	Kentucky	35.3
29	Colorado	509.6	Kansas	5.8	Indiana	130.2	Washington	305.6	Alabama	35.2
30	Mississippi	493.7	Washington	5.5	Arkansas	128.7	New Jersey	296.2	California	34.9
31	Ohio	485.8	Colorado	5.4	Oklahoma	128.1	Nebraska	280.2	Georgia	34.7
32	Kansas	478.7	West Virginia	5.4	Delaware	125.9	Mississippi	270.5	Wyoming	33.6
33	Connecticut	455.5	New Jersey	5.0	Kansas	119.8	Rhode Island	256.8	Illinois	33.3
34	Pennsylvania	426.7	Oregon	4.9	Minnesota	117.6	Ohio	245.1	North Carolina	33.0
35	Nebraska	389.5	Delaware	4.7	Wisconsin	112.9	Iowa	243.0	Nebraska	30.8
36	Rhode Island	375.5	Wisconsin	4.5	Colorado	106.9	Connecticut	236.5	Hawaii	30.4
37	Minnesota	359.0	Hawaii	4.2	Hawaii	103.6	Idaho	235.9	Massachusetts	30.2
38	Virginia	357.7	Rhode Island	4.1	Kentucky	93.9	Wyoming	218.9	Virginia	28.5
39	Iowa	315.1	Massachusetts	3.5	Rhode Island	87.3	Pennsylvania	208.0	Idaho	27.9
40	Utah	304.5	Idaho	3.5	Nebraska	75.4	Utah	195.8	Vermont	27.6
41	Idaho	285.8	Wyoming	3.4	Utah	63.6	Virginia	187.6	Rhode Island	27.4
42	Wyoming	272.5	Montana	3.3	Iowa	46.9	Minnesota	178.6	Montana	27.2
43	Wisconsin	270.5	Minnesota	3.2	West Virginia	42.4	South Dakota	165.5	Pennsylvania	26.1
44	Hawaii	262.2	Nebraska	3.1	Montana	32.7	West Virginia	147.6	New York	25.9
45	South Dakota	227.6	Utah	2.9	New Hampshire	27.1	Wisconsin	129.7	Maine	25.6
46	West Virginia	215.8	Maine	2.3	Maine	22.4	Hawaii	123.9	New Jersey	24.9
47	Montana	177.1	Iowa	1.7	South Dakota	18.7	Montana	113.8	Connecticut	24.6
48	Maine	129.9	New Hampshire	1.4	Idaho	18.4	Maine	79.6	Iowa	23.5
49	New Hampshire	116.8	South Dakota	1.4	Wyoming	16.6	Vermont	56.0	Wisconsin	23.5
50	Vermont	96.9	Vermont	1.0	Vermont	12.2	New Hampshire	52.5	North Dakota	23.4
51	North Dakota	81.8	North Dakota	0.2	North Dakota	11.1	North Dakota	47.2	West Virginia	20.3

Note: These data were compiled by the National Rifle Association of America, Institute for Legislative Action. Research and Information Division from data provided by the Federal Bureau of Investigation's Uniform Crime Reporting Program. Where rates for States are reported as equal, rank was determined by calculating the rate to the decimal place necessary to make a distinction. Counts for murder and non-negligent manslaughter include certain homicides later ruled as self-defense or other justifiable homicides. Complete data were not available for Illinois, Kansas, and Montana; therefore certain crime counts were estimated by the FBI's Uniform Crime Reporting Program.

[a]Includes murder, nonnegligent manslaughter, rape, robbery, and aggravated assault.
[b]Includes offenses reported by the Zoological Police.

Source: Table provided to SOURCEBOOK staff by the National Rifle Association of America, Institute for Legislative Action; data were made available through the Federal Bureau of Investigation's Uniform Crime Reporting Program.

Table 8

Number and rate (per 100,000 population) of violent crime and murder and nonnegligent manslaughter, and number and percent of firearm-related violent crime and weapon-related murder and nonnegligent manslaughter

By State, 1994

State	Violent crime[a] Number	Violent crime[a] Rate	Firearm-related violent crime Number	Firearm-related violent crime Percent of all violent crime	Murder and nonnegligent manslaughter Number	Murder and nonnegligent manslaughter Rate	Murder and nonnegligent manslaughter Percent of all violent crime	Percent of all murder and nonnegligent manslaughter Firearm-related	Handgun-related	Shotgun-related	Rifle-related	Knife-related	Fists/feet-related
United States, total[b]	1,864,168	716.0	552,669	29.6%	23,305	9.0	1.3%	70.0%	56.5%	4.3%	3.3%	12.5%	5.3%
Alabama	28,844	683.7	7,085	24.6	501	11.9	1.7	74.5	62.9	7.4	4.2	10.8	6.2
Alaska	4,644	766.3	1,262	27.2	38	6.3	0.8	64.9	51.4	5.4	5.4	18.9	16.2
Arizona	26,653	703.1	10,313	36.0	426	10.5	1.5	72.6	54.4	4.1	5.5	11.2	5.5
Arkansas	14,598	595.1	5,014	34.4	294	12.0	2.0	72.4	51.9	8.9	6.1	9.9	3.1
California	318,395	1,013.0	87,634	27.5	3,703	11.8	1.2	75.2	66.1	4.4	3.8	11.5	4.2
Colorado	18,632	509.8	4,883	26.2	199	5.4	1.1	63.5	53.9	3.9	1.7	16.3	5.6
Connecticut	14,916	455.5	3,640	24.4	215	6.6	1.4	73.6	64.8	2.3	3.2	13.9	6.5
Delaware	3,961	561.0	830	21.0	33	4.7	0.8	46.2	23.1	0.0	0.0	15.4	7.7
District of Columbia[c]	15,177	2,662.6	4,974	28.4	399	70.0	2.6	77.4	76.2	0.8	0.0	11.8	1.8
Florida	160,016	1,146.8	45,415	28.4	1,165	5.3	0.7	54.8	37.3	2.8	2.3	13.1	4.8
Georgia	47,103	667.7	17,167	36.4	703	10.0	1.5	72.6	62.2	4.9	2.7	12.7	4.9
Hawaii	3,091	262.2	459	14.8	50	4.2	1.6	48.0	38.0	6.0	4.0	12.0	14.0
Idaho	3,238	285.8	907	28.0	40	3.5	1.2	60.0	50.0	0.0	10.0	17.5	10.0
Illinois	112,928	960.9	42,492	37.6	1,376	11.7	1.2	69.0	55.3	1.3	1.1	12.5	5.4
Indiana	30,205	525.1	7,293	24.1	453	7.9	1.5	74.0	61.4	5.8	1.6	12.1	4.2
Iowa	8,914	315.1	1,481	16.6	47	1.7	0.5	47.7	25.0	13.6	2.3	22.7	9.1
Kansas[d]	12,226	478.7	NA	NA	149	5.8	1.2	NA	NA	NA	NA	NA	NA
Kentucky[d]	23,165	605.3	NA	NA	244	6.4	1.1	NA	NA	NA	NA	NA	NA
Louisiana	42,369	981.9	17,210	40.6	856	19.8	2.0	82.8	72.0	3.5	3.9	7.3	3.8
Maine	1,611	129.9	159	9.9	28	2.3	1.7	40.7	29.6	11.1	0.0	22.2	-4.8
Maryland	47,457	948.0	17,106	36.0	579	11.6	1.2	70.3	65.8	2.9	1.0	13.0	5.7
Massachusetts	42,749	707.6	5,676	13.3	214	3.5	0.5	72.3	52.4	7.3	3.6	11.5	4.4
Michigan	72,751	766.1	25,130	34.5	927	9.8	1.3	72.3	42.8	8.7	5.8	20.3	5.8
Minnesota	16,397	359.0	3,633	22.2	147	3.2	0.9	57.2	42.8	3.1	2.2	11.4	3.1
Mississippi	13,177	493.7	5,911	44.9	409	15.3	3.1	79.0	72.1	5.3	3.4	12.2	4.1
Missouri	39,240	743.5	15,358	39.1	554	10.5	1.4	64.3	51.3	NA	NA	NA	NA
Montana[d]	1,516	177.1	NA	NA	28	3.3	1.8	NA	NA	NA	NA	NA	NA
Nebraska	5,322	329.5	1,598	25.3	51	3.1	0.9	60.0	33.3	2.7	20.0	6.7	13.3
Nevada	14,597	1,001.9	4,587	31.4	170	11.7	1.2	66.3	55.6	5.3	4.1	10.7	11.8
New Hampshire	1,328	116.8	182	13.7	6	1.4	1.2	54.0	49.5	2.0	0.5	16.9	10.9
New Jersey	48,544	614.2	12,622	26.0	396	5.0	0.8	61.7	45.8	5.6	9.3	15.9	6.5
New Mexico	14,708	889.2	4,418	30.0	177	10.7	1.2	68.1	61.3	1.9	1.4	14.6	6.0
New York	175,433	965.6	45,215	25.8	2,016	11.1	1.1	63.8	51.4	5.4	6.5	14.1	5.4
North Carolina	46,308	655.0	15,822	34.2	772	10.9	1.7	63.8	51.4	5.4	6.5	14.1	5.4
North Dakota	522	81.8	40	7.7	1	0.2	0.2	0.0	0.0	0.0	0.0	0.0	0.0
Ohio	53,930	485.8	16,466	30.5	682	6.0	1.2	72.8	59.5	5.5	1.2	9.0	6.2
Oklahoma	21,225	651.5	5,745	27.1	226	6.9	1.1	70.0	52.4	8.8	7.5	13.7	5.7
Oregon	16,067	520.6	4,266	26.5	150	4.9	0.9	65.3	46.0	5.3	8.7	20.0	6.0
Pennsylvania	51,425	426.7	16,003	31.1	712	5.9	1.4	66.5	59.7	3.1	2.0	14.0	8.2
Rhode Island	3,744	375.5	618	16.5	41	4.1	1.1	51.2	41.5	4.9	4.9	19.5	4.9
South Carolina	37,756	1,030.5	10,183	27.0	353	9.6	0.9	72.2	55.7	7.1	5.7	11.4	5.4
South Dakota	1,641	227.6	291	17.7	10	1.4	0.6	44.4	33.3	0.0	11.1	11.1	22.2
Tennessee	38,705	747.9	13,479	34.8	482	9.3	1.2	70.1	59.1	6.2	3.3	14.8	5.5
Texas	129,838	706.5	43,319	33.4	2,022	11.0	1.6	73.3	54.2	5.9	4.0	13.3	4.8
Utah	5,810	304.5	1,270	21.9	56	2.9	1.0	68.3	52.4	4.8	6.3	14.3	4.8
Vermont	562	96.9	104	18.6	6	1.0	1.1	33.3	16.7	16.7	0.0	33.3	16.7
Virginia	23,437	357.7	6,800	29.0	571	8.7	2.4	73.3	64.1	4.4	3.0	11.7	5.4
Washington	27,317	511.3	7,271	26.6	294	5.5	1.1	62.8	50.2	1.4	7.8	14.7	6.8
West Virginia	3,931	215.8	796	20.2	99	5.4	2.5	77.8	57.6	11.1	8.1	4.0	5.1
Wisconsin	13,748	270.5	4,705	34.2	227	4.5	1.2	52.9	47.1	3.1	2.2	18.2	10.2
Wyoming	1,297	272.5	209	16.1	16	3.4	1.2	62.5	37.5	6.3	18.8	12.5	18.8

Firearm-related figures are projections based on Uniform Crime Reports data showing incomplete reports from the States and the District of Columbia. Not all States report each year; therefore comparisons between years should not be undertaken, except for States that have reported consistently.

For detailed information on State and Federal restrictions on the purchase, carrying, and ownership of firearms, see table 1.110.

[a] Includes murder and nonnegligent manslaughter, robbery, aggravated assault, and rape.
[b] Firearm-related violent crime figures for "United States, total" are projections based on reports from 47 States and the District of Columbia.

[c] Data on weapons used were provided by the Metropolitan Police Department of the District of Columbia.
[d] Kansas, Kentucky, and Montana did not provide data on weapons used in violent crimes.

Source: Table provided to SOURCEBOOK staff by the National Rifle Association of America, Institute for Legislative Action; data were made available through the Federal Bureau of Investigation's Uniform Crime Reporting Program.

❖ BIBLIOGRAPHY ❖

Adler, P. S. (1977). Beyond Cultural Identity: Reflections Upon Cultural and Multicultural Man. Health Education and Health Promotion. New York: Harper & Row.

Alcoholics Anonymous. (1976). (3rd Ed.). New York: Alcoholics Anonymous World Services, Inc.

Allio, R. J. (1988). Thinking and Planning Strategically. Research Report. New York: Conference Board, Inc.

Amaro, H. (1995). Love, Sex, Power: Considering Women's Realities in HIV Prevention. American Psychologist, 30, (6), 437-447.

Baker Eddy, M. (1994). Science and Health: With Key to the Scripture. Boston: The First Church of Christ.

Baranoski, T. (1992). Beliefs as Motivational Influence at Stages in Behavior Changes. Int'l Quarterly of Community Health Education, 13, (1), 3-29.

Bassuk, S. S. et al. (1997). Homelessness in Female-Headed Families. American Journal of Public Health, 87, (2), 242-248.

Bastien, R. (1961). Haitian Rural Family Organization. Institute of Social and Economic Research. Jamaica: University College.

The Bay State Banner. (Feb. 13, 1997). Damages Awarded in O. J. Case. Boston, Massachusetts, pp. 1, 12, and 14.

Beatrice, M. (1989). Codependent No More & Beyond Codependency. New York: MJF Books.

Bender, D. L. et al. (1988). Poverty: Opposing Viewpoints. San Diego, CA: Greenhaven Press, Inc.

Bondurant, J. V. (1965). Conquest of Violence: The Gandhian Philosophy of Conflict. Los Angeles: University of California Press.

The Boston Sunday Globe, Parade Magazine. (1997, September 7). I Didn't Have Time For Anger. By D. Rader, pp. 12 & 13.

Brewer, R. (1988). The Science of Ecology. Philadelphia: Saunders College Publ.

Brynteson, P. et al. (1985). Fitness & Faith: The Complete Book of Health for the Whole Person. Nashville, TN: Thomas Nelson Publishers.

Capps, C. (1976). The Tongue: A Creative Force. Tulsa, Oklahoma: Harrison Publishing House, Inc.

Carlson, N. R. (1986). Physiology of Behavior. Boston: Allyn and Bacon, Inc.

Carter, J. (1982). Keeping Faith: Memoirs of a President. Toronto: Bantam Books.

Chapman, S. et al. (1993). Self Exempting Beliefs About Smoking and Health. American Journal of Public Health, 83, (2), 215-219.

Charonko, C. (1992). Cultural Influences in Non Compliant Behavior. Holistic Nursing Practice, 6, (3), 73-78.

Compayre, G. (1893). Abelard and the Origin of Early History of University. New York: Greenwood Press.

Conger, J. A. (1992). Born or Made? Forces that Foster Leadership, Learning to Lead. San Francisco: Jossey-Bay, Publisher.

Cooper-Patrick, L. et al. (1997). Exercise and Depression in Midlife: A Prospective Studies. Am. Journal of Public Health, 87, (4), 670-672.

Cosby, B. (Ed.) (1989). Love and Marriage. New York: Doubleday.

Cummings, P. et al. (1997). The Association Between the Purchase of a Handgun and Homocide or Suicide. American Journal of Public Health, 87, (6), 974-78.

Daco, P. (1988). Les Voies Etonnantes de la Nouvelle Psychologie. Belgium: Collection Marabout.

Danishelsky, I. (1980). Biochemistry for Medical Sciences. Boston: Little, Brown and Co.

Davis, M, A. et al. (1997). Living Arrangements, Changes and Survival Among Community Dwelling Older Adults. Am. Journal of Public Health, 87 (3), 371-377.

Dawes, R. M. et al. (1977). Behavior, Communication, and Assumption about other People's Behavior…Journal of Personality and Social Psychology, 35, 1-11.

Dawkins, P. and J. (1994). Together Toward Success. Primerica Financial Services.

Dawkins, R. (1976). The Selfish Gene. New York: Oxford University Press.

Devins, G. M. et al. (1997). Cross-Cultural Measurements of Psychological Well-Being. American Journal of Public Health, 87, (5), 794-799.

Diener, E. et al. (1979). An evaluation of the Jamaica Anti-crime Program. Journal of Applied Social Psychology, 9, 135-142.

Dinitto, D. M. et al. (2nd $^{Ed.}$) (1987). Social Welfare: Politics and Public Policy. Englewood Cliffs, New Jersey: Prentice-Hall, Inc.

Dollar, J. et al. (1939). Frustration and Aggression. New Haven, CN: Yale University Press.

Dorfman, L. et al. (1997). Youth and Violence on Local Television News in California. American Journal of Public Health, 87, (8), 1311-1316.

Duckett Cain, J. (March 1994). We wear the Pants. Essence, 24, (11), 92-101.

Duncan, E. V. (1995). Forgiveness Unlimited. Trinidad, W. I.: Exousia Books.

Dunlop, D. D. et al. (1997). Disabilities in Activities of Daily Living: Patterns of Changes and a Hierarchy. Am. Journal of Public Health, 87, (3), 378-383.

DuRant, R. H. et al. (1997). Tobacco and Alcohol Use Behaviors Portrayed in Music Videos: A consent Analysis. American Journal of Public Health, 87 (7),1131-1135.

Eagly, A. H. (1982). Inferred Sex Differences in Status as a Determinant of Gender Stereotypes...Journal of Personality & Social Psyhology, 43, 915-925.

Editors of Time-Life Books. (1996). The Medical Advisor: The Complete Guide to Alternative and Conventional Treatments. Alexandria, Virginia: Time Life Inc.

Edson, C. H. (1989). Toward Multiculturalism. Coalition Quarterly: A Publication of the Tech. Assistance for Parents Programs Project. Boston, 2 & 3, (6).

Ellyson, S. L. et al. (1985). Power, Dominance and Nonverbal Behavior. New York: Springer-verlag.

Erickson, B. et al. (1974). Functions of the Third Party in the Resolution of Conflict. Journal of Personality and Social Psychology, 30, 294-306.

Eshleman, J. R. et al. (1983). Sociology: An Introduction. Boston: Little, Brown and Company.

Fairholm, G. W. (1994). Leadership and the Culture of Trust. Westport, CN: Praeger Publishing Co.

Federal Bereau of Investigation. (1985). Uniform Crime Report for the United States. Washington, D. C.: U. S. Government Printing Office.

Feldman, R. S. et al. (1982). The Teacher and the Student as Pygmalions: Joint Effects of Teacher and Student Expectations. Journal of Educational Psych., 74, 217-223.

Felson, R. B. (1984). The Effect of Self -Appraisals of Ability on Academic Performance. Journal of Personality and Social Psychology, 47, 944-952.

Fichten, C. S. (1984). See it from my point of view: Videotape and attributions in happy and distressed couples. Journal of Social and Clinical Psychology, 2, 125-138.

Fiedler, F. W. (1981). Leadership effectiveness. American Behavioral Scientist, 24, 618-632.

Fletcher, R. H. (1988). Clinical Epidemiology: The Essentials (2nd Ed.), Baltimore: Williams & Wilkins.

Fontana, A. et al. (1997). Posttraumatic Stress Disorders Among Vietnam Veterans. American J. of Public Health, 87, (2), 169-175.

Freedom: From Stress and Pressure. (1995). Boston: The Christian Science Publishing Society.

Fritz, R. (1984). The Path of Least Resistance: Principles to Create What you Want to Create. Salem, Massachusetts: DMA, Inc.

Gates, M. F. et al. (1933). Conditioned behavior of isolated and grouped cockroaches on a simple maze. Journal of Comparative Psychology, 15, 333-354.

German, C. (1992). Cultural Care: A Bridge Between Sickness, Illness and Disease. Holistic Nursing Practice, 6, (3), 1-9.

Graham, N. (1988). Psychological Stress as a Public Health Problem. Journal of Community Health Studies, 12, (2),151-160.

Green, L. W. et al. (1991) Health Promotion Planning: An Educational and Environmental Approach (2nd Ed.), Toronto: Mayfield Publishing Co.

Greene, J. M. et al. (1997). Substance Use Among Runaway and Homeless Youth. American Journal of Public Health, 87, (2), 229-235.

Grodin, A. (1993). Religious Directives: Law, Religion, Medicine, and Public Health. American Journal of Public Health, 83, (6), 899-903.

Guyton, A. C. et al. (1985). Anatomy and Physiology. Philadelphia: Saunders College Publishing.

Hallak, J. (1990). Investir Dans L'Avenir. UNESCO: Institut International de Planification & de L'Education. Paris: Editions L'Harmatten.

Hamilton, D. L. et al. (1976). Illusory Correlation in Interpersonal Perception: A Cognitive Basis of Stereotyping. Journal of Experimental Social Psych., 12, 392-407.

Harkins, S. G. et al. (1980). Social Loafing: Allocating Effort or Taking it Easy? Journal of Experimental Social Psychology, 16, 457-466.

Harrison, N. (1985). Winnie Mandela. New York: George Braziller.

Hart, A. D. et al. (1992). Mastering Pastoral Counseling. Portland, Oregon: Multnomah Press.

Haskins, C. H. (1923). The Rise of University. New York: Henry Holt & Co.

Hole, J. W. (1987). Human Anatomy and Physiology. Dubuque, Iowa: Wn. C. Brown Publishers.

Jefferson, T. President. (1973). The Man, His World, His Influence. New York: G. P. Putnam's Sons.

Kemper, D. W. et al. (1997). Healthwise handbook: A Self Care Manual for You. Boise, Idaho: Harvard Pilgrim Health Care.

Kinston, R. S. et al. (1997). Socioeconomic Status and Racial and ethnic Differences in Functional Status Assoc. with Chronic Disease. Am. J. of P. H.,87, (5).

Kobasa, S. C. (1979). Stressful Life Events, Personality, and Health: An Inquiry into Hardiness. Journal of Personality and Social Psychology, 37, 1-11.

Laguerre, M. S. (1981). Haitian Americans: Ethnicity and Medical care. In: A Harwood. Boston: Harvard University Press.

Legerman, C. J. (1975). The Haitian Potential: Research and Resources of Haiti. In: Vera Rubin. New York: Teachers College Press.

Leininger, M. (1981). Cross-Cultural Hypothetical Functions of Caring and Nursing Care. In Leininger, M. (Ed.), Caring: An Essential Human Need. Proceedings from Conferences. Thorofare, N. J.: Slack.

Leland, J. (November 29, 1993). Criminal Records: Gangsta Rap and the Culture of Violence. Newsweek, 60-64.

Louis Cole, E. (1985). Courage: A Book for Champions. Tulsa, Oklahoma: Harrison House Inc.

Mandela, Nelson Rolihlahla. (1994). Long Walk to Freedom: The Autobiography of. Boston: Little, Brown and Co.

Martin, F. P. (1979). Hang by the Tongue: A Study of the Words of Your Mouth. Lafayette, Louisiana: Bible Teaching Seminars.

Massachusetts Dept. of Public Health. (1994). Substance Abuse Report. Boston.

The Medical and Health Encyclopedia (1987). The Endocrine Glands, Mental and Emotional Disorders, Substance Abuse. Chicago: J.G. Ferguson Publishing Company.

Miller, J. B. (1976). Domination-Subordination. Toward a New Psychology of Women. Massachusetts: Beacon Press.

Minkler, M. (1986). People Need People: Support and Health. American Journal of Health Promotion, 1, (2), 33-38.

The Minnesota Lawyers International Human Rights Committee: Report Series. (1990). Restavek: Child Domestic Labor in Haiti. Minnesota, U. S. A.

Morales-Gudmundsson, L. (Sept. 1995). La Femme Face a L'An 2000. La Sentinelle,19, (9), 2-5.

Morganthau, T. (November 29, 1993). The Crisis of Black-on-Black Violence. Newsweek, 65-67.

Morrow, L. (Feb. 14, 1994). Are Men Really that Bad? Time, 143, (7), 52-59.

Mottaz, P. et al. (1991). Stress of Effects of Sampling and of Anesthesia on Metabolic Status of Sucking Rabbits. Archives Internationales de Physiologie, de Chimie et de Biologie, 99, 265-268.

Newsweek Poll (1993). November, 22, 1993. Young People Growing Up Fast and Frightened. Reported in Newsweek.

Paymar, M. (1993). Violent No More: Helping Men End Domestic Violence. Alameda, California: Hunter House, Inc.

Perkins, R. (1991). Into the Great Solitude: An Arctic Journey. New York: Henry Holt and Company.

Powell, M. What Makes a Man Great in Bed? Emmaus, PA.: Men's Health Books

Raskin, N. J. and Carl R. Rogers. (1988). Person-Centered Therapy. New York: Praeger.

Raybon, P. (1996). My First White Friend: Confessions on Race, Love and Forgiveness. New York: Penguin Books.

Revue Internationale des Sciences Sociales. (1989). Reconcilier la Sociosphere et la Biosphere. UNESCO.

Robbius, S. L. (1974). Pathological Basis of Disease. Philadelphia: W. B. Saunders, Co.

Rodriguez, W. (August 1995). Pour Rester en Bonne Sante Mentale. La Sentinelle, 19, (8), 5-7.

Roussel, A et al. (1979). Philosophie: Notions et Textes. France: Editions Fernand Nathan.

Schelling, T. C. (1984). Choice and Consequences: Perspectives of an Errant Economist. Cambridge, MA.: Harvard University Press.

Schuller, R. H. (1988). Success is Never Ending: Failure is Never Final. Nashville, TN: Thomas Nelson Publishers.

Schultz, T. W. (1983). Il n'Est de Richesse que d'Hommes. Paris: Bonnel Editions.

Schur, E. M. (1980). The Politics of Deviance. Stigma Contests and the Uses of Power. Englewood Cliffs, NJ.: Prentice-Hall, Inc.

Schutz, S. P. and Stephen Schutz. (1994). Be proud of all you've Achieved: Poems on the Meaning of Success. Boulder, Colorado: Blue Mountain Press.

Seage III, G. R. et al. (1997). The Boston AIDS Survival Score. American Journal of Public Health, 87, (4), 567-573.

Shaw, J. E. (1972). The Justice Machine. Boston: The Tower Press.

Sidney, S. et al. (1997). Marijuana Use and Mortality. American Journal of Public Health, 87, (4), 585-590.

Snyder, N. H. et al. (1994). Vision, Values and Courage. New York. The Free Press.

Solara, A. A. (1989). The Descent into Matter. The Star-Borne: A Remembrance for the Awakened Ones. Virginia: Star-Borne Unlimited.

Spitzer, R. L. (1983). Psycho-Pathology. New York: MaGraw-Hill Book Co.

Staub, E. (1989). The Roots of Evil. Cambridge, MA.: Cambridge Univ. Press.

Strawbridge, W. J. et al. (1997). Frequent Attendance at Religious Services and Mortality Over 28 Years. American. Journal of Public Health, 87, (6), 957-961.

Suinn, R. M. (1986). Seven Steps to Peak Performance: The Mental Training Manual for Athletes. Toronto: Hans Huber Publishers.

Taylor, R. L. (1990). Distinguishing Psychological from Organic Disorders. New York: Springer Publishing Company, Inc.

Thomas, S. B. et al. (1991). Public Health Then and Now: The Tuskegee Syphilis Study, 1932 to 1972. American Journal of Public Health, 81, (11), 1498-1505.

Tortora, G. J. et al. (1984). Principles of Anatomy and Physiology. New York: Harpers & Row, Publishers.

Trouillot, Ex-President Ertha Pascal. (1990). Des Lois Usuelles. Port-au-Prince, Haiti: Editions Henry Deschamps.

United Nations. International Charter for Human Rights/Charte Internationale des Droits de L'Homme.

Ury, W. (1991). Getting Past No: Negotiating with Difficult People. New York: Bantam Books.

U.S. Dept. of Health and Human Services. (1995). NIH Consensus Statement: Physical Activity and Cardiovascular Health, 13, (3), Washington, D.C.: Gov't. Press.

U. S. Dept. of Justice. (1995). Source Book of Criminal Justice Statistics. Washington, D. C.: Government Press.

The Virginia Pilot. (October 2, 1995). Maybe a Little Stress isn't Bad After All. By L. S. Kadaba, pp. E6.

Vos, L. De et al. (1980). Atlas D'Embriologie des Vertebres. Paris: Masson.

White, R. W. (1962). Lives in Progress: A Study of the natural Growth of Personality. New York: Holt, Rinehart and Winston.

Wirt, F. M. et al. (1972). Political and Social Foundations of Education. Berkeley, California: McCutchan Publishing Corporation.

Wolff, R. P. (1976). Philosophy: A Modern Encounter. EngleWood Cliffs, NJ.: Prence-Hall, Inc.

Woolfolk, A. E. (1990). Educational Psychology. Englewood Cliffs: Prence-Hall.

Zimmerman, T. C. et al. (1993). Social Support, Adversities and Emotional Distress in an Italian Community Sample. Journal of Clinical Epidemiology,46, (1), 65-75.

ABOUT THE AUTHOR

Eno Mondésir is a native of La Gonave, Haiti. After finishing secondary school in his country of origin, he attended Rutgers, The State University of New Jersey. He later transferred to Oral Roberts University in Tulsa, Oklahoma, where he received a Bachelor of Science in Biology. For his graduate work, he completed his Master's in Public Health at Boston University in Boston, Massachusetts, and he is about to fulfill the requirements for his Doctorate in Clinical Psychology from the National Christian Counselors Association, a U. S. based institution.

In addition to his active service on several boards, he has served as a consultant, lecturer, and talk-show host in both Haiti and the United States. Also, his academic interests and travel to different parts of the world have not only broadened his cultural views but also led to his fluency in the English and the French languages, as well as in the Haitian Creole. As a Public Health Specialist, Mondésir has been affiliated with The Boston Public Health Commission since 1997, where he has designed, developed materials and conducted training on prevention and health education, as well as overseeing HIV/AIDS grants. As of 2000, he has also joined Roxbury Community College, Roxbury, Massachusetts, as adjunct faculty.

His love for writing inspires provoking thoughts. His previous book, **Enrichissez Vos Relations Intimes et Conjugales,** was published in 1993.